WORLD ASSEMBLY EDITION

CITIZENS

STRENGTHENING GLOBAL CIVIL SOCIETY

Coordinated by

Miguel Darcy de Oliveira
Instituto de Ação Cultural

and

Rajesh Tandon
Society for Participatory Research in Asia

CIVICUS
World Alliance for Citizen Participation

919 18th Street, N.W.
3rd Floor
Washington, DC 20006
U.S.A.

Printed in the United States of America by McNaughton and Gunn, Inc.

Publication design by Page Design Services

ISBN 0-9644001-0-3

CONTRIBUTORS

African Women's Development and Communication Network (FEMNET)

Alain Anciaux
CRITIAS, France

Miguel Darcy de Oliveira
Instituto de Ação Cultural, Brazil

Rubem César Fernandes
Instituto de Estudos da Religião, Brazil

Dirk Jarré
International Council on Social Welfare, Germany

Amani Kandil
National Center for Social and Criminological Research, Egypt

Michael Keating
Independent Consultant, Canada

Ewa Les
Institute of Social Policy, Warsaw University, Poland

Amaury Nardone
DMG Avocats, France

Isagani R. Serrano
Philippine Rural Reconstruction Movement, Philippines

Rajesh Tandon
Society for Participatory Research in Asia, India

Sylvie Tsyboula
European Third Sector Training Network, Belgium

Edited by Linda Starke

WORLD REPORT COMMITTEE

Miguel Darcy de Oliveira, chairperson
Instituto de Ação Cultural
Rio de Janeiro, Brazil

Farida Allaghi
Arab Gulf Programme for the U.N. Development Organizations
Riyadh, Saudi Arabia

William Dietel
Independent Consultant
Virginia, United States

Eddah Gachukia
Forum for African Women Educationalists
Nairobi, Kenya

Milad Hanna
Supreme Council of Culture
Tawfik Coptic Society
Cairo, Egypt

Sylvie Tsyboula
European Third Sector Training Network
Brussels, Belgium

Rajesh Tandon
Society for Participatory Research in Asia
New Delhi, India

TABLE OF CONTENTS

PREFACE

This book is a collective effort to capture the almost impossible: the common trends behind and beneath the richness and diversity of Third Sector activities in various parts of the world. In its way, the report is a truly global and cross-cultural attempt to deal with the complexity of the Third Sector.

However, this is more than a book. It is part of a *process* developed by CIVICUS that reaches toward a global alliance in the Third Sector, which, in turn, with its strong voice, promotes the strengthening of civil society world-wide.

In this process, the primary building blocks were the regional reports on the state of the Third Sector in six regions — Asia-Pacific, Latin America and the Caribbean, Africa, the Arab region, North America, and Eastern and Western Europe. In order to ensure compatibility, the reports were guided by a framework developed by the CIVICUS World Report Committee in March 1993 in Budapest, Hungary. Additional chapters addressing overarching issues were combined with condensed versions of the regional reports to create the World Report.

The process leading to the World Report was designed, approved, and implemented by the Board of Directors of CIVICUS. Among the Board members, none was more instrumental than Brian O'Connell, one of the five co-chairpersons and Chair of the Executive Committee of CIVICUS. His commitment and gentle but firm diplomacy was absolutely essential in making the dream of CIVICUS become a reality.

As to the World Report, intellectual guidance, true leadership, and practical responsibility were provided by Miguel Darcy de Oliveira and Rajesh Tandon. They took on the immense task of coordinating the whole process from the regional reports to the finishing touches of the World Report. CIVICUS owes much to their energy, vision, and cross-cultural experience. Without their dedication, this report would simply not have been completed. Of course, they were not without help. Farida Allaghi, Eddah Gachukia, Milad Hanna, Sylvie Tsyboula, and Bill Dietel, CIVICUS' World Report Committee, took their share in designing the report and taking responsibility for the individual regions. In addition, Éva Kuti helped us greatly during the Budapest meeting of the Report Committee, where the overall structure of the reports was first drawn up.

The authors of the regional reports -- Rubem César Fernandes, Ewa Les , Isagani Serrano, Michael Keating, Amani Kandil, Alain Anciaux, Amaury

Nardone, Dirk Jarré, and the African Women's Development and Communication Network (FEMNET) -- made it possible that what has been written about the Third Sector and civil society is deeply rooted in the everyday reality of the regions. Many thanks go to the funders who provided financial support to CIVICUS. Without their generous support and involvement, neither CIVICUS nor the report could have been realized.

Special thanks must go to our editor, Linda Starke, for making such a large cross-cultural undertaking coherent to the reader. During this project, she had the remarkable ability to view the project as a whole, and to convey this picture to us throughout its development.

Finally, let me mention the obvious: without a committed and skillful staff, this report would not have been completed on time. Considering the complexity of this international enterprise, Theresa Siegl, Jo Render, and Jennette Smith went above and beyond their routine tasks to ensure the project's completion.

Miklós Marschall
Executive Director of CIVICUS

FOREWORD

The emergence of a global civil society and the opportunities this opens for the democratization of global economic mechanisms and political structures are at the roots of CIVICUS: World Alliance for Citizen Participation. As one of the first major attempts to establish a worldwide framework specifically geared to the promotion of civil society, CIVICUS is a bold new idea. The decision to launch this initiative was taken by an international group of civic leaders and activists. At the end of a two-year consultation process, these individuals felt that building a global citizen alliance was an opportunity and a challenge whose time had come.

The process leading to CIVICUS started in April 1991, when two major U.S.-based institutions (Independent Sector and the Council on Foundations) and the European Foundation Centre accepted an invitation from 10 private philanthropies to survey the need for and viability of creating a new framework for bringing nonprofit organizations together on a worldwide basis. The survey detected a consensus among both donors and donees that there should be some new mechanism for sharing and capacity building within the various "independent sectors" throughout the world, and that a process of planning and developing an international mechanism should be set in motion within the global independent sector community.

These findings were further discussed by an Exploratory International Committee, which ratified the idea of building a Global Citizen Alliance. In November 1992, a follow-up Organizing Committee was established to enlist a core group of founding members, propose an organizational framework, and take other necessary steps leading to a formal constitution. In May 1993, in Barcelona, the alliance was formally launched under the name of CIVICUS: World Alliance for Citizen Participation.

Consistent with the idea of building an inclusive organization, CIVICUS' constituency was defined from the outset as including key components of the nonprofit, nongovernmental sector, such as nongovernmental organizations (NGOs), civil associations, philanthropic institutions, foundations, and corporate grantmakers. The presence of this broad cross-section of civil society institutions in a common platform is one of CIVICUS' most distinctive elements and the springboard for opening up much-needed meeting and networking opportunities.

CIVICUS' founders were also aware that it is one thing to formally establish a global institution. Another quite different thing is for this institution to gain recognition, legitimacy, and support in the eyes of its constituency. Despite the recent emergence of several international citizen coalitions and sectoral networks, civil society is a stronger reality at the national rather than the regional or global levels. In this sense, to be more than a name, CIVICUS was immediately confronted with the challenge of demonstrating that an international citizen alliance could be an effective mechanism for enhancing national and regional action to strengthen civil society.

This challenge led to the establishment of a process approach to build CIVICUS based on four building blocks:

- the production of reports taking stock and making sense of the status of civil society in six regions of the world: North America, Latin America, Europe (East and West), the Arab world, Africa, and Asia-Pacific;
- the preparation of this World Report, outlining the risks and opportunities for strengthening global civil society in a world in transition;
- the organization of a series of consultations in different parts of the world to evaluate CIVICUS' significance as a global alliance and its potential role at the regional level; and
- a World Assembly in January 1995 in Mexico City to determine CIVICUS' priorities and action agenda on the basis of the proposals and ideas contributed by the regions.

CIVICUS' first major international initiative was the preparation throughout 1993 of the regional reports. Data collected in the most diverse cultures and societies confirmed beyond doubt that citizen participation is a deeply rooted human phenomenon. It has frequently been restrained, coerced, or forced underground, but it has always managed to survive and prosper. CIVICUS' goal, therefore, is to build on what is already happening at the local and regional levels.

The publication of the World Report is another step in this ongoing process. It is an attempt to capture the challenges and opportunities for global citizen action at the eve of CIVICUS' first World Assembly. It is also an invitation for all citizens to participate in and contribute to an initiative deemed viable and necessary.

Miguel Darcy de Oliveira
Rajesh Tandon

1

AN EMERGING GLOBAL CIVIL SOCIETY

Miguel Darcy de Oliveira
and Rajesh Tandon

"Our world cannot survive one-fourth rich and three-fourths poor, half democratic and half authoritarian, with oases of human development surrounded by deserts of human deprivation"

Human Development Report 1994

"Neither Prince nor Merchant: Citizen." Written seven years ago by Marc Nerfin, these words capture the emergence of an unprecedented worldwide phenomenon—men and women, groups and individuals, getting together to do things by themselves in order to change the societies they live in. In the last two decades, people of all classes, creeds, and ethnic backgrounds have organized themselves to defend democracy and human rights, to fight for more equitable development and a safer environment, or, more simply, just to help those in need or improve the quality of daily life in their neighborhoods and communities.

People coming together and helping each other solve problems is by no means a novelty. Since time immemorial, human beings have banded together for caring and mutual protection. Compassion for one another is a distinctive attribute of humanity. Solidarity and cooperation have always characterized relationships and social ties within families, communities, and friendship networks. The concerns and obligations that we feel toward our relatives, friends, and neighbors are not determined by self-interest nor imposed by an external coercive authority. We help those close to us on a spontaneous, sympathetic, and reciprocal basis.

What is distinctive about today is the extension of these virtues of solidarity and responsibility to the public sphere on a global scale. True enough, faith and revolution also had a global outreach. Missions of different religions inspired many to leave their homes to bring conversion and, therefore, salvation to strangers. The socialist internationals tried to link all the oppressed in their quest for a "promised land" in the here and now. In both cases, the global drive was promoted by a centrally organized institution, be it a church or a political organization, spreading its compass to the periphery.

Today's massive, almost universal movement toward greater citizen participation and influence is a new phenomenon. It is not being promoted by one all-encompassing structure. It has no fixed address. It seeks neither converts nor political militants. Its target is not state power. At its center is the figure of the citizen. And there are many citizens, with their myriad faces, concerns, and sources of inspiration in today's world.

Citizen action is as multidimensional as the diversity of human endeavors. It may be local or global, small or massive, permanent or ephemeral, highly dramatic or almost invisible, confrontational or collaborative, spontaneous or organized, promoted by associations of like-minded individuals or by large civic movements. Or any combination of these, depending on the needs of the moment.

Its breadth and diversity range from women in India hugging trees to save them from being felled to global environmental organizations lobbying governments to come to terms with ecological imbalance. From students in Scandinavia donating the proceeds of their voluntary work for educational projects in the Third World to the mothers of political prisoners in Argentina barehandedly confronting a ferocious military dictatorship. From Polish workers challenging a totalitarian regime to entire villages in Asia mobilizing for self-governance and self-development. From medical doctors disregarding national frontiers to rescue the victims of civil strife to millions of Americans reading for the blind, collecting money for a health charity, or doing volunteer work in the local library, art gallery, or soup kitchen. From courageous Arab women standing up for their rights to citizens worldwide demanding the safeguard of the physical integrity of persecuted people whose names they can hardly pronounce and whose political beliefs they often do not share.

The sources of inspiration may be spiritual, religious, moral, or political. The common thread, however, in this ever-changing quilt is to be found in the realm of values: solidarity and compassion for the fate and well-being of others, including unknown, distant others; a sense of personal responsibility and reliance on one's own initiative to do the right thing; the impulse toward altruistic giving and sharing; the refusal of inequality, violence, and oppression. These are the compelling moral values that generate people's social energy and enhance the texture of civil society. The themes and concerns vary from place to place and from time to time, but citizen movements are now a constant, global phenomenon.

In counterpoint both to the power and the impersonal rules of governments and to the quest for profit and personal gain intrinsic to the market, a third sector—nonprofit and nongovernmental—now coexists in practically every society. All over the world, civil society now interacts with and exercises a countervailing power to markets and government.

Yet the richness and diversity of citizen initiatives still far outweigh their public visibility and recognition. "Private action for the public good" is a new concept in many parts of the world. Despite the recent multiplication, at the local and national levels, of innovative experiences that cut across the boundaries of class and culture, cross-sectoral partnerships and interactions among the different components of the nonprofit sector are still the exception rather than the rule.

In the countries of the South, NGOs possess a rich history of solidarity and collaboration with popular movements, but have so far had little contact with the emerging initiatives of corporate philanthropy. Private foundations and development agencies have been actively supporting civil society associations, but donors and donees hardly ever share equal responsibility for joint programs on issues of common concern. Only now are the government and business sectors, the academic world, and the media beginning to acknowledge the role and potential of the third sector. Many countries lack the appropriate legislation to encourage citizen action, private giving, and volunteering.

Challenges and Paradoxes of Globalization

These emerging needs represent opportunities for citizen action in a world in transition. CIVICUS' international initiative coincides with the growing realization that neither the market nor the state alone can meet the challenges of equitable and sustainable development.

In many areas of the world, governments in the past tended to oppose civil society. The collapse of the communist regimes and of many repressive military dictatorships in Latin America and Asia, combined with the crisis of the welfare state in the North and of state-promoted development in the South, has given rise to a much more open and complex political environment.

Governments' traditional suspicions regarding NGOs, often accused in the past (because of external funding) of pursuing a non-national agenda, are gradually being replaced by a recognition of the role of civil society institutions as agents of change and partners in development. In Latin America, for instance, where NGOs built their institutional identity in open resistance and opposition to an authoritarian state, recent trends point to experimentation with flexible, innovative forms of interaction and partnership among civil society institutions to deal with social reform and poverty .

Under heavy criticism for their bureaucracy and inefficiency, and confronted by a shortage of funds and credibility, governments can no longer pretend to monopolize the development process. Systems and structures of governance have lost most of their credibility and legitimacy worldwide. The question to be asked is whether this withdrawal of the state is only opening space for the affirmation of unbridled market values. Or whether it also creates unprecedented opportunities for the global emergence of a third sector.

Globalization confronts us with the paradox of an expanding international consensus in favor of democracy, pluralism, and respect for human rights coexisting with unprecedented levels of human suffering and environmental degradation. Rapid technological change is leading to growing structural unemployment. Patterns of production and consumption are depleting the planet's life-support systems. The preeminence of western paradigms of politics, science, and economics are fostering, in reaction, the phenomena of religious fundamentalism and ethnic exclusiveness.

Two or three decades ago, people in the North looked at the South, at the emergent societies in Latin America, Africa, and Asia, as sources of inspiration and commitment. Solidarity with the Third World and its struggles for liberation was a powerful mobilizing force. This generous view of a common future for all humankind is being replaced by pervasive feelings of indifference toward and rejection of the outcasts.

In the same sweeping movement by which capital and technology, abolishing distances and frontiers, tend to integrate national markets into a single all-encompassing global market, the logic of profit and the imperatives of technological competition fracture into two every society, generating an ever-growing number of useless people.

In terms of the global economy, we all live indeed in one world; in terms of the human condition, however, a new dividing line, larger and deeper than the traditional East-West and North-South rifts, separates those who live with freedom and dignity from those who cannot satisfy their most basic survival needs. These two worlds not only coexist, they are drifting farther apart. Our global village has an expanding slum area. And many of those who live in the world's affluent neighborhoods are either indifferent to or afraid of the poor. It is as if the poor themselves—wherever they are—North or South—had become a problem, not to say a threat. They are the ones to blame for over-population, environmental pollution, illegal immigration, narcotics trafficking or religious fanaticism. In view of their reckless behavior, they must be closely watched and controlled. Their migration to the rich neighborhoods of the world must by all means be prevented. Their economy is to be structurally adjusted and monitored to ensure that they do not mismanage resources and do not leave their debts unpaid. Even their sexuality is considered too exuberant: their very numbers threaten the fragile limits of the Earth.

The weaker, the more vulnerable, the powerless, those who do not produce or consume anything of value for the world market, those who can hardly be privatized or internationalized, are becoming expendable. Their labor is useless, their buying power is negligible. They are no longer even worth exploiting. In Africa, the entire population of some countries is facing the threat of extinction, in the same way as, in the past, indigenous civilizations were wiped out in the Americas. What is being done to prevent this human disaster? How can we understand the widespread apathy about this major sociological and ecological catastrophe?

Social fragmentation, economic instability, and uncertainty about the future are breeding prejudice, intolerance, and racism. Peace and democracy are not compatible with ever-increasing poverty and exclusion. The social and geographic segregation of a growing number of individuals can only fuel ethnic tensions and violence. From the moral and ethical standpoint, global apartheid is absolutely unacceptable.

The same processes that globalize problems also globalize their possible solutions. Global civil society is a new concept. Will it be capable of generating the energy and resources needed to cope with global problems and concerns? Recent history gives us reasons for hope. And hope can also be strengthened by inspired, principled human action.

Civil Society, State, and Market

Civil society institutions may be fragile but they are many and have been growing steadily in scope and reach during the last two decades. The breathtaking peaceful revolutions in Eastern Europe, the democratic transitions in so many countries of the South, and the dramatic changes in South Africa all bear witness to the strength of civic action.

Governments are showing greater openness to cooperation with citizen associations. The matter of corporate social responsibility has gained space on the agenda of private enterprises. These changes are paving the way for broader, innovative forms of interaction between civil society, state and market.

For these partnerships to materialize, it is also necessary for civil society institutions to overcome some ingrained prejudices and misconceptions. We must be cautious not to idealize and therefore falsify the reality about what the third sector is and what it can achieve.

Power and money also play a role within civil society associations. "For all their much-vaunted flexibility," notes Lester Salamon, "nonprofit organizations remain organizations. As they grow in scale and complexity, they are vulnerable to all the limitations that afflict other bureaucratic institutions— unresponsiveness, cumbersomeness and routinization, lack of coordination. Nonprofit organizations may be less prone to these disabilities than government agencies, but they are hardly immune to the inevitable tensions that arise between flexibility and effectiveness, grassroots control and administrative accountability." Hence the urgent need for the third sector to define its own ethical standards, patterns of openness and accountability, as well as the means to enforce them.

The bitter experience that many NGOs and civil associations had of fighting authoritarian regimes led some to equate state authority with repression. Times have changed, however, and democratically elected governments have a legitimacy that cannot be overlooked. The collapse of governments can only lead either to chaos and anarchy, as in some African countries where central authority has practically ceased to exist, or to a radically laissez-faire economy, where the unchecked prevalence of market values would transform every social good into a commodity.

The drastic slashing of public expenditures and the total deregulation of the economy, advocated by the neoliberal approach, can only undermine the capacity of both state and society to reverse the trends toward increasing national and global poverty. Recalling that "support for the voluntary sector has at times been used to rationalize assaults on government social welfare spending, as was the case in the United States in the 1980s," Salamon calls attention to the risk of rhetorical praise for the nonprofit sector serving as a smokescreen for indiscriminate anti-state crusades.

Private initiatives for the public good are evidently not incompatible with responsible and efficient public policies. In fact, for the non-governmental sector to function properly, it is essential that the governmental sector also fulfill its irreplaceable role in the provision of the most basic social services, from health and education for all to public safety and protection of the environment. Not less, but more and better public initiative is needed in today's complex societies.

The same rethinking of basic assumptions is valid for the relationship of the nonprofit sector to profit-making corporations. In many countries of the South, NGOs allied themselves with popular movements to oppose the state while, for all practical purposes, ignoring the market and its institutions. The transition to democracy and the magnitude of the postauthoritarian social agenda is giving rise to a new climate where past mutual prejudices are gradually being overcome. Indeed, as the *Human Development Report 1993* aptly put it, "the ideological battlelines of the past are being replaced by a more pragmatic association between the efficiency of the market and social solidarity."

It is quite true that there are at least two things that markets cannot guarantee on their own: equity and fair competition. The pressure from civil society and the regulatory authority of the state are both indispensable to promote social justice and balance the power of private monopolies. But it is equally important to acknowledge that, in the same way that they often aggravate poverty and inequality, market mechanisms are also capable of injecting vitality and dynamism in society by taking risks and promoting innovation.

For this to happen, however, it is essential that global economic mechanisms do not overwhelm and stifle the dynamics of local and regional development. The global market accounts for one relevant dimension of economic activity. It cannot, however, subordinate to its logic the infinite diversity of people's strategies for generating wealth and well-being. There are as many markets in the world as the circuits linking producers and consumers. Some are rigidly structured; others are informal and barely visible. Here again, a dynamic balance and complementarity must be explored between the formal and informal sectors as well as between the local, national, regional and global levels of economic activity.

There is no reason whatsoever for relieving the private sector and its institutions from addressing the challenges of citizenship and social responsibility. On the other hand, the exploration of opportunities for cooperative action does not imply that citizens should renounce their right and duty to question and oppose corporations—and states—whenever their behavior proves detrimental to the common good. In any case, labor disputes and conflicts over environmental or consumer issues will hardly disappear from the agenda of civil society.

In the last five years, we have been consistently moving beyond the market-versus-state polarization that was intrinsic during the cold war and closer to a less doctrinarian, more action-oriented approach. The narrow ideological alternative between market and state can now be transformed into a broader, contextual kind of questioning: What kind of state? What kind of market? And, therefore, what kind of third sector?

The Case for Global Civil Society

Given the global interconnectedness of contemporary civilization, the prevailing movement toward poverty, ecological imbalance and exclusion cannot be reversed by actions taken only at the local and national level.

Global market mechanisms and structures of world governance can only be democratized through concerted global citizen action. This is the lesson that popular movements have learned in their long struggles to democratize government, the market, and society within each country. The challenge to planetary citizenship is, therefore, to expand to the global arena the struggle for democracy and human development that has so far been carried out basically at the national level.

It is also true that civil society institutions so far have not reacted quickly enough to the challenges of globalization. Even though still lagging behind transnational corporations in terms of building a capacity to act at the world scale, citizens have been trying hard in the last 10 years to build their own linkages and mechanisms for consultation and joint action.

Regional coalitions and sectoral networks have recently been formed in many parts of the globe to address specific themes and concerns such as protection of the environment; human rights; adult, nonformal and popular education; the rights of women, children, and indigenous peoples; health and habitat issues; and so on. Networking has become the key word for the emerging global civil society.

As stressed by Marc Nerfin, networks, in contrast to the international mechanisms created by corporations and governments, tend to operate horizontally. Their centers are eveywhere; their peripheries, nowhere. Similar to local civil society institutions, they exercise an inner power over themselves. Communication is one of their primary concerns. Leadership is shifting. There is no networking for networking's sake. Their rationale is not in themselves, but in a job to be done. Networks adjust quickly to changing circumstances but are also transient. If and when they are no longer needed, they disappear.

Women have taken the lead in this process. For two decades now they have been pursuing, with energy and consistency, an action agenda of their own targeted at the elimination of gender-based discrimination. Similarly, the actions of Amnesty International in the defense of political prisoners and of Médecins Sans Frontières in favor of civilian victims of armed conflicts have broken new ground in terms of affirming the right of the world citizen community to overcome claims of national state sovereignty when human lives and people's essential rights are at risk.

An innovative experience in terms of coalition-building comes from the Asia-Pacific region with PP21, the People's Plan for the 21st Century. Cutting across different categories of sectors within civil society, PP21 has attempted over the past five years to gather citizens, women, indigenous peoples, workers, human rights groups, and social activists in an alliance to propose an alternative development paradigm.

On another level, the global networking and advocacy efforts of NGOs to influence the agenda and outcome of major U.N. global conferences have produced some landmark events. The most comprehensive and best planned of these processes was developed in preparation for and during Rio's Global Forum and Earth Summit in June 1992. It is fair to say that citizens at those events not only educated the public about the issues at stake but also and, for the first time, really asserted their right of sharing responsibility with states for the governance of the planet. Similar mobilization drives were carried out for the Vienna Human Rights Conference and the Cairo Population and Development Conference, and are being implemented in 1995 for the World Summit on Social Development in Copenhagen and the Beijing Women's Conference.

The process of building such global networks is also occurring in relation to the institutions of the market. Besides lobbying and calling for transparency and accountability from multilateral development banks, including the World Bank and the International Monetary Fund, strong associations of consumer groups are also acting at the global level. The International Organisation of Consumers' Unions, for example, has contributed significantly to ensuring greater public accountability of market enterprises.

The fact that parts of the North are also being exposed to the global phenomenons of structural unemployment, urban violence, drugs, AIDS and environmental degradation is paradoxically providing untapped opportunities for more horizontal international cooperation among donors and donees beyond the grant-making/grant-seeking pattern.

All these changes indicate that the time is ripe for citizens to act boldly to strengthen the trends toward global solidarity and planetary citizenship.

Implications for Global Citizen Action

Expressing this new global spirit in deeds is one of the foremost challenges to citizens and civil society institutions. Private action for the public good has been lost in the shrill of public for public good or private for private good. Citizens' actions for public good are conceptually and qualitatively different from private, profit-oriented initiatives. Likewise, the government is not the sole repository of all wisdom, concern, and capacity to act for the common good.

Citizen initiatives aimed at addressing public issues and problems are no longer to be considered residual actions. They are now in the center, not the periphery. The actors of civil society are not following the prescriptions of the state or of the market, but creating their own initiatives. In this sense, the nonprofit sector can be said to be not the third, but the primary sector of society.

Global citizen participation is rising at a time marked by the sharp decline, especially in the North, of many more traditional forms of political participation, such as voting, party affiliation, and labor union membership. While the struggle in the South is to extend newly gained democracy and citizenship to the economic and social spheres, the North is confronted with an increasing drift toward civic disaffection and apathy. There is a growing disillusion with politics. Many citizens feel that they have lost control over the political and economic mechanisms that determine their lives.

Threatened by processes that seem beyond their understanding and capacity to influence, suffering from the alienation produced by global cultural homogenization, many react defensively by going back to ethnocentrism and parochialism. A renewal of the sense of concern and solidarity among citizens could be a powerful alternative to both social fragmentation and the aggressive affirmation of ethnic or religious identities.

This sense of common belonging, however, cannot be sustained by ignoring differences in cultures, religions, languages, or ethnicity. Cutting across traditional boundaries of caste, class, religion, and nation-state, the notion of global citizen action, rooted in a common set of values, implies the acknowledgment and acceptance of diversity as one of the most distinctive characteristics of humankind.

Articulating morality is another emerging challenge for global civil society. In the transition to postmodernism, the traditional value system has almost crumbled. A new ethical and moral code has not yet been universally established. In many parts of the world, the dominance of the state and governmental bureaucracy has promoted a culture of dependence, apathy, secrecy and corruption. The recent dominance of market enterprise has also resulted in individual self-centeredness, profit-over-people orientation, and widespread alienation.

The reassertion of the primacy of civil society calls for the articulation of a set of universal human values. The current crisis of morality is being countered by inspired and value-based citizens' actions worldwide. The source of inspiration for human response to the needs and suffering of individuals and groups is essentially spiritual throughout the world. Spontaneous and committed citizen initiatives are premised on love, compassion, concern for others. These values and inspirations provide meaning and substance to people.

In a world where material acquisitions and consumptions are becoming the dominant ethos, there is an urgent need to bring spirituality to the core of human endeavor. This will constitute the fountainhead of a universal moral code based on our common humanity. The values of diversity, of tolerance and pluralism, of peace and justice, of solidarity and responsibility to unknown others and to future generations need to be proposed and practiced as the anchor for universal humanity and global citizen action.

CIVICUS as a Tool for Strengthening Global Solidarity

As a World Alliance for Citizen Participation, CIVICUS is a global mechanism within civil society. Its own functioning and posturing need to reflect the values and thematic concerns felt by citizens. A global citizen alliance is also a new concept. As such, it requires new modes of operation.

CIVICUS' strength lies in its broad constituency and global outreach. The joint presence of NGOs and civil associations, of foundations and corporate grantmakers, and of charities and service organizations opens up untapped opportunities for dialogue and cooperation between the components of the nonprofit sector. In particular, it provides a more horizontal and substantial platform of action for both donors and donees as equal and full partners in development.

The strengthening of the institutions of civil society enables them to explore innovative forms of interaction with business and governments. The relationship of the third sector with corporations and states will probably always be marked by tension and complementarity. The conceptual novelty here is that tension, or even conflict, does not mean negation or exclusion of the other. Nor does it preclude synergy and cooperation. Each of the three sectors of society is autonomous of and interdependent on the other two.

The creation of CIVICUS means that we come together as an international alliance. The roots of civil society, however, are at the local and national levels. Hence CIVICUS' first challenge is: How can a global alliance support emerging national and regional agendas to strengthen civil society? How can local and national initiatives be reinforced by linkages with global processes? How can citizens be empowered to address emerging global problems and influence distant economic institutions and structures of governance?

Broadly speaking, these are not challenges merely for CIVICUS as a citizen alliance but for global civil society as such. The question for CIVICUS then becomes what role can it play within this larger context and what it cannot and should not attempt to do.

CIVICUS cannot be a centrally organized, all-embracing formal institution. It cannot be the equivalent of the United Nations for civil society nor the network of networks. Governments have a mandate to represent their nation in the field of international relations. No equivalent formal representation exists for the nongovernmental sector yet.

The many institutions that compose the third sector follow very diverse organizational patterns. Some are connected to well-established hierarchical structures; others are extremely zealous of their autonomy. Some cherish egalitarian legal structures; others follow charismatic leaders. Some deal with specific questions; others have a broad, cross-sectoral agenda. Some have grown through decades of institutional building; others have recently been formed in response to emergent needs. Some are large membership organizations; others are flexible action-oriented small groups.

Any attempt to amalgamate all this diversity under a single umbrella organization runs the risk of giving rise to hollow structures. Nor is there any point trying to bring together this immense variety of citizen groups and initiatives in order for all to pursue a common global course of action. Revolutionary parties, in the past, invested themselves with the task of organizing the whole people around a cohesive political project. History has delivered stinging blows to such arrogant grand designs.

CIVICUS cannot pretend to be the one and only legitimate representative of the third sector or of any of its constitutive segments. If CIVICUS has no reason for seeking to control or vertically integrate a process that is too diverse, complex, and unpredictable to be handled by any one organization, what can it hope to achieve? CIVICUS is what it does, and its legitimacy can only be validated by those who feel it provides them with a useful tool of action.

Its role might be described as that of a catalyst. In chemistry, catalysis occurs when a given element acts as a starter of a molecular reaction, thus being the determinant of a change into a new and very different condition. Maybe the notion of a planetary third sector and, within it, a citizen alliance such as CIVICUS might be understood in similar terms—not as an objective reality, whose existence is a given fact, but as an open, evolving possibility; not as a solid structure, but as a powerful dynamic process. We have learned that, sooner or later, "all that is solid melts in the air." On the other hand, the interplay of certain elements, under certain conditions, can unleash interactive chain reactions that would indeed give substance and shape to an emerging global civil society.

To be a catalyst is not to be an overall, ever-present organizer. The sector is made up of countless initiatives, experiences, projects, movements, and networks that are happening simultaneously in different places, cadences, and levels. Such a phenomenon can hardly be coordinated, let alone centrally controlled.

Communication is a more appropriate operational word for CIVICUS than coordination. New channels can be opened to foster dialogue, exchange, and cooperation among the institutions of civil society at the different levels in which they function: local, national, regional, global. For such communication to take hold, however, a single language or unidimensional symbolic code is not enough. Communication within the sector will have to overcome the differences of culture and class. It will also have to open channels for a creative interaction between the cosmopolitan discourse of modernity and the many local voices of tradition.

The polarities of the cold war accustomed us to thinking in terms of inflexible ideological dualities. Within this frame of mind, allegiances were exclusive, all-encompassing, and durable. This paradigm has been shattered, but we are still relearning how to engage in simultaneous, multiple, partial alliances. Partnerships, both within and outside the sector, depend on the parties involved, the circumstances, and the needs at stake. Confrontation does not exclude compromise and cooperation.

In such a volatile, changing field, citizens' common values—peace, responsibility, solidarity, compassion—are the safest compass to chart CIVICUS' course of action. There is much that a global citizen alliance cannot do but it is also true that values are of no use if they are not put into practice. Therefore,

CIVICUS has a duty to take a stand on limited cases, on extreme situations, whenever essential values are being threatened or negated.

Beyond emergency action on test cases, CIVICUS will have to develop its own action agenda. This most likely will be as open and evolving as the needs and concerns of civil society itself. It will also have to find the most appropriate balance between support for on-going local, national, and regional processes and the promotion of fresh global initiatives.

CIVICUS is moving forward in a still largely unchartered landscape. At this point, the most we can do is to outline some challenges and opportunities for action to be explored by this emerging global citizen alliance.

- *Enhancing the sector's visibility.* Our sector is what it does. The most profound messages of human courage and compassion are propagated through the stories of inspired and exemplary human action based on moral and spiritual grounds. The human face of citizen action demands greater visibility insofar as the very essence of planetarian citizenship is the initiative of inspired and committed people.

    At the local and national level, innovative forms of interaction within the sector and of partnerships with governments and business around burning social issues are increasingly being explored. The systematic dissemination of information about these groundbreaking social experiments would also enable the media, decision-makers, and the general public to gain a clearer understanding of the moral texture and potential of civil society.

- *Promoting interaction and partnership.* The diverse components of the nonprofit sector are not used to talking to each other, let alone to cooperating in flexible, creative ways. In some parts of the world, NGOs and popular movements see themselves as the cornerstone of civil society. In others, there is a strong tradition of volunteering, private giving, and corporate philanthropy, with no equivalent elsewhere. Many charities and service organizations operate informally at the community level, with effectiveness but little visibility.

    This absence of dialogue within the sector can be countered by the opening up of new opportunities for cross-sectoral meetings and interaction. Person-to-person exchange of knowledge and experiences would enhance cooperation and mutual learning, thus helping build a common sense of identity and purpose among the institutions of civil society.

• *Encouraging private giving and voluntarism.* The significance of voluntary efforts is getting lost in modern utilitarianism. Giving of time, energy, capacity, and resources for the promotion of the common good is the cornerstone of the sector. Some countries have a rich historical experience of large campaigns to enhance private giving and voluntarism. This includes public pressure and advocacy geared to removing legal barriers and devising tax inducements to private giving and corporate responsibility.

Sharing of knowledge and information about these matters would help the nonprofit sector launch national drives aimed at building the cultural and political environment most favorable to spontaneous citizen action and philanthropy.

• *Promoting and nurturing an enabling environment.* Since many countries and regions do not have the appropriate legal, political, and fiscal environment for the development and growth of civil society, CIVICUS could play an effective role through sharing experiences and examples of good practice. CIVICUS could also promote effective policy advocacy and policy formulation with governments, regional, and international agencies and other key decision-makers to promote an enabling legal, political, and material context (such as registration laws, tax laws, public policy on government posture toward civil society and so on) for the evolution and strengthening of actors in civil society.

• *Promoting research and outreach.* As noted earlier, private action for the public good is a new concept in many parts of the world. In the same sense, civil society and the third sector have not yet been widely acknowledged as objects for in-depth study. Relevant information is dispersed and often unreliable. Issues are not clearly defined. Alternatives are barely beginning to shape up. Hence the need to map the contours and dimensions of the sector as a means of understanding its importance.

Building the information and knowledge basis about the sector would give added credence to citizens' claims about the role and responsibility of a vibrant civil society in strengthening democracy and human development. It was not until Independent Sector in the United States began research in 1988 that the amazing figures of more than $85 billion worth of annual household donations in that country and over $184 billion worth of voluntary hours came to light.

• *Engaging in dialogue with major international agencies.* Agencies of the U.N. system, multilateral financial institutions, regional development banks, and global business associations are creating mechanisms for consultation and, eventually, joint policy initiatives with institutions of civil society. CIVICUS, as a global citizen alliance, can play a significant role in terms of being a counterpart to these large institutions, giving voice to the sector's needs and exploring new forms of international cooperation.

• *Enhancing citizens' power to act.* People have the power to act as citizens. This is not power over other things or beings. It is the power to create, to innovate, to engage with other citizens. This power carries with it a responsibility toward nature, toward future generations. The power to act responsibly is rooted in the spiritual and moral fabric of global citizen action. It is not derived from the state or the market. Its inspiration comes from deep within the human spirit.

Citizen associations' programs are increasingly combining direct involvement in projects at the microlevel with participation in large-scale processes of change. This expanded, more complex action agenda requires qualitative organizational improvements. Sharing of knowledge and expertise in areas such as leadership training, management skills, fundraising and the self-enforcement of ethical standards are capacity-building needs that could also be addressed by CIVICUS.

Being a tool for citizens' empowerment is the basic reason CIVICUS exists. Translating these concerns into a plan of action is the task of the first World Assembly of CIVICUS.

Citizens are at the center of the global drama unfolding today. They are the lead actresses and actors in building global democratic governance and human development. The state and the market, and their related institutions, must serve the citizens, not the other way around. The security of our common future lies in the hands of an informed, inspired, committed, engaged citizenry. This is the dream of CIVICUS. This is our hope.

Bibliography

Independent Sector. "Ethics and the Nation's Voluntary and Philanthropic Community—Obedience to the Unenforceable, A Statement by Independent Sector." Washington, D.C.: 1991.

Independent Sector. *Giving and Volunteering in the United States.* Findings from a National Survey. Washington, D.C., 1992.

Inter-American Development Bank and U.N. Development Programme. *Social Reform and Poverty—Towards a Comprehensive Agenda for Development.* Washington, D.C., and New York: 1993.

Ministry of Foreign Affairs. *A World of Difference - A New Framework for Development Cooperation in the 1990s.* The Hague: 1991.

Nerfin, Marc. "Neither Prince nor Merchant: Citizen—An Introduction to the Third System." *Development Dialogue.* 1987, No. 1, pp. 170-195.

Salamon, Lester M. "The Rise of the Nonprofit Sector." *Foreign Affairs.* July/August 1994.

U.N. Development Programme. *Human Development Report 1993.* New York: Oxford University Press, 1993.

Wolfe, Alan. *Whose Keeper? Social Science and Moral Obligation.* Berkeley and Los Angeles: University of California Press, 1989.

2

PRIVATE BUT PUBLIC: THE THIRD SECTOR IN LATIN AMERICA

Rubem César Fernandes

In the 1960s, Latin America was the source of images of promise that combined the vigor of material progress with the romantic and willful generosity of youth. The region not only enjoyed positive rates of economic growth but also evoked deep humanitarian feelings. Around the world, Guevara's smiling countenance hung on the walls of bedrooms, living rooms, and studies, a symbol of the youthful disposition of those who lived there. Latin American song, made up of a cosmopolitan poetry combined with the exoticism of local sounds and rhythms, propagated a solidarity of sentiments around European and North American campuses. "Guantanamera," Victor Jara, the Parras, Arturo Piazzola, bossa nova—this music aroused solidarity everywhere. The best and most generous minds in the North dreamed of a long trip through the interior of Latin America. Many learned Spanish and came to establish lifelong personal (and professional) links with the region.

Alas, these images belong to the past. The enchantment is gone, and the wheel that combines actual events and social fantasies has turned, so that now a quite different figure represents this continent before international public opinion. A "lost decade" for the economy, environmental devastation, drug trafficking, children roaming the mean streets, corruption—such is now the stereotypical image of Latin America worldwide. The romantic promise of the earlier period was replaced by the challenge of a pragmatic question: Can they really cope with their own problems? After the nostalgia is gone, vital signs begin to manifest themselves, and other scenarios invite us to look toward the future on different terms.

The focus here is the relevant and concrete social action in the nongovernmental spheres. The expectations raised in the 1960s provide the backdrop, and each section roughly coincides with a decade, in a cumulative process of dismantling and rebuilding the parameters that made up the initial discursive horizon.

Key words are isolated that deconstructed one by one the overpoliticized parameters of the previous age and opened up further spheres, further possibilities of action: "community" and "social movements" in the 1970s, under the pressure of authoritarian regimes; "citizenship" and "civil society" with the processes of democratization of the 1980s; "nonprofit and nongovernmental," or simply "Third Sector," with its multiple and innumerable expressions, in the last few years. These well-known words have implied profound changes in action and thinking.

Social Movements

"Community work" is a frequently used term in the Third Sector. It denotes a concrete, localized activity of reasonably small dimensions, in which relationships are personalized. Work on this level, however modest, carries an unequivocally positive aura. The "community" is made up of a number of families, and it defines a residential space. It is near home and, at least in urban centers, far from work. The situation is different in rural areas, where home and work make up a differentiated but continuous space. But in the city, a taste for the "community" is associated with a certain distancing from the world of "labor and business."

Curiously enough, it was during authoritarian rule that the term community acquired more weight, attracting countless social agents in Latin America. In the 1970s, the military dominated the political system in key countries— Brazil, Argentina, Uruguay, Chile, Peru, Bolivia—while Central America was violently divided by cold war confrontations. Together with the guerrilla movements in Colombia and Venezuela, it all added up to a region taken over by the force of guns. The mechanisms of civil communication with political parties, the media, and so on were paralyzed, and the opposition groups that resorted to armed struggle experienced a series of tragic defeats. The trade union movement, which in the past had been the backbone of popular mobilization, was violently repressed. In short, civil participation in the state and the private sector was reduced to a bare minimum.

Since the drive to participate that had been so strong in the previous decade had been effectively contained, the only way out now was to look to the local plane, to "communities." There were dangers here, too, but the risks were unquestionably smaller. The military dictatorship had no direct access to the inner core of institutions. When it barged in, it always caused a traumatic intervention. Therefore it did so selectively, in response to demands or in preventive measures informed by maps of social conflicts. In this sense, it differed from totalitarian regimes, in which control is exercised from inside institutions.

Community work escaped controls, and thus it managed to expand under the most violent regimes, as in Pinochet's Chile. Even as the police persecuted political activists and kept an eye on unions, a different brand of activism found a fertile ground on which to grow. The newness of this saved it from police persecution.

The Roman Catholic Church—more particularly, Liberation Theology—gave the movement its widest spreading streams. The intensity and scope varied considerably from one diocese or nation to another. Nevertheless, there were significant exponents of Liberation Theology in every subregion of Latin America: Gustavo Gutierrez (Peru), Leonardo Boff (Brazil), Pablo Richards (Chile/Costa Rica), Otto Maduro (Venezuela), Juan Luiz Segundo (Uruguay), Javier Gorostiaga (Nicaragua), and others.

Pastoral agents renewed the term "community," stressing the sacred and prophetic value of the "Church base communities" (CBCs): sacred, because they were Church communities; prophetic, because they expressed the conviction that it was on the "grassroots" level that the true Church was to be found, the announcement and expectation of the Kingdom that gives meaning to the Christian faith. Hence its mystique. Renewed by circumstances, the term "community" in the 1970s was infused with the breath of religious revival. In this new context, it was more than a sociological expression associated with social projects: it was "a new way of being a Church."

In spite of the efforts of the last hundred years, the parish network in Latin America remains inadequate, in vivid contrast with its European counterpart. In 1987, for example, France registered 1,283 Catholics per parish and an average size of 15 square kilometers (sq. km.) per parish; Central America, in contrast, had 17,005 Catholics per parish, with the average parish spread over 416 sq. km., while the equivalent figures for South America were 14,036 Catholics and 1,000 sq. km.

The problem was well known, but the renovation of the 1970s gave it a new sense of urgency—the Church had to develop proper ecclesiastical roots or else lose its very reason of being. The CBCs were to be the seeds; they were to multiply like small vital circles in the territory of the old parishes, making intensive use of laypersons and breaking the inertia of traditional structures. In actual practice, the results varied widely.

In most countries (Chile, Uruguay, Argentina, Peru, Ecuador, and others), the movement remained circumscribed to a few dioceses directed by bishops attracted by the idea. In others (Mexico, El Salvador, and Brazil), it exerted nationwide influence. A 1993 survey found an impressive 46,000 CBCs in Brazil. Even if the initial momentum has died out and the impact has been differentiated, there is no doubt that CBCs wrote a new chapter in the history of local associations in Latin America.

What the CBCs aspired to was a Church built on the participation of the faithful. The magic of the rites did not matter so much. True, there were not enough priests, and in Catholicism a good Mass requires a priest. But what the movement emphasized was something else: in the CBCs, the voice of the faithful would finally be heard. Their distinguishing mark was Bible study, in groups, with the participants forming a circle, using the Scriptures as the starting point for an exchange of views concerning the oft-repeated question: what does God's Word say to us who are here, in this particular place, with these particular problems and hopes? In its own way, Liberation Theology propagated in Catholic circles a genuine belief that if people think together, they can change circumstances, the Church, and the world.

There was a symbolic emphasis on "the poor"—not people in general, identified with society itself, but the poor, those in the bottom of the social pyramid, who have no property, those who most suffer the consequences of an unjust society, the oppressed. In dramatic contrast with the mercantile mentality and the defense of affluence that animated the ruling classes, the movement was able to revive the generous mystique that has marked the figure of "the poor" in Catholic culture since the Middle Ages.

Since the 1970s, Church reaction and the rise of other processes, made more visible by redemocratization, have made it clear that the CBCs were just one alternative among many, even within Roman Catholicism. Marxists analyses were discredited, at least as regards the notion of historical dialectics. Other, less intellectualized, religious revival movements came to the fore. Organized crime grew among the poor, robbing them of part of their innocence. The notion of "the people" integrated as a sovereign collective subject was noticeably undermined.

Nevertheless, the Church Base Communities did not disappear. There is talk of their decline, but they continue. If they no longer live up to messianic expectations, they still count. Anyone doing social work in the poor neighborhoods of Latin America knows what a difference it makes to find a Church community formed in the spirit of Liberation Theology. In social matters, results hardly ever correspond to original intentions. But that is how history proceeds.

The scale and style of the movements in the 1970s pointed to the emergence of a new phenomenon, and a new phrase was coined to describe it: "social movements." They were "movements" because of their unstable, ever-changing nature, quite different from structures organized for the long haul; they were "social" because they kept their distance from the state machinery. Although they were constantly involved with public issues, they were not "political movements" because they lacked connections to integrate them into a systematic government policy. The scope of their action was limited to what could effectively be said about the local society in which they found themselves.

Mobilizing a few dozen people (hundreds made for a strong movement, thousands was more than daring) in connection with supposedly local problems, these movements saw the national state as a practically inaccessible level. Conversely, if they were able to emerge in an authoritarian context, it was probably because, seen from above, they did not seem threatening. In contrast with trade unions, in which local conflicts could rapidly escalate into national issues, social movements were typically perceived as expressions of localized problems.

From the very beginning they were conceived in the plural. Land issues, rural and urban squatting, security problems, water shortages, lack of sewers, energy blackouts, excessive pollution, sky-high prices, uncontrolled traffic in densely populated neighborhoods, and a variety of other such topics made up the agenda of these various movements. Typically, even when they existed side by side in the same part of a city, they did not join into formal structures.

In this same period, neighborhood associations, micro-institutions of a civil nature, arose. They were created in accordance with legal and egalitarian rules, with elected, rotating directorates and a mandate to care for the neighborhood's collective interests. They form, on the grassroots level, the rudiments of democratic rule of the law. Their elected leaders have a mandate to negotiate with third parties, particularly government agencies that are locally relevant. Whenever possible, protests reach authorities through neighborhood associations. Local development projects must reckon with them. The existence of so many problems and such grassroots penetration lend neighborhood associations a unique importance among social movements. Though they existed before, they grew in numbers and significance in the 1970s. A 1986 survey in Rio de Janeiro and São Paulo found that 90.7 percent of the neighborhood associations had been created since 1970. Two terms had dominated the political imagination in the preceding period: the Nation and the People. Political leaders were called on to build (strengthen, defend, and so on) the Nation in the name of the People. In the 1970s, however, this ideological equation was seriously disrupted. "The People" were replaced by this or that "popular movement." Although still important, "the People" became less visible and less effective as a concept, and gave way to a weaker notion: the adjective "popular," which served to qualify a variety of singular social subjects—shantytown-dwellers, landless peasants, rubber tappers, miners, gold prospectors, Native Americans, fishers, street children, streetwalkers, and so on. The nongovernmental stage made room for a variety of "social actors."

It is only a short step from this to admittedly contrasting identities. "Women," "Native Americans," "blacks," and "gays" appeared on the public stage, in an array of alternative identifications; these categories and others, such as "senior citizens," "children," "ethnic minorities," and "handicapped people," made their way into the lexicon of subjects that should be reckoned with and to whom something was owed.

The rise of "women" as an autonomous social subject brought along a review of values that affected the entire set of known human societies. "Native American" called into question the history of colonial America. "Blacks" brought to light the traumas of modern slavery. The history of childhood, like the history of old age, became illuminating to the extent that it provided other angles from which to see the dilemmas of today. In short, the multiplication of collective actors accustomed us to the idea that social reality is intriguingly made up of multiple points of view.

The movements internalized a few profound dilemmas. If singular identity gave them access to the space of public policies, the uniqueness was not a self-evident given. The women's movement, for example, is a worldwide phenonmenon. Two U.N. conferences and the priority given to the theme in international cooperation agencies are clear indicators of this fact. Exile during the authoritarian period turned out to be an important experience for the constitution of the movement, since it gave Latin American women an opportunity to participate in women's groups in North America and Europe.

In the very beginning of the democratization process, when civil society was being reorganized, associations of the most varied kinds included sections specializing in women's affairs. Councils dedicated to changing the situ-

Housing Cooperatives in Uruguay

The building of housing developments by nongovernmental initiative is a unique and dramatic chapter in Uruguayan history. In the late 1960s, cooperatives were started that received state credits to build popular housing. Most of the associates were unionized workers who brought with them the habits of an advanced trade union culture. Individual property was allowed, but the dominant system was joint ownership by the cooperative, the families enjoying usufruct of their homes. As late as 1986, when given the opportunity of choosing, 95 percent of associates preferred the collective-property system. In 1970, the cooperatives joined to form a federation, FUCVAM, which in 1975 had 194 members representing over 10,000 families. At the time, FUCVAM accounted for 41 percent of all housebuilding activity in Uruguay.

At first, FUCVAM managed to escape the repressive effects of the 1973 military coup. While political parties and trade unions were outlawed and leftist activists became urban guerrillas, FUCVAM went on functioning as an articulating agency for the building and management of popular housing. But its very survival burdened it with political significance. It became the major example of civil autonomy in an authoritarian state. Its stance of overt opposition was increasingly intensified in the 1980s, and FUCVAM began to clash with the government, which struck back, raising costly obstacles to autonomous enterprises.

A significant number of cooperatives went bankrupt, and construction work stopped. Cooperatives, being among the most active forces in the process of redemocratization, are now trying to regain their autonomy from politics, deemphasizing their union connections and moving closer to neighborhoods. But their most difficult task is to recover their economic effectiveness, threatened by scarcities and the high cost of available credits.

ation of women were created on the governmental level in several countries, such as Brazil, Chile, Nicaragua, and Argentina (in Buenos Aires Province). Such themes as birth control, violence against women, and equal rights were introduced in the public agenda. Research in and teaching of subjects of interest to feminists gained space in universities.

The movement, in short, for all the usual difficulties that characterize periods of change, progressed fast and in a relatively effective way in the space between organized civil society and government. But a whole sea of challenges slowed it down on other levels, where most Latin American women actually lived. Inertia, though, is not stagnation. It would be misleading to speak of a contrast between women on the move in the North and stagnant women in the South. Major changes took place in the behavior of Latin American women during this period. Take the issue of population, for one. Between 1960 and 1990, the population growth rate dropped almost 30 percent in the region as a whole—about 40 percent in Colombia, Venezuela, and Brazil, and 25 percent in Argentina and Mexico. People live longer, children die less often, and nevertheless the population growth rate is falling because women are having far fewer children. Unless women are totally passive in the face of the aggressive sterilizing zeal of doctors—a supposition that seems too one-sided—large-scale, long-run strategic changes have clearly occurred among the women of the continent.

Urban social movements took place preferentially in the sphere of the neighborhood, a territory in which women have ample power. Such issues as water, garbage collection, security of children, day care centers, school, and food that were responsible for many of the mobilizations of the period all directly interest and involve the women living in a neighborhood. Squatting on farmland, on plots of urban land, or in buildings combines the elements of struggle with those of domestic space and requires the involvement of women to an unusual degree. In fact, the female component of social movements was most significant.

The problem, however, is more subtle and more complex, for the presence of women in these movements is usually associated with their traditional function in the hierarchy of genders. The responsibilities, the charisma, and the skills of motherhood lend women more authority in the territory of the home and its immediate surroundings; this authority tends to increase when men are unable to carry out their functions as providers adequately, as is often the case in very poor neighborhoods.

Some of the most creative responses to this dilemma have been tried in Peru. In a supportive climate provided by a city government dominated by the United Left and with funding from European agencies, some nongovernmental organizations (NGOs) developed an extensive network of mothers in the shantytowns of Lima in two major projects: the distribution of one glass of milk per day to each child, and "popular eating houses" in which women took turns in the kitchen, offering a daily meal to a small number of neighboring homes. Relying on the initiative of women who had no problems of local integration, acting mostly as vehicles of communication, these NGOs were able to manage in a simple way a huge public service with connections on the local, municipal, national, and even international levels.

Instead of simply questioning traditional female roles, the projects managed to re-enhance them, giving them a public dimension. This paradoxical solution generated a number of more comprehensive offshoots that brought to the popular sphere the civilizing challenges posed by the movement. Thus in Peru and elsewhere the denunciation and control of domestic violence, a perverse manifestation of "male honor," became a major theme of feminine identification in all segments of society.

Other positive experiences can be found within the Roman Catholic Church. Church base communities tend to be predominantly made up of women. Seen from the inside, CBCs are organizations with clearly feminine connotations. This is not, however, the impression they give from the outside. They see themselves and present themselves as "the people" congregated in a community. Yet many pastoral agents are nuns who were freed from isolation by the internal reforms of the Church (for instance, as regards wearing the traditional habit) and who implemented many changes in their work.

In addition, Liberation Theology opened up a space for academic theological reflection by Catholic female intellectuals. These women are active on various levels of the Church; in spite of their differences, they share a common problem, particularly as Catholics, with ample implications for the regional culture. The growing communication among these women through meetings, spiritual retreats, assistantships, training courses, and so on promises to open new alternatives.

In a word, dilemmas are not culs-de-sac. However, they do call for the ability to assimilate contradictory principles and logics, as well as openness to processes and dynamics on which systematic control cannot be ensured from the outset.

A schematic approach suggests that the case of Native Americans is the opposite of women. They are attaining international prominence as they structure a "Native American movement." But their weight and significance is mostly local. In opposition to the cosmopolitan character of the women's movement, which makes it difficult for feminism to take root, the assertion of an indigenous identity largely depends, in Latin America, on acknowledgment of its rootedness in the land.

The movement is also characterized by the huge diversity of its circumstances. The demographic distribution of Native Americans is unequal. They make up a large part of the population in some Andean and Central American countries, where they have a conditioning impact on the population. It is impossible to think of "the people" in Bolivia, for instance, without calling to mind the Aymara, the Quechua, and the Guarani. But they are small minorities in such countries as Chile, Argentina, Brazil, or Venezuela. Even here, however, they may be a significant presence in certain subregions—in Amazonia, for instance, or on the Atlantic coast of Nicaragua.

Native Americans also vary widely as to language, social organization, power structures, beliefs, and rites. Attempts to find common elements in South American Native mythologies must abstract the concrete connotations of symbols. For instance, neighboring peoples often interpret and respond in radically differently ways to the same outside provocation.

A recent case in the Brazilian state of Mato Grosso do Sul, near the Paraguayan border, provides a dramatic example of this. The Kaiowa and the Terena share the same reservation outside the city of Dourados, in a region witnessing an aggressive capitalization of agricultural activities. The Kaiowa became profoundly depressed, and many of them have resorted to suicide; the Terena, however, managed to rise to the challenge, and have had some success in economic terms (using tractors and relying on exploitation by nuclear families) and in generating important leaders. Although subjected to the same colonial process, the history of each group is characterized by the uniqueness of its circumstances, conflicts, reconcilements, and alliances.

There are many different kinds of intertribal relationship, ranging from complex systems of multicultural exchange and integration to systematic antagonisms or indifference. Again, each group has had a unique history of relationship with colonial society. Different segments of the same tribe, competing with one another for internal reasons, interact with different agencies—some with Evangelicals, others with Roman Catholics, still others with some NGO. It makes a difference whether the group in question is a majority or a minority, whether their land is coveted by prospectors, peasants, or a major multinational project, and whether they collect Brazil nuts or raise coca.

In the 1970s, more and more Native leaders showed an interest in problems on the level of national society as a whole, or even beyond. It was then that the Native American movements arose, attempting to find means to defend their interests and speak in the name of all Natives to the outside world. This is a new requirement, one that implies more than a change of scale. It implies fluency in the national language, ability to circulate around the national territory, a generic discourse, forms of association that will face the problems of representing a multi-ethnical universe, knowledge of national mechanisms of decision, attunement to public opinion in order to influence it, and so on.

In short, the Native American movement implies awareness of the problems and possibilities of social movements in general. The affirmation of a "Native identity" that can subsume differences in a generic image can make sense only as a specific form of participation in the common struggles of the larger society. By affirming its difference, the movement heightens the value of its participation.

The passage from exclusion to participation included, significantly, the support of missionary organizations, always committed to the integration of native societies. Salesians in Ecuador, Jesuits in various countries, the Indian Missionary Council (CIMI) in Brazil, among others, translated Liberation Theology into a new style of mission: first to identify with Natives, then to seek out with them the ways of redemption. The Indian Mass composed by the poet-bishop Pedro Casaldaliga is a significant example of the transfiguration of the names of the many tribes into a universalist symbology. The first assemblies of Native American leaders in Amazonia were made possible by the boats and the organizing efforts of pastoral agents.

Anthropologists associated with NGOs have also been instrumental in this process, providing assistance to economic projects and acting as mediators with various national and international agencies. Finally, legal associations have been formed to provide an articulated and representative sense to the movement; among them are the Federation of Shuar Centers and the Confederation of Ecuadorian Indian Nationalities, in Ecuador; the Coordination of Indian Organizations in Brazilian Amazonia and the Union of Indian Nations, in Brazil. The Nobel Peace Prize awarded to Rigoberta Menchu, a Guatemalan Native American leader, and her nomination as U.N. "Goodwill Ambassador" are indications of the movement's symbolic value in the international conscience.

The brilliance and agility of the movement, however, contrast with the slow and often tragical rhythm of local history. Violence remains the predominant form of solving conflicts, particularly when the right to use land is in question. Traditional Native authorities, for the most part, are humiliated. Cases of stimulating economic integration are rare. Mediating agents are needed between the inner dynamics and the numerous plans of articulation with the outside world. Latin America's fragile liberal democracy is only beginning to think about the implications of a multiethnic, multicultural society. Despite

---

A Native Ritual in the Brazilian Constituent Assembly

The Native American lobby was among the most effective during the 1988 Brazilian National Constituent Assembly. It obtained far more than the 30,000 signatures needed for the proposal of "popular amendments," and ensured the enactment of a number of laws protecting their rights to traditional territories.

When the amendment was to be officially presented, the audience of Congress was filled with bare-chested Native Americans, their bodies painted, wearing their traditional ornaments and feather headdresses. Expectations ran high when the representative of the Native peoples came forward to present the case for the amendment. To everyone's surprise, he was impeccably dressed, wearing an elegant suit, tie, and shoes.

With a grave expression on his face, he walked up the aisle and took the tribune. He turned to the chairman as if he were asking authorization to begin his speech; then, instead of speaking, he took from his pocket a small box of paints and silently began to color his own face with the ritual colors of his tribe. He spent the full twenty minutes allotted to his speech painting himself, a serious expression on his face. Then he faced the audience, still silent, exhibiting his war paint.

Without a word, he left the tribune and walked away, proudly, leaving the members of the Assembly stunned by the eloquence of his performance.

---

these uncertainties, "Indians" are no longer thought of as a "species doomed to extinction."

In contrast with the Native Americans, who are typically distinguished by territory, language, or even social organization, blacks are dispersed throughout the poorest regions of national societies. Racism in Latin America does not conform to the Anglo-Saxon pattern. Instead of isolating a black community, making it clearly identifiable, it weaves it into a complex structure of hierarchies. Skin colors combine in mixed marriages; an intermediate category is formed—the "mulatto"—which makes the game of racial identifications more fluid. But the stigmatizing polarity is always present (the whiter, the better), although its specific application varies on different steps of the social hierarchy, generating a wide array of personal strategies.

The black movement spoke up against this cultural pattern, denouncing the persistence of the polarity that justifies the stigma. It revolted against the hypocrisy of a kind of interracial intimacy that does not allow us to forget the unequal values attributed to the differences. It has even been suggested that this hierarchical and inclusive kind of racism, being more covert, is more cruel and effective than the explicit segregation of the Anglo-Saxon model. Like other movements, it achieved major advances in legislation and formal representation. Antiracism organizations multiplied in the 1980s, attaining a degree of prominence in organized civil society and government agencies. The movement gained the support of the small intellectualized sector of black youth in universities and in the clergy. But it proved unable to expand to any significant degree.

On the other hand, some large-scale sociocultural dynamics point to the emergence of symbols and values associated with negritude. Afro-American religions are acquiring a following among the middle classes, even in a few countries that have no significant black population, such as Uruguay and Argentina. But these new followers adopt the inherited patterns of inclusiveness. In Brazil, blond-haired, blue-eyed priests and priestesses incorporate deities in the African pantheon. For them, African religiosity has truth value, explains and helps, order behaviors, shapes tastes and styles, and is open to any one, independent of gender, background, or race. The African origins are not forgotten, but they do not define a separate identity.

Other cultural movements follow a similar path. Reggae music, which in the Caribbean is associated with the Ras Tafari movement, finds adherents among young people of all races. Rap music fascinates the youth of the lower-class suburbs, assimilating the rebelliousness that simmers among the poor population of big cities.

Notwithstanding all this, racism is still present in the intimacy of Afro-American temples and discotheques frequented by young people. As in the case of women and Native Americans, the black movement faces the challenge of establishing a connection between the egalitarian values of modern social movements and the deep-seated dynamics of Ibero-American hierarchies.

Social movements during the authoritarian 1970s tended to adopt the logic of radical protest, and in one way or another incorporated the ideology of the Left. In spite of the absence of vertical structures to integrate them, the rhetoric of movements actualized the expectation of a union to be achieved in the future. The key word in this integrating rhetoric was the adjective "popular." However diversified, movements were predominantly "popular," a characteristic that placed them in a historical dimension oriented by class struggle. This idea was substantially developed by intellectuals with a Marxist background. Gradually, researches and theoretical debates began to follow in other directions, but the leaders of the movements, for the most part, continued to be oriented by Marx's tragic and apocalyptic image of a system that behaves like a grave digger digging his own grave. To work in "popular education," to stimulate "consciousness-raising among the people," acquired a larger sense as a preparation for the day after the collapse to which the system seemed to be doomed. Flourishing in the margins and cracks of dictatorial regimes, movements continued to cultivate the expectation of a revolution.

This ideological scheme was weakened during the 1980s, however, and the phrase "social movements" began to elbow out the older "popular movements" for several reasons. For one, some of the most important movements did not fit the "popular" mold. Such is the case of the women's movement, which includes all strata of society. Neighborhood associations were formed in middle-class areas and raised issues of relevance to the whole city.

The environmental movement arose, opening up a new discursive dimension. The first unmistakably environmental organization in Latin America was created in 1971, a contemporary of the other movements. But from the beginning it was founded on values that transcended the division between "Right" and "Left." It questioned patterns of "development" in the East and in the West, and stressed issues of individual habits that simply had no place in the agenda of class struggle. It generated a circuit of communication that, particularly in the beginning, could not identify and had hardly any communication with the lower strata of the population. The growing visibility of the environmental movement in the 1980s was a sign of new times and new sensibilities. Even when, at a later stage, it incorporated the challenges of social rootedness, the movement never relied on the rhetorical and organizational resource of the "popular."

Other movements opened yet other lively circuits of participation. One of the most disturbing of these was brought about by the AIDS epidemic. The disease highlights certain "risk practices," the demarcation of which has no direct relationship with the division of social classes. Nevertheless, their significance to life in society is extreme. Unexpectedly, particularly in the context of Latin culture, persons identified with unorthodox sexual habits become for this very reason the public figures most qualified to express in words the meaning of solidarity in a context of plague. Reverting deep-rooted tendencies, an international network of activists is able to oppose the forces of prejudice. The slogan created by Herbert Daniel, a Brazilian gay leader, was proclaimed with such force and dignity that it came to be heard in the most unlikely quarters—The real question: is there life before death?

In short, the phrase "social movements" has become more relevant, among other reasons, because it is more inclusive. It does not deny the "popular" but includes and surpasses it. It does not deny class struggle, but shifts it from the central and structuring position it held in the earlier pattern. What is lost in terms of a general view is compensated for by the present relevance of newly emphasized words.

Nongovernmental Organizations

The first generation of NGOs in Latin America typically arose as an ad hoc solution when few alternatives existed—as provisional research centers developing in the margin of universities submitted to the pressures of the authoritarian state, popular education centers outside the official school network, groups providing support to emerging social movements without any links with legal political organizations, and so on. These were not expected to last long. They were not expected to vindicate themselves as such. It was felt that the proper place for research was the universities; for popular education, the public schools; for the articulation of social movements, the political parties.

As the original restraints were gradually lifted during the 1980s, however, the founders encountered reasons to establish themselves positively as "NGO cadres." This was a crucial decision, the existential subtleties of which provide many anecdotes in the memories of this first generation. Even as they developed closer ties with large institutions, those who decided to remain expressed a new conviction: small is not all bad.

The taste for smallness, in this case, seemed to be associated with a well-known characteristic of small organizations: institutional instruments are brought down nearly to the scale of individual decisions. The red tape is reduced. On the other hand, NGOs have no representative character. Unlike trade unions, neighborhood associations, or even social movements, NGOs cannot speak for or act on behalf of others. They only speak and act for themselves. Consequently, they do not rely on the complex political game that is obligatory in representative systems in order to legitimate their decisions.

Further, being private, in principle they can multiply indefinitely, a function of demands and initiatives. The credit they are given is a function of the responses to the services they offer. Last—and this is the other side of the coin—it was realized that a job well done may have repercussions surprisingly larger than the means employed. Working for (and with) unions, associations, movements, social networks, churches, government agencies, the media, businesses, and so forth, NGOs amplify their capabilities. It was thus found that public interest activities may be performed outside government, and in a measure that exceeds the expectations of a lifetime. In short, without the major actors realizing it, NGOs brought to the sphere of social work significant elements of what is usually referred to as "free enterprise." The main tool of this process of institutional innovation was "the project." Funding was provided for specific projects, and consequently researchers and social activists had to learn to define their work in terms compatible with a schedule, in which there was consistency between ends and means. Above all, projects should be translatable into budgets that quantified the financial resources necessary to reach the desired goals, in terms sufficiently specific to allow reliable accountability. The consequences of the introduction of this seemingly innocent figure—the "project"—in the institutional culture of Latin American activists cannot be overestimated. Thanks to it, those who worked in NGOs had to swallow, however unwillingly, a large spoonful of pragmatic logic.

Unlike other segments, NGOs give rise to more questions than answers, and they require a more descriptive approach. Given the fragmentary nature of the available information, primary sources are used for a generic, if tentative, profile of Latin American NGOs. This section is based on a review of 32 NGO directories covering 24 countries and a total of 4,327 NGOs and 5,860 other nonprofit groups. The extent of each directory depended on the purposes and capabilities of the editors, as well as on the level of visibility of the organizations to be listed. Every entry was classified according to date of foundation, thematic sphere of action, and main groups benefiting from their action.

One pattern is clear: NGOs became a massive phenomenon in Latin America from the 1970s on. About 68 percent of them appeared after 1975. A significant number (17 percent) date from the 1950s and 1960s, and the remaining 15 percent are distributed irregularly among earlier decades. Simplifying, it may be said that certain organizations created before 1970 were assimilated into the NGO circuit, which became visible as such in the late 1970s or early 1980s. The term itself, which comes from U.N. terminology and is still a matter of debate, became generally recognized in the mid-1980s.

The spheres of action least covered by the NGOs in the directories are crime, violence, and drugs. Fewer than 1 percent of Latin American NGOs are reported here. This is a shocking state of affairs, considering the importance of these issues, particularly among the poor. It calls for comments and explanations. It is also interesting for comparison purposes: the drug problem is a classical theme of civil movements in Germanic and Anglo-Saxon countries. Alcohol, in particular, was the object of large-scale programs in the previous century and the beginning of the present century. The moral dimension in which these problems acquire urgency has not proved attractive to Latin American NGOs.

Blacks and Indians are the next least covered topics—by only 1.6 percent of the NGOs in the lists. Only in the Brazilian directory is the theme of negritude present—5.5 percent of the organizations listed are associated with the black movement. The theme is not mentioned in other countries' lists. The subject of Native Americans is more widely distributed, but again the Brazilian directory stands out. Only 0.44 percent of the Natives in the region live in Brazilian territory, but 37 percent of the NGOs dealing with them are Brazilian.

In terms of the fields with the most entries, two categories stand out: qualified training/consultancy (41 percent) and Education (36 percent). NGO growth in Latin America was associated most of all with education. "Popular education" is often mentioned, a term extended beyond the context of formal schooling, along the lines defined by authors such as Paulo Freire and Ivan Illich. Research, mentioned by a large number of NGOs (16 percent), is frequently qualified as "participatory"—that is, involving pedagogical interaction between subject and object during the research. Development/welfare is another recurring category (30 percent), often in combination with rural development (16 percent). Considering the categories mentioned most often, the major thrust of NGO activity in Latin America can be summed up as education for development with emphasis on social justice.

Health is also important: more than one-fifth of all NGOs perform some sort of health service. In some countries the percentage is much higher: 44 percent in Bolivia and 51 percent in Guatemala. Indeed, health is a top-priority field for all kinds of agents in the Third Sector—whether traditional or modern, poor or rich, all are concerned with health.

It is worth noting that in Central America the term NGO has been avoided by some centers that prefer to describe themselves as OPDs—Organizations for Promotion and Development, emphasizing productive programs. The approach of these organizations is closer to the North American outlook, whereas the "human rights" approach has mobilized European solidarity in particular.

Who are the direct beneficiaries of the NGOs' work? The "community" is the most frequent reply. About one-third of all NGOs claim to work for it. The importance of this concept for social movements in the 1970s and 1980s is clear; now the NGOs are following suit. Three basic ideas seem to be related to the concept: seeing the totality rather than specializing on a segment, valuing face-to-face interactions rather than a formal and bureaucratic approach, and focusing on home instead of workplace. In terms of their relationship to the world of labor, the emphasis is on the rural environment. In spite of the importance of urban workers in leftist ideology, NGOs have made little investment in them. In addition to conjunctural reasons (more control over companies in the authoritarian period), Latin America's strong trade union tradition probably had an inhibiting effect here. Urban workers already had organizations able to respond to their associates' demands for services. In the country, however, the fragility of existing organizations resulted in a fertile ground for NGO action. In addition, an emphasis on "the poor" is indicative of the general orientation of the organizations of the period.

"Civil associations" is another important category, which calls for a brief comment. In our sample, 621 organizations give support of such associations as their professional objective. This is particularly important among Southern Cone NGOs—41 percent in Uruguay and 25 percent in Chile. Although the concept is more comprehensive, it should be observed that most associations mentioned center on neighborhood problems, and NGOs act as sources of technical assistance to improve their performance and increase their legitimacy. NGOs strengthen associations vis-à-vis communities. Mediating between personalized community ties and the formal rules of civil associations is a typical NGO task. They may be thought of as small vehicles moving systematically between romantic traditional communities and the businesslike offices of citizenship.

In short, Latin American NGOs have addressed particularly the poor, with a civil rights agenda, concentrating on homes. They tend to give priority to the regions and functions that are weakest in the social structure—the poor in general; children and women in the family; rural workers in the productive sector.

NGOs concentrate on the values and institutions of citizenship—community centers, neighborhood associations, cooperatives, unions, and so on—which operate better in daylight. When night falls, NGO cadres go to meetings, or home to rest. This selective approach clearly implies a major limitation in the NGOs' field of work, for marginalization has grown extraordinarily in Latin America in the last few decades.

The little interest manifested in ethnic groups (3 percent) is even more surprising. The directories of three countries present somewhat higher figures—Paraguay (11 percent), Guatemala (7 percent), and Brazil (5 percent)—

but this is still far too little, considering the high proportion of Natives among the poor in Paraguay and Guatemala. NGOs do extensive work with them in such countries as Bolivia, Peru, and Mexico. But this does not show in the directories. This work has apparently been classified by NGOs under such categories as "rural workers" or "peasants." In other words, the ethnic dimension is underrepresented, being included in a socioeconomic category.

This suggests a comment that qualifies an earlier conclusion: in general, NGOs have assimilated the modernist bias common among development agencies. They find it hard to perceive and think positively about the margins of society, as well as about traditional cultures. Mediating between "community" and "citizenship," they define the limits of the legitimacy of their movement: the limits of rational and egalitarian forms. The mediation is one-sided. Although they often visit the villages of tradition, NGOs tend to behave as agents of modernity, which, like so many others, lack the necessary time to appreciate and learn traditional customs.

All these movements would not have taken place with the intensity and in the form they have without "international cooperation" and funding. The "nongovernmental" character of the funding agencies was decisive in these circumstances. Financing supplied by foreign governments must be received by national governments, but nongovernmental agencies may deal directly with civil groups, as long as this is not expressly forbidden by law; in most of Latin America such relationships were ignored by existing legislation. In certain extraordinary situations, nongovernmental international agencies established covert relationships with movements, such as those in defense of the rights of political prisoners in dictatorial regimes. In an authoritarian context, the existence of this kind of "nongovernmental" support seemed to many local actors a precious discovery. Thanks to this, movements and small organizations realized that they could also be seen in these terms.

More than money, then, it was the institutional form and concept that took to the untrod road of "nongovernmental" financing. This was the relationship that, among other things, gave rise to NGOs. International cooperation agencies needed local partners able to formulate projects, monitor their execution, and give account of their finances. They needed to deal with legal entities, with minimal administrative structure and congenial goals. They could not establish relations directly with social movements, for these had no institutional stability. So Latin American NGOs were born in a game of reciprocal support, as partners in international cooperation, aiding community action and social welfare movements.

Financing Projects in the Informal Economy

Although little developed in comparison with the situation in Africa or Asia, economic support to the popular economy in Latin America has been the object of some significant NGO experiments. With support from the International Labour Organization and the U.N. Development Programme, IDESI (Institute for Development of the Informal Sector) was created in Peru in 1986.

By 1992, IDESI had 29 offices in 19 regions of the country and liabilities amounting to US$30 million distributed as credit to small businesses. COPEMI, a Peruvian organization, specializes in mediating between private banks and poorer clients who would not be able to get financing without the NGO's assistance and participation as cosigner. According to reports, the rate of repayment on these loans is higher than the national average.

Another Peruvian organization is CLAE, a people's savings-and-loan institution that in only a few years acquired over 600,000 clients. Pressured by banks, the Fujimori government intervened in CLAE, but was forced to back down when small investors protested.

On the other hand, dealing for the most part with recently created organizations and interested in achieving the goals of cooperation, agencies preferred financing specific projects rather than supporting institutions. Instead of funding NGOs as such, they financed projects, reinforcing the pragmatic logic of these new organizations.

The nongovernmental character was associated with another typical aspect: cooperation agencies were many and diversified, for they reflected the variety of the civil traditions of their respective countries. From the United States came private foundations supported by philanthropical industrialists. Ford, Rockefeller, Kellogg, MacArthur are among the most active in the continent, in addition to the Inter-American Foundation, which is unique in that it is associated with the U.S. Congress.

In addition to major divisions reflecting the main traditions of European social history, numerous NGOs are organized in function of specific topics or mandates. There are organizations to provide support to victims of disasters, to refugees, needy children, women, old people, or invalids; others are concerned with the environment, public health, AIDS prevention, human rights, and so on. Each of these themes is reproduced in a variety of countries and traditions.

Given such a segmented situation, Latin American NGOs developed relationships with multiple foreign partners, each with its own language, its networks, its priorities, its assets, and its difficulties. They learned to distinguish between them and argue with each. They specialized in themes of mutual interest. Conversely, they furnished the foreign partners with a set of themes and priorities that made up the discourse of social movements. They became accustomed to interacting amid a veiled competition between projects and partnerships. In short, the multiplicity typical of social movements found its match in the segmentation of international cooperation, generating an open field of alliances and disputes that extended from the local plane to the most distant and diversified international connections.

There is a clear predominance of countries with a basically Protestant culture, where individualism is more highly valued—a survey in Brazil found 250 cooperative relationships with these countries, against 66 with countries with a dominant Catholic culture. Another question in the same survey reinforces this point: when questioned about the relative importance of the various kinds of agency for the income of NGOs, the directors of these organizations reported that ecumenical agencies were of major importance in 45 percent of cases, Catholic agencies in 25.5 percent, private foundations in 23.5 percent, multilateral agencies in 9 percent, and governmental agencies in 3 percent.

Since most nongovernmental cooperation comes from Europe, Latin America is a minor partner among developing regions. Due to historical reasons and to the magnitude of their needs, Africa and Asia have greater priority and are allotted more resources. Similarly, within Latin America the poorer subregions tend to get more attention from Northern NGOs—Andean countries rather than the Southern Cone, Nicaragua and Guatemala more than Mexico, the Northeast and Amazonia more than southern Brazil, and so on.

This is not a rigid rule, for the segmentation of agencies corresponds to the interweaving of a variety of criteria. Chile, for instance, has attracted more interest because of its dramatic recent history and the prolonged nature of its exile period. After democratization, though, it has been losing rather than gaining importance. In short: in addition to the segmentary form, international cooperation has reinforced a pattern of thinking in which need, not profitability, is the number one criterion when it comes to defining priorities for nonprofit, nongovernmental initiatives.

Civil Society and Citizenship

In the late 1970s, the phrase "civil society" became current in the discourse of Latin American social activists, in contrast to "popular movements" and "social movements." The earlier phrases referred to a part only, whereas "civil society" denotes the whole; likewise, "poor," "woman," or "black" brings to mind a specific class of people, whereas "citizen" should refer to all individuals above a certain age, whether rich or poor, man or woman, black or white or yellow. When they began to speak of "civil society" and "citizenship," the movements adopted a universalist perspective, and were forced to see themselves as parts of a larger whole.

In addition, in Spanish and Portuguese, "civil" means both "civil" and "civilian" as opposed to "military"; so a contrast is made between the rule of law and the rule of force. The concept also has a clear legal connotation. In "civil society," individuals and groups relate according to acquired rights that are spelled out in the law. Further, the reference to law becomes constitutive of the way of conceiving of life in society. Thus, although the concept does not deny the existence or the relevance of "popular movements" or "social movements," it effectively interferes with their meaning, placing them in the totalizing context of a legally constituted society. In order to have a legitimate existence, these movements, however valid their claims, must behave according to the law. The adoption of the concept expresses the need and the desire of political participation.

A wave of democratization swept through Latin America in the 1980s; very few countries were untouched. In some, such as Brazil, Uruguay, Argentina, and Chile, what happened was a return to a tradition interrupted by military coups. In others, like Paraguay and Nicaragua, it was the beginning of a democratic experience. Even the Mexican one-party system, legitimated by its revolutionary roots, is pressured to adapt to the plurality of an emerging civil society. Some Mexican NGOs have specialized in monitoring elections, and have even conducted plebiscites in Mexico City.

Everywhere the question "How to vote?"—meaning not "Whom to vote for?" but rather "What does voting mean?"—is inspiring a number of educational initiatives. The state, the Church, the parties, the media, and the NGOs all are explaining how one should vote. In Chile, a number of NGOs joined to create a new organization ("Idea") to engage in this kind of work. The general trend has been to expand the universe of those who take part in elections—lowering the voting age to 16 (as in Brazil), giving illiterates the right to vote, dropping restrictions to the equality of women's participation (which still existed, for instance, in Argentina in the 1970s), and including Native American populations. Adding these new voters to the generation that grew up under dictatorial rule and to the various countries with no previous democratic traditions, it is clear that for the vast majority of Latin Americans, these have been the years of a first contact with the rules and concepts of liberal democracy.

Even in Brazil, with a liberal tradition that, however checkered and imperfect, dates from the first half of the nineteenth century, the political "opening" of the 1980s brought about a marked increase in the number of voters. In the last election before the dictatorship, in 1960, there were 16 million voters; in 1989, there were 80 million. Voters were less than one-fourth of the population in 1960 but more than half in 1989.

Whereas the authoritarian period gave us a taste for "community" and local "movements," democratization opened up spaces for the participant presence of individual citizens. Although communities and movements were not to be forgotten, whoever wished to speak of public affairs had to learn the appropriate language for communicating with this unique, diffuse character. It was also necessary to resort to the mass media, the only vehicles that could establish with individuals a permanent communicative relationship on a scale in which they really count.

Having been trained to specialize in face-to-face relationships and the discourse of the collectivity, activists now find themselves at a loss before the wider channels of communication opened with the demise of authoritarianism. The dim lights that shone in the darkness of the 1970s run the risk of being dazzled by the solar brightness of the communications made possible by democratic individualism.

When "voluntary associations" are included in the Third Sector, an incomparably more diversified view becomes clear of the organizations that proliferate in the "grassroots" of society. Indeed, associations project the variety of individualization onto the plane of collective forms, and enhance the value of individual options. They emphasize the voluntary dimension, a consequence of strictly individual decisions. They imply a membership equally responsible for being there, since, in principle, people are there only because they want to be.

In this sense, the rules for participating in voluntary associations tend to be egalitarian. They internalize, in miniature, the democratic forms of government. Democratic forms take root in everyday practices and are modified by them. It seems that voluntary associations are expressive presences in major Latin American urban centers today, and the rate of their growth has quickened since the 1970s.

Democratization has brought more than openness; it has also brought confusion. Instead of returning to previous patterns, it set about dismantling the populist heritage. New political competitions arose; in many cases, national constituent assemblies redefined the fundamental laws of the country; neoliberal strategies of economic policy were adopted. To the uncertainties brought about by the redefinition of laws and political partnerships were added the "structural adjustments" with the systematic removal of the regulating and protectionist functions of the state. Instead of reinstating the links of protection taken over by the military, democratization gave a radical turn to the break with past integrating patterns.

Adding to the uncertainties of such a transition, changes took place at a time of grave economic difficulties. Economies built on the basis of expected growth faced prolonged stagnation. Whereas for developing countries as a whole the per capita gross national product grew annually 2.5 percent from 1980 to 1990, in Latin America it fell -0.3 percent. With resources growing scarce and currencies being eroded by soaring inflation, the adjustments cut deep into the flesh of national budgets. In the midst of democratization, public services deteriorated. The combined effect of stagnation, inflation, adjustments, and crisis in public services caused a huge increase in mass poverty, both in absolute and in relative terms. According to the World Bank, the number of persons below the poverty line in Latin America increased by 25 percent between 1985 and 1990.

Thus an extremely dangerous situation developed. With few exceptions, during the period of democratic transition the public and legal system suffered a loss of credibility. Services still exist, but in a terrible condition. Fresh faces abound among politicians, but as a class they have not won credit among the population. The judicial system is independent, but the impoverished majority does not trust it. Except for a few occasions, such as elections, citizenship has not truly reached the lower classes. And, in counterpoint to the crisis of institutions, the circuit of parallel and marginal powers financed by the drug trade kept on growing, unaffected by the depression.

Such major difficulties require urgent solutions. Suggestions of a return to authoritarianism are often heard. There is another kind of solution, though, that is closer to the spirit of citizen participation. The insecurities of the state enhance, in contrast, the value of civil initiatives, free of the traditional dependence on government agencies. The ineffectiveness of public services encourages the search for independent alternatives that reinforce the ideas of mutual support and self-help. The budgetary scarcities of governments have led some of the more enlightened sectors of business to invest in social programs. Given the impasses of politics, some segments that were once antagonistic to one another are beginning to assert the advantages of cooperation.

In short, the concept of "civil society" is advancing. The end of the cold war has certainly removed a number of ideological obstacles to the idea of belonging to the same society. But business and labor are only beginning to try this approach, which is crucial for the enhancement of a "Third Sector" in the region.

Business philanthropy, the source of many foundations, has deep cultural roots in North America, but not south of the Rio Grande, where in the Catholic tradition, charity works are an obligation of the clergy. In the twentieth century, through revolution and populism, the state assumed responsibilities previously attributed to the Church. Church and state divided between them responsibility for meeting people's needs, so that businesses were left to take care of business.

The cold war had the effect of making businesses invest even less in social projects. The best ideologues of the period saw public life as an arena for the struggle over the right of property. Placed at opposite poles, accusing each other of the worst sins (often justifiably), social activists and business leaders rarely met, even when they belonged to the same families. Isolated from religion, fighting socialist ideas, counting on state protection, the business class felt free and justified to indulge in unbridled capitalism. There are exception in various countries, of course. In Brazil, for instance, some companies (Shell and Antarctica) have had philanthropic programs for over 50 years. But this is not the rule. The idea that since we already have capitalism it would be nice to have philanthropy too is only beginning to take root.

The generalization of the concept of "citizenship" seems to make a positive contribution here. Not only individuals, with their moral conscience, but also corporations and private institutions are beginning to be valued. Like any citizen, private groups, whether or not for profit, have rights and duties vis-à-vis others. From the viewpoint of "civil society," horizontal lines are positively valued, encouraging actors to question their relations with the world around them.

Concern about the environment easily translates this perception into practical directives. The factory that pours wastes into a body of water can be accused of trespassing on the rights of others, and as such may be accused of a crime. Ultimately, it may even be convinced that by acting so it is acting against its own possibilities of surviving in the long run. If it cannot take the long view and refuses to be persuaded, it may be forced to act through legal coercion.

Similarly, urbanization constantly conveys messages of clear relevance to the civil behavior of companies. Each new building may be questioned as to its relationships with its surroundings. If shared responsibility for the natural and human-made environment becomes evident, it takes only a short step for shared responsibility to develop beyond the company grounds.

In addition to commitments to workers, businesses are called on to assume a commitment to the society. Technological advances require constant and renewed investments in personnel training, which puts pressure on firms to take an interest in the education of the new generations. Investment in research is vital to the most dynamic sectors.

Further, the quality of the sociocultural environment interferes, in the most unexpected ways, with the chances offered to and lost by business groups. According to exporters, worldwide news reports on violence in Latin American cities have a negative effect on their daily business. Closer to home, the growth of poverty and urban violence poison the existence of the elites, forcing them to wonder what can be done. All this requires thinking about the future, beyond immediate gains and losses, something that is not easy to do, particularly in critical circumstances, but that is precisely the ampler perspective expected of a "citizen."

There is a growing conviction that it simply will not do to just pay taxes and wait for government action. In this context, the elaboration of tax legislation that will encourage private investments in the social sector is of utmost relevance. Earlier laws, usually complex and ineffective, that sometimes even discouraged such investments—as was the case in Mexico—are being progressively revised.

Business philanthropy in Latin America is only beginning to be studied. But there is evidence of a positive trend in Chile, Brazil, and Mexico, while in Peru and Nicaragua, it remains a distant perspective. The kind of conflict experienced by these countries, which threaten the very unity of the body politic, does not make for broader views among businesspeople, nor does it encourage communication between the private sector and social activists. The instability of the state, with its direct consequences on micro-relations, increases the dependence of the whole on specific political actors and events, inhibiting strategies of cooperation. But in Chile, Brazil, or Mexico, civil society—with its increased solidity—is beginning to promote cooperative efforts to rise to the tremendous challenges posed by abusive and unbearable inequality.

With support from North American foundations (Inter-American, Kellogg, and Ford), studies of this topic were recently conducted in Mexico and Brazil.

The Mexican Center for Philanthropy, responsible for the research in Mexico, is itself a pioneering institution. Founded by business leaders and directed by people familiar with NGOs, it is conceived as a catalyzing agent for philanthropic initiatives in the private sector. Among its major partners in this effort are such private institutes as Domecq, Mexican Foundation for Rural Development, Mexican Health Foundation, Miguel Aleman Foundation, Arturo Rosemblueth Foundation, Foundation for Community Support, the Mexican Center for Philanthropic Institutions, and the Social Union of Mexican Businessmen.

Brazil seems to be having the most dynamic experiences in these matters. Recent studies show that new initiatives began to grow in the 1980s, gaining momentum in the last few years. The local branch of the American Chamber of Commerce created in 1982 an annual prize (ECO) to be awarded to the best works in business philanthropy. About 500 companies contended for the prize in the last 11 years. The meetings of this organization gave rise to a network of large corporations to exchange information and promote this kind of work. It is known as the Group of Institutes and Foundations (GIF). About 60 percent of GIF-affiliated programs began after 1980.

A survey sponsored by the Inter-American Foundation and conducted by ARCO in 1993 gathered information on 58 business philanthropy programs in Brazil (only 19 of which were GIF members). These programs invest more than US $115 million a year in sociocultural projects. It is not much, but it is more than Brazilian NGOs were getting from international cooperation per year up to the late 1980s. According to ARCO, most of the programs (67 percent) follow no clear criteria or procedures for choosing programs. Only 17 percent have mechanisms for evaluating the performance of the projects being financed. They still largely depend on individual contacts and decisions. On the other hand, about 27 percent of them maintain regular relationships with NGOs and other civil associations. GIF members are generally better structured. In short, it is reasonable to conclude that business philanthropy in Brazil is in a transition period that may lead to more business investments in nonprofit ventures.

The changing role of unions in an era of citizenship is also noteworthy. In countries such as Mexico, Venezuela, Brazil, Argentina, Chile, and Uruguay, being a unionized worker used to mean quite something. It ensured the individual not only the protection of labor laws but also a considerable degree of social security. In popular language, to claim to be a "worker" was the equivalent of claiming to be a "citizen," a "decent person" who deserved the protection of the law. This perception grew through out the twentieth century in

Latin America, which in turn is strikingly different from its older tradition, also present in memory, that associated work with the condition of slavery. Unions became more powerful in Latin America as industrialization gained momentum. In contrast with the European pattern, where unionization required a long struggle, in Latin America unions were quickly integrated into state politics, and in this way acquired status. Populists leaders gained popular support by winning measures of social protection and integrating unions into the apparatus of state support. In this way, while losing much of their autonomy, unions also gained access to the highest spheres of power. Labor-business negotiations could then take place under the protection of higher arbitration. Through unions, a number of free public services were created that acquired importance among the distribution of collective goods to the working class population. Legal and health services, in particular, gave unions a truly public function.

Due to this unique history, Latin America was ahead of other developing regions as far as social security of workers was concerned. In 1950, for instance, 16 countries in the region already had laws ensuring social security pensions, whereas only three in Africa and two in Asia had such laws. The long history of support for social security in the region includes some dozen countries that had programs for workers' compensation in the 1920s and for old age and disabled citizens in the 1950s; by the 1990s, more than 30 countries had these.

But the entire union structure has been undermined over the past few decades. Unions were among the top targets of repression in the 1970s. Conversely, in Chile, Argentina, Uruguay, Brazil, Bolivia, and other countries, union leaders were active participants in the struggle against military dictatorships. But the democratization of the following decade did not make things easier for them either. "Structural adjustments" cut deep into the central mechanisms of the older system, which depended on state subsidies, corporative negotiations, and protectionist legislation.

The dismantling of this institutional system, combined with the economic crisis, had a tremendous impact on the condition of workers. Employment fell and the informal sector grew geometrically, so that the world of labor was flooded with alternative forms of work devoid of legal protection, and salaries were lowered to unprecedented levels. In some countries, the legal minimum wage fell dramatically: in Argentina in 1990, for example, it was 58 percent lower than in 1985; the equivalent figure for Uruguay was 27 percent, and for Brazil, 24 percent.

Another dramatic chapter is the story of state companies and public servants. People used to be proud of being employees of the state, and there were high levels of identification with state-owned companies. A number of legal privileges (such as lifelong employment) were associated with public jobs. All this is threatened by privatization. Further, global technological changes devalued some sectors that once had strategic importance in industry and the trade union movement. The crisis of mining in Bolivia, for instance, had devastating effects on a sector of the organized working class that played a fundamental role in the history of the country.

No wonder, then, that most members of the union movement are radically opposed to neoliberal policies. Violent protests erupted in Bolivia, Colombia, Argentina, Brazil, and elsewhere. But unionists' resistance seems to be on the wane. They lack not only the state support of the past but also the active support of the working masses. A large part of the union structure seems to be affected by the general loss of credibility that characterizes public institutions.

The crisis of unions suggests a wide range of questions about one of the major segments of civil society in Latin America. Which way is the new unionism heading? How can salaries be protected without the state's mediation? Exposed to market pressures, how can organized workers redefine the terms of their relations with their employers? How can they combine confrontation and cooperation in their relations with business? Given the fall of socialism and the ideological crisis of those parties that have traditionally identified with the working classes, how should their relation to politics be redefined? How can they escape corporate isolation and conquer the support of public opinion for sectorial causes? How can they incorporate the new agendas (environment, women, computerization, and so on)? How to compensate for labor-saving technological progress? What new forms of struggle and persuasion can be used? How should they participate in broader causes for which new partnerships and alliances may be formed?

In short: In order to find their place in civil society, union leaders must consider the meaning of a "citizens' unionism"—in other words, unions that even as they defend their associates' interests will also aim at the whole of society and that, as autonomous bodies, will establish alliances beyond the interests not only of their sector, but also of the working classes themselves, thus contributing to the consolidation of a "civil society."

During the 1980s, the idea of a "civil society" spread fast, but it still lacked density. It predominated among intellectuals and gained followers among organized circuits of social activists, whether among business leaders, workers, associations, or NGOs. It influenced the public discourse diffused by the press and parliamentary leaders. But it was not fully understood or taken seriously by the majority of the population, including the elites, the middle classes, and the lower classes. "Civil society" glimmers like the tip of an iceberg floating above the deep-seated beliefs and practices of Latin Americans.

The insistent appeal to "grassroots participation" soon finds its limits. Considering that the laws do not function as they should, it is often more sensible to take a different path. Citizenship runs the risk of generating an empty discourse, artificially rhetorical, unreal. Meeting resistance, it is subject to the temptation of authoritarian solutions, along the lines of enlightened despotism. Popular activism runs similar risks. In spite of all these difficulties, there are good reasons to expect positive interactions and the expansion of civil society, even if tempered by unexpected cultural combinations.

Other Dynamics

The traditional forms of mutual help remain quite alive, being among the most important forms of support in times of trouble. The needs are so many and so urgent that the protagonists of civil society are beginning to take an interest in the reserves of social caring that flourish outside typically modern institutions.

In that regard, any discussion of "health" often takes us beyond medicine. It must include the environment, family relationships, lovesickness, financial hardships, tension at the workplace, fears, and mystical hopes. For this reason, sessions of spiritual healing and magic tend not to isolate the patient as a separate individual. Good shamans and spiritual advisors are recognized specialists in human drama on the interpersonal, everyday scale. In poor neighborhoods, but also among the middle classes, this kind of practice is increasingly accepted in Latin America.

Such beliefs may look silly and superstitious to a Puritan mind content to say "Thy Will be done," but the merging of Iberian, Native American, and African traditions has resulted in a different sensibility (and understanding) in Latin America. Between the Almighty and frail human endeavors, a forest of symbols, to use Baudelaire's phrase, grows with the exuberance typical of tropical regions. The dynamic power of this symbolism in a changing society may be estimated by the performance of the mediumistic religions of Brazil. They come in a wide array of forms, ranging from the Spiritualism of Allan Kardec, of French extraction, to Candomble, Tambor de Mina, and Batuque, of African origin, and the native Umbanda. All are growing in metropolitan areas and moving upward through the social hierarchy.

Of all Brazilian religions, Kardecism's followers have the highest education. A survey in the southernmost state of Brazil, Rio Grande do Sul, a region mostly populated by European immigrants, found about 16,000 legally registered Umbanda centers. Afro-Brazilian cults are expanding in Uruguay and Argentina. A census of religious institutions in Greater Rio de Janeiro arrived at some impressive figures on the growth of mediumistic religions in the city: 1,201 new centers (including Kardecism, Umbanda, and Candomble) have been formally organized in the Rio metropolitan area in the last 10 years. That amounts to an average of 10 new mediumistic centers per month, or one every three days. Here is one tradition that is certainly not dying out.

Spiritual healing and protection must have some degree of effectiveness. But what deserves attention here is not exactly the results but the sort of sociability they involve. Mediums or shamans are not, properly speaking, "altruistic." They do not renounce their own interests in order to serve others. They may even perceive themselves or be perceived in this way, but their work is based on another dimension, independent of subjective intentions. They speak of their work as a "duty," a commitment that cannot be neglected, or else they may suffer severe punishment. They also speak of "karma," an onerous mission that is imposed on them by higher reasons. "Altruism" is the reverse of "egoism"; the two are opposite and complementary sides of an individual consciousness that sees itself as autonomous and sovereign in relation to other individuals.

In the sphere of healing and protection, however, people do not imagine themselves like this. Mediums are called mediums because they mediate between different levels of a spiritual hierarchy. It implies the ultimate degree of self-giving; one annuls oneself so that Another can manifest in one's place. Seeing oneself as a "medium" makes it possible to establish an exceptional form of communication, which transcends individual options and autonomy.

In similar ways, rites and prescriptions interfere in the links between people, enhancing their value to the point of investing them with extraordinary powers. Whether the links are of kinship, neighborhood, or some other kind of proximity, they make up the prime material of attention and care, for depending on how they are positioned and manipulated, they may bring about evil or act as a healing principle. These ritual agents revive the links of mutual dependence among people; they function as veritable sources of symbolic support for a kind of sociability that theories of modernization saw as doomed to extinction.

Giving, receiving, and returning a gift make up a simple form of communication that underscores the relationships that make a personal life. It is different from the anonymous exchange of the marketplace, which is effected by means of an abstract and generic instrument—money. In reciprocity relationships, on the contrary, the object of the exchange is specific, personalized, and always meaningful. Gifts should be carefully chosen, for there is always the risk they will cause a serious misunderstanding. Gift-giving may be a competitive gesture, as exemplified in the excessive expenditures of carnival celebration in Brazil. It may be a sign of authority (the Pope is called the least of the servants, the one who has the most to give). It may be a source of power (populist leaders are notorious givers). And there are no healing and protection sessions that do not involve in some way the activities of giving, receiving, and returning the gift.

Giving, then, is not just the manifestation of a benevolent inner disposition toward others. Through giving, relationships are asserted, confirmed, and renewed, for good and for evil, even beyond individual choice. Ultimately, one does not choose to become a relative, a medium, or the "son" of a spiritual entity (as they say in Afro-Brazilian religions). Once involved in reciprocity relationships, expressed through gifts and countergifts, the obligation toward the other is internalized as part of what one is.

If such is the case, there is a possible field of positive interactions between the priesthood of traditional religions and the publicly minded initiatives that are typical of civil society. Beyond the logical and institutional differences, both must face the challenge of opposing the dissociating forces of extreme selfishness. Combining languages and sociologies, they may occasionally meet in common initiatives. For this to occur, however, the dominant part, being oriented by the ethical and legal principles of modern individualism, must find forms and formulas for associating with the complex, mysterious spirit of the gift.

The theme of charity was apparently appropriated after the ideological debates of the postwar period by the conservative end of the spectrum. Its old paradox was attacked by progressives as a part of the culture that should be left behind. All charity did was to mop up the perverse consequences of a structure it was a part of. For all its good intentions, it had the actual effect of reproducing the very causes that had generated the consequences in question. New public policies, together with the productive energies freed by development, would abolish the causes and, with them, the very need for charity work.

Almost half a century later, the ideological wars having been largely outgrown and with poverty growing faster than ever, more attention is being given to those who, in spite of all the rhetoric, went on caring for the poorest of the poor. Here, too, there are profound differences to consider, but since they are more familiar they can be approached with less difficulty.

Although medieval in its origin, charity work has played a prominent role in the Church's modernizing efforts in Latin America in the present century. It underwent a serious crisis with the wars of independence at the same time that the Church in Europe was suffering its gravest crisis ever; it was only in the twentieth century that recovery took place. Reinforced by new missionary congregations, with the restoration of discipline and the links with Rome, the Church has been consciously investing in the promotion of social services—schools, hospitals, orphanages, and homes were created in large numbers.

Even today, it may be said that practically every parish in each country in the continent promotes some sort of social work. The articulation of so many institutions and projects within the Church is the object of a specialized organization, CARITAS. Founded in 1950 on a worldwide basis, CARITAS INTERNATIONALIS has a complex structure closely modeled on that of the Church, opening offices in each country and, whenever possible, in each diocese. In Brazil alone there are 120 offices.

Clearly, despite all the changes that have occurred, the Roman Catholic Church still carries the heaviest load in the sphere of nongovernmental social services in Latin America. And in spite of all the attacks against charity among socialist and liberal circles promoting development, charity has kept on working.

At the same time, Protestantism has exploded in Latin America. Indeed, Evangelical growth is the most spectacular sign of change in the region's mentalities at the end of the century. Started by foreign—mostly North American—missions, Evangelicalism has become an endogenous phenomenon, growing mostly by local means. It is still a minority movement, but its persuasive power is tremendous. The main thrust is Pentecostal, and it speaks primarily (although not exclusively) to the poor.

A census of religious institutions in the Rio de Janeiro Metropolitan area (13 cities, 10 million souls) found in the Evangelical institutional network almost 4,000 temples, 45 publishing houses, 38 bookstores, 12 radio stations, one television station, 295 weekly radio programs, 41 centers for theological training, 89 philanthropic organizations. In 1992 alone, 307 new Evangelical churches opened in Rio de Janeiro—an average of six new churches per week.

Conversion to Evangelical faith implies a major change in traditional religious culture. It turns the convert into a regular member of a specific congregation and of a voluntary religious association. So Evangelical growth opens a new symbolic territory where individuals get together by their own indi-

Hogar de Cristo—A "Charity Corporation"

Founded in Santiago, Chile, by the Jesuit priest Alberto Hurtado in 1944, Hogar de Cristo has grown into a huge charity organization with 37 offices distributed around the entire country and with a "preferential option for the poorest of the poor"—destitute old people, terminal patients, homeless children and teenagers. In a country marked by intense ideological polarization, Hogar de Cristo has managed to emerge from all conflicts unscathed and reach almost universal approval.

Father Hurtado, who worked in the Catholic Action for young people and workers, always made a point of drawing a clear line between such polemical activities and his work in Hogar de Cristo. Father Hurtado died at the age of 51, and in 1976 his canonization process was started in the Vatican.

In 1992 Hogar de Cristo provided daily care to about 7,200 children, 2,900 adults, and 2,000 old people. It keeps an old people's village made up of 110 houses, donated by construction companies. There are 40 shelters for destitute people in 30 cities. There is a funeral service for the extremely poor, which held 275 funerals in 1992. Hogar provides scholarships for poor youngsters and credit on a small scale for unemployed people seeking to start a business. There is a foundation for building prefabricated houses on rented land, or even on plots occupied by squatters. In 1982, 8,930 such houses were built.

Hogar de Cristo has 541 paid employees and about 1,200 permanent volunteers. Most of the organization's resources come from local voluntary donations. About 200,000 associates give monthly contributions (which account for 40 percent of the budget) and receive regular information through a magazine for members. A marketing council, consisting of volunteer professionals, develops advertising for radio, television, and the press. Additional funding is raised by selling various printed items and bouquets for brides, by fundraising dinners attended by thousands of people, and by yearly sales of Christmas cards. In a country with a population of 13 million, Hogar de Cristo sold 5 million Christmas cards in 1992.

There is also Program One-To-One, in which employers commit themselves to match every donation made by an employee of their companies. The scale and the professionalism of the enterprise justify the proud boast of one of its directors, Father Van der Est: "We are a major charity corporation!"

vidual choice and, in a congregation, face the challenges of life. They assimilate the cultural logic of participation, with its typical voluntarism, the stress on self-rule, individual initiative, and ascetic discipline in everyday affairs. Severe cultural confrontations are involved. Exorcism is revived as a relevant form of symbolic confrontation. Sectarian intolerance takes root. The break is dramatized by the demonization of traditional beliefs. The difficulties are many. But possibilities for cooperation in broader civil causes are also present. If the right words are said by the right people and communications are handled carefully, Evangelicals may add a tremendous potential to some of the issues concerning civil society in Latin America.

Growing mostly among the poor, the movement builds a dense social network in areas lacking in institutional support. On the grassroots level, Evangelicals may be called upon to help in any number of difficult situations. Health problems have a prominent place among them too. Healing by divine means is one of their most important kinds of charisma. Evangelizing zeal, expressed in the message that each believer must be a missionary, presses Evangelicals to present themselves as role models in all situations. They must prove in everyday life that they are not only good for themselves, but also for their families, neighborhoods, and countries. This may have conservative and negative connotations, but it may also make for eminently positive civil behavior.

The Third Sector in the 1990s

The idea of a "Third Sector" presupposes the existence of "First" and "Second" sectors, the state and the market. But it does so indirectly, by means of negation—"nongovernmental and nonprofit." In explicit, positive terms, the concept refers merely to a set of private, public-minded initiatives. Whereas the notion of a "civil society" involves complementary and systemic opposition to the state, the idea of a "Third Sector" points in other directions, with no clearly established boundaries.

Following this direction takes us beyond the field of institutions to a variety of services not usually included in conventional directories of "nongovernmental agents." Many are not even legally registered anywhere. They operate outside the reach of formal controls. Others have institutional status, but do not distinguish between different services with the sort of analytical precision required of civil agencies. A healing session has many simultaneous functions, and it is simply impossible to draw the line between worship and healing. Cures involving witchcraft, which are so popular, are expressed in a ritual language that aims to reach the totality of circumstances of the client's life. The secret of many of them is to do precisely the opposite of specialization: they underscore the points where the most diverse domains intercommunicate. In much of this field, the distinction between the public and the private is not fully assimilated.

By incorporating informal structures, the Third Sector becomes even more complex and heterogeneous than is usually acknowledged. Indeed, the services that make up everyday sociability are countless and extremely diversified. In each family, in each neighborhood, persons of social significance— mostly women—have a vocation that extends beyond the circle of private interests. Acknowledging this fact is conceptually important. It widens our understanding of the *res publica*, and it changes the scope of the question concerning actual and potential interactions in the Third Sector.

To summarize what has been said so far, four major segments may be distinguished in Latin America: traditional forms of mutual help, social movements and civil associations, NGOs, and business philanthropy. How did the agents of these segments interrelate in the 1970s and 1980s? The pattern is clear: the two middle sectors were closely associated, reinforcing each other in a powerful relationship, but they had hardly any communication with traditional groups or the business community.

Movements, associations, and NGOs asserted their vocations, breaking explicitly with the traditional charity approach known as "assistencialismo". Even when they originated in this tradition, as was the case of many Church organizations, their intention and their rhetoric pointed to a break with the past. The emphasis on this break even had the effect of seeing traditional charity negatively. "Assistencialismo" became a derogatory term.

On the other hand, authoritarian regimes created a situation in which the business sector had to defend its interests by means of covert negotiation. Discreet lobbying and corruption became regular practices, without which nothing could be done on the government level; this made business even more cautious in its relations with opposition groups. Accordingly, social movements and NGOs saw themselves as participants in a global class confrontation—which was indeed the case on several occasions.

Further, under authoritarian regimes, the most dynamic segments of the Third Sector kept government at arm's length, reducing to a minimum the relations (usually hostile) in this sphere. Typically, social movements felt happy and victorious whenever they managed to step into the local seat of authority and present some sort of complaint. Cooperating with the government was simply out of the question.

Major NGO Networks in Latin America

The first networks were formed on the basis of common areas or themes, such as "social development" or "popular education." A good example is ALOP, formed by 33 NGOs from 18 Latin American countries, which concentrates on the participation of popular movements in development strategies. Another is CELADEC, which involves progressive churches dedicated to popular education. Thematic networks include organizations dedicated to such issues as women, children, health, and ecology, among others. Some are ephemeral groupings, as were those formed around the 1992 U.N. Conference on Environment and Development and the Global Forum; others acquire the status of minor traditions, as is the case of Chile's Rural NGO Network.

Peru's COPEMI is made up of NGOs specializing in small businesses. In Costa Rica, the Coordination of NGOs for Appropriate Technology emphasizes another important field of work. In Brazil, the issue of street children has achieved such prominence that it gave rise to a National Movement dedicated to providing support to various local projects.

Some networks, then, are local, while others are regional, and yet others international with a Latin American basis. Thus EL TALLER has headquarters in Tunisia, IRED has regional offices, and the CULTURES AND DEVELOPMENT NETWORKS, for promotion of cultural themes in development strategies, has its headquarters in Brussels.

Relations of mutual trust, which introduce a curious personal dimension in networking, favor the creation of NGO associations for the development of common projects. In Brazil, FASE, IDAC, IBASE, and ISER have engaged in several such projects in the last few years. In Peru, some of the country's major NGOs—DESCO, CEPES, CEDEP, ILEP, IBC, and CIDCA—associated in the PROPOSAL group in order to formulate alternatives to the government's constitutional project. In Nicaragua, FACS, ADP, and CEPAD jointly proposed to the European Community a project of support for the victims of the civil war.

Continued on next page

Continued from previous page

Northern Hemisphere NGOs and foundations that finance Southern Hemisphere NGOs have formed networks with their counterparts, in which they discuss common problems of cooperation. ICCO, NOVIB, EZE, Christian Aid, Inter-American Foundation, and others sometimes organize meetings with their partners.

More recently, government agencies interested in international cooperation have begun to operate as catalysts of NGO networks. Program SEDESOL/PRONASOL, in Mexico, provides support to a new Social Fund of Co-Investments. The Chilean government has created a Consulting Commission in the Ministry of Economic Planning (Oficina Enlace), including 16 representatives of the Third Sector and chaired by the Minister, to discuss priorities and criteria for the government's social investments. It has also created an International Cooperation Agency to attract funding for projects to be jointly implemented by the government and NGOs.

This formula of three-part cooperation, involving government, NGOs, and international agencies, is beginning to bear fruit. A Bilateral Sustainable Development Agreement with these characteristics has been signed by the governments of Costa Rica and the Netherlands. In Mexico, Project Ba Asolai involves the major networks of NGOs and Civil Associations, government agencies, and international cooperation agencies in a program of evaluation and joint decision-making on social projects.

Also in Mexico, the country that seems to make the best use of networking, the Mutual Support Fund created by the Church gathers about 200 NGOs and civil associations through the major networks to raise international funds. In Paris in May 1993, the Fund brought representatives of the government and various sectors of civil society to meet with European banks and other financing agencies. Swap operations—that is, the conversion of foreign debt in social investment in the country—were one of the major topics discussed.

Interactions were intense, however, among the recently emerging segments of the nongovernmental universe. NGOs became centers of human resources (assistance, information, preparation of educational material, training, projects, and so on) at the service of community associations and social movements.

Thus a nongovernmental circuit of cooperation was formed that has been able to articulate initiatives originating on the various planes of civil society. The improbable connection between local microprojects and international campaigns proved perfectly feasible.

The key word in this new process came from the world of computers: the formation of "networks" that combined the autonomy of each point in the system with an intense flow of information. Multiple and transverse, NGO networks combined in various ways; belonging to one of them did not rule out the possibility of belonging to another.

Social movements and NGOs suffered from isolation: breaking with traditional forms of mutual help and assistance, they unintentionally separated themselves from the poor majority; attacking business and government, they moved away from the elites. Isolated from the masses and the upper classes, they finally came to the limit of their mobilization potential. The promising climate, with almost messianic overtones, that characterized the 1970s gave way in the late 1980s to the awareness of a "crisis of paradigms." Yet the 1990s has seen the emergence of an increasing number of vital signs of what has been called here the Third Sector. The interactions are multiplying in various directions, surpassing old barriers. This review of the Third Sector in Latin America concludes with brief descriptions of some of these interactions.

• Recently elected rulers ask for the support of "organized civil society" to implement some project of local relevance. This has been happening everywhere, in different forms and to different extents, with varying degrees of success.

• NGOs compete for government contracts with other public or private institutions to conduct research, to coordinate projects, to implement segments of larger projects. According to some estimates, at present about 40 percent of the budget of Chilean NGOs comes from government funding.

• Some multilateral agencies, such as the Pan-American Health Organization and the World Health Organization, support national projects under the condition that NGOs take part in their implementation.

• A province is mobilized to assert its rights vis-à-vis the central government. Local authorities, businesspeople, civil associations,

NGOs, and public opinion join forces in defense of their province. This has happened in Chile and Peru.

• The Sendero Luminoso simultaneously attacks two neighborhoods in Lima—Miraflores, an upper-middle-class district, and El Salvador, a poor area. The submayors of Miraflores (a successful businessman) and El Salvador (a well-known popular leader) jointly plan a public demonstration against terrorism. A large number of residents of both neighborhoods march to a central common place.

• National pacification is a growing concern in different segments of the Third Sector. The slogan "Peru, Life, and Peace" has brought the traditional human rights approach to the issue of political violence, which is an obstacle to the functioning of national institutions. In Nicaragua, a number of NGOs are conducting a project named Pacification of Peasant Families, aimed at former members of Sandinista and contra forces. The Institute of Women develops a project for the Pacification of Nicaraguan Women with the participation of Suscena Ferray, former leader of a contra organization, as well as various former Sandinista guerrillas. The Viva Rio campaign mobilizes several organs of the press, businesspeople, unions, NGOs, and public opinion in a search for nonviolent ways of facing urban violence in Rio de Janeiro.

• Large national and multinational corporations adopt social investment policies. They begin to invest in environmental protection and social campaigns as a marketing strategy, in order to improve their public image.

• North American financing agencies support projects for encouraging business philanthropy in Latin America. The Inter-American, Ford, and Kellogg foundations and Synergos support projects of this kind.

• The World Council of Churches creates a network of Pentecostal ministers in the region, trying to associate the Gifts of the Spirit with an ethics of social responsibility. The Brazilian Evangelical Association, with a charismatic and Pentecostal tradition, drops its iso-

Private But Public: The Third Sector in Latin America

lationist stance and actively participates in such citizen campaigns as For Ethics in Politics, Against Hunger and For Life, and Viva Rio.

* Spiritualist leaders in Brazil, members of a sect traditionally associated with spiritual healing, also take part in citizenship campaigns, trying to bring together "charity" and "civil rights."

* An interreligious movement created at the '92 Global Forum in Rio brings together more than 20 religious traditions, with support from both official hierarchies and alternative movements. Catholics, Evangelicals, Jews, followers of Afro-Brazilian religions, Spiritualists, Hindus, Buddhists, and others establish an Interreligious Fund for fundraising and financing projects against hunger.

* Organized crime and terrorist groups kidnap family members of rich businesspeople, exchanging their lives for money. This traumatic experience results in various kinds of reactions. In several countries, a number of them become active in business philanthropy.

* Five-star hotels finance projects for combating violence and improving the social conditions in tourist areas of Rio de Janeiro.

* Private banks in Peru open special credit lines for small businesses using NGOs as mediators, technical assistants, and cosigners.

* The campaign Against Hunger and For Life, in Brazil, mobilizes an unprecedented number of initiatives. According to an IBOPE survey, about 38 percent of Brazilians personally participated in the campaign, with donations or practical action against hunger. The decentralized style of the movement and the appeal to moral consciences set off an unexpectedly large wave of local interactions involving various institutions—large corporations, condominium buildings, groups of friends, schools, social associations. Voluntary commissions of advertising executives provided quality marketing for the campaign and ensured free space in the media. The leader of the movement, Herbert de Souza (known everywhere as "Betinho"), was presented by the Brazilian government as a candidate for the 1994 Nobel Peace Prize.

59

Many more examples of interactions such as these could be cited. All illustrate the tendency to break previously insurmountable barriers, which defined alliances and oppositions in terms of fundamental political party and ideological divisions. They also point to a search for forms of interaction that are less cumbersome and more circumstantial, and that can express a diffuse feeling of urgency when approaching socio-institutional problems.

Bibliography

Directories

ARGENTINA - *Directorio de Organizaciones No-Gubernamentales Argentinas de Promoción y Desarrollo.* Serie Documentación nr. 1, Buenos Aires: GADIS, 1989.

BOLIVIA - *395 ONGs en Bolivia, Catálogo.* La Paz: Coordinadora de Redes, Estudios y Proyectos, Coordination of José Antonio Perez, 1990.

CHILE - *Registro de Fichas de Identificación de los Organismos No-Gubernamentales (ONG) de Chile,* Santiago de Chile: MIDEPLAN, División Social, Oficina de Enlace ONG-Govierno, 1992.

CHILE - *Directorio de instituciones de Chile.* Silber Editores Limitada, Mayo 1990.

COLOMBIA - *Directorio Nacional de Entidades Sin Animo de Lucro de Beneficio Social, 1990.* Bogotá: CIDESAL.

COSTA RICA - *Directorio Parcial de Organizaciones Privadas Voluntarias.* San José: Coalición Costarricense de Iniciativas de Desarrollo (CINDE), 1986.

DOMINICA - Borland, Barry and Jerry La Gra. *Profiles of Farmer Organizations in Dominica.* IICA, 1989.

DOMINICAN REPUBLIC - *Directorio de Instituciones Privadas de Interés Social de la República Dominicana, 1986-1988.* Santo Domingo: CEDOIS, 1988.

ECUADOR - Foro de organizaciones Privadas Sin Fines de Lucro.
Guayaquil: Fundación Eugenio Espejo, 1989.

EL SALVADOR - Private Organizations with US Connections, Directory
and Analysis. Albuquerque, N.M.: Inter-Hemispheric Education Resource Center, 1988.

GUATEMALA - Directorio de Organizaciones Privadas Voluntarias de
Servicio a la Comunidad de Guatemala. FUNDESA, 1986.

GUATEMALA - Private Organizations with US Connections - Directory
and Analysis, Albuquerque, N.M.: Inter-Hemispheric Education Resource Center, 1988.

HAITI - Haitian Association of Voluntary Agencies, Rapport Annuel, 1987-
1988.

HONDURAS - Ramirez, Pedro Pablo and Joaquin Picht. Características
Generales de la Comunidad de Organizaciones Privadas de Desarrollo
en Honduras. Tegucigalpa, F.M., Honduras, 1988.

HONDURAS - Private Organizations with US Connections, Honduras -
Directory and Analysis. Albuquerque, N.M.: Inter-Hemispheric Education Resource Center, 1988.

HONDURAS - Directorio de Organizaciones Privadas de Desarrollo de
Honduras. IISE, 1989.

JAMAICA - Brownell, Jennifer M. Directory of Jamaican Development
NGOs for Inter American Foundation.. 1989.

MEXICO - Lopezllera Mendez, Luis. Sociedad Civil y Pueblos Emergentes
- Las Organizaciones Autónomas de Promoción Social y Desarrollo,
Promoción del Desarrollo Popular (PDP), AC, Mexico

MEXICO - Directorio de Instituciones Filantrópicas. Centro Mexicano de
Instituciones Filantrópicas, Mexico, 1990.

PANAMA - Castro, Carlos and José Grenard, Estudio de las

Organizaciones No-Gubernamentales de Desarrollo de Panamá. Informe de AVANCE, 1990.

PERU - *Directorio de Organismos No-Gubernamentales de Promoción Social, Investigación y Desarrollo del Perú.* Lima: Asociación Nacional de Centros ANC, Sétima Edición, 1988.

PARAGUAY - *Directorio de Organizaciones Privadas de Desarrollo en el Paraguay.* Comité Paraguay-Kansas, Centro de Información y Recursos para el Desarrollo.

SAINT LUCIA - La Gra, Jerry et al. *Profiles of Farmers Organizations in Saint Lucia.* IICA Office in Saint Lucia, 1989

ST VINCENT AND THE GRENADINES - Rittgers, Rob and Jerry La Gra. *Profiles of Farmer Organizations in St Vincent and the Grenadines.* IICA Office in Saint Vincent and the Grenadines, 1991.

TOBAGO - *Profile of Rural Development Agencies/Groups in Tobago.* The Caribbean Network for Integrated Rural Development, 1990.

TRINIDAD - *Trinidad Profiles - A survey of 39 Agencies/Groups engaged in Rural & Commuity Development in Trinidad.* The Caribbean Network for Integrated Rural Development, 1991.

URUGUAY - Barreiro, Fernando and Anabel Cruz, *Entre Diversidad y Desafíos - Organizaciones No-Gubernamentales de Uruguay - Análisis y Repertorio.* Montevideo: Instituto de Comunicacion y Desarrollo, Agencia Española de Cooperación Internacional, Comisión de las Comunidades Europeas, 1991.

Buckley-Ess, Julie, ed. *Natural Resources Directory - Latin America and the Caribbean.* Natural Resources Program, Partners of the Americas, 1988.

NOVIB/PROTERRA, *Peruvian Environment Network.* Lima: 1990.

Directory of Environmental NGOs in the Eastern Caribbean. Island Resources Foundation, 1991.

OECD, *Directory of Development Research and Training Institutes in Latin America*, Paris, 1992.

Abugattas, Juan et al. *Estado y Sociedad: Relaciones Peligrosas.* Lima: DESCO, 1990.

General Works

Agencia Latinoamericana de Información. Quito, Ecuador.

Amnesty International. *Amnesty International Annual Report, 1993.* London.

Annuarium Statisticum Ecclesiae. Vatican: Secretaria Status, Rationarium Generale Ecclesiae, 1987.

ARCO. *A Filantropia Empresarial no Brasil: Estudo Preliminar.* São Paulo: 1992.

Bailey, Michael. "Notes on NGOs In Brazil." Save The Children Fund, Brazil Programme Discussion Paper, mimeographed, 1992.

Beekman, David et al. *Friday Morning Reflections at the World Bank, Essays on Values and Development.* Washington, D.C.: Seven Locks Press, 1991.

Borja, Jordi. *Movimientos Sociales Urbanos.* Buenos Aires: Ediciones SIAP Planteos, 1971.

Boschi, Renato Raul. *A Arte da Associação - Política de Base e Democracia no Brasil.* São Paulo: Vertice, 1987.

Bustamante, Alberto. *De Marginales a Informales*, Lima: DESCO, 1990.

Camacho, Daniel. "Movimientos sociales, algunas definiciones conceptuales," *Revista de Ciencias Sociales*, No. 37-38, 1987, Editorial de la Universidad de Costa Rica, Costa Rica.

Castells, Manuel. *La Cuestión Urbana.* Buenos Aires: Siglo XXI, 1974.

Cavarozzi, Marcelo and Vicente Palermo. "Estado, Sociedad Civil Y Organizaciones Populares Vecinales en la Transicion a la Democracia en la Argentina", Tepoztlán: InterAmerican Foundation, mimeographed, 1991.

Centro Ecuménico Antonio Valdivieso *Incidencia del Centro Ecuménico Antonio Valdivieso en la Sociedad Civil.* Managua: Documento de Circulación Interna, CAV, 1993.

Centro Mexicano para la Filantropia. *La Filantropía Mexicana: Diagnóstico Y Propuestas.* Mexico.

Centro Mexicano para la Filantropia. *La Filantropía en México.* Mexico. A study complementary to the above.

Darcy de Oliveira, Miguel "Crisis or Transformation? The Answers Change the Question", in Several Authors, *Development, International Cooperation and the NGOs.*

Diaz-Albertini, Javier. "Non-Governmental Development Organizations and the Grassroots in Peru." *Voluntas*, Vol. 2 No. 1, Manchester University Press, 1991.

Dimaggio, Paul J. and Helmut K. Anheier, "The Sociology of Nonprofit Organizations and Sectors." *Annual Review of Sociology*, 1990.

Duarte, Luis Fernando Dias et al. "Vicissitudes e limites da conversão à cidadania nas classes populares brasileiras." *Revista Brasileira de Ciências Sociais*, No. 22, 1993.

Edwards, Michael and David Hulme. *Making a Difference - NGOs and Development in a Changing World.* London: Earthscan Publications Ltd., 1992.

Eckstein, Susan. "Poor people versus the state and capital: anatomy of a successful community mobilization for housing in Mexico City." *International Journal of Urban and Regional Research*, 1990.

Ezcurra, Ana María. *V Centenario de la Conquista de América*. Buenos Aires: Guía Bibliográfica, Rei Argentina SA, Instituto de Estudios y Acción Social, Aique Grupo Editor s.a.

Fernandes, Rubem César and Leandro Piquet Carneiro. *NGOs in the Nineties, a Survey of their Brazilian Leaders*. Rio de Janeiro: Textos de Pesquisa, ISER, 1991.

Fernandes, Rubem César. "Wishes for a New Decade," in Several Authors, *Development, International Cooperation and the NGOs*.

Finkler, Kaja. *Spiritualist Healers in Mexico - Successes and Failures of Alternative Therapeutics*. New York: Praeger, 1985.

Francchia, Emilio. *CARITAS en América Latina, Itinerario Historico Doctrinal*. Quito: SELAC, 1987.

Franco, Maria A. Ciavatta (org.). *Estudos Comparados e Educação na América Latina*. São Paulo: Cortez Editora, 1992.

Fundaçao Emilio Odebrecht. *Perfil do Grupo de Institutos e Fundações*. GIF, 1993.

Gomez, Sergio. *Dilemas de Los ONGs Rurales en el Contexto Democrático*. Santiago de Chile: FLACSO, Serie Estudios Sociales no 41, 1992.

Gonzales, Mariana. *Las Redes Invisibles de la Ciudad*. Montevideo: CIESU, 1992.

Gorostiaga, Xabier. *Entre el desastre y la Esperanza, Centro América y América Latina frente al Desafío de los Años 90*. Managua: CRIES, mimeographed, 1991.

Gutierrez, Carlos Rojas. "O Programa Nacional de Solidaridade: fatos e idéias em torno de um esforço." *Estudos Avançados*, Vol. 6 No. 16, USP, São Paulo, 1992.

Grubb, Michael. "The Greenhouse Effect: Negotiating Targets." *International Affairs*, Vol. 66, No. I, 1990.

Hugarte, Renzo Pi. "Cultos de Posesión y Empresas de Cura Divina en el Uruguay: Desarrollo y Estudios." Facultad de Humanidades y Ciencias de la Educación, Universidad de la Republica, Montevideo, mimeographed, 1991.

InterAmerican Foundation. *Grassroots Development.*

Hodgkinson, Virginia et al. *The Future of the Nonprofit Sector, Independent Sector.* San Francisco: Jossey-Bass Publishers, 1989.

Ibarra, Miguel Santibañez. *El Nuevo Orden Internacional y el Desarrollo Local.* Santiago de Chile: JUNDEP, 1991.

Instituto del Desarollo del Sector Informal. *Rostros de la Informalidad (Testimonios).* Lima: IDESI, 1992.

International Labour Organization. *Work in the World, 1993.* Geneva, 1993.

Jacobi, Pedro. "Movimentos Sociais Urbanos no Brasil: Reflexão sobre a Literatura nos Anos 70 e 80." *BIB*, No. 23, ANPOCS, Rio de Janeiro, 1987.

Lojkine, J. *Le marxisme, l'état et la question urbaine.* Paris: Presses Universitaires de France, 1977.

Landin, Leilah. *Defining the Nonprofit Sector: Brazil.* Working Paper No. 9, The Johns Hopkins Comparative Nonprofit Sector Project, Baltimore, 1993.

Landin, Leilah. *Para Além do Mercado e do Estado? Filantropia e Cidadania no Brasil.* Rio de Janeiro: Textos de Pesquisa, ISER, 1993.

Landin, Leilah. *A Invenção das ONGs, Do Serviço Invisível à Profissão Sem Nome.* Doctoral Dissertation, PPGAS, Museu Nacional, Universidade Federal do Rio de Janeiro, 1993.

Loveman, Brian. *Private Development Organizations and International Cooperation: Chile 1973-90.* InterAmerican Foundation, mimeographed, 1991.

Lopezllera Mendez, Luis. *Autogestión de los Pueblos, organizaciones civiles y gente comum.* Mexico: Promoción del Desarrollo Popular (PDP), 1993.

Mainwaring, Scott and Eduardp Viola. "Novos Movimentos Sociais: Cultura Política e Democracia: Brasil e Argentina." In *Uma Revolução no Cotidiano?*, Brasiliense, São Paulo, 1987.

McCarthy, Kathleen D. et al. *The Nonprofit Sector in the Global Community, Voices from Many Nations.* San Francisco: Independent Sector, Jossey-Bass Publishers, 1992.

Nerfin, Marc. "Neither Prince nor Merchant: Citizen, An Introduction to the Third System." *IFDA Dossier*, 1986.

Obando Bravo, Cardenal Miguel. *Agonía en el Bunker.* Arquidioceses de Managua, 1990.

Oro, Ari Pedro. *As Religiões Afro-Brasileiras no Cone-Sul.* Porto Alegre: Cadernos de Antropologia 10, UFRGS, 1993.

La Otra Bolsa de Valores. Mexico, Promoción del Desarrollo Popular (PDP).

Panhuys, Henry et al. *La Prise en Compte des Facteurs Culturels dans les Programmes de Developpement.* Brussels: South/North Cultures and Development Network, 1993.

Przeworski, Adam. "The Neo Liberal Fallacy." *Journal of Democracy*, July 1992.

Salamon, Lester and Helmut K. Anheier. "In Search of the Non-profit Sector. I: The Question of Definitions." *Voluntas* 3/2, Manchester University Press, Manchester, 1992.

Santos, Wanderley Guilherme. *Razões da Desordem.* Rio de Janeiro: Rocco, 1992.

Several Authors. *Development, International Cooperation and the NGOs.* Rio de Janeiro: IBASE/UNDP, 1992.

Several Authors. *Una Puerta Que Se Abre - Los Organismos No Gubernamentales en la Cooperación al Desarrollo.* Santiago: Taller de Cooperación al Desarrollo.

Several Authors. *A World of Difference - A New Framework for Development Cooperation in the 1990s, Policy Document.* The Netherlands, government publication.

Several Authors. *Neoliberales y Pobres, el debate continental por la justicia.* Bogotá: CINEP, 1993.

Several Authors. *La Violencia Política en el Perú, Análisis y Perspectivas.* Lima: CEPES, mimeographed, 1993.

South/North Cultures and Development Network. *Quid Pro Quo, Cultures & Development.* Brussels.

Thompson, Andrés A. "Democracy and Development: The Role of Nongovernmental Organizations in Argentina, Chile, Uruguay." In McCarthy, Kathleen et al.

Torre, Gabriel Quadri. "Movimientos Sociales: el ecologismo en México." Mexico: SEP, 1992.

Touraine, Alain. *Em Defesa da Sociologia.* Rio de Janeiro: Zahar Ed., 1974.

Valdes, Teresa and Enrique Gomariz (coord.). *Mujeres Latino Americanas en Cifras - Brasil.* Santiago de Chile: Ministerio de Asuntos Sociales, Instituto de la Mujer, FLACSO, 1993.

Valladares, Licia and & Flávia Impelizieri. *Invisible Action - A Guide to Non-governmental Assistance for Underpriviledged and Street Children of Rio de Janeiro.* Rio de Janeiro: IUPERJ, 1992.

Verhelst, Thierry G. *Des Racines pour Vivre.* Paris-Gembloux: Editions Duculot, 1987.

Vicente Parada, Santiago. *Indianidad y Sociedad en México.* Promocion del Desarrollo Popular (PDP), 1992.

Viola, Eduardo J. *O Movimento Ecológico no Brasil (1974-1986).* Campos do Jordão: ANPOCS, 1986.

UNDP. *Human Development Report 1993.* New York: Oxford University Press, 1993.

UNFPA. *The State of World Population, 1993.* New York, 1993.

United Nations. *The World's Women 1970-1990 Trends and Statistics.* Social Statistics and Indicators, Series K, No. 8. New York: 1991.

Weffort, Francisco. *O populismo na Política Brasileira.* Rio de Janeiro: Paz e Terra, 1978.

Weffort, Francisco. *Qual Democracia?,* Companhia das Letras, 1992.

World Bank. *World Development Report 1992.* New York: Oxford University Press, 1992.

World Council of Churches. *Discerning the Way Together,* Southern Perspectives, WCC, Unit III, 1993.

3

NORTH AMERICA'S INDEPENDENT SECTOR

Michael Keating

The popular images of the United States and Canada include cowboys and polar bears, Wall Street in New York and the CN Tower in Toronto, presidents and prime ministers, industrialists and entertainers. They can easily give the impression that North American society is shaped mainly by big government, big business, and the entertainment industry. But these countries run on a lot more than political declarations, the stock exchange, and Hollywood. There is a deeply important third sector that binds communities together, does work that governments and business cannot or will not do, and gives participants an important sense of accomplishment.

The sector is so large and varied that it has no single image or spokesperson. It is a vast network of mediating institutions that lie between the citizen and the state. Because the sector is so diverse, people tend only to see some of its parts, but the whole itself remains almost invisible to most people.

This part of society has been called the independent, nonprofit, nongovernmental, voluntary, and charitable sector. These are all aspects, but no one description tells the whole story. One of the major characteristics is that it is separate from government and from business, leading to another description— the third sector.

One important distinction is between two major groupings: organizations that exist to help others, and those that exist to represent or meet the needs of their own members. Both may serve a community good, but the motivations are different. A Chamber of Commerce or trade union can be a nonprofit organization, but it is organized primarily for the benefit of its members. A charity is created for the benefit of the community at large.

The sector can also be looked at as having two streams: charity and empowerment. There is the simple giving of food, clothing, and money to those in need. There is also the training and advocacy side to help people learn better how to help themselves and society. Many organizations play a variety of these roles. Some collect money for their own use, while others pass on some of the funds to yet other groups.

This chapter deals primarily with the charitable sector that works for the community at large. Within this category are found charities, such as food banks, educational organizations that help people help themselves, and advocacy organizations that push for changes in society.

Characteristics and Role in Society

In both the United States and Canada, most people are touched by the independent sector. The vast majority of people donate to at least one cause, and most people have done some volunteer work. Giving to a cause is an important part of North American culture. It is all philanthropy, whether it is a large donation from a foundation or wealthy individual, a small donation to a canvasser at the door, or "sweat equity" in the form of free labor to help a cause. About 90 percent of U.S. nongovernmental funds for voluntary nonprofit groups come from individuals, with the balance coming almost equally from corporations and foundations.

Involvement in the charitable sector often starts in childhood with organizations such as scouting or guiding, religious organizations or Little League sports. Even children collect money for charities or for services for the community, learning the basic concepts of doing something for their neighbors. It might be a tag day to raise money for the scouts or to buy a resuscitator for the local fire brigade.

For most people, giving consists of putting money in the collection plate during religious services, handing money to a neighbor canvassing door to door, or writing checks for charities that solicit by mail. But "giving" is taking many new forms in our evolving society. It ranges from supplying a credit card number to turning over frequent flyer points to a charity so that very ill children can have a holiday. While the image of corporate giving is often that of a big check, companies make very large donations in the form of equipment, loaned employees, advertising space, and other services.

The concept of giving springs from humans identifying with one another in a time of need. That was evident during the disastrous Mississippi River floods of 1993, when neighbor helped neighbor pile sandbags or rescue people from the worst American flood in living memory. It was an emotion that reached far afield. A Canadian man bought 20,000 liters of bottled drinking water and rented a truck to ship it across part of a province and several states to reach flood victims whose drinking water was contaminated. When asked in a radio interview why he dug into his own pocket to do this, he replied, "I don't know how to answer that, except...they are neighbors."

Volunteering also takes many forms. It may involve providing expertise at the board meeting of a large charity, going door to door for a health charity, coaching a local baseball or hockey team, providing first aid and rescue services for a community, fetching mail and groceries for an ill neighbor, or wading into a stream to clear it of garbage and re-establish fish habitats. Many volunteers serve as teachers, passing on their expertise not only to the community but to the next generation of volunteers. In many cases, people use their work skills. A lawyer may donate legal expertise or a writer, free writing skills, but in many cases, the volunteer organization is a place to develop other skills. Rick Hayward, a Toronto investment manager, was delegated by the executives in his company to get more donations from coworkers for the Metro Toronto United Way. He succeeded, and recalls that he satisfied an altruistic urge, met more people in the company and demonstrated his organizational skills.

People go to great lengths to help their communities. While big cities have professional fire departments, many small communities still rely on the volunteer fire brigade. In Canada, 80 percent of the country's firefighting forces are volunteers—some 94,000 people who risk their lives for their fellow citizens.

There are important parallels between business and the independent sector. Both sectors include big and small organizations responding to a wide variety of human needs and aspirations. In many ways, the independent sector is a parallel economy in our society, but one run for the common good rather than for individual or corporate profit. It has been described as "the charitable economy." In *Canada's Charitable Economy*, Larry W. Smith notes that "we see in the activities of volunteers the full range of variety and diversity that is the hallmark of humanity's creativity and initiative."

Indeed, one of the important characteristics of the sector is its tremendous diversity. "The landscape of the Third Sector is untidy but wonderfully exuberant," wrote Waldemar Nielsen, a well-known American commentator on the sector. "What counts is not the confusion, but the profusion. There is literally something in it for everyone." It includes donors and donees. It ranges from Alcoholics Anonymous to Zero Population Growth. It encompasses such different approaches as Rotary and Greenpeace, amateur astronomers and the Flat Earth Society. It provides thousands of outlets for expression and service to others.

As John W. Gardner, a founder of the organization Independent Sector, put it, "Perhaps the most striking feature of the sector is its relative freedom from constraints and its resulting pluralism: within the bounds of the law, all kinds of people can pursue any idea or program they wish. Unlike government, an independent sector group need not prove that its idea or philosophy is supported by some large constituency, and unlike the business sector, they do not need to pursue only those ideas which will be profitable."

The fact that anyone can create an independent organization for almost any purpose means that this sector is the essence of pluralism. People band together to influence every aspect of the human condition, and to speak out on any public issue. Citizens can organize to tackle a small neighborhood problem, such as illegal parking, or a serious national issue, such as the carnage of drunk driving, or a global issue such as climate change. When they succeed, they can change the course of history. Our educational, medical, artistic and cultural institutions, many of them now partly or wholly government supported, were initiated by volunteers trying to improve their society. Environmental, social welfare, and international assistance movements largely began in the nonprofit sector, and often maintain strong ties in this part of society.

Typically, the creation of a new group begins when someone responds to a need or a problem in their community. Often, the first task is to educate other people of the need. This leads to the formation of a core group, and, if it is successful, the organization grows, seeks more funding, and becomes more professional. Most nonprofit organizations are formed on the initiative of one person, a leader. A charismatic leader may be able to create an organization but not able to run it, and when that person retires or quits a small organization, there is often the problem of who will be the successor. In many cases, the organization goes into decline or even collapses at this point.

This is a random process, and there is no central authority to define what organizations should be created or stopped. Even tax-exempt status does not ensure that this is the best way to spend money, only that the organizations have goals that meet government criteria, and have some sort of governing structure that can be held accountable for misuse of funds.

There is a great deal of growth in the mutual help movement as people who have survived heart attacks, divorces, drug abuse, firings, and assaults band together to create support groups. These groups then help other people with advice, expertise, and the comfort of knowing they are not alone with

---

Examples of Changing Society Through the Voluntary Sector

Drinking and driving were, until a decade or so ago, considered a somewhat risky but widely tolerated activity. "One more for the road" was taken literally. In response to the carnage on the highways, groups such as Mothers Against Drunk Driving (MADD) were formed by parents of children killed by intoxicated drivers. The bereaved parents not only campaigned for stricter enforcement of laws against impaired driving, they helped change the way people think, so that drinking and driving is much less socially acceptable and less frequent.

A similar change in social attitudes surrounds smoking. Groups such as the Non-Smokers' Rights Association have won smoke-free areas in many public buildings. As often happens over a contentious issue, groups spring up to espouse the other side of a cause. The Smoker's Freedom Society is campaigning for lower taxes on tobacco.

In the early 1980s, AIDS burst onto the scene, threatening people with an incurable disease that wasted them away. People involved in the AIDS movement created a powerful lobby, pushing governments and the medical profession to control the effects of the disease, to make experimental drugs available earlier, and to find a cure. This pressure has reoriented significant amounts of health care spending.

---

their problems. The black community, working first mainly through the churches, formed a number of self-help organizations in the last century. Black churches, one of the few black institutions that were not banned in some parts of the United States, were supported by charitable giving, and gave to other institutions. They fostered the development of education and training systems that produced black leaders in ever greater numbers.

The Hispanic community has been doing the same since the 1930s. Cuca Robledo Montecel, Executive Director of the Intercultural Development Research Association in San Antonio, says that the Hispanic nonprofit sector has roots in social philanthropy organizations originally interested in such issues as the care of Hispanic war veterans. During the past 30 years, this has evolved more activist civil rights groups. Montecel feels it is important for the nonprofit sector to lobby on behalf of people of color who, as minority groups, often have poorer living standards than Americans in general. She believes in empowerment as a major role for nonprofits. One way to empower people is to see that they have a good education.

At times, those who started the movements were seen as unpopular, troublesome, and even dangerous by the "establishment" of the day. Members of some groups have broken the law because of their beliefs. However, the democratic structures of North America have allowed nonprofit groups to operate, within the law, and when their ideas were valid they often flourished, and even became official policy.

Sometimes, the sector draws people who wrap themselves in the mantle of public service while seeking self-aggrandizement, money or a platform to play out pet fantasies. In the main, however, the independent sector has been a powerful force for good in North America, and most of its members work for low pay. Opinion surveys routinely show charitable organizations near the top of a list of institutions that people trust the most, ranking higher than government, business, and the media.

The independent sector plays an important role in the democratic system of government in North America. Its organizations are usually small and therefore less encumbered by tradition and bureaucracy. This allows them to research and innovate ideas much more quickly than government or large businesses. Many of its members deal with such fundamental issues as hunger, shelter, and disease. They form a vital part of our educational, medical, artistic, and cultural life. The independent sector has had an impact on almost every field of endeavor, including architecture, agriculture, arts, cancer research, historic preservation, the homeless, sports, education, international understanding, physics, and zoology. The role of the independent sector is not to replace government, but to provide an additional support service for the community, and an outlet for people's desires to do good and to express themselves.

Nonprofits are sometimes created specifically to lobby governments to enact new policies or change old ones. This can lead to a partnership arrangement in which nonprofits work closely with government, carrying out public policies with government funding. This is very common in social services, where nonprofit groups provide health care and adult education services. The nonprofit workers are closer to the public, and sometimes more trusted than government officials. These arrangements are often cheaper than creating a government department, and allow governments to try new policies without committing to maintain them indefinitely.

There is a certain tension among government, business, and the independent sector. Often the nonprofit sector works in partnership with and depends on the other two for technical support and funding. At other times it acts as a critic of government and business. These relationships can exist at the same time.

In many cases, the nongovernment sector acts as the catalyst that changes public policy. Volunteers led civil rights demonstrations that broke racist laws in the southern United States in the 1950s. Over time, popular opinion came to support the volunteers, and pushed governments to change their policies. Similarly, for years Spanish-speaking Americans had been lobbying for the right to education in their first language as well as in English. The Bilingual Education Act of 1968 created a national office to promote the issue and train people in the skills needed. It was a federal government court challenge in 1973 that required San Francisco to provide bilingual education for Spanish-speaking children, helping the cause of many voluntary groups.

When the U.S. Government gives money to nonprofit groups, it is generally as a fee for services, not for lobbying activities. Since the late 1960s, the Canadian government has been more willing to provide support to advocacy groups who are trying to change public policy. Grants have gone to such groups as the National Action Committee on the Status of Women and the Canadian Coalition on Acid Rain.

Another important characteristic of the independent sector is that it lives because people voluntarily support it. Government has the power to raise money by taxes, and business lives by selling goods and services. Nonprofit organizations depend on donations, which is money people are not obligated to give, and which provides benefits that often go to other people. Donations are often acts of faith, since it is impossible for the average person to measure the impacts. In many cases, the organization asking for money is known only by the solicitation it sends through the mail. Often, organizations get prominent people to lend their names to causes as a way of legitimizing their appeals.

People give for many reasons: religious belief, personal philosophy, or a family tradition of helping others. Some give because they feel a debt to their university, their community, or their nation. Many give to medical charities to find a cure for a disease that killed a loved one or that threatens their own health. Sometimes people support the nonprofit sector because they believe it is important to maintain alternatives to government.

Many people volunteer because they like the companionship of working with a group, and often join voluntary groups to be with friends and colleagues. Few people give money just because of tax incentives, but tax deductions help to increase the amount that people donate. Most volunteers find that they not only gave but gained. This voluntary nature of the sector is both a strength and a weakness. People join in because they want to, and can leave when they wish. There is no constitutional guarantee that these services will be provided in the amount needed—or at all.

Americans and Canadians are similar in language, dress, politics, and culture, and the similarities are often mirrored in their nonprofit sectors. But the history of these sectors also reflects some of the fundamental differences in the two cultures: while the United States has strong traditions in the civil rights movement, based on the reaction against slavery, Canada's independent sector involved cooperatives, whose grain silos dot the Prairies and whose banks are important in Quebec.

The United States, born in revolution more than two centuries ago, forged a tradition in which citizens cherish and fiercely defend the freedoms of religion, speech, and assembly. Their basic distrust of authority fostered a society in which self-help groups were a natural development. Canada evolved slowly from a colony to an independent nation in a peaceful transition. Canadians more than Americans look to governments to provide services, with charities trying to fill in the gaps.

A major difference between the two countries is shown by the approach to a social welfare system. In Canada, the government takes the lead responsibility for such services as medical care and universities, while the American system places much more reliance on private institutions. In the social services sector, the Canadian government provides a greater percentage of the funds for nonprofit organizations than is the case in the United States. Similarly, the Canadian Broadcasting Corporation is largely publicly funded, while the United States has a relatively smaller public broadcasting system, funded mainly by philanthropy.

History and Evolution

The native peoples of the Americas had their traditions of sharing. Without help and advice on how to live off the land, use indigenous plants as medicines, make canoes and moccasins, and a thousand other wilderness skills, the Europeans arriving on this continent would have had a very difficult time surviving. From indigenous peoples come concepts such as the importance of the community and a sense that people must consider the impacts of their decisions on future generations.

When the first European settlers were building farms, towns, and cities, government was small and often distant. People had to band together to govern themselves and provide services for their communities. People cooperated in barn-raisings and quilting bees. They built and created churches, schools, hospitals, unions, libraries, fire companies, and dozens of other organizations that provided essential services and became networks for socializing the next group of immigrants into a new culture. Often churches created the foundation for voluntary action, helping to create schools and hospitals, or simply providing a way to bring relief to the poor and hungry.

Volunteerism often led to the formation of local government. Town meetings were held in Massachusetts as early as 1633, when people met to work out such problems as how to control farm animals that were running loose. The idea spread as a way of defining common, shared interests. When he wrote *Democracy in America* in 1835, Alexis de Tocqueville reported a strong network of voluntary organizations. He said these were "the moral associations" where such values as charity and responsibility to others are taught and where the nation's crusades took root. De Tocqueville believed that voluntary associations helped to maintain democracy and limit the growth of the power of central governments.

Canada's first voluntary agency was likely the Bureau des Pauvres, created in 1688 to help those left homeless by a fire that devastated the town of Quebec. A board of volunteer directors oversaw the collection and distribution of money, food, clothes, shelter, and tools. One of the oldest voluntary traditions in North America is the Town Watch, now often called Neighborhood Watch. The concept was borrowed from England, and first introduced in Philadelphia in 1704 by William Penn, the city's founder. Today, more than 2,000 town or neighborhood watches in the United States and Canada organize citizens to observe and report crimes to police, thus helping to keep communities safer.

One of the early activist roles of the independent sector was in the antislavery movement. The first U.S. antislavery group was founded in 1775, and in 1833 the American Anti-Slavery Society was formed in Philadelphia. This was also the period of the Underground Railroad, a volunteer movement that helped fugitive slaves from states where slavery was allowed reach freedom in states where it was abolished, or to escape to Canada. The issue of minority rights, particularly for African Americans, arose again after World War II in the form of the civil rights movement, which was pushing for equal rights and desegregation. This was led by a number of groups, including the National Association for the Advancement of Colored People. This organization, founded

---

The Cooperative Movement in Canada

For Canada, the cooperative movement has been a very important part of nation-building. The principles of the cooperative movement, which evolved in nineteenth century England in response to industrialization, were that anyone could join, everyone could vote, and profits would be shared among members. From 1860 to 1900, farmers in Atlantic Canada, Quebec, and Ontario formed more than 1,200 cooperative creameries and cheese factories. They developed mutual insurance companies to protect themselves against early frost, hail, and fire. In the early 1900s, Prairie farmers organized the first of many grain handling and marketing cooperatives, whose silos still dot the western landscape along the rail lines that bound the country together.

In 1900, Alphonse Desjardins, a parliamentary reporter concerned that the high interest rates prevented poor people from getting loans, developed a "people's bank," called the Caisse populaire, in his native Levis, Quebec. The goal was to help working people save and plan for the future. The caisse movement, which started off with working capital of $26.40, has grown into a network of hundreds of financial institutions providing financial services to millions of people.

In Atlantic Canada, the Antigonish Movement, an adult education organization, used study clubs to help people to organize credit unions, and cooperatives to make it easier to build homes and to sell their produce and consumer goods. The group developed in the 1930s, and was known in a number of countries by the following decade. More recently, it was supported as part of Canada's foreign aid program.

---

in 1909, was pushing for "equal citizenship rights for all American citizens by eliminating segregation and discrimination in housing, employment, voting, schools, the courts, transportation, and recreation."

Another important advocacy movement has been for the rights of women, who in the last century usually could not legally control property, the future of their children, or their own destiny. In 1848, feminists called suffragettes, because of their struggle for the right to vote, met at Seneca Falls in New York, and issued a declaration of independence for women. This movement, led by Susan B. Anthony and Elizabeth Cady Stanton, spread through the United

States. In 1876, Dr. Emily Howard Stowe, Canada's first woman doctor, created the Toronto Women's Literary Club, which was actually an organization to get the vote for women. Just as the abolitionist movement was echoed a century later by the civil rights movement, the suffragette cause was echoed by the women's rights movement that built momentum in the 1960s.

Typically in the independent sector, various groups have supported one another. Women campaigning against unjust marriage laws and for the vote were sometimes also involved in fighting slavery, and in creating the temperance movement. The Woman's Christian Temperance Union was founded in Ohio in 1874 to educate the public against the abuses of liquor, and it became an important women's pressure group devoted to many types of social reform in both Canada and the United States. It promoted such reforms as female suffrage, sex hygiene, and mothers' allowances, and it operated residences so that single women could have safe places to live.

War led to the formation of what became the great public welfare appeals of today in Canada and the United States. During World War I, appeals led to the formation of some 400 community "war chests" to raise funds to help people overseas. These campaigns established a model for the creation of "community chests" for local welfare, and this has evolved into the United Way movement of today.

The formation of foundations and trusts is an important part of the independent sector history. Organizations such as the Slater, Peabody, and Jeanes funds supported schooling for blacks in the southern United States after the Civil War, but foundations in North America are largely a twentieth century phenomenon. The major trigger for their creation was the great fortunes amassed in the United States during the second half of the last century. People such as steel magnate Andrew Carnegie, oil baron John D. Rockefeller, and financier Andrew W. Mellon began some of the large trust funds that support parts of the independent sector.

Foundations introduced a new approach to giving. Carnegie, Rockefeller, and Margaret Olivia Sage organized philanthropic giving like business corporations, run by boards of directors. The idea of foundations was not so much to give money to needy individuals, but to fund research into problem solving by understanding and attacking the root causes of hunger, poverty, and disease. This research led to public policy recommendations to improve living conditions. These reports spurred the formation of advocacy groups that pushed governments and the business community to improve social conditions. Money from foundations has sometimes been called "society's risk capital" because it allows people to experiment, research, and produce programs to expand knowledge and cope with problems.

At the same time that wealthy families were creating private foundations, the community foundation movement was started by Frederick H. Goff, in Cleveland, Ohio. These public organizations, formed for the benefit of a community or region, are generally based in cities but can have as broad a scope as a whole state. Community foundations can have one fund or a number of funds donated by people or businesses for specific purposes. This enables people to target their donations over a long period without going to the expense of creating their own foundations. Corporate foundations were created after changes in U.S. tax law in 1935.

In Canada, foundations are mainly recent institutions; only 2 percent existed before 1940, and most have been created since the 1960s. Canada's largest, the J. W. McConnell Family Foundation, was established in 1937 by a wealthy Montreal businessman and owner of the Montreal Star, then Quebec's largest English-language newspaper. The Winnipeg Foundation, Canada's first community foundation, was created in 1921 by local banker William F. Alloway. Canada's foundations underwent rapid growth after World War II, when the federal and provincial governments imposed very heavy succession duties, something they have since repealed.

The concept of the foundation keeps evolving. In Canada, provincial governments have got into the lottery business in a big way. They created charitable foundations to put some of the money they raise back into hospitals and other community works. Parallel foundations allow a charity to set up a fund for a specific project, ensuring that endowments and large donations will remain separate from the regular operating funds of the institution, and will be used for the project. Crown foundations allow people to receive a higher tax deduction, by giving to the government but targeting their donations to specific public institutions, such as hospitals and universities.

The Size and Shape of the Sector

In the United States, there are about 1.14 million registered nonprofit organizations. Some 400,000 are primarily member-serving organizations, including social clubs, business associations, labor unions, professional associations, and cooperatives. The other 740,000 groups were created to serve the public at large rather than a specific group of members. Some 47 percent of these public-serving organizations are religious-based.

Canada has about 70,000 registered charitable organizations, the public-serving category, 45 percent of which are religious institutions. The federal government estimates that there is an equivalent number of nonregistered voluntary organizations. Some are created for a specific purpose and disappear within days, weeks, or months. Others simply do not bother to apply for or have been refused registration because they do not meet official criteria. Some 1,300 new charities are registered each year, about half the number that apply. The greatest growth in registered charities in Canada has been in the field of education.

Americans make individual annual contributions totaling more than $100 billion, an average of $899 per contributing family. U.S. nonprofits get another $22 billion in donations from foundations, corporations, and bequests. Nonprofit groups also receive money from governments, for services or special programs, and sell services and products to the public and private businesses. Although Americans on average give more than people in other countries, more than a third of contributors felt they did not give enough. Giving is not restricted to the rich: people with incomes under $10,000 gave more than twice as much of their income (3.6 percent) as people with incomes of $50,000-100,000 (1.7 percent).

Individuals contributed 81.9 percent of the $124.31 billion given in the United States in 1992, while foundations gave 6.7 percent, bequests accounted for 6.6 percent, and corporations contributed 4.8 percent. In addition, 51 percent of adults are volunteers and 14 percent give at least five hours a week, which has been estimated as worth at least $176 billion.

The $124 billion went to the following causes and groups:
- religion, 45.6 percent;
- education, 11.3 percent,
- human services, 9.3 percent
- health, 8.2 percent,
- arts, culture, and humanities, 7.5 percent,
- public or societal benefit, 4.1 percent,
- environment and wildlife, 2.5 percent,
- international affairs, 1.4 percent, and
- undesignated, 10.1 percent.

There is a recent trend to give more money to social justice issues, such as the rights of the disabled or minority groups, environment, youth programs, and community development. At the same time, there have been some declines in contributions to the arts, education, religion, and international issues.

There are about 32,000 grant-making foundations in the United States, including some 1,600 corporate and 282 community foundations. They hold about $138 billion in assets, and make $8.3 billion a year in grants. Three quarters of the foundations had less than $1 million in assets and made grants of less than $100,000. The 7,500 largest foundations hold 95 percent of assets and made 87 percent of the grants. Just 100 foundations hold almost half the $138 billion of assets. Corporations provided $6 billion in donations.

In Canada, individuals, foundations, and corporations donate about CDN$5.6 billion a year, with CDN$3.2 billion of this going to religious organizations. Corporations and foundations contributed, respectively, CDN$406 million and CDN$303 million of the total.

Individual Canadians give about CDN$4.87 billion a year, 87.3 percent of the total. Of those who claimed charitable donations on income tax returns, 67 percent gave to religion, 10 percent to welfare, 9 percent to education, 8 percent to health, 3 percent to benefits to the community, and 3 percent to other causes.

The CDN$406 million in corporate donations to charity represented 1.28 percent of pre-tax profits. It was allocated as follows: education, 27 percent; social services, 20 percent; health, 20 percent; arts and culture, 13 percent; civic causes, 8 percent; and the balance to a number of causes, such as environment and sports. A survey of 300 Canadian leaders found their favorite charities were the United Way, health care and disease research, and education. Half the leaders felt charitable donations were an essential corporate obligation to society, and 85 percent said their companies gave.

In Canada, there are about 850 active foundations, which had CDN$3.23 billion in assets and gave almost CDN$303 million in grants. Most of these are small, and only 10 percent have a full-time staff. The 50 biggest foundations had 70 percent of the assets, and gave 70 percent of the grants. These ranged from hundreds of thousands of dollars to a single dollar provided for a subsidized rent for an Edmonton group running a shelter for battered women and children.

Surveys have found that 96 percent of Canadians believe that supporting charities is important, and 91 percent believe that charities and nonprofit organizations make a positive contribution to society. Canadians volunteer an estimated CDN$13 billion of their time. This work is the equivalent of 617,000 full-time jobs or 6 percent of the full-time labor force.

The number of registered charities has been growing dramatically in Canada in recent years. There were 35,000 in 1974 and there are more than 68,700 now. Of these, about 49 percent are religious, 14 percent welfare-related, 14 percent educational, 9 percent offer "benefits to the community," and 7 percent are health related. The final 7 percent are categorized as miscellaneous. Although religious charities predominate in these figures, they have dropped from being nearly two thirds of the total just 20 years ago.

Some organizations have a steady income from fees and grants, but most charities have to constantly work to keep donations coming in. For many groups, telephone solicitation has replaced door-to-door canvassing. Another technique is the repeated mailing of requests for funds. Some organizations send people a half-dozen or more mailings in a year in an effort to raise funds.

Only a very few organizations, such as United Way, have succeeded in turning canvassing into a relatively stable source of revenue. They have done this by getting large employers to allow payroll deductions to be sent directly to the charity. The United Way and similar movements, such as the United Jewish Appeal, began decades ago. The aim is to have a single fund-raising organization that can raise millions of dollars in contributions, and distribute them to a number of nonprofit organizations in the health and welfare fields.

Many different techniques are now used to raise funds, however. In its search for support, the independent sector has developed such new devices as charitable mutual funds to encourage individual and corporate donations. Since more than 80 percent of every charitable dollar in the United States comes from individuals, these and other innovative approaches are bound to remain popular with fund-raisers.

Charities have been regulated at least since the 1601 Statute of Uses in England, which was written to control abuses related to charitable activity, especially improper uses of charitable property. One of the major ways that U.S. and Canadian charities are regulated is through income tax laws, which date from the early part of this century.

Under U.S. federal law, there is tax exemption for a number of different types of organizations, including "corporations, and any community chest, fund, or foundation, organized and operated exclusively for religious, charitable, scientific, testing for public safety, literacy, or educational purposes."

The Canadian government lists four categories of tax-exempt charity: the relief of poverty, education, religion, and the good of the community. The last definition is a broad one that allowed the growth of a number of new forms of nonprofit organization. Cultural activities and promotion of the arts fall under education, while libraries and museums fall under "benefit to the community." So do protection of animals, charitable trusts, recreation, temperance associations, and community organizations. The other category includes service clubs, employees' charity trusts, registered Canadian amateur athletic associations, and a number of other organizations. According to the Canadian Centre for Philanthropy, "Charitable organizations are corporations or trusts constituted and operated exclusively for charitable purposes; there is to be no self-interest, but altruism and benefit to the community."

Revenue Canada and the Internal Revenue Service in the United States oversee the activities of foundations and groups that have been registered as nonprofits. Registration means that the income of foundations is not taxed, and people who donate to registered charities are allowed to deduct at least some of their gifts from their income when calculating their income taxes. The regulations are to ensure public accountability for money that would otherwise have gone, at least in part, to government in the form of taxes. The sector is regulated by the U.S. states, Canadian provinces, and some municipal governments. These multiple levels of regulation have created a sometimes inconsistent patchwork of rules that is difficult to understand.

A Picture of the Independent Sector Today

This section profiles some of the major categories of organizations in the tax-exempt philanthropic sector, particularly in the public-benefit side. The categories have been selected to give a sense of the diversity within this vast sector.

Although foundations only provide 5-7 percent of donations to nonprofit groups, these funds play a special role because they are independent and relatively stable. Philanthropic organizations support a wide variety of activities, including research, health, education, arts, and culture. They give money for conferences to promote research and innovative thinking. They provide scholarships and fellowships and supply other organizations with management assistance and training. Although most foundation funding goes to traditional institutions, they are able to provide "venture capital" for innovative programs, and can support new, even unpopular causes.

Most foundations are small organizations run by the donor or that person's family, sometimes with the part-time help of accountants, lawyers, and consultants. Larger foundations have boards of directors or trustees, and are often run by a professional staff. A few large foundations are as big and as professionally run as companies. The Ford Foundation has more than 500 employees, for example, and offices in several countries.

Foundations have often put money into trying to find solutions for basic social problems. Before World War I, the Russell Sage Foundation showed

---

Categories of Organizations

The organization Independent Sector has developed a list of categories of organizations in the tax-exempt philanthropic sector in the United States. The list, called the National Taxonomy of Exempt Entities, includes:

- Arts, culture, and humanities
- Education
- Environmental quality
- Animal-related
- Health
- Consumer protection, legal aid
- Crime prevention and public protection
- Employment
- Food, nutrition, and agriculture
- Housing
- Public safety
- Emergency preparedness and relief
- Recreation, leisure, sports, and athletics
- Youth development
- Human services
- International
- Civil rights, social action, and advocacy
- Community improvement and capacity building
- Grant-making organizations
- Research, planning, science, technology, and technical assistance
- Voluntarism
- Religion and spiritual development

---

how governments could deal with wretched living and working conditions. Between the wars, the Rockefeller and Rosenwald funds were pressing for new opportunities for blacks. In more recent decades, foundations have promoted improvements in fields as diverse as education, civil rights, environmental protection, public interest law, the status of women, housing, broadcasting, deficit reduction, and tax simplification. Grants are provided for an extremely wide range of research, including aeronautical, agricultural, auditing, behavioral science, communications, education, energy, environment, medicine, social science, theology, and transportation.

The importance of religion in North American life is shown by the fact that the bulk of individual donations are given to religious institutions. Part of that is used to support the institutions, and part is used for general community welfare. Religious institutions have long been centers both of faith and of charity. They often serve as community centers, opening their doors to believers and nonbelievers to participate in everything from food banks to choral societies within their walls. It was often religious people who started basic services such as hospitals or schools. It is in religious congregations and gatherings that people learn and are reminded of responsibility to others, and where moral issues are raised, debated, and reinforced. Religion not only develops a system of belief, it fosters an attitude that supports service to community, creating a more caring and moral society.

The United States has become "by far the most religious of all major industrial countries," according to Benton Johnson, a sociologist at the University of Oregon. Since 1960, church membership has increased 37 percent, reaching 156 million. An estimated 350,000 religious congregations are found in the United States, representing more than 100 denominations. The picture is different in Canada. While close to 60 percent of Americans rank religion "very important" in their lives, only 30 percent of Canadians accord it the same importance, according to a 1993 public opinion poll. Yet only 7 percent of Canadians say they have no religion.

People who identify themselves as religious are the most generous when it comes to giving time and money. According to *From Belief to Commitment*, Americans gave $39.2 billion to congregations and donated time worth close to another $20 billion. An estimated 49 million people volunteer to or through religious organizations. The same people who made donations to congregations also made 73 percent of all the contributions to other charities. "The natural affinity between religious beliefs and improving the human condition is probably stronger than most people think," notes Virginia Hodgkinson of Independent Sector.

Although the bulk of the money and time given to the religious organizations was for religious ministry and education, a very important amount went for such community work as housing programs for the homeless, food kitchens, youth groups, and family counseling. A great number of these programs are run in affiliation with other organizations. This community service accounted for about $6.6 billion in funds and 43 percent of volunteer time.

Religious institutions have played an even more important role in some minority communities. Since the beginnings of the Black church in eighteenth-century United States, religious congregations have provided both faith and substance. Although African Americans could not head banks and insurance companies, the churches could create mutual aid associations that lent money and provided insurance. This helped blacks gain experience that proved useful when they could move into businesses, such as banking, when racial barriers finally were lowered.

Health care has become one of the largest components of national spending in North America as the population ages and people demand the benefits of new and expensive medicines, machines, and treatments. It is a complex area involving government-run institutions, those run by nonprofit organizations, and for-profit private institutions. This field shows differences in how Canada and the United States treat the role of government in relation to their people.

In the United States, the government pays most of the cost of health care for the elderly, the poor, and the disabled. Just over half the nation's 6,700 hospitals are organized as nonprofits, and they account for two thirds of the short-term general hospital beds. About a third of the hospitals are operated by governments, mainly state and local authorities, and the remaining 17 percent of hospitals are run by for-profit corporations. The nonprofits also play a major role in outpatient and home health care activities that involve such services as blood banks and kidney dialysis centers.

In Canada, the government pays most of the cost of health care for everyone out of taxes, and the government sets all fees charged by doctors and hospitals. There are 1,093 public hospitals, 52 private hospitals, and 44 under the jurisdiction of the federal government. Hospitals now receive the vast bulk of their funds from governments through Canada's medical care system, but many also raise funds through charitable donations, which help them buy equipment or expand. Volunteers donate millions of hours and millions of dollars of time to help operate hospitals.

Fund-raising for research into cures for diseases has a long tradition and is one of the common ways in which volunteer organizations maintain direct contact with the public. Voluntary funding agencies, which are generally disease-specific, play an important role in medical research. There is a fund-raising effort for virtually every major disease or affected part of the human body, as well as many for injuries to the human spirit. Some organizations deal with both. Alcoholics Anonymous, founded in 1935 and operating in more than 90 countries, helps alcoholics to help themselves stop drinking.

Gamblers Anonymous helps people deal with a compulsion that can lead them to wager away all they possess.

Some diseases, in particular cancer, draw a great deal of support. In Canada, charitable donations finance about 60 percent of cancer research, and the federal government provides most of the remaining money. The world's largest single one-day fund-raising event for cancer research is the annual Terry Fox Marathon of Hope. Each September, more than 500,000 people in Canada and around the world run, walk, roller skate, and even walk with crutches to earn money pledged for the distance they can cover. By 1993, the annual event had raised more than CDN$106 million for cancer research. Jim Terrion, a deaf runner from Prince Rupert, B.C., collected more than CDN$46,000 in pledges in one run.

In education, private nonprofit schools have a smaller part of the enrollment than public schools, but they play a critical role. Just over 10 percent of the U.S. school population goes to more than 27,000 private nonprofit schools, and 5 percent of Canadian pupils are in 800 similar institutions. In both nations, most of these schools are affiliated with religions. Private school enrollment has been rising steadily in both countries. In the United States, the number of public schools declined by 3 percent during the 1980s, while the number of private schools jumped 29 percent. In Canada, private school enrollment has doubled since 1970.

At the post-secondary level, there are great differences between the two countries. In the United States, 49 percent of the more than 2,000 higher education institutions are private and nonprofit. They are generally smaller than public colleges and universities and, as a result, have only 20 percent of post-secondary enrollment. But some of the most prestigious U.S. universities are private nonprofits—including Harvard, Princeton, University of Chicago, Johns Hopkins, Duke, Massachusetts Institute of Technology, Wellesley, and Stanford University.

Despite the lower enrollment, U.S. nonprofit universities give half the nation's doctoral and professional degrees and absorb about one third of higher education spending. The figures have been changing. In 1950, two thirds of universities and colleges were private nonprofits, and they had half of all students. Since then, there was a building boom of colleges and universities by state and local governments, although that tapered off sharply after governments began to restrain spending in the past decade or so. Now, public colleges and universities have 78 percent of students while profit-making institutions, mainly technical and vocational schools, have 2 percent.

Helping People to Help Themselves

The Highlander Research and Education Center, on a 105-acre farm near Knoxville, Tennessee, is in its fourth stage of evolution. It started in 1932 by teaching people how to get access to clean well water and to protect water quality. During the 1930s and into the 1940s it was one of the most important training centers for labor organizers in the U.S. South. By the 1950s, Highlander turned its attention to desegregation, and became one of the main incubators of the civil rights movement. At times, classes were held on buses, and the blackboard was a large paper bag.

Since the 1970s, the center has been working on such problems as health, safety, poverty, and land rights issues, particularly in the mining country of Appalachia. The goal is to help people find ways of getting companies to protect the environment without driving employers away. Highlander does this by getting people who have had success in resolving such problems to share their experiences with others.

The center brings together working people with social activists, educators, and grassroots leaders mainly from the South and Appalachia, but also from other countries.

In Canada, by contrast, there are no large private universities. Canada's higher education students are virtually all in the 60 universities and 210 community colleges, which are largely publicly funded. The closest that Canada has to private universities is 16 religious colleges, which have less than 1 percent of post-secondary students. In addition, there are about 3,500 private, for-profit trade and vocational colleges.

Most of our cultural and artistic institutions, including art galleries, libraries, symphonies, and theaters, were created by private families or nonprofit organizations, and are still supported—often to a great degree—by foundations, corporations, and donations of citizens. In some cases, families have needed public funding to maintain a private collection, and the collection became a public one. Sometimes homes have been expanded into larger buildings. The names of such institutions as Guggenheim Museum in New York and Roy Thomson Hall, the home of Toronto's major symphony orchestra, are permanent records of donations by wealthy families. A large number of libraries in Canada and the United States were built early in this century because of the philanthropy of Andrew Carnegie, who endowed 2,500 libraries in the United States and Canada.

While philanthropy and the arts may be associated with grand museums and collections of rare works of art, most activities occur in small local centers. It is local artists and art supporters who raise funds to open a small town gallery. It is volunteers who run the little local theater, and local citizens who donate artifacts to the community museum, proud to share their history with their neighbors.

In recent years, arts and cultural institutions have been scrambling for dollars as governments cut funding. Since the 1970s, government grants to the arts have fallen behind the rate of inflation, and in recent years there have been outright reductions. This is clear in the ever-increasing appeals for funds to keep public broadcasting stations on the air. Other institutions suffer, too. In Toronto, the city's largest, not-for-profit summer theater closed its doors after 21 years. In the past five years, 23 nonprofit U.S. theaters closed.

The corporate world has long been a patron of such arts and cultural institutions as symphony orchestras, museums, art galleries, theater, dance, opera, choirs, libraries, and archives. But as corporate revenues fell in recent years, companies began to seek more than a mention in the program. In recent years, the foyers of some opera and symphony halls began to resemble new car showrooms as performance sponsors show their wares, or as the arts institution itself raffles off an expensive vehicle to raise funds.

Community organizations, another major category in this sector, help poor people develop the power and capacity to improve their communities, and to change policies and institutions that affect their lives. The roots of many community organizations go back decades. Some trace them to social reformer Jane Addams and her efforts to involve poor people in the creation of settlement houses such as Hull House at the turn of the century. Another source was the work of union organizer Saul Alinsky in creating neighborhood organizations in 1940s Chicago. There was a great expansion of American community organizations during the War on Poverty in the 1960s. The groups range from Positive Women United, in Washington, to the Concerned Citizens to Save West Dallas, from the United Hands Community Land Trust in Philadelphia to Napa Valley Ecumenical Housing.

Community organizations deal with such diverse issues as civil rights, the settlement of migrant families, crime, hunger, Indian rights, rural development, voting rights, and housing in blighted urban neighborhoods. Often, they are working in the toughest neighborhoods, such as Watts in Los Angeles, to help people rebuild a sense of community and deal with problems such as unemployment.

Organizations such as the National Urban League, founded in 1910, show how strong this movement can be. The League has 3,000 paid staff and 50,000 volunteers in 112 cities across the United States. It spends $80 million a year, which it receives from foundations, corporations, individual donations, and government contracts. Its president, John E. Jacob, said one of its major functions is to train people with "work readiness skills" so they have a better chance getting jobs. Jacob said they get 85-95 percent job placement rate as they take people off welfare and put them on payrolls all over the country. He said the organization acts as a buffer between government and individuals.

The independent sector also encompasses groups that work on political action and human rights issues. One way of getting change is to help people register to vote, and to understand how the political system works. Minorities have become more involved in the political system as a way of reducing discrimination. Groups such as the Southwest Voter Registration Project register Hispanic voters in order to increase their influence in the political institutions that govern their lives.

These groups also work to improve education. The dropout rate for Hispanics in the United States is more than double the national average. Organizations such as the Intercultural Development Research Association in San Antonio have lobbied hard for better school funding for poor areas, such as Edgewood District. This San Antonio district lacks the tax base of richer neighborhoods in the same region, and the school dropout rate is very high. Such activism is fairly recent in the Hispanic community, according to Raul Yzaguirre, president of the National Council of La Raza. He said that Hispanic people grew up in a Catholic tradition in which the church set most of the priorities for charitable action. In recent years, the Hispanic sector has started to evolve a culture that is more activist, and based on group decisions.

In the environment field, it is nonprofit groups that most often publicize environmental issues, obliging governments and businesses to respond. The result has been a public deeply concerned about environmental degradation, and a series of major changes in public policy and business practices.

Environment groups have been the catalyst in turning science into attention-getting headlines and television documentaries that alert the public to the dangers of environmental degradation. For many people, the image of the environmentalist is the Greenpeace demonstrator hanging an anti-pollution banner from a smokestack, or a protester chaining herself to a tree to stop logging in old forests. But the environment movement is maturing rapidly,

---

Trying to Help People Understand How to Save the World

While many environmental groups are known for their confrontational tactics, Worldwatch Institute uses facts and figures on the state of the environment to reach policymakers. The goal is to show decision-makers the connections between economic and environmental systems, so that governments and businesses will see the need to protect and conserve natural resources.

Over the past two decades, the institute has become one of the world's foremost sources of informed commentary on such key indicators of planetary well-being as deforestation, soil loss, species extinction, energy use, and the amount of food being produced. It draws the information from the United Nations and the World Bank, as well as a global network of research institutions.

With support from the Rockefeller Brothers Fund, Worldwatch was founded in 1974 by Lester Brown, formerly a farmer and U.S. government agriculture specialist, who believed people needed to know how growing human impacts were undermining the environment. He and his staff are constantly speaking to policymakers in government and business in a number of countries, and appearing in the news media.

Worldwatch is best known for its annual State of the World report, published in 27 languages. It also produces Vital Signs, which tracks such key indicators as global temperature, fish catches, population growth, and military spending, and World Watch magazine, with articles distributed to nearly 100 leading newspapers around the world. State of the World is a textbook in more than 1,300 U.S. college and university courses.

---

and includes a number of large organizations who wield influence as much by publishing detailed scientific reports as by picketing the polluters or burying old cars as a protest against air pollution. The field is no longer one inhabited solely by young radicals.

Now the sector is struggling with its identity as it evolves from a group that is mainly a bearer of bad news to one that is trying to propose constructive solutions, sometimes under the rubric of sustainable development. While many groups continue to protest against polluting industries or dumps, others spend more time at the negotiating table with business and government, working out agreements on how to make the economy more environmentally sustainable. Environment groups have even been invited into negotiations over international agreements between Canada and the United States over water quality. They participated in discussion with these two countries and Mexico over the environmental implications of the North American Free Trade Agreement.

Complementing the work of environmentalists and others seeking to influence policy are research organizations, sometimes popularly known as think tanks and among the most prestigious of nonprofit groups. Although they are not voluntary groups, they provide independent advice to governments, businesses, and the public. Often they are funded by major foundations that want experts to investigate new issues on behalf of society.

One of the top think tanks is the Brookings Institution. It began in 1916 as the Institute for Government Research, with help from the newly established Rockefeller Foundation. Its first task was to study ways to run government more efficiently, a problem it and many other groups are still working on. What later became Brookings is known internationally for its research on economic issues at a global level.

There is a very wide range of policy institutes across the United States. Some focus on political and economic issues while others, such as Worldwatch Institute and World Resources Institute, analyze the state of the planet, working in cooperation with international agencies, including the United Nations.

In Canada, there are a number of policy institutes, ranging from the Royal Society of Canada to the Institute for Research on Public Policy and the Fraser Institute. While some rely mainly on private funding, a number depend heavily on government grants and fees.

The volunteer efforts of Americans and Canadians do not stop at their borders. People have been sending famine relief and other forms of voluntary help abroad for decades, both on an emergency basis, and through long-term programs. Often the help goes through such well-established organizations as the Red Cross. Emergency relief for natural disasters and longer term hunger is necessary, but it is the equivalent of giving someone a fish so he or she can eat for a day. People in poor nations also need to learn how to be self-sufficient, and, according to the reports from the 1992 Earth Summit in Rio de Janeiro, they need a chance to escape from the crushing burden of foreign debt and to sell their products on world markets at fair prices. Despite foreign aid programs, the poor are getting poorer, and poor nations are sending more money to the rich, mainly in debt repayments, than they are receiving in assistance.

The first American and Canadian groups to send assistance abroad on a systematic basis were church missions, while governments began foreign aid programs later, particularly after World War II. In 1961, the United States created the Peace Corps to send trained volunteers overseas. The same year, CUSO was created by 21 universities and 22 other nonprofit organizations, and it placed thousands of Canadian volunteers, mainly teachers, overseas.

North American nonprofit organizations play an important role in what is often called capacity building—helping people develop the skills, knowledge, and technical know-how to be self-sufficient. Large advertisements have regularly appeared in the Globe and Mail, Canada's national newspaper, saying, "Give us the tools, and we'll finish the job." CARE Canada is inviting people to donate used tools and equipment for shipment to small-scale entrepreneurs in Latin America. The Calmeadow Foundation specializes in "banking the unbankable" by providing loans, sometimes of less than CDN$100, that enable poor people to start or improve small businesses. This micro-banking for micro-enterprise started in Asia with such organizations as the Grameen (rural) Bank in Bangladesh. The concept has been imported into poor regions in Arkansas and native reserves in Ontario.

With the collapse of the Iron Curtain, the opportunity has opened up for nonprofit organizations to work with East European nations. A group called the Center for Citizens' Initiatives, based in San Francisco, is working to provide seeds so that Russians can plant food gardens. It has also established centers in Russia to teach people accustomed to a centrally planned economy how a free market operates. Some Russians are brought to the United States for training.

The Sector's Future

North America has been through 50 years of industrial expansion and population growth that began after World War II. The nonprofit sector has flourished in a climate of democracy, which has given the region more nonprofit organizations for its population than other parts of the world. Now Canada and the United States are becoming less an industrial society and more an information society that processes ideas rather than steel, concrete, and wood. Major shifts in employment patterns have left hundreds of thousands of people unemployed, which increases the demand for help, and at least as many more underemployed—working at lower skilled jobs than they should. At the same time, governments in both countries are struggling with a combined national debt that is larger than the gross domestic product of Africa and Latin America combined. As a result, governments at all levels are cutting budgets, and this reduces the flow of money into the economy. Tough economic times mean the sector is facing potentially wrenching changes.

Both U.S. and Canadian charities have felt the pinch of two recessions in a decade. In some cases, donations to charities stagnated, and even fell when compared with inflation. Nonprofit groups in Canada appear to be even more vulnerable to cuts, because they depend relatively more on government for funding than do their U.S. counterparts, and the Canadian debt and unemployment rates are relatively higher. The federal Department of Canadian Heritage, for example, provides CDN$45 million a year to nearly 10,000 nonprofit groups. That budget was cut 10 percent for 1993, and is to drop another 20 percent by 1997, based on current government policy.

A 1992 poll of charities by the Canadian Centre for Philanthropy found that 80 percent of those replying said they had been forced to make changes because of the recession. Half the groups had cut or postponed spending, and a third had cut staff. One-fifth of the organizations responding said they knew of a group that had been forced to shut down principally because of lower revenues.

At the same time, the Centre found that "Demand for charitable services is up across the board. Increased demand was most pronounced for respondents active in basic and emergency needs." The number of people they have served has risen by as much as 25 percent within six months. There is one encouraging sign. In 1992, charities surveyed in Canada said that individual donations were rising despite the recession.

All these pressures are forcing the independent sector to articulate more clearly what it is, what it does, and what it cannot take over from government. Facing growing financial constraints, the sector had to become more efficient. More and more charities are selling products and services in order to raise more money. Often it is on a small scale, in the form of T-shirts, calendars, or mugs carrying their message. In the case of a YMCA that operates a sports complex, it could be seen as competition for private health clubs. There have been some complaints from the private sector that nonprofits, which get tax breaks, are invading the terrain of private business, which does not get such advantages. The Mountain Equipment Co-op, a Canadian chain of nonprofit outdoor stores, competes directly with commercial camping stores, sometimes located just a few steps away.

Representing the Sector

By the late 1970s, a number of American nonprofit leaders were concerned about a relative decline in giving, greater government regulation of the sector combined with its greater dependence on government funding, and limited public awareness of the sector's importance for individual freedom and fulfillment.

The Coalition of National Voluntary Organizations and the National Council on Philanthropy joined forces in 1980 to revitalize the sector. Originally the new body was called A National Forum to Encourage Voluntary Support and Service for the Public Good. It rapidly became Independent Sector because organizers felt this name represented the most important common characteristic.

The new group was chaired by John W. Gardner, a former secretary of the U.S. Department of Health, Education, and Welfare, with Brian O'Connell, former executive director of the Mental Health Association, as president. Among its goals were to:

• preserve and enhance the tradition of giving, volunteering, and not-for-profit initiative;

• improve the public's understanding of the independent sector' contributions and problems;

• improve the management of the sector and promote access, accountability, openness, and disclosure; and

• provide commentary on a such issues as equity, openness, potential for usefulness, standards, tax policy, health of volunteering, and the relationship of the nonprofit sector to business and government.

Independent Sector grew rapidly to become a respected center of expertise on this part of society. One of its most recent activities was to foster the development of CIVICUS as an independent organization.

Nonprofits are drawing more on the expertise of business people, asking them to sit for free on advisory boards. In some cases, they have developed what amounts to a business partnership. One of the more visible examples of this is the appearance of the names of a nonprofit and a profit-making business together. The company often pays for the ad, which is usually to promote the nonprofit cause. And both benefit from the association. Similarly, when the Consumers Association of Canada found its funding drying up, it cut staff and began to do something that would have been considered heretical a decade ago—solicit funds from business in return for services such as consumer advice panels. The partnership allows the organization to maintain a watchdog role, and gives businesses an insight into consumer concerns.

The very face of the nonprofit sector is changing. Minority groups were often asked to give and volunteer less often. But when they are asked, they give and volunteer at a higher rate than average. Now their participation rate is increasing. Among African Americans, the rate of volunteering went from 28 percent in 1988 to 43 percent in 1992. Among Hispanic Americans, the comparable change was from 27 percent to 38 percent.

The nonprofit sector has long been associated with women's issues, and women have often formed the majority of the workers in this field. But some U.S. commentators have noted that although women make up two thirds of the paid employees of nonprofit groups, they do not seem to have parity with men in senior positions. This is noticeable in the executive levels and boards of directors of large organizations, such as universities, hospitals, and foundations, although more women have been promoted in recent years, particularly in the senior staff levels.

The independent sector evolves with society, and such developments as the personal computer have spawned a new branch. Electronic bulletin boards, which people reach by using computers connected to telephone lines, are used to help people with information on a wide variety of subjects. This has created what one computer writer calls online or electronic volunteerism—a reference to the fact it takes place "on" the telephone line. It has led to the creation of "virtual groups," which exist via the computer connections but which rarely if ever meet in person. When people post electronic calls for information, they not only get electronic messages, but what one writer called "random acts of kindness." These can include a jar of spices in the mail, phone calls and flowers sent to a hospital room, and invitations to visit. A group called CompuMentor in San Francisco helps other nonprofit organizations, such as the American Civil Liberties Union and California's Foundation for School Services, in dealing with the often confusing world of computer technology.

Another aspect of the evolution of the sector involves groups that have had to adapt to the fact that the problem they were created to cure has been "solved." There are few needy war veterans now, for example, so the War Amputations of Canada now provides services for child amputees with programs such as CHAMP and JUMPSTART. Donations are used to provide specially designed artificial limbs, and training on computers that can be operated without limbs. By the same token, the largest U.S. medical charity used to be the March of Dimes, which fought infantile paralysis caused by polio. Now that the disease is almost eradicated, the organization has set its sights on birth defects. In Canada, the largest part of the March of Dimes is in Ontario, where it works to help adults with physical disabilities in general.

At the same time, the nonprofit sector keeps adding new members. It is likely to keep growing as people realize they will have to provide some services that governments cannot or will not pay for. Governments are faced with invidious choices: whether to cut funding to education, or to health care, or to social services for the poor. Legislators are trying to make current services more efficient in order to maintain services with less spending. However, there is increasing pressure on the independent sector to pick up services that governments have decided to cut or drop entirely. In mid-1973, the health minister for Ontario said she wanted to transfer government funding for homemakers for the aged and handicapped from private, profit-making companies to nonprofit operators, which she believes can do the work more cheaply.

Business leaders surveyed in 1992 said they believed in giving to charity, but corporate donations would likely drop by 5.5 percent in 1993. When asked how donations would change, companies said they were more likely to increase support to education, United Way, and the environment, while cutting support to sport, arts and culture, hospitals, civic causes, and other health and social services.

People are concerned that if the lingering recession and government cutbacks in spending continue, the independent sector faces a kind of triage. Under this scenario, the type of service that provides food for the hungry would likely be saved, but those that provide for quality of life, such as children's day camps, may not survive. The Canadian Centre for Philanthropy warned of changes ahead, saying "if the demand for social services is likely to increase and grow more complex, but public funding is likely to decrease, how can individual Canadians be encouraged to provide more charitable support?"

Although the nonprofit sector receives billions of dollars a year, this is still a tiny sum compared with the revenues of government and industry. In the United States, in terms of national income, commerce represents 79 percent, government 15 percent, and the independent sector only 6 percent. During the 1980s, a number of U.S. politicians felt that foundations and corporations should help government keep schools, libraries, and parks open and maintain other public services. Once people looked at the amounts of money needed and available through philanthropy, however, it became obvious that donors can deal with emergencies, but that the small amount of money available could not possibly take over large public programs.

An Independent Sector report says: "Public trust stems from our willingness to go beyond the law or even the spirit of the law. We act ethically because we have determined that it is the right thing to do." But in recent years, parts of the sector have been challenged over the efficiency of their operations and the size of salaries paid to some of their executives. Groups that started as loose coalitions around a kitchen table face issues of governance, accountability for their revenues, annual reports, and even investigations by governments and the news media. And some observers feel that there are too many organizations doing the same thing; they point to groups that seem to be organized more to obtain grants than to fill a pressing public need. Others question if large donations should keep being used to build additions to hospitals and universities at a time when governments are reducing operating grants for such institutions.

There is no simple measurement of what the sector provides to society because—unlike private business—there is no simple profit and loss sheet at the end of the year. In some cases, nonprofits are not living up to the goal of doing "the right thing." John Gardner once wrote that "some nonprofit institutions are far gone in decay. Some are so badly managed as to make a mockery of every good intention they might have had. There is fraud, mediocrity and silliness. In short, the independent sector has no sovereign remedy against human and institutional failure."

Periodically, governments move to exert greater control. Since the 1970s, there have been proposals to strip or limit tax exemptions and deductions for U.S. organizations that emphasize advocacy and activism. Sometimes, proposals to limit nonprofits are aimed at ensuring that the groups are fulfilling a public service. This is fair, since many nonprofits benefit from tax deductions, but it is essential to leave such groups the freedom to innovate and sometimes to criticize government policies.

What are some of the directions the independent sector can take to cope with difficult economic times, and to demonstrate accountability?

John Jacob of the National Urban League believes the not-for-profit sector must build more partnerships with government and business. He says that U.S. society is moving through major changes as, for example, minority groups become larger and more influential. The independent sector can play an important role in shepherding the nation through this period of change. Jacob sees this sector also taking on more responsibilities that have been handled by families, such as child care and elder care.

Nathan Gilbert, Executive Director of the Laidlaw Foundation in Toronto, echoes this sentiment, saying that members of the nonprofit sector need to "partner, share, collaborate and merge." He said that the nonprofit sector cannot expect any increase in income, but it can expect a growth in demand for services. As a result, it will have to become more efficient, and avoid waste and duplication of services. Just like big companies such as IBM, the independent sector will have to restructure to face changing needs and demands. Linda Mollenhauer of the Canadian Centre for Philanthropy predicts that nonprofits will be forced to charge higher fees for services such as art galleries, to seek even more donations, and to reduce services.

In a period of recession, there is growing competition for donations among organizations, and they will have to differentiate themselves. Mollenhauer adds that nonprofit organizations will also have to be more accountable in showing how they brought about real change. Donors will demand more proof of the effectiveness of organizations before they hand over their money, and will be asking, "What's the benefit for me or for my family?"

William Dietel, former president of the Rockefeller Brothers Fund, stresses that it is vital that nonprofit organizations, particularly the large ones, have first-class management. They must manage finances even more carefully than in the past, and this will lead nonprofits to adopt more of the procedures of business. There will be less of a tendency to run over budget, and then to try to raise more money to cover the deficit. As donations become harder to raise, Dietel adds, there is a need for more expertise in fund-raising—the equivalent of marketing for a corporation.

One problem facing nonprofits is relatively low salaries. Leaders of these organizations need to find other rewards for their staff, such as the knowledge that their actions are influencing government policies or helping people to live better lives. Management duties are sometimes seen as a burden by the people who create voluntary organizations in order to deal with problems in society. Some leaders learn management skills, and others delegate the tasks. In some cases, the management problems are not dealt with, and this can handicap the organization.

One sign of the increasing professionalism is the creation of university programs on the independent sector. Yale University was the first to get into this field in an organized way in 1982, and now there are 25 U.S. universities with specialized centers for voluntary sector studies. In Canada, York University's Voluntary Sector Management Program, started in 1983, is the only one of its kind focused exclusively on the sector. In addition, the Canadian Centre for Philanthropy has a non-degree certificate course, delivered through the continuing education departments of 13 universities.

Closing Thoughts

The independent sector is a constantly evolving organism—far different today than it was a generation or two ago. It is always risky to predict how a sector, let alone a single organization, will evolve in the future. It is certain that the independent sector will remain a major driving force in such fields as education, environment, health, and caring for the needy. It is likely to expand in other fields as the need arises.

The voluntary and nonprofit sectors of North American society are a strong antidote to many of the ills of modern life, including cynicism, powerlessness, and despair. As John Gardner noted in a speech at the time of the founding of Independent Sector, more than a decade ago, myriad organizations scattered across the continent and representing all parts of our societies "permit the expression of caring and compassion; they make possible a sense of belonging, of being needed, of allegiance and all the other bonding impulses that have characterized humans since the prehistoric days."

The independent sector has been an important part of North American life for centuries. The continued health of this sector will be a barometer of the health of the cultures in the United States and Canada in the future.

Bibliography

Boris, Elizabeth. *Philanthropic Foundations in the United States, An Introduction.* Washington, D.C.: Council on Foundations, 1992.

Brodhead, Tim and Brent Herbert-Copley. *Bridges of Hope? Canadian Voluntary Agencies and the Third World.* Ottawa: North-South Institute, 1988.

Canadian Centre for Philanthrophy. *Law, Tax, and Charities: The Legislative and Regulatory Environment for Charitable Nonprofit Organizations.* Toronto: 1990.

Canadian Centre for Philanthrophy. *The Canadian Charitable Sector: Giving and Volunteering by Individual Canadians in March 1991.* Toronto: 1991.

103

Canadian Centre for Philanthrophy. *Charity Facts, 1993.* Toronto: 1993.

Duchesne, Doreen. *Giving Freely: Volunteers in Canada.* Ottawa: Statistics Canada, 1989.

Marsh, James H., ed., *The Canadian Encyclopedia.* Edmonton: Hurtig Publishers Ltd., 1988.

Independent Sector. *Ethics and the Nation's Voluntary and Philanthropic Community: Obedience to the Unenforceable.* Washington, D.C.: 1991.

Independent Sector. *From Belief to Commitment.* Washington, D.C.: 1993.

Lautenschlager, Janet. *Volunteering: A Traditional Canadian Value.* Ottawa: Multiculturalism and Citizenship Canada, Voluntary Action Directorate, 1992.

Lipsett, Seymour Martin, *Continental Divide: the Values and Institutions of the United States and Canada,* New York: Routledge, 1991.

Martin, Samuel A. *An Essential Grace, Funding Canada's Health Care, Education, Welfare, Religion and Culture.* Toronto: McClelland and Stewart, 1985.

Nielsen, Waldemar. *The Third Sector: Keystone of a Caring Society.* Washington, D.C.: Independent Sector, 1990.

O'Connell, Brian, ed., *America's Voluntary Spirit: A Book of Readings.* New York: The Foundation Center, 1983.

O'Connell, Brian. *Origins, Dimensions and Impact of America's Voluntary Spirit.* Washington, D.C.: Independent Sector, 1993.

O'Connell, Brian. *State of the Sector: With Particular Attention To Its Independence.* Washington, D.C.: Independent Sector, 1987.

O'Connell, Brian and O'Connell, Ann Brown. *Volunteers in Action.* New York: The Foundation Center, 1989.

Ross, David P. *Economic Dimensions of Volunteer Work in Canada.* Ottawa: Department of the Secretary of State of Canada, 1990.

Royal Bank of Canada. *Royal Bank Reporter.* Toronto: Spring 1991.

Salamon, Lester M. *America's Nonprofit Sector: A Primer.* New York: The Foundation Center, 1992.

Smith, Larry W. *Canada's Charitable Economy.* Toronto: Canadian Foundation for Economic Education, 1992.

4

THE STATUS OF THE THIRD SECTOR IN THE ARAB REGION

Dr. Amani Kandil

The third sector—or the "indigenous sector," as it is commonly known in Arab countries—is characterized by a wealth of experience and a wide spectrum of organizational structures. (Indigenous here implies strong links to the broad base of the population or "grass roots," and is used in terms of initiatives emanating from the people or the community rather than the state.) The sector will be referred to in this chapter as private voluntary organizations (PVOs), meaning associations and institutions at both the official and the popular level. This usage is justified by the fact that all associations and private institutions for public benefit in Arab countries are privately initiated by individuals (or by other institutions) for the provision of services and not for the generation of profit. Laws are enacted to confer legality on such institutions.

Since the early 1970s, third-sector organizations have tended to develop and to assume a variety of patterns and organizational structures. Although the experience of several Arab countries in this area dates back as far as the nineteenth century, during a "revival" over the last two decades this sector began to assume different forms. It is still taking shape.

The changes that the third sector has undergone have not been restricted to increases in size or variations in patterns; they have radically affected its concepts and underlying philosophy, modifying its course. The concepts of "philanthropy" and social care, which once constituted the major thrust of the third sector, have been replaced by the concepts of development and community participation as crucial approaches capable of optimizing the sector's role. Although the problems of the third sector and its effectiveness were once the concern of the few, concern about this issue has expanded to large and varied groups of the public and policymakers today.

The changes in the third sector reflect to a great extent social, economic, and at times political changes in society as some countries have reverted to a multiparty system. They may not be ignored because they reflect a worldwide trend of the third sector and international nongovernmental organizations (NGOs) playing a greater role in addressing problems related to population growth and distribution, the environment, disadvantaged and marginalized groups, human rights, and so on.

What socioeconomic factors have precipitated the change in the status of the third sector in Arab countries? The major factors may be divided into two groups: the first relates to the socioeconomic policies adopted by most Arab countries in recent years; the second relates to the changes that have occurred in the structure of the population and consequently in people's needs and requirements.

Most Arab governments adopted financial and monetary policies aimed at addressing the problems of inflation and debt. In this context, government spending for public services such as health, education, and social welfare has been relatively reduced. Thus the role of the third sector in meeting part of people's needs has been enhanced. It seems normal that the role of the government was complemented by the third sector on the one hand and by the private sector on the other. State policies have no doubt encouraged the third sector to fill the gap or gaps in public policies, particularly in health care, education, and disadvantaged groups.

On the other hand, the shift in certain Arab countries toward privatization—in Egypt, Tunisia, Morocco, and Algeria—have positively affected the business environment of the private sector in both its nonprofit and its profit-generating organizations. During the initial years, these policies led—by their very nature—to the marginalization of certain sectors of the population, a rise in unemployment rates, the increase in prices, and the deterioration of the condition of the poorer classes. It is anticipated that such economic policies will inevitably enhance and expand the role of the third sector to new areas of activity (particularly in the face of unemployment, transformative training, and poverty).

While these reductions in public spending for public services and social welfare were enthusiastically pursued by Arab governments, the populations of these countries steadily increased (to 229 million in 1991). The population growth rate soared to 2.1 percent. Population growth obviously implies more needs to be satisfied, specifically needs of a young society (approximately 40 percent of the population is under 15), which governments usually fail to satisfy. The age composition of the population explains the tendency of indigenous organizations to focus on children's issues as well as those of the elderly in general. These conditions provide the justification for the growing concern in Arab countries with issues related to family planning, child labor, street children, and so on.

Finally, we should highlight the prominent role that the third sector played in providing relief works in Arab countries exposed to hardships due to natural or environmental disasters or to wars (such as Lebanon, Palestine, and Sudan). Activities of this sector have been characterized by flexibility in dealing with problems and changing situations.

An Overview of the Third Sector

In Arab countries, as in the West, third-sector organizations fall between government organizations and private, profit-seeking concerns on the other. Accordingly, the third sector covers voluntary organizations that do not seek profits and that are active in the fields of social services, welfare, community development, and relief work. Whatever term is used, the important fact remains that third-sector organizations in the Arab countries mean to a great extent what they mean in western countries.

Being designated as private voluntary organizations, associations and institutions share many features. Yet there is a slight difference between them in the Arabic context. Institutions are considered more complex, possibly consisting of a number of organizations. But more important, institutions rely for funding on resources allocated for humanitarian, cultural, or scientific activities. Associations, on the other hand, although they may target similar causes, are financed by donations by the state or subscriptions of their members but have no allocations as such to realize their purposes. Members in an association are natural persons not legal entities, as is the case with members in an institution (which may include a number of organizations). Hence, associations and private institutions for public benefit are the closest structures to the concept of a PVO. It is a comprehensive concept that encompasses the various structures operating within the third sector, whether they be philanthropic organizations, public service organizations, or NGOs.

Generally speaking, activities undertaken in this sector are aimed at:
- child and maternity care;
- family welfare;

- care of the aged, the disabled, and orphans;
- charities and philanthropic activities;
- social and health care;
- cultural, educational, artistic, literary, educational, and environmental activities;
- activities to promote friendship between peoples;
- religious services (classes to teach religion and the recitation of the Koran and to organize pilgrimages to the Holy Places);
- protection of inmates in correctional institutions and prisons;
- vocational training;
- community development;
- training women; and
- consolidating relations between neighbors or workmates.

While these may be the activities common to most PVOs in Arab countries, particular activities distinguish certain countries. These may be dictated by the peculiar conditions prevailing (wars or natural disasters), the intensification of social or economic problems, or possibly historical or social experiences.

In the Sudan, for example, emergency conditions caused by drought, famine, and the war in the south gave rise to scores of organizations providing food and emergency assistance to the population in the disaster-stricken areas. Environmentally active organizations are also on the rise. And in Egypt, PVOs were created to address social and economic problems. Thirty-two associations were established to address drug abuse, which has become dangerously widespread among youth.

Difficult environmental conditions in Yemen have given rise to certain customs and traditions that consolidated cooperatives as the mainstay of third-sector organizations. In the understanding and experience of the West, cooperatives stand on the borderline. Yet the case of Yemen highlights the particularities of such organizations in that they are a popular initiative, a voluntary action, and a collective effort. They play a prominent role in addressing the needs of the community in building schools, hospitals, roads, and houses. Private voluntary organizations have complemented the work of cooperatives, contrary to the situation in other Arab countries. A similar self-initiated and voluntary system exists in some parts of the Sudan based on participation and volunteering, with the aim of finding community-initiated solutions to problems.

The Effect of War on PVO Activities

The war in Lebanon that lasted for almost 18 years created the need for relief activities, which have become the main concern of associations and private voluntary organizations. About 30 percent of the PVOs in Lebanon (some 1,302 organizations) are active in addressing the consequences of the evacuation of the population to escape the destruction and brutality of the war.

The deterioration of the environment induced 15 percent of organizations to adopt the cause of environmental protection.

Conditions of the war also enhanced the role of organizations for the disabled, and those providing health services and medicines. This pattern exists nowhere else in the Arab region.

Historical and Philosophical Background

The creation and development of the third sector are both rooted in the divine religions and inspired by religious principles and moral thought. The Arab region shares one culture, in which religion carries a great deal of weight. Thus private voluntary organizations have, since the nineteenth century, assumed a religious character (both Christian and Moslem) in the Arab region. Despite the religious sources of the third sector, PVOs have exercised functions of a secular nature. They have struggled to assert national identity in the face of colonialism, to implant the concepts of citizenship and national belongingness, and to provide health care, education, and social welfare services.

Islam, the faith of most people in the region, advocates charity and voluntarism, which are among the very pillars of the faith. "Zakat" (tithing) and "sadaqa" (almsgiving, mentioned 30 times in the Koran) are intended to help others with cash and personal involvement in a system of "social interdependence." This philosophy, which is deeply rooted in religion, propagates solidarity and the support of the needy. Even before the emergence of private voluntary organizations in the nineteenth century, mosques since the dawn of Islam have been the mediators between the donors and recipients of charity. They were not only places of worship, but also educational, cultural, and social institutions. In times of decline and deterioration of society, mosques were places of learning where students sat at the feet of eminent scholars and teachers who provided their services on a voluntary basis. Scores of such "schools" are represented by the "zawaya" in Libya and Algeria, "al-mahdara" in Morocco and Mauritania, and the "kuttab" in Egypt. Mosques were virtually institutions for education at the grassroots level.

The "wakfs" or "ahbas" played a historical role in organized charity and voluntarism and in the implementation of the philosophy of social interdependence in the Arab region. Wakf is a system of religious endowment by which real estate is bequeathed for a purpose. Cash funds, agricultural land, or buildings may be consecrated under the wakf system to help the poor and needy. Wakf allocations were used to build schools, hospitals, and places of worship as well as institutions for homeless children, the aged, and the disabled. In the nineteenth century, however, wakf allocations were directed to finance PVOs active in the fields of health, education, and social welfare.

The first private voluntary organization in the Arab region was linked with Sufi orders (Islamic mystical orders) and manifests the association between belief in Islam and its teachings on the one hand, and charity and social interdependence on the other. Sufi orders are voluntary organizations that came into being during the first two centuries of Islam. Members usually gathered at the feet of a "master" who enlightened them into the path of the mystic so as to grow closer to Allah through a life of prayer and charity. Sufi organizations have been and remain the most prominent PVOs with a large-scale membership in the Arab region (as well as in Islamic countries). Members of Sufi orders in Egypt were estimated to number approximately 3 million in 1989. Organizations affiliated to Sufi orders feature as borderline cases in the third sector in Arab countries.

The impact of the religious component on the third sector in Arab countries must be studied to determine the actual weights of religious associations within the total array of PVOs. In 1990, Islamic associations in Egypt constituted some 34 percent of the total number of associations (51 percent of all associations in certain localities), and Christian associations constituted 9 percent. The figures reveal the continued impact of the religious component on private voluntary organizations. In Lebanon, there are 18 formally acknowledged religious sects that have their own PVOs each distinguished from the other but all pursuing humanitarian ends. The same is the case in the Gulf countries and North Africa, confirming the fact that a great number of organizations established in the third sector have religious origins.

The development of private voluntary organizations in the Arab region was championed by the educated classes and religious leaders (particularly in Egypt, Syria, Lebanon, Iraq, and the North African states), as well as by the traditional elite and members of the royal family. Women played a prominent role in the movement as pioneers and leaders. In Saudi Arabia, for example, women participated actively in the establishment of philanthropic associations, and Palestinian women in the 1920s and 1930s bore the brunt of social work when political conditions prohibited men from assembling. In Egypt, women were among the social and political vanguards working through the channels of private voluntary organizations.

The arrival of western religious missionaries in Arab countries from 1815 and the gradual expansion of their role and influence posed a threat to Arab communities. As a reaction, PVOs sprang up in Egypt, the Sudan, Jordan, Lebanon, and Iraq. In Egypt, for example, the increasing flow of foreign communities in the nineteenth century (from 3,000 in 1836 to 91,000 in 1881) establishing organizations to serve the interests of their members spurred the rise of PVOs of a similar nature to counter their expanding influence and the increasing privileges they enjoyed. (Al-Jamia Al Khayria Al Islamia was established in 1887 and Jamiat Al-Masai Al Khayria Al Qiptia was set up in 1881 in Egypt. And in Jordan, Jamiat Al Ihsan was established in 1912 and Al Nahda Al Orthodoxia, in 1912.) Their main thrust was to protect the faith and assert the identity of the respective countries through education and care for the poor.

Religious and ethnic minorities in Arab countries took part in the shaping of private voluntary organizations over the years. Each ethnic or religious community sought to establish its own network of relationships. The most prominent example occurred in Lebanon, where voluntary organizations are still dominated by a sectarian spirit; the 18 officially recognized sects there each have their own organizations. In Jordan, religious sects as well as ethnic groups have set up organizations to serve their members (Jamiat Al Nahda Al Orthodoxia established in 1920 and Jamiat Al Ikhaa Al Sharkasia, in 1932).

A close review of the development of PVOs and the movement of grassroot organizations that preceded it in the nineteenth and early twentieth centuries reveals that the entire sector is blended with political action. The weakness that characterized the Arab region at the time and the deep and far-reaching influence of colonialism played a prominent role in shaping this sector and in setting its priorities for action. Private voluntary organizations and popular community organizations generated a political, cultural, and social elite. It was not by chance that pioneers of nationalism and proponents of Arab revivalist movements were founders of "associations." These replaced organs in safeguarding nationalism and in mobilizing national forces to defend national identity. Hence education was accorded top priority on the agenda of these organizations, both religious and secular. Indigenous community organizations have contributed to fulfilling this role (philanthropic associations, the village Koranic schools or "kuttab," and the "zawaya" or small village mosques where classes were taught by voluntary teachers).

Since the advent of colonialism to the Arab region in the nineteenth century, education assumed vital importance in each and every Arab country. However, education in Tunisia, Algeria, and Morocco took a different turn, basically due to the fact that education was tied to charitable services and was typical of French colonialist policy posing a threat to Arab Islamic culture.

The Arab intelligentsia conducted, through PVOs, a reform movement aimed at breaking the shackles of backwardness that prevailed, particularly during the latter part of the nineteenth century. The three major trends in Arab society that developed were a liberalist trend, an Islamic trend (revivalist and orthodox), and a progressive socialist trend. Private voluntary organizations posed as meeting places where political, social, and cultural activities blended together. Arab identity was an issue soon introduced into the agendas of these organizations. Scores of groups interested in Arab culture and in propagating the concepts of Arab unity and nationalism appeared.

It is interesting to note the interaction and the dialogue that for the first time was established between PVOs and associations on the level of the Arab region. We may cite in this connection Jamiat Tawheed Al Thakafa Al Arabiya (the unification Arab culture) in 1937 and Jamiat Al Wihda Al Arabiya (Association of Arab unity) in 1936. The two organizations were first established in Egypt, then expanded to Syria, Lebanon, Iraq, and Palestine. The organizations and the intellectuals who presided over them have produced a deep impact on the cultural life in certain Gulf countries such as Bahrain and Kuwait. The cultural clubs were the first fruits in a series of organizations that subsequently appeared.

In sum, this brief historical review indicates that the seeds of current PVOs were sown in the nineteenth or the beginning of the twentieth century. Private voluntary action in the Gulf region arose at a later date, and was influenced by the national role these organizations had played in Egypt, Syria, Lebanon, and Iraq. Religion—both Moslem and Christian—played and is still playing a significant role in the development of such organizations in all Arab countries. Its role transcended that of religious advocacy and charity to the provision of social and health services as well. In addition, throughout this history, organizations of the third sector played—explicitly or implicitly—a political role in addressing social and political challenges.

A Contrast in Funding Groups in Lebanon

Two large organizations active in social and health services provide an interesting contrast in funding. Dar Al Aytam Al Islamia (the Islamic Orphanage) and the Young Men's Christian Association each provided services evaluated at some $5 million in 1992.

The difference between the two organizations in terms of the weights of local donations and resources is striking: Local donations and resources constitute 65 percent of the funds available to Dar Al Aytam, while 20 percent is from foreign sources. Yet 87 percent of the funds of the YMCA are derived from foreign sources, compared with just 2 percent from local resources.

These results may be due to a number of factors. The most prominent is that zakat money constitutes almost half the resources of Islamic organizations in general. Christian organizations, on the other hand, totally rely on assistance from abroad. These findings are in line with the very composition of Lebanese society.

Understanding this historical background of private voluntary organizations will certainly help in understanding the phenomenon prevailing in Arab countries today—most prominently, the effectiveness of organizations with a religious inclination and the relationship between them and the state.

Legal Status, Economic Value, and Funding Sources

The national constitutions of Arab states provide for the right to establish private voluntary organizations—associations or private institutions—for public benefit. Constitutions ensure that aspects related to incorporation, relationships with the state, and the extent of control and supervision will be governed by pertinent legislation. Since the beginning of the twentieth century, certain constitutions have provided the right to establish such organizations (the Egyptian Constitution in 1923 and the Lebanese Constitution in 1926). At the end of the nineteenth century, laws were enacted in certain Arab countries (Tunisia in 1888) to regulate and control the establishment of PVOs. The early enactment of relevant legislation by some states confirms the legal status that PVOs enjoy.

All legislation enacted in Arab countries is aimed at nonprofit-oriented organizations. It may be noted that the laws do not require that the objective of the activity be the general interest or public benefit, but associations could be established to serve the interests of the members. All laws, however, prohibit objectives that violate the law, disrupt public order, undermine moral standards, or harm the political regime. In some countries (Egypt and the United Arab Emirates), laws have been flexible in providing lists of the possible objectives to be adopted by the association, while elsewhere laws have tended to impose constraints on the objectives to be pursued and pose the threat to abolish the association in case of contravention.

In general, the legislation does not differentiate clearly between private associations and institutions. Hence, there is no legal status for NGOs, charities, private foundations, or corporate philanthropies. Arab legislation addresses only institutions for public service that are established to allocate funds for realizing certain goals. Public service institutions may include judicial persons, whereas associations include natural persons and rely on subscriptions of members, donations, grants, government support in cash and in kind, and so on.

The law sets the conditions for the incorporation and registration of associations, control of their activities, and the relationship between the associations and the state. Control may be tight or more relaxed. Only recently in some Arab countries have certain associations acquired legal status by registering themselves as nonprofits. The aim of this move on the part of associations is to liberate themselves from the constraints placed on third-sector activities as well to free themselves from state bureaucratic procedures. This new development is more pronounced in Egypt, where there is a strong urge for the modification of the law on the grounds of its incompatibility with social, economic, and political development and its negative effect in hampering the liberation of third-sector potential.

Studies on the economic value of the third sector are very scarce in the Arab region. Unlike western countries, most Arab countries do not include the third sector in their national accounts or national income statements. For most countries, there are only some indicators about the income, expenditure, and funding sources of this sector.

The economic value of private voluntary organizations in Jordan is estimated at approximately $40 million. A field study on the economics of social work done in 1986 found the income of organizations was about $28 million and their expenditures reached almost the same level. Self-generated income represents almost 94 percent of the total, being the revenue from the educational and health services provided by the organizations as well as from interests on bank deposits and real estate. Subscriptions constituted only 10 percent of the self-financed portion. The rest consists of private donations from citizens (68.3 percent), assistance from the General Federation (17.6 percent), and subsidies from the Ministry of Social Development (6.4 percent). The government's support to PVOs is not limited to financial assistance; it includes the supply of employees paid by the government to work in the third sector on secondment.

In Lebanon, the third sector was evaluated at $100 million in the 1993 budget. The government's contribution represents almost 11 percent of the resources; the rest is derived from donations from local and foreign sources, as well as self-generated revenue from the sale of commodities and services. No data are available about the distribution of the funding sources, since the law does not require private voluntary organizations to disclose information about their budgets or funding sources.

Tithe payments of "zakat" are still considered an important source for funding associations and PVOs in Arab countries. In Lebanon, for example, a good 50 percent of the resources of social welfare institutions (Islamic organizations) are derived from zakat funds. Further, the Zakat revenue collected by 3,000 mosques in Egypt that are controlled by special zakat committees totalled the equivalent of $5 million in 1989. In these mosques, the zakat committees collect the revenue and deliver it to the Naser Social Bank, which channels the funds to the beneficiaries. Special legislation was enacted to regulate the operations of the bank. This type of organization, which is based on the concept of social interdependence in Islam, may also be classified as a borderline third-sector case, since it is both governmental and active in philanthropic fields and deals with private voluntary organizations.

In the Gulf States, zakat also constitutes one of the major sources of financing. Zakat committees are the channels that collect or receive funds and deliver them to the organizations, which in turn distribute the funds to needy families. These committees have acquired experience in the process of collecting donations and zakat. The committees are usually headquartered in mosques and Islamic centers. This practice prevails in Saudi Arabia, Bahrain, and the United Arab Emirates. In Kuwait, however, Bayt Al Zakat—an autonomous government body—distributes zakat funds to needy families, and to orphanages as well as to mosques both domestically and outside the country. Bayt Al Zakat is another government borderline third-sector institution.

In addition to zakat in the Gulf states, government support may constitute the major financing source, as it does in Qatar. Data about this support are not available so that we could assign it a weight as against other sources of funds. However, we know that government support varies from one country to another, as well as from one field of activity to another (organizations active in providing services to the disabled receive far greater assistance than those devoted to cultural fields).

Financing institutions such as Bayt Al Tamweel Al Kuwaiti, Bayt Al Zakat, banks, and similar institutions provide regular cash support to PVOs as well as to specific projects and programs. Private voluntary organizations are also financed from subscriptions and income-generating activities such as bazaars and the sale of their services.

Islamic associations in the Gulf countries are capable of securing resources for their activities. Their quest is for regular financing from guaranteed sources, but without compromising their independence from the state. Several Islamic associations own residential buildings and shopping malls and have bank deposits, while certain of them have economic investments abroad.

In Egypt, Law 32/1964 has established these possible sources for funding associations and private voluntary organizations: subscriptions of members; revenue from sale of commodities and services; donations; allocations for charitable purposes (wakf); income generated from bazaars, tombolas, and exhibitions; and donations from foreign organizations subject to the approval of official authorities, represented by the Ministry of Social Affairs. Subject to their compliance with certain requirements, mainly to cater to the needs of the community as a first priority, private voluntary organizations may receive regular or occasional government support. Official reports for 1990/91 indicate that some 30.4 percent of 4,034 associations have received $6.5 million in aid. However, the value of official aid has taken a descending curve over the past five years due to the economic constraints.

Annual subscriptions are a very meager and highly uncertain source of funds. Donations carry an important weight in the financing of charitable societies that cater to the poor. Private voluntary organizations selling services or commodities do well. A survey conducted on a sample of 1,172 associations revealed that the revenue generated from the sale of services alone was the equivalent of $4 million. Although this may be astonishingly large, we should bear in mind the vital health services provided by these organizations as well as by the numerous health centers affiliated to associations and mosques in the fields of maternity, child care, and family planning.

While the contribution of local resources has declined, foreign assistance (from governments, international organizations, and NGOs) has acquired

---

PVO Estimates

The number of private voluntary organizations (and the date for which data are available) is as follows:

- Bahrain—66 (1992)
- Egypt—13,239 (1991)
- Jordan—587 (1992)
- Kuwait—29 (1988)
- Lebanon—1,302 (1993)
- Mauritania—7 (1988)
- Morocco—159 (1993)
- Palestine—444 (1992)

- Qatar—3 (1988)
- Saudi Arabia—104 (1991)
- Sudan—262 (1991)
- Sultanate of Oman—16 (1989)
- Syria—628 (1992)
- Tunisia—5,186 (1993)
- United Arab Emirates—89 (1992)
- Yemen—223 (1992)

---

greater weight as a funding source (as discussed in the section on international connections).

Details of budgets of Egyptian PVOs receiving subsidies from the government must, by law, be disclosed. The income and expenditure of 4,077 organizations that received subsidies in 1991 was estimated at $33 million and $28 million respectively. The largest income was realized by social welfare organizations that offer health services to the community. In Egypt, as in the Gulf countries, religious organizations are the most autonomous because they can raise funds to cover their needs, and to recruit volunteers.

Number and Size of Third-Sector Organizations

Estimates of the size of third-sector organizations rely on official data published on legally registered associations and private institutions, although obtaining accurate information on even these categories is difficult. In some cases, we must rely on certain partial indicators to help clear ambiguities (such as the number of volunteers, paid labor, the economic value of the organizations, and so on).

Official estimates in some Arab countries may consider certain types of third-sector entities as associations and private institutions, while in other countries such groups are classified differently because of their independent legal status. A prominent example of this is professional groups, which constitute a large share of officially registered associations (in accordance with the Associations Law) in Bahrain, the United Arab Emirates, and Kuwait. Elsewhere, such as in Egypt and Jordan, they are considered professional syndicates subject to an independent legal system. Hence estimates of the size of PVOs depend on the mode of registration in accordance with the laws regulating associations and private voluntary organizations in each country.

The variations in the size of the sector from one country to another are due to the length of time the official sector has existed and the size of the population. Although Egypt may have the largest number of organizations, they are scarce in proportion to its population (estimated at 56 million in 1992) and the magnitude of its needs.

On the other hand, PVOs in the Gulf States are generally speaking few. This may be attributed to the relative novelty of the third sector in these countries and to the nature of their population structure. But there are indications of an increase in the number and diversity of groups in this region. In Palestine (the West Bank and Gaza), the number increased from 272 in 1987 to 444 organizations in 1992—a doubling within five years to respond to the mounting needs of the Palestinian population. The same may be said of Jordan, where the number went from 221 associations in 1980 to 364 in 1985 and then to 587 in 1992—a 300-percent increase in a decade.

In Tunisia, the number of private voluntary organizations suddenly soared in the past three years, from 1,886 in 1988 to 5,186 in 1993. The increase may be attributed to the trend of the new regime to encourage organizations within the general democratization process taking place. Further, the legislation concerning associations was amended on 2 August 1988 to reflect the new policy. Last, in Egypt, the number of associations and private organizations increased from 11,471 in 1985 to 13,239 in 1991, which was below the growth rates in other Arab countries.

It is difficult to estimate the size of human resources involved in PVOs in the Arab countries because of the scarcity of data, its untimeliness, and its lack of reliability. We will therefore try to estimate these resources on the basis of available data, while at the same time highlighting their shortcomings.

In Egypt, there were about 3 million members of associations in 1992, according to the records kept by the associations. These figures seem somewhat inflated, however, because a field survey revealed that about 40 percent of active members had not paid their subscriptions, which reduces the actual number of members to approximately 2 million. The survey found that about 65 percent of the associations employed paid staff (on a full- or part-time basis), and that the average number of paid workers was 13. (The Ministry of

---

PVOs in Yemen and the Sudan

In Yemen, there are about 18,000 association members, compared with 130,145 registered in cooperatives. The figures reveal the greater appeal of cooperatives in view of their popular character, which is more in harmony with the tribal traditions. In Sudan, too, cooperatives have an extensive membership (2 million in 1990), whereas PVOs have a much smaller membership.

A survey of associations in the Sudan found that 42 percent of associations have 300 registered members each, and the remaining 58 percent have between 100-150 members each. The total is estimated at around 50,000, distributed between 262 associations. The survey showed that 77 percent of members are male, and that most female members have an intermediate level of education.

Social Affairs, the administrative authority, also subsidizes the organizations by supplying them with staff who are paid by the Ministry on the basis of secondment.)

In Lebanon, there were about 6,458 workers in PVOs in 1979, an average rate of 5 workers per group. The greater part of the work is shouldered by the paid staff. It is difficult to assess the number of volunteers, because these are recruited on the spot whenever there is need. An official in one organization noted that voluntary work in Lebanon is offered at two levels: policymakers, who constitute the board members in associations and organizations, and implementers, who deliver the relief services according to the orientation of the service. Relief works in the south of Lebanon, including medical services and campaigns to provide medical supplies, were undertaken by young volunteers.

Reliable information exists for Jordan. Private voluntary organizations employed 4,214 paid staff (69 percent females and 29 percent males) in 1986. One quarter of these work part-time. Volunteers are estimated at 62,000, almost equally divided between the two sexes. They are involved in fund-raising campaigns to help in the execution of programs of the organization. For example, 22,000 students volunteered to help in the campaign launched by the General Federation for Philanthropic Associations to assist Al Amal Cancer Institute in 1992.

In the Arab Gulf states, the number of members is as follows: Kingdom of Saudi Arabia, 25,157; Kuwait, 18,813; Oman, 1,500; Qatar, 500; and Bahrain, 5,420.

In certain Arab countries, it is difficult to mobilize volunteers for activities that are not religiously oriented. This may be explained by the low level of awareness of the value of voluntary action and popular initiatives in general, the inability of the organizations to mobilize volunteers, and the limited role of mass media in highlighting the social and ethical value of voluntary action. Yet in most Arab countries, even in those that adopt political pluralism, the overall reaction to voluntarism is negative, the general feeling being that the government alone is the active agent and is solely responsible for providing all services to the people.

This attitude is particularly true of the Gulf countries, where per capita income is high and the state pledges to provide all possible services. Thus the main focus in such countries is on charitable efforts in their traditional sense without any relevance to development. Voluntary activities in the Gulf countries have a peculiar profile, as they are linked with Islamic associations. In other Arab countries, where per capita income is low and the state is committed to reduce public spending—as in Egypt, Tunisia, Morocco, and Jordan—people are occupied with making ends meet every month and have no time for volunteer work. In addition, other factors related to the political education in general are not conducive to the contribution of time or effort, and people are generally satisfied with doing nothing rather than observing their religious obligation of "zakat" and charity.

In light of this, it is important to raise awareness of voluntary work through the media and through prominent figures in this field. The value of voluntarism, its forms and concepts, and its levels, channels, and institutions should be made known to the public.

Objectives and Target Populations

The poor and disadvantaged are the object of charitable activity, which confirms the thesis that the third sector is rooted in religious belief. The term "charitable society" is usually used for all PVOs, denoting their religious origin in Arab culture. On the other hand, the religious connotation attached to many groups has meant altruistic activities are held in high esteem even if they are oriented to educational, social, or economic objectives.

The actual percentages of PVOs in selected countries that are classified as charitable organizations aimed at helping the poor (in cash or in kind) are as

---

Examples of Charitable Organizations

The National Project for the Development of Traditional Handicrafts in Jordan is sponsored by the Queen Noor Al Hussein Institution. It is virtually a counterpart of the Egyptian Productive Families project. It was established in 1985 to provide income-generating opportunities to the poorer sectors of the population, and at the same time to revive the traditional handicrafts of Jordan.

The Institution markets the products at home and worldwide. The number of beneficiaries of the project was estimated at 2,000 in 1992, (included 740 women) distributed throughout Jordan.

In Yemen, the Social Household Development Association was established in 1990, targeting the poor sectors of the population and the residents of slum areas. It established a vocational training center with the support of international organizations such as Oxfam.

The center implements vocational training programs to form cadres in areas for which there is a demand on the labor market. These are also helped to find suitable work opportunities.

---

follows: Lebanon, 45 percent; Jordan, 37 percent; Syria, 20 percent; Palestine, 64 percent; Egypt, 23 percent; Tunisia, 10 percent; Kuwait, 78 percent; United Arab Emirates, 31 percent; Saudi Arabia, 78 percent, and Yemen, 43 percent.

In Lebanon, the relatively high percentage is attributed to the conditions precipitated by the civil war that destroyed and devastated many homes, leaving families unprovided for. Similarly, in Palestine the high percentage of 64 percent is understandable in view of the emergency conditions and their social and economic impact on the population (loss of household head, loss of job, the nonexistence of even a minimum level of social services and social security).

In Egypt, charitable organizations account for one quarter of total private voluntary organizations. The share would be higher if it included religious societies, which, in official statistics, are classified as cultural associations and religious organizations, not as social welfare organizations. Religious associations in Egypt—both Moslem and Christian—focus on the administration of charity.

In some Arab countries, the poorer classes who have been traditionally targeted by charitable activities are today reached by an innovative approach. This seeks to provide new training and work opportunities for members of poorer households with the view to generate income, on the one hand, and to integrate them into the development process on the other. In Egypt, for example, where the percentage of the population below the poverty line has increased to 23 percent in urban and 25 percent in rural areas, and where unemployment rates soared to 14 percent in 1986, the government is cooperating with a large number of PVOs in implementing the Productive Families project.

Productive Families is a social project with an economic dimension. It aims at capitalizing on the household resources by converting the home into a unit of production. Income is thus generated, human resources are used, and the resources of the environment are tapped. The project is implemented through thousands of associations spread throughout the country, within the umbrella organization known as the General Association for Vocational Training and Productive Families. The Association will assist persons who satisfy the requirements by giving them loans for raw materials, equipment, and working capital. The Association undertakes the marketing of the production both at home and abroad.

The Productive Families project has achieved astonishing results. It has received substantial amounts in aid from local and external donors. More than 250,000 households benefitted from the project in 1990, compared with 7,001 households in 1985, and officials expect the number to reach 1 million in 1993.

The disabled are a second basic group targeted by PVOs. The share of services going to the rehabilitation of the disabled has been mounting since the early nineties. Although these are common in most countries of the Arab region, the weight accorded to such services varies from one country to another: Palestine (West Bank and Gaza), 20 percent of total organizations; Jordan, 6.5 percent; Lebanon, 6 percent; Egypt, 1 percent; Yemen, 3 percent; and Morocco, 17 percent.

The high share in Palestine can be explained by the political unrest that has lasted for many years, leaving large numbers of disabled. In the absence of state efforts, PVOs were established and received regional and international assistance; care of the disabled requires substantial funds to cover material costs as well as personnel training. In Egypt, in contrast, the share of the total going to this sector is small, estimated at 150 private voluntary organizations.

In Lebanon, where years of civil war have left large numbers of disabled, one of the organizations established is Muassassat Amel. This was set up in 1980 by a group of medical doctors, university professors, journalists, and social workers under the slogan "For country and fellow citizen." Al Amel has opened 27 centers to provide health, social, vocational, and educational services, but the most effective has been in the field of the disabled. The organization was assisted by western governments and international NGOs such as the Arab American Committee for the Prevention of Racial Discrimination in the United States, which undertook the treatment of 200 disabled persons abroad. From 1983 to 1990, Muassassat Amel provided medical treatment, including artificial limbs, to approximately 2,000 people, for a total cost of $2 million.

In the Sudan, civil strife is also responsible for the rapid increase in the number of disabled (estimated at 2.3 million in 1983). The problem was addressed by traditional and nontraditional methods administered by charitable associations as well as by popular unofficial groups, such as neighborhood organizations. In recent years, however, there was a surge in PVOs providing rehabilitation services to the disabled through unions established by the disabled themselves. In villages and cities, these are sponsored by an umbrella organization that manages a communication network to probe the needs and implement rehabilitation programs accordingly. This seems to be a unique example in the Arab countries of a national communication network that links the disabled to private voluntary organizations.

Some PVOs provide health and educational services and cater to basic needs of the local communities, thereby filling gaps created by state policies. A major sector of private voluntary organizations, largely Moslem and Christian, started administering basic health services. In Egypt, about 3,000 mosques annexed health centers to their premises. These are staffed by part-time doctors who work on a voluntary basis or for nominal fees. Inadequate data on this activity are available because the centers are involved in more than one field. However, beneficiaries were estimated at 4.5 million in 1979 and at more than 10 million within a decade.

In Jordan, the number of PVO health and feeding centers was estimated at 101 in 1991, reportedly serving 176,000 beneficiaries. In Palestine, health services along with educational services, food supply, housing, and health education constitute the major field of activity of private voluntary organizations. There is not a single city or village where refugee camps exist without a multipurpose PVO providing health services.

Including Women in Development

Private voluntary organizations are active in the field of women in two directions: first, in advocating protection of their rights (Tunisia, Morocco, Egypt, Jordan, and Lebanon), and second and more often, in advocating the integration of women in the process of development. Organizations concerned with women's issues vary in number: 19 in Morocco (12 percent of total organizations), 2 in Tunisia (0.09 percent), and 22 in Egypt.

In the Gulf States, there is a relatively high percentage of organizations concerned with women with the view to enhance their role in development. Out of 16 organizations in the Sultanate of Oman, 13 are concerned with women; there are 7 in Bahrain (10.6 percent). In Saudi Arabia, where women play an active role in social work, women's associations account for 21.8 percent of the total.

In Jordan, the Business and Professional Women's Club was established in 1976 to protect the rights of women and to integrate them into the development process. Women's organizations seek to enhance women's awareness of their legal rights and duties, to propagate legal understanding, and to follow up certain cases in the courts. To realize these objectives, a number of methods are applied—mainly holding seminars and issuing a comprehensive directory of laws relating to women and conducting field activities.

A program to distribute medicine and aid to the poor and to those suffering from chronic diseases was established by the YMCA in Lebanon, and its beneficiaries are estimated at 22,000 Lebanese citizens. The conditions of the war had caused shortages in imported medicines, and donations from states and major pharmaceutical producers failed to address the situation. The program was able—in cooperation with all other medical centers in Lebanon—to draw up a list of the medicines needed. It financed shipments of medicines worth $6 million in 1990 and distributed the medicines to the centers according to need.

Educational services have been launched in two directions: to eliminate illiteracy among adults and to establish day care centers and kindergartens. In Jordan and Lebanon, loans and fellowships are granted to university students. Some 18,000 students are said to have benefitted from this program in Jordan in 1991, and 12,000 in Lebanon during the war. In the latter case, one institution alone—Al Hariri Corporation—financed the costs of university education for students specializing in different fields from 1983 to 1992.

In the Gulf States, major groups fall into two categories: trade unions, and professional associations and associations concerned with foreign labor working in the Gulf. In the United Arab Emirates, professional associations are estimated at 42 percent; in Bahrain, 39 percent; and in Kuwait, 55 percent. Private groups that safeguard the interests of foreign communities are usually called cultural or social clubs and account for 18 percent in the United Arab Emirates and 11 percent in Bahrain. The weights reflect the impact of the population composition on the establishment of voluntary organizations.

Two new fields of interest have surged recently in the Arab region: protection of the environment and human rights. The mounting significance of the two types of organizations is reflected in the steady increase in their numbers and their impact as they have come to exercise pressure on decision makers. However, the weight of advocacy organizations is still limited as compared with that of other organizations. Advocacy organizations are totally nonexistent in certain Arab countries.

One characteristic common to all PVOs is their lack of equitable geographic distribution. They all tend to be more concentrated in the capital and other urban centers, and are almost nonexistent in the hamlets and villages, where the need for their service is greatest. This reflects the positive correlation between the existence of these organizations and cultural and social levels. As noted earlier, PVOs have been established by the higher middle-class professionals, who are mainly urban. The inequitable distribution is a major shortcoming that minimizes the effectiveness of these organizations, narrows their scope of influence, and excludes large sectors of the rural population who may be in dire need for their services. This phenomenon is noticeable in certain Gulf States (Saudi Arabia and the United Arab Emirates), in Egypt (34 percent of organizations are located in Cairo and Alexandria), in Jordan (42 percent of organizations are in Amman), and in the greater part of Arab countries.

Disparities in Social, Economic, and Political Variables

Despite the common characteristics among PVOs in the Arab region, differences are found in terms of social, economic, and political variables that affect the patterns and fields of activities of the organizations.

Private voluntary organizations within Arab countries in the process of democratization, such as Egypt, Lebanon, Jordan, Tunisia, Algeria (prior to the restrictions on the Islamists), Morocco, and Yemen, tend to grow faster than groups in other Arab countries. With a larger margin of freedom, PVOs can be active in a wider range of fields, such as human rights, women's rights, and "enlightenment," which propagates secular concepts and calls for the respect of human freedoms in an endeavor to counter the extremist Islamist movement (examples in Egypt are Jamiat Al Mara Al Jadida and Jamiat Al Nida Al Jadid).

Under conservative political systems in the Gulf countries, PVOs are fewer in number and in diversity. Organizations propagating human rights and advocacy organizations are minimal. Most are charities (in Saudi Arabia, Kuwait, Bahrain, and the United Arab Emirates) expressing deep religious feeling.

In countries with a third political system—that is, popular authority—the state does not permit PVOs that represent private initiatives. In those countries, popular committees are established (in Libya) considered as extensions of the state, or unions that are controlled by the state (in Iraq).

As noted already, religious trends dominate the attitudes and activities of a large number of private voluntary organizations in Arab countries. There are many indications of this. First, the group's name (for example, the Islamic Charitable Association, and the Orthodox Association) and the teaching of religious classes with the view of sowing the seeds of the faith. Apart from this activities, such organizations may engage in charity works and health and child care services. Organizations with a religious inclination are very prominent in Egypt as well as in the Gulf States and Lebanon. In Egypt, where data are available, organizations of an Islamic inclination accounted for 35 percent and Christian organizations accounted for 9 percent of all groups in 1991.

The surge in the political Islamist movement over the past five years is a deviation from the traditional movement pioneered by the Moslem Brothers. The new radical movement is characterized by violence. The concepts as well as the means for the realization of goals differ from those held by previous Islamic movements. The new movement rejects cooperation with any government and seeks to change the political system by the use of force. The "new Islamist movements" come out of mainstream Islamic movements as represented by the Moslem Brothers (in Sudan and Tunisia) or are an offshoot of a national socialist party (in Egypt) or a coalition between Islamist movements (Algeria). The increasing weight of the Islamist movements in the Arab region raises certain questions about their relationship with private voluntary organizations.

In all Arab countries, whether they are witnessing a surge in Islamist movements or not, Islamic organizations operate side by side with nonreligious charities. Islamic organizations can mobilize people and raise funds to finance their goals and reach their target populations. PVOs of a religious orientation are common in all Arab countries, particularly in Egypt and the Sudan.

Certain organizations established in Arab countries reflect specific Islamic reform movements. They are found in some Gulf countries, Egypt, Tunisia, Jordan, and Algeria. For example, the Tunisian Islamist Movement, which emerged in the seventies, stemmed from the Society for Teaching the Koran, an organization found in numerous Arab countries that became widespread in Tunisia in the eighties within the context of the Islamic Tendency Movement. Its name was changed in 1988 to Al Nahda (the Islamic Revival). In Algeria, the elections of 1990 and subsequent events (the success of the Islamic Salvation Movement in the municipal elections) brought the government into a confrontation with the Movement.

Being denied the right to form political parties, the Islamist Movement attempts to use PVOs as a tool to realize its political ends. In Egypt, for example, many private voluntary organizations are financed by the Moslem Brothers, and most health services provided by mosques are delivered by the clinics annexed to mosques and staffed by members of the Moslem Brothers. The health and social services provided by PVOs to the poor extend the influence of the Islamist movement and pave the way for the realization of their political designs to reach the seats of government. In the Sudan, PVOs mobilized the support of the middle classes, particularly professionals, to become an organized entity addressing the public. Since the Islamist Movement came to power in the Sudan in 1989, it has succeeded in rallying the public around it on the question of "identity." The Islamist identity consequently became the identity of the private voluntary organizations.

To sum up, there is significant interaction between PVOs and the Islamist movement in most Arab countries. Such organizations are used as channels to reach a wider sector of the population. The significance of their services increases in countries where free government services are inadequate or nonexistent (as in Egypt). In such cases, the organizations play a sociopolitical role in rallying support for the Islamist movement and paving the way for a shift of influence from social to political (for example, in the case of Tunisia).

In terms of socioeconomic variables, Arab countries may be classified in four groups: rich oil-producing countries (Gulf States); moderate oil-producing countries (Iraq and Algeria); countries with a varied economy (Egypt, Syria, Jordan, Lebanon, Palestine, Morocco, and Tunisia), where the share of the population below the poverty line varies from 14 percent (in Jordan) to 48 percent (in Morocco); and poor countries with scarce resources (Somalia, the

Sudan, Djibouti, Yemen and Mauritania), where a large share of the population is below the poverty line.

In the first group of countries, the number of organizations and their average growth is limited. The groups rarely need to provide health or social services because government services are sufficient. But PVOs here are active in the areas of the handicapped, female education, child care, cultural clubs, professional clubs, and ethnic associations (due to the large number of migrant workers from Southeast Asia).

In the third group of countries, PVOs have to address the problem of poverty through traditional (charity) and nontraditional means (vocational training and the generation of work opportunities). Population growth, one of the problems plaguing this group, is handled by organizations providing family planning and related services in Egypt, Jordan, Tunisia, and Morocco. The problems that follow the economic reform policies of these governments are addressed by PVOs that help marginalized groups and poor families to become productive by training them in certain skills. Work opportunities are generated by encouraging small industries. Child labor, street children, and squatter areas are all issues unknown in the first group of countries. PVOs provide health services free or at nominal cost to the lower and middle classes, where they are greatly needed in view of the tightening of government spending, the rise in the price of these services, and the absence of a health insurance umbrella.

In the fourth group, where a large sector of the population is below the poverty line, the number of PVOs is small given the size of the population and magnitude of the needs. Financing these organizations is difficult; they depend mostly on external funds. Foreign NGOs are numerous and are the most effective agencies operating in this group of countries (particularly in Somalia, Djibouti, and Mauritania).

Interactions of the Third Sector

Since their inception, private voluntary organizations have been confronted with challenges both at the internal and external levels. Their reaction has been positive, consolidating cooperation and integration. Most Arab countries have at some point fallen victim to a form of colonialism, either religious missions or foreign minorities who exercised their influence on the population and jeopardized its national identity. On the other hand, the social and political reform movements in the region since the end of the nineteenth century have all relied on PVOs as channels capable of conveying their message to a wider public and mobilizing the efforts of society.

Within this framework, the relationships among PVOs were dominated by a strong tendency to cooperate and to adopt a common stance in the face of political and social dangers. In part, this was possible because the number of organizations was limited. A remarkable phenomenon of this period was the solidarity and cooperation between religious and secular organizations on the one hand, and between Moslem and Christian organizations on the other. Competition and conflict had no place in the face of a common danger. The pattern of interaction between third-sector organizations that had prevailed during the early years lasted almost until the 1940s, after which a new stage began.

The most prominent changes of the new stage were the disappearance of the challenges that had fostered solidarity in the face of threats to national identity and expansion in the size and scope of PVOs. The emergence of the state as an effective party capable of influencing the nature of the relations between third-sector organizations and between them and the society at large is another change. The dwindling resources available to groups, particularly from foreign sources, further fuelled competition and sharpened tensions. There was a need for cooperation and coordination between organizations operating in the same field or in the same geographical area. These changes affected the pattern of interaction and had a negative impact on the performance of organizations of this sector.

Legislation was one of the measures to promote coordination and cooperation. It created two patterns: the first allowed groups performing the same activities or located in the same geographical area to become unions; the second was optional, whereby a number of organizations could form a union or an umbrella organization to ensure cooperation and integration between organizations. The former is what prevails in Egypt, and the latter is found in Jordan and Lebanon. Apart from the two patterns, some countries (the Gulf States, Tunisia, and Morocco) have not sought to regulate the formation of unions or umbrella organizations by law, but have left this matter for the third sector to decide.

The trend today in most Arab countries is that of diminished levels of cooperation and coordination between PVOs, even among those bound together in a union or an umbrella organization. The current stage therefore is characterized by a revision of interactions both in terms of legislation and fact.

In Lebanon, the Corporation of Civil Lebanese and Foreign Organizations was established in 1985. In 1989, it was converted into the Corporation of

Voluntary Organizations in Lebanon, consisting of 16 voluntary and 8 foreign organizations. In the same year, the Forum for Nongovernmental Humanitarian Organizations was established, consisting of 13 Lebanese organizations.

In Egypt and Jordan (both of which have enacted laws to establish unions on the basis of type and geographical locations), there is a call for the revision of restrictive laws that do not give unions the right to participate in making decisions concerning their groups or to cement cooperation and coordination between organizations.

In Tunisia, the Meeting of Tunisian and Foreign Organizations was held in 1991 to consolidate relations. Among its recommendations was the formation of a preparatory group to establish a body to coordinate between the activities and objectives of various organizations, and to compile a directory of all who are involved in the field.

In Sudan, the Sudanese Council for Voluntary Organizations (SCOVA) was established recently. Its aim is to unify the efforts of various organizations, promote cooperation, and encourage the exchange of experience in order to address the series of disasters that the Sudan has experienced (drought, desertification, floods, and torrential rainfall) and to mitigate the effects of the war in the south. The Council is in the process of establishing regional unions between private voluntary organizations on both the national and the community level.

To sum up, coordination between private voluntary organizations is inadequate in most Arab countries. This is true both for countries where there are regional federations (geographical or by type of activity) representing all or some organizations, and in countries where no federations exist. Coordination should therefore be accorded high priority.

The relationship between organizations and governments is determined by a number of factors. First, the government enacts the laws that regulate the sector, including the establishment of private voluntary organizations, government control and monitoring, and, in some cases, the dissolution of the organizations. In addition, the government sets the rules on such measures.

The government is also one of the financing sources of private voluntary organizations, and therefore often sets funding priorities according to the urgency of the social needs and the significance of projects to be implemented by these organizations. It often gives the organizations technical support through the secondment of experts and personnel.

The government may enter into direct relations with PVOs by assigning them the implementation of certain social welfare projects or programs. In such cases, the government confers on the organizations the title of "public" or "public utility," which is a widespread practice in Arab countries, including Egypt, Jordan, Syria, and Lebanon. In political science, such cases are known as "functional integration" of PVOs into the government system on the grounds that the organizations are undertaking "partially" the functions of the government.

The government designates the authority or authorities that monitor the work of organizations. These bodies are endowed with the powers and functions to realize their mandate. In most cases, monitoring is carried by an administration in the Ministry of Social Affairs, as well as by other government bodies concerned with local government, health education, and so on.

The nature of the relation between governments and PVOs varies from cooperation at one extreme and tension on the other. Cooperation characterizes direct relations. It is also seen in the technical and financial support the government provides, and in the monitoring of state projects implemented by the organizations. Other modes of cooperation came into being over the past few years. Private voluntary organizations became a means for the government to implement economic reform and privatization policies.

The most prominent examples are drawn from Egypt and Tunisia, where certain organizations are implementing huge projects—financed by foreign funds—in the field of small industries. These projects aim at bringing down unemployment rates that have increased as a result of structural adjustment programs. Another of these projects is in the field of transformative training open to workers who have been made redundant in the process of privatization.

Modes of cooperation between the government and third sector organizations may be said to be partly traditional and partly up to date, dictated by social and economic changes. Strained relations between the two parties may be explicit or implicit, for numerous reasons. First, the laws that let government monitor PVO activities have, in actual practice, become a bureaucratic exercise, greatly undermining the autonomy of the organizations.

Second, in certain countries, governmental supervision and monitoring is carried at a number of levels, creating numerous problems that hamper the organizations in implementing projects.

The government's power to dissolve or merge private voluntary organizations—as is the case in Egypt, Syria, the United Arab Emirates, and Algeria—may lead to mutual distrust and a strained relationship. This authority can be used by governments to threaten the organizations.

Last, the distribution of foreign funds between PVOs has become another source of tension. On the one hand, foreign assistance flows must, in most

---

Private-Sector Funding

In Lebanon, a great portion of PVO funding comes from individuals and private-sector firms. Commercial and economic firms reap benefits in the form of publicity from their donations (in cash or in kind) to nonprofit organizations. A new form of contribution is for major commercial firms to finance housing projects for displaced persons or to pay for students to go to university.

In Jordan, apart from the private sector, chambers of commerce and industries have financed the costs of seminars and conferences held by private voluntary organizations. The Businesswomen's Club provides technical advice through private-sector leaderships, with the aim of promoting small industries.

---

cases, obtain the approval of the government. On the other hand, agreements concluded with foreign governments regarding assistance to PVOs provide that the government administers the distribution of the assistance (an example is an Egyptian-American agreement for the support of PVOs signed in 1991).

Cooperation is stronger between governments and organizations where the latter fill the gaps in government services, or where organizations are entrusted to implement state plans or programs. But relations become strained if governments start feeling that their activities are somehow threatened or challenged by those of the organizations. The leaders of organizations can also pose a threat to the regime, so PVOs tend to appoint as leaders people who are on good terms with the government.

Regarding relations with the private sector, the fact that secular and religious motives induce the private sector to donate to PVOs makes it difficult to get accurate data on the nature of the funds and the value of donations. Donations and the allocation of zakat funds are usually undeclared, and it is not considered proper in Islamic culture to exploit such funds for commercial purposes, as is common in western societies, where market mechanisms could be influential.

Still, there are a few remarkable examples that highlight the nature of the interaction between the private sector and PVOs. In Yemen, for instance, the private sector finances certain PVO projects. Chambers of commerce representing the business sector may finance some project phases. Private voluntary organizations have of late tended to appoint prominent businessmen to their boards of directors; at the same time, businessmen have established PVOs.

In the Gulf States, contributions from the private sector and from businessmen constitute the major funding source for associations (or private voluntary organizations). Contributions may be given on a regular, temporary, or occasional basis. Islamic financial institutions in the Gulf provide funding for specific projects and programs.

In Egypt, the private sector finances specialized health centers (for cancer, kidney, and liver diseases). The centers are sponsored by PVOs or by the government. The private sector has extended substantial assistance to the Red Crescent Society, which has streamlined the efforts of PVOs in relieving earthquake victims in October 1992.

International Connections

Until recently, cooperation between the U.N. Development Programme (UNDP) and Arab countries was channelled through the government and its organs. Today, UNDP cooperates directly with private voluntary organizations. The organizations present project proposals to the United Nations, specifying the objective of the projects and an estimate of the support needed (financial, technical, or both). Scores of such projects are now being implemented in the fields of maternity, child care, the environment, population, community development, and so on. The relationship between UNDP and private voluntary organizations has become a direct one, an important step in the process of consolidating the ties between the common citizens and PVOs on the one hand and the United Nations on the other.

Other U.N. organizations and agencies also maintain relations with PVOs in the Arab region. UNICEF cooperates on projects relating to children. The International Labour Organization is involved with a number of Arab organizations in implementing programs to improve training and upgrade vocational skills (in Egypt, Lebanon, and Jordan). The World Food Programme works with private vocational organizations in the implementation of feeding programs. UNESCO is involved with local organizations in cultural and scientific activities. The World Health Organization is involved in health-related fields, including a rural development project being implemented in a number of Arab countries. And the U.N. Population Fund is cooperating in the fields of population and of women and development.

Despite these interactions, only 17 Arab organizations are accorded consultative status with the U.N. Economic and Social Council. Among these is the Federation of Arab Lawyers, the Arab Council for Childhood and Development, and the Arab Human Rights Organization.

International nongovernmental organizations cooperate with Arab organizations in various fields, and Arab professional unions are members of international federations. NGOs generally work through local bureaus or branches. Examples are CARITAS, CARE, and the Catholic Relief Organization. Those without offices or branches in Arab countries supply PVOs with technical and financial support. Unfortunately, the number of such organizations in the region is unknown, but we know that they are active. We estimate that there are about 200 foreign organizations in Lebanon, 25 in Egypt, and 24 branches of organizations in Tunisia. Conferences, seminars, and training programs are among the fields of activity of such organizations.

In view of its geographical location, extending into Asia and Africa, and its population of both Christians and Moslems, the Arab region interacts in diverse ways. An international nongovernmental network links Arab organizations to Asia and Africa, as well as Islamic (the Islamic Relief Organization) and Christian (the World Council of Churches) groups. Regional Mediterranean networks also interact with Arab organizations in specific fields of activity.

States may enter into relations with PVOs in Arab countries either directly or through governments. The major ones maintaining such relations are the United States, which acts through the U.S. Agency for International Development (USAID); the Netherlands; Sweden; France; and the United Kingdom. USAID, for example, implemented a three-staged, $15-million project in Egypt in 1988-90 to finance more than 1,497 associations in the field of community development. And the Egyptian-American agreement concluded in 1991 provides for the payment of $20 million in aid to support productive projects through PVOs. In 1992, USAID cooperated with the Union of Charitable Associations in Jordan in financing productive projects to benefit 14 percent of total associations in Jordan. Similar projects are in operation in Tunisia, Morocco, Lebanon, and Yemen.

In addition to the global networks found in the area, regional networks bind organizations to one another. Yet there is no Arab umbrella organization to cement cooperation between organizations, nor a regular implementation mechanism. An umbrella organization would strengthen the position of PVOs vis à vis governments, the private sector, and international financial institutions. At the Conference of Arab Non-Governmental Organizations, held in Cairo in 1989, the need for the establishment of an umbrella organization was raised. Various collective efforts between Arab countries have been established in this direction.

One of the recommendations of the conference was for a follow-up committee, which since then has organized training courses for paid employees and PVO volunteers, and has sponsored a number of studies in this field. Further, the committee has mobilized the efforts of private voluntary organizations for the representation of Arab organizations in international forums and the establishment of an effective Arab communication network between these organizations. To date, however, no official regional union or umbrella organization has been established.

There are a number of professional unions in Arab countries, such as the Federation of Arab Engineers, the Federation of Arab Lawyers, the Arab Social Science Association, the Arab Political Science Society. NGOs active in the Arab region include the Arab Council for Childhood and Development, which was established in 1987 to initiate and coordinate efforts for improving the conditions of Arab children.

The role of certain Arab institutions in financing and supporting PVOs should be noted. One of these is the Arab Gulf Programme for United Nations Development Organizations. This was established in 1981 to finance humanitarian and relief programs in developing countries. Funds come from subscriptions paid by member states (Saudi Arabia, Bahrain, United Arab Emirates, the Sultanate of Oman, Qatar, Kuwait, and Iraq), donations from governments, and public and private institutions both in member states and elsewhere. The Programme aims at consolidating development projects undertaken by international, regional, and local organizations. It focuses on the delivery of basic services in the fields of health, education, culture, and food, giving particular attention to women and children. By 1990, the Programme had funded 47 projects implemented by NGOs in 15 Arab countries. The Programme's contribution is assessed at $8 million. Two additional projects conducted at the regional level are the Centre for Training and Research on Arab Women and the Documentation Centre of the Arab Council for Children and Development.

Other institutions and funds provide technical and financial support to PVOs. Among these are the Arab Monetary Fund, the Arab Fund for Social and Economic Development, the Islamic Development Bank, and the Kuwait Fund for Arab Economic Development. The League of Arab States has played a limited role in supporting PVOs in Arab countries. Efforts are being made to enhance this role in the future.

To sum up, Arab private voluntary organizations have been more involved with international than with regional networks. There is hope that an Arab umbrella organization would mobilize and coordinate the efforts of these organizations.

Visions for Tomorrow

The 1980s revealed that popular participation and voluntary initiatives play a major role in inducing social and economic changes. The events in Eastern Europe and the collapse of the Soviet Union are clear evidence that the lack of popular participation can destroy government regimes and ideologies alike. The decade further highlighted the development crisis in the Third World. The crisis may be partly attributed to the fact that the government alone bears the brunt of development. Further, the trends toward the "capitalist state" and privatization have turned certain international NGOs into mechanisms for precipitating this shift.

Arab countries have naturally become affected by such trends. Foreign assistance flows into several Arab countries suffering the hardships of the economic crisis have at times been used to finance PVOs. These organizations served as a way to penetrate the private sector in general and as a possible tool in the shift toward democratization. Funds from USAID to private voluntary organizations had a twofold effect—fostering decentralization and accelerating privatization, which, according to this thesis, promotes democratization.

As a result of the growing government awareness of the significance of popular participation, and of the limited role that intermediary organizations between official authorities and the grass roots can play, the need to consolidate PVOs gained momentum. We should consider these realities in the Arab context, in which political parties (in multiparty systems) and interest groups play insignificant roles. At the same time, several Arab countries (Egypt, Morocco, Tunisia, and Jordan) have become conscious of the burden of development, particularly in view of their commitment to the International Monetary Fund and the World Bank to adopt structural adjustment policies.

Regional and international pressures have spurred private voluntary activity as a mechanism to bring about change in the Arab region. PVOs, at the same time, are aware of the global and regional changes and of their own societal conditions. Hence, they have sought to capitalize on these changes and benefit from the prospects offered to solve social and economic problems. Addressing poverty and the development impasse has therefore been a priority for PVOs, which became the mechanisms to realize these ends. In some other Arab countries, PVOs became the channels for the participation of the population in development and the realization of democracy at the community level through grassroots organizations. Yet dependence on foreign aid has raised the question of whether donors would not have a say in the priorities for action, and if their priorities would necessarily match those of the society. External aid flows have also raised the question of self-reliance and the extent to which funds could be raised at the community level.

Beyond this, a number of challenges and obstacles to the third sector in Arab countries can be identified. First, there is a shortage of data and statistics about societal problems as well as about PVOs, which constrains third-sector prospects. Lack of information was consistently a problem in preparing this chapter. The absence of a standard regional or international classification of PVOs has made it difficult to evaluate the performance of this sector. The shortage of information or simply aversion to the study of social phenomena has led many officials to believe, according to Abdalla El Khatib, that "poverty and disability are far below the levels claimed. No doubt that the lack of information is a major shortcoming which social work is confronting both in its official and unofficial aspects."

Concerning the relationship between the third sector and the government, the problems are basically related to government monitoring and supervision of activities. The mode is usually bureaucratic, which hampers the work of the organizations and undermines their autonomy. The relationship is at times competitive rather than complementary, thus creating a strained and uneasy environment. Laws that bear on the effectiveness of the organizations and govern their creation should be revised. Such procedures are contingent in the first place on government's awareness of the challenges and problems, and its desire to change.

A second challenge in this relationship is manifested in the participation of the organizations in policymaking and their usefulness to the government on account of their field work experience. The relationship with the government varies within the same circumstances. Hence on a continuum of PVOs there are, at one end, organizations that have lost their autonomy and have been functionally integrated into the government, and, at the other end, those that still enjoy autonomy. This issue is of major concern both to specialists and the public at large.

Another problem to be addressed is the lack of coordination and cooperation between private voluntary organizations, particularly between those operating in the same field. This should be fostered to optimize the material and human resources. New institutions may be needed for this in Lebanon, Tunisia, and the Gulf countries. Where they already exist (Egypt and Sudan), it may be necessary to reconsider their situation to empower them further and to improve their capabilities to function effectively. Under the present world system, which is more and more distinguished by governmental and nongovernmental blocs, the need for coordination at the Arab and regional level is clear.

Since NGOs have some reservations on Arab coordination efforts under the "umbrella" of unions or institutions, certain organizations in the region have established mechanisms, such as the Follow-up Committee for Non-Governmental Organizations that was established after the 1989 conference in Cairo. The Committee has approved a project for management and institutional development for the training of staff and volunteers in PVOs in the Arab world. It also established a group of Arab academic researchers to provide the basic studies for the sector and hopes to set up a regional network that can contribute actively in Arab and international forums.

Volunteer recruitment and the provision of funds is another problem confronting PVOs. However, countries and organizations vary in terms of the intensity of the problems. Volunteers are less available due to the pressures of everyday life and the conditions for voluntary work. Also, there is a weak sense of social and political involvement, which is the outcome of the political culture and socialization and the deep conviction that the state is the major initiator of any action. Recruiting volunteers is more of a problem for some countries (such as the Gulf States), while for others, funds may be the constraint (as is the case in Egypt). Solving the problem of human and material resources requires institutional building, management development, upgrading awareness through the media and socialization channels, and the development of fund-raising skills to confront the financing difficulties at local, regional, and international levels.

Democratic self-management systems adopted by PVOs may pose a problem for a number of reasons. First, the managers in the organizations hold office for long periods, leaving no chance for new blood and frustrating ambitious youth. Second, decision making is often an individual process. Despite the fact that the statutes of Arab organizations provide for the convening of general assemblies and define their relationship to boards of directors, there is a gap between the statutes and their application. Decisions regarding programs and activities may be taken by individuals, not by collective action.

Codes of conduct and ethical values complement the management effort exerted by PVOs operating in social work and in the third sector in general. Such values define the relationships between organizations, and between them on the one hand and their society on the other. It further determines relationships between management and the remaining staff within an organization, as well as between volunteers and paid staff. Consensus should be developed regarding a code of ethics, asserting the values that should guide the steps of nongovernmental organizations, particularly in a period witnessing the expansion of organizations as well as social, economic, and political changes that could undermine those values.

A final problem facing the sector is maintaining a balance between rural and urban areas. PVOs are poorly distributed geographically. Despite the fact that rural areas have a larger percentage of their population living under the poverty line and a higher illiteracy rate, organizations are concentrated in urban areas. This imbalance should be redressed.

In several countries, social disparities and the nature of the social and cultural composition of the population have weakened and constrained private voluntary organizations, as is the case of Qatar. In Lebanon, there is fear that after years of full-force activity, the third sector will be curtailed because of the diminishing flow of assistance available from both external and internal sources.

These problems and challenges can only be addressed by the coordinated efforts of both the organizations and the state. Maintenance of the third sector also depends on the possibility of winning over new sectors of the population, particularly youth and women, to participate in its different activities. Cultural changes in terms of the value ascribed to the third sector and its role in accelerating development are also needed.

Still, the growing awareness on the part of the third sector of the problems of society and the flexibility of its response to these problems, particularly during the last decade, augurs well for the future. The third sector has a long experience in social work, and is rooted in religious teachings advocating "giving," social solidarity, and interdependence, which greatly enhances the possibilities of a positive role in the future.

The third sector is benefitting from certain policies adopted by the state, such as encouraging the participation of the population in social and economic development and sharing the burden that government alone had been carrying. All these factors together open up new horizons of hope for private voluntary organizations in the Arab region.

A new trend may be detected in governmental policies pertaining to the third sector. This is seen in the elimination of legal obstacles, the provision of financial and technical support, and the reaction to growing public opinion about the effectiveness of the sector and the government's responsibility toward it. Examples of this new trend are found in Egypt, Lebanon, Jordan, and

Tunisia, where third-sector problems and issues arouse the concern of the public and are discussed in the legislative assemblies in those countries. The changes expected to follow these discussion seem promising for the future.

Generally speaking, the third sector has interacted effectively with the social, economic, political, and cultural changes that have taken place in Arab countries. The response to societal changes is manifested in the patterns and volume of the sector's activities—in its embrace of women's issues and the environment, of care of the disabled and the victims of civil unrest and natural disasters, and of cultural objectives. The response has been characterized by flexibility that at times has been faster and more effective than government responses, particularly in reaching the most deprived sectors of the population.

The awareness and interaction exhibited by the third sector to these changing social conditions is no doubt promising. It will open new vistas of hope for this sector in Arab countries in the future.

Bibliography

Afifi, Mohamed. *Al Wakf and Economic Life in Egypt*. Cairo: Egyptian Book Organization, 1991.

Arab Council for Childhood and Development. *Annual Statistical Report on Arab Children*. Cairo: 1992.

Arab Gulf Programme for United Nations Development Organizations. *Annual Report 1989-1990*. Riyadh: 1990.

Arab Monetary Fund. *Arab Economic Aggregate Report*. Kuwait: 1992.

Barakat, Mohamed. Director of Islamic Orphanage in Lebanon. Interview, Beirut, July 1993.

Bold, Soliman Ali et al. "Local Non Governmental Sector in Sudan. A Critical Survey." Khartoum: unpublished, 1992.

Director of Association of Business Women. Interview. Amman, July 1993.

El Baba, Wafa. "The Situation of the Third Sector in Lebanon." Beirut: unpublished, 1993.

El Dahan, Omayma. "The Situation of the Third Sector in Jordan." Amman: unpublished, 1993.

El Khatib, Abdallah. *The Mechanics of Social Work*. Amman: General Union of Philanthropic Associations Research Centre, 1992.

El Khatib, Abdallah. Director of the General Union of the Philanthropic Associations in Jordan. Interview, Amman, July 1993.

El Nagar, Baker. "Volunteer Social Work in the Arab Gulf Countries." Bahrain: Follow Up Office, Council of Social Welfare Ministries in the Arab Gulf, 1988.

El Nagar, Baker. "Associations in the Arab Gulf." Studies presented to the Conference of Arab NGOs. Cairo: 1989.

El Romeihi, Mohamed. "The Mass Media and Indigenous Activities: Issues, Rules, and Future." Studies presented to the Conference of Arab NGOs. Cairo: 1989.

Farahat, Nour. "The Legal Status of Associations in Arab Laws." Studies presented to the Conference of Arab NGOs. Cairo: 1989.

General Union of Associations. *Directory of Philanthropic Associations in Palestine*. Gaza: 1992.

General Union of Philanthropic Associations. "Study on the Economics of Social Work in Jordan." Amman: Centre for Social Studies, 1988.

Hussein, Raoufa. Director of Women's Studies in Yemen. Interview. Cairo, September 1993.

Hussein, Raoufa. "The Situation of the Third Sector in Yemen." Sanae: unpublished.

Kandil, Amani. "Professional Groups and Democratization in Egypt." Conference on Democratization in the Arab World. Cairo: Centre for Political Development, 1992.

Kandil, Amani. "Survey on Private Voluntary Organizations." Cairo: unpublished, 1992.

Kandil, Amani. *Civil Society in Egypt.* Cairo: unpublished, 1993.

Kandil, Amani. "Defining the Non Profit Sector in Egypt." Working Paper No. 10. Baltimore: The Johns Hopkins University Institute for Policy Studies, 1993.

Kandil, Amani. "The Role of Islamic Non Profit Organizations in Egypt and Promoting the Caring Society." Spring Research Forum Working Papers, on Transmitting the Traditions of a Caring Society. Texas: Independent Sector, 1993.

Mehna, Kamel. "The Role of NGOs in Social Development. A Factual Experience." Presented to Conference on Coordination Between NGOs, Beirut, 1992.

Ministry of Social Affairs. *Social Welfare Indicators in Egypt.* Cairo: 1993.

Moteleb, Rashida Abdel. "Theoretical Framework: An Action Plan to Study Volunteer Work in Sudan." Studies presented to the Conference of Arab NGOs. Cairo: 1989.

Nafis, Saraha Ben. "The Situation of the Third Sector in Tunisia." Tunis: unpublished, 1993.

Naser, Serri. "The History of Philanthropic Work in Arab Mashrek." Studies presented to the Conference of Arab NGOs. Cairo: 1989.

Rashid, Mohamed Abdel. *Sufi Orders and Development.* Egypt: Menia University, 1988.

Soulha, Gassan. Director of the Christian Youth Association. Interview, Beirut, July 3, 1993.

"Status Report: United States Economic Assistance to Egypt." Cairo: 1991.

Wanas, El Munsef. "The History of Indigenous Work in Arab Maghreb." Studies presented to the Conference of Arab NGOs. Cairo: 1989.

5

THE VOLUNTARY AND NONPROFIT SECTOR IN SUB-SAHARAN AFRICA

African Women's Development and Communication Network

Before the 1980s, African governments were responsible for offering social services. A great deal was achieved in education and health. The literacy rate and life expectancy increased while infant mortality was reduced greatly. Yet a decade after the introduction of structural adjustment programs to the continent, the social conditions of the poor have deteriorated substantially. These people continue to suffer due to eroded income levels and the lack of basic services such as health care and education.

The 1980s will be remembered as a decade of unprecedented crises in Africa, a "lost decade." The Ethiopian disaster shocked the world, and the dismal economic, social, and political performance of many African countries was a major concern. The state and its institutions showed signs of retreat from micro-development activities, especially in regard to the provisions of basic services. Moreover, the institutionalization of economic stabilization measures since the early part of the decade caused governments to withdraw from some basic aspects of development.

Africa could become the backyard of the Third World unless appropriate measures are taken toward sustainable development, which is defined as the ability of the present generation to meet their needs without compromising the ability of future generations to do the same. Sustainability of growth becomes critical if the poor cannot afford to meet the basic necessities and participate in national development.

In addition to the subsistence nature of the economy, the region is also fragile in many other ways. For instance, most of the countries emerged recently from colonialism, while South Africa is in the process of dismantling the inhumane apartheid system. The democratic structures and political participation by the masses that marked the transition to independence collapsed during the 1960s and were replaced by military and one-party dictatorships.

The region has also experienced frequent civil wars and other catastrophes such as severe droughts and famines, resulting in death and suffering of millions of people. Although there has been tremendous pressure to move toward democracy since the collapse of the Soviet Union, the ruling elites have been extremely resistant to change and seem to cling to power at all costs.

Nevertheless, in Africa, as elsewhere in the world, people have made efforts individually and collectively to forge a healthy and sustainable future. This effort to identify and seek solutions is a significant factor in contemporary society. In light of this, the voluntary sector is rapidly providing an alternative vision as the shortcomings of states and their ideologies increasingly become clear. More and more people are having to fall back on the basic human resource of collectivism and communality in search of solutions to the overwhelming variety of human problems.

Thus the voluntary and nonprofit sector in sub-Saharan Africa is receiving more attention than ever today. Furthermore, voluntary organizations seem to represent a truly hopeful complement to the highly centralized, government-centered approaches that have come under critical scrutiny since the early 1980s. The sector is viewed as having advantages over government institutions. Indeed, many observe that the kind of micro activities favored by voluntary organizations give priority to development at the grassroots and use participatory, bottom-up approaches as opposed to top-down, government-engineered activities. On account of this, donor organizations today put an enormous amount of aid through voluntary channels rather than through the state.

The voluntary sector in Africa is highly decentralized and different: no single definition or classification can capture the labyrinth of organizations involved. The heterogeneity of the sector is in fact an impediment to achieving an articulate definition and picture of the sector. Nevertheless, within the broad purview of the voluntary sector, several structures can be identified that are engaged in nonprofit, charitable, and human development activities.

The terms voluntary and nonprofit are used here to refer to a combination of various organizations formed by individuals on a voluntary basis and without the intention of realizing a profit from such organizations. Their aim is people-centered development. In Africa, there are various actors in this sector.

They include traditional welfare associations, self-help groups, and nongovernmental organizations (NGOs) focused on development.

In Africa, the voluntary sector can be categorized in numerous ways. Some organizations are indigenous and grassroots-oriented. They have emerged out of African people's need to respond to the neo-colonial ravages, according to Paul Wangoola. They are "African conceived, African propelled and African directed at all levels and in totality, i.e process, policy, management and execution." These organizations are built on people's capacities, capabilities, and resources—their culture, existing structures and organizations, technology, skills, leadership, enthusiasm, and spirit of solidarity.

Grassroots organizations cover a wide range of institutions. Included here are women's groups, traditional labor exchange groups, women's saving organizations, local religious groups, and other community-based organizations started by the people for their own development. Since they are the initiative of the people and are managed by the people themselves, they are referred to as people's organizations. These are concrete attempts by people to provide for themselves through collaborative efforts.

Other organizations operating at the national level include umbrella NGOs servicing grassroots organizations in the areas of administration, finance, and organization. These groups, which can be called national NGOs, include organizations such as the Voluntary Agencies Development Association, Kenya Energy and Environment Organizations, Tanzania Non-Governmental Organizations, Development Network of Indigenous Voluntary Association of Uganda, and Federation des Associations des Femmes de Senegal. These type of organizations may be formed on local initiative, but they tend to be associated with external influences, especially from donors.

International NGOs are also active in Africa. They are involved in development projects, either on their own or in conjunction with grassroots organizations, religious groups, and national NGOs. Examples of organizations in this category include World Vision, Oxfam, World Neighbors, Ford Foundation, Save the Children, Action Aid, Amnesty International, and Christian Aid.

NGOs are distinguished from self-help groups on the basis of being formally registered as voluntary development organizations or as a body with either national or international legal status. They have both national and international sources of funding and their broad development activities are not restricted to any particular area or beneficiary. This distinction obviously excludes traditional welfare organizations and autonomous self-help groups.

The priority for self-help groups—informal community-based organizations and associations of members brought together by immediate common concerns—is their members. They have local activities that rely on limited amounts of local resources and, in some cases, provide membership-restricted benefits. Though concerned with development activities, they are accountable to their members and act for and on behalf of the members' benefits.

Voluntary citizens' associations are support structures formed by the people themselves to tackle various problems. They were mostly formed as a result of disruptions starting from the colonial days. They first appeared in urban centers as part of the struggle for independence and adjustments to a new sociocultural milieu.

Philosophical Concerns and Sources of Inspiration

The need for associational life is as old as humankind. People find themselves helpless on their own against the vagaries of nature and against other individuals, especially powerful ones. To survive in the face of this immense opposition, humans have to struggle. There is greater chance for success if the struggle is done in collaboration with other people. Thus the spirit of collectivism is the basis of individual strength when it comes to working with nature. As an African proverb puts it, one finger cannot kill a louse.

In the traditional social setup in Africa, established communal structures absorbed societal or community problems. Traditional structures arose out of strong communal bonds. Africans regarded one another as brothers and sisters, and this meant they had to come to each other's assistance in the hour of need. An African belonged to a community and not just to a family. The individual was therefore the community's concern and responsibility. This interdependence was articulated by Nigerian novelist Chinua Achebe in 1966: "Whereas an animal scratches itself against a tree, a human being has a kinsman to scratch it for him."

Many African communities believed that the welfare of an individual meant the welfare of the whole community and that individual tribulations were tribulations of the whole society. An article in the African Association for Literacy and Adult Education Newsletter captures this point well: "The African person was subordinate to the community. If an individual suffered in any way, the community also felt the pain. It was thus the responsibility of the community to protect the individual as a means of protecting itself. An individual was born to a clan, to an age-group, to a community; not to a nuclear family."

Herein lies a philosophical background to traditional African communities. It is supported by a rich mythology and folklore. Myths and stories abounded of selfish and generous people. In some folklore, the hyena became a major symbol of selfishness and greed in society. This was the type of character to be detested and avoided. Characters who were generous were regarded as being rewarded with wealth and prosperity.

When Christian missionaries came to Africa, they worked to help Africans in the fight against poverty, sickness, and illiteracy. Churches became very active in the fields of education, health, relief, and welfare. The inspiration behind these efforts was the teachings of Christianity that emphasized the need to be mindful of a neighbor's welfare and the value of taking care of the sick, the orphaned, the poor, and the oppressed. Religious charity was viewed as godly and a passport to heaven. A person who engaged in good deeds toward another, especially the helpless, was viewed as being nearer to heaven.

Discussions about the potential of the voluntary sector to function now as agents of social change center around the failure of the state to foster social, economic, and political changes. The argument in many such discussions is that all over Africa governments have shown limited capacity to raise rural standards of living and have been helpless in the face of natural disasters. Roles in these fields have been diligently taken over by the voluntary organizations. NGOs are seen by many as providing a more effective and efficient means of promoting micro-development goals than government institutions essentially because the latter are concerned with large-scale projects that rarely involve beneficiaries in their initiation and implementation.

Most researchers agree that the kind of micro-activities NGOs usually engage in constitute a development priority, and that these groups have an advantage over other agencies in that they:

- are at the grassroots and therefore better situated to respond to the needs of the people,
- by design recognize people as protagonist of development,
- reach the marginalized groups of society who are rarely reached by other agencies,
- use a bottom-up approach through which people actively involve themselves in development,
- break patterns of "dependency,"
- complete and supplement government's development initiatives, and

149

• have independent operations and are autonomous of host governments' control, which is a source of their motivation.

One major challenge for NGOs is to satisfy these expectations. In many respects, these groups have broadened the institutional framework of development operations. Their development activities and their role in the democratization of rural development are frequently referred to. In the 1987 conference on South-South NGO cooperation, for instance, it was stressed that NGOs in the South should operate in areas not adequately served or reached by the governments, with a view to providing people with basic services and improving their development opportunities.

Thus NGOs fill the development gaps left by the state. They aim at providing the three major core values of development to poor communities: life sustenance through the provision of basic needs; self-esteem, by allowing the poor to have control over their lives; and freedom from servitude. They has build capacity for development by enabling communities to make choices.

Community and Voluntary Associations

As noted earlier, the voluntary and nonprofit sector in Africa predates modern governments. Before the advent of colonialism, African people had structures that catered to the needy among them. Communal living characterized all communities.

One component of this sector is mutual assistance groups. These are based on the traditional spirit of communalism, which involves doing things together and sharing communal and family burdens. Many such groups are widespread in rural villages and are confined to kinship and clan ties. Activities for such groups do not have a long-term focus. They are intuitively founded to respond to immediate needs of particular members of the community. Some researchers suspect that this describes a majority of the people's organizations found in the continent. Examples of this type, which is common in East Africa, include burial societies, childbirth networks, and organized agricultural work groups.

Some of the most important social institutions in Africa have been age-group work parties and the clan. The age-group was made up of people born around the same time who went through initiation ceremonies for transition into adulthood together. Members of an age-group were bound to each other, and these bonds demanded that they took care of each other. If one of them suffered, the others had to come to the rescue.

Civil Society in South Africa

Civil society has come to represent one method of deepening democratic participation in political, economic, and social life both through and outside primary and constitutional forms of political representation. As such, its current importance rests on the perceived need to supplement conventional popular democracy with other forms of voluntary or associational activity. The result of this desire has been the development of voluntary associations and institutions.

Through four decades of apartheid rule, for example, churches played a major role in supporting NGOs to advance the course of the oppressed. This brought religious institutions closest to the efforts of NGOs to create a civil society. Further, some NGOs exist entirely as a vehicle to create civil society with the moral justification of challenging apartheid. Hence the need to create a civil society that could ensure the accountability of government institutions and provide avenues and opportunities for participation at every level of society.

In East Africa, the age-groups among the Maasai of Kenya and Tanzania and among the Kikuyu, Kalenjin, and Luhyia of Kenya are well documented in historical and anthropological/sociological literature. In West Africa the age-group institution is still alive in rural areas of Burkina Faso, Mali, Senegal, Gambia, Guinea Bissau, and the Republic of Guinea. In Mali and Bukina Faso, among the Joola, the Serer, the Mandinka, the Jula, and the Fulaani, the age-group institution provides an excellent support system to the people who migrate to big cities.

Other community organizations were also found in East Africa. The spirit of communalism was prevalent in East Africa. The idea of "pulling together" is not new to Kenya, for instance. This is a spirit that "embodies mutual assistance, joint efforts, mutual social responsibility, community self-reliance," according to P. Mbithi and R. Rasmusson. Many local languages have a word for the concept of mutual social responsibility and joint effort: the Luo call it Konyier Kende; the Luhya, Obwasio (Bulala among Babukusu); the Kikuyu, Ngwatio; the Kamba, Mwethia; and the Maasai, Ematonyoki. The groups among the Kamba people were traditional mutual aid institutions that today have been transformed into modern self-help groups. They are now wider in coverage and scope, and address modern-day development challenges.

151

In West Africa, these indigenous structures still exist both in rural areas and in big towns and cities. In Senegal the mutual assistance groups are known as Mbootaay from the Wolof word "boot," which means "to carry on the back" or "to nurture," referring to the way a mother carries or nurtures a baby. The deeper meaning of the concept therefore is the support or the nurture that the structures offer to the beneficiaries. In urban areas, for example, the indigenous structures offer people something to lean on as support against the problems of living away from one's original home.

Presently in Senegal, these groups are the main socioeconomic support network of the people. They carry out all cultural activities that help people keep ties with their rural base. Women play an essential role in terms of general management of the groups, information circulation, and implementation of a program of activities.

The name of the group usually refers to the village or area the people are originally from; for example, Khaley Lebouga is a Mbootaay of young people from the zone of Lebou in the town of Mekhe. They carry out mainly sociocultural activities and sports. Gouney Ngaay, a Senegalese Mbootaay of young people from the town of Ngaay Mekhe, has as a main objective to keep in touch with young people from Ngaay Mekhe who are away. They also have sociocultural and economic activities.

The clan was another institution supporting the needy. It was responsible for the welfare of its members. Anybody in distress could approach the clan for assistance. In West Africa, and in Senegal in particular, the traditional spirit of helping the needy or disadvantaged is best captured by the Wolof word Sarax, meaning "to give to someone." Sarax is taken as a duty or moral obligation that every member of society should observe. In traditional Senegalese society, if a woman delivered twins, the community would come together and help her, that is, give her Sarax. This system has continued to date because it is believed that "on the day of judgment, God will ask you if you do the sarax or not. If you do not, you will be punished."

In the Southern Africa region there are Nhimbe Amalima groups. Their main purpose is to share labor during peak agricultural seasons. Among communities that keep cattle, groups such as the majana were common for dividing labor and making the best use of time.

Across the continent, ample evidence has documented that traditional society thrived on an acute awareness of corporate existence, a strong sense of common destiny among people. In general, African communities were characterised by a sense of interdependence and communal living. On this ethos, Africans used to mobilize communities to achieve common goals. They

---

Tontine

In West and Central African French-speaking countries, there is the phenomenon of "tontine." This is a self-help group of citizens organized to set up a revolving fund of equal financial contributions from members and used by them in turns. It acts as their "savings bank." It works extremely well in big cities such as Douala, Yaounde, Libreville, Cotonou, Abidjan, Dakar, and Conakry. In these groups, women are the most active members and managers.

---

had myths, beliefs, and sayings that supported voluntary and non-profit service to the needy. Hence in many African communities, traditional rainmakers, herbalists, healers, and birth attendants served their respective communities for a token or no fee.

With the advent of colonialism and the weakening of community structures such as these, new ones evolved. The introduction of the cash economy, and migration (in some cases across borders) to farms, mines, and cities resulted in other new indigenous structures to address new challenges. These often took the form of home-area associations. Workers from Malawi, for instance, formed social clubs to cater for the needs of fellow migrants in the new urban environment. These developed into burial societies and stockvels; they became the social welfare and insurance mechanism for workers away from their homes. People living in urban centers formed new support structures to help tackle the problems facing them in the urban environment. This whole process was speeded up as the nationalist struggle for independence gained momentum.

The colonialist era also brought in an internationalized form of charity that was targeted at people with physical disabilities: the blind and the deaf, the physically handicapped and the socially disadvantaged, such as the aged and orphans. Schools were set up specifically for these groups. They operated in similar ways as institutions in their home countries. Most of them were aligned to the churches' responsibility to cater for the disadvantaged. Funds were raised in Europe and North America to run these institutions. These church activities were the first voluntary and nonprofit sector services from Northern countries.

The two main categories of voluntary action present an extremely complex institutional structure. For instance, many mutual assistance groups do not have a clear organizational structure as their formation was mainly intuitive and spontaneous, sometimes evolving to reflect urgent communal or societal members' needs. On the other hand, there are the semistructured and formal voluntary associations and organizations such as trade unions and various types of cooperatives.

In East Africa, the following types of organizations are easy to discern, particularly in Kenya:

- community initiatives for survival;
- institutions created to cater for migrants after colonialism;
- institutions for the socially disadvantaged, which were spearheaded by the churches and colonialists;
- trade unions;
- consumer councils and associations; and
- producers' associations and cooperatives.

The historical background of voluntary associations and other citizens' collective initiatives vary by region. For instance, the rise of trade unions can be traced from early nineteenth century, when workers felt the need of form unions to register their complaints and to be vehicles for fighting for economic, political, social, and cultural freedom.

Cooperatives were started as early as 1909 through a promulgation of the Co-operative Agricultural Societies Act. They were exclusively for white commercial farmers. As more Africans got involved in the armed struggle, however, the need to start cooperatives arose. The African peasants' struggle to form cooperatives was legalized in the Southern Africa sub-region in the 1950s. As more Southern Africa states became independent, cooperative movements were promoted as the focus for the transformation of the country's socioeconomic basis, as a vehicle for the promotion of the government's socialist ideology, and as a way to create egalitarian society, for most governments had adopted socialist economic policies.

Social justice groups have a relatively short history, which can be traced to the 1970s and 1980s. They were formed mainly to protect and safeguard people's rights, especially those of women against sexual harassment. They promoted gender sensitivity, and helped people needing legal advice or other human rights assistance.

The major themes in voluntary citizens associations are:

- Equal employment opportunities for all, irrespective of race, sex, religious belief, political affiliation, or beliefs, as in the case of trade unions.
- Observance of international labor regulations as set out by the United Nations.
- Unity in diversity in promotion of economic levels and market opportunities.
- Consumer education to all in order to enlighten buyers on how to increase the value of their money.
- Understanding and practice of human rights as documented in the United Nations Charter.

The target groups for the voluntary citizens' association are varied.

- Trade unions target all workers, especially those below management levels. They also target the self-employed, especially micro-entrepreneurs and hawkers.
- Cooperatives target both commercial farmers and very small-scale producers in virtually all fields—agriculture, construction, mining, manufacturing, and the service industry.
- The consumer council targets all consumers, particularly the middle class and ordinary people who are sensitive to any price changes.
- Social justice groups target the lower class and ordinary people who have limited money and are not fully aware of their rights.

All the informal grassroots social groups and institutions operate under traditions of the local communities. Their legal status depends on the type of organization. For instance, a majority are registered as social clubs although most of them have developed into credit and savings unions and burial societies, which command large followings and amounts of money. Similarly, institutions such as centers for the handicapped were the first to be registered as welfare organizations.

The registration of these associations has not always been easy. There were several papers to be filled in, and if just one was not completed properly, the application could be rejected and the entire process started all over again. This was an attempt to discourage associations from obtaining legal recognition, so that when they carried out programs these could be termed illegal and hence liable to prosecution. This procedure did not, however, deter associations from seeking registration, regardless of the time it took.

In total, indigenous grassroots structures bring together millions of people in the communities. For instance, in Zimbabwe in 1992, it was estimated that there was at least one women's club in each village in a total of 6,000 villages in the country. And in Kenya, grassroots organizations such as women and youth groups number in thousands. The number of self-help groups in Kenya was estimated to be over 30,000 in 1990, with a membership of more than 1 million.

Data from Zimbabwe demonstrate the growth of cooperatives. The number of supply and marketing cooperatives rose from 22 in 1956 to 597 in 1985, the last year for which data are available, while only 1 farming collective society was registered in 1980, compared with 275 in 1985. And the number of nonagricultural cooperatives went from 3 in 1960 to 634 in 1985. This means that by 1985, more than 1,500 primary cooperative societies existed in Zimbabwe.

The dynamism of the interaction between the indigenous structures of collective action and the new forms of voluntarism provided a basis for widespread political, religious, and social movements against colonial domination and for development during the post-colonial era. A typical example of this interaction is the Harambee (self-help) movement in Kenya.

Harambee means pulling together of resources by people to accomplish some basic communal tasks. It reflects collective and cooperative social values of a people in the sense that it is a process whereby they mobilize themselves and their resources to form on-the-ground structures to meet their needs. In this context, Harambee is essentially a modernized version of the traditional mutual assistance process because it engages people in modern activities that are based on modern values. In the Harambee process, resources are voluntarily contributed by community members and the benefits are broadly distributed.

In the post-independence political and ideological context, Harambee began to play an absolutely central role in local development activities and later in the national development process, serving as a major focus of popular participation. The Harambee movement is supported by a wide spectrum of people and almost everybody at the local level is involved, although the degree of involvement varies considerably. Ordinary community members, particularly the lowest and middle-range peasants, participate more because they have more to gain from the enterprise. Their contributions are labor, money, or material in kind. Local elites also make contributions, mainly in the form of financial resources obtained through state patronage relations.

To date, Harambee is the foundation along which basic service facilities are built at the local level. Educational facilities, health posts, water projects, and numerous other community-focused facilities are built through the Harambee process. Perhaps as a result of declining abilities of the state to nurture such structures, government officials vigorously support Harambee. Senior politicians and state officials are in many cases chief guests at many fundraising events, demonstrating that Harambee, as a voluntary spirit, is a key feature in the country's development efforts. One role it is playing, arguably, is redirecting focus from national social and political problems to local ones, sparing the state the blame for poor development returns.

Beyond lineage-focused spontaneous groups, community-based organizations have evolved over time, flourishing out of the need to accomplish collective goals, mainly the provision of collective goods. Such self-help organizations are important ways to mobilize local resources for the betterment of people's lives. They represent structures through which members collectively participate in activities geared toward the improvement of their lives.

Ideally, such groups constitute membership organizations, acting on behalf of the members and accountable to those who constitute the group. Many are founded on the basis of mutual aid and are devoted to provision of basic services to members, as such benefits are sometimes restricted to the group. The spread of benefits to other members, of course, depends on the nature of the enterprise undertaken, as there are some projects ostensibly motivated by the need to benefit the local community at large while others direct benefits to individuals in the group. This graduation from member-focus to community-focus is seen in many Harambee projects.

Self-help groups are the best example of traditional welfare associations. In most cases, they are community-based. In rural areas, for instance, a village would have several such collective actions. The groups are not gender-conscious in either activities or membership. This ideally differentiates them from the mutual assistance (ephemeral) groups whose formation was spontaneously aroused by sudden need to help a member of the community. But in some communities, the activities performed rationalized the gender role—that is, some activities were preserved for men and others for women.

Nevertheless, most self-help groups in Kenya are women's groups. Women organize themselves into small associations to help each other or their communities. In other words, many women are involved in the collective action of the women's groups movement. The role of self-help groups in the country

157

Maendeleo Ya Wanawake

The change of shape and form of many groups in Kenya is associated with the growth of Maendeleo Ya Wanawake (MYW, Progress for Women), an umbrella women's body. This was formed in 1951 by the colonial government to promote the interests of women's clubs, some of which had been formed during World War II by the wives of African soldiers. The clubs together with settler farmers' wives were the initial members of MYW.

The significance of the association led the colonial administration to set up a women's activities desk with the Department of Community Development, an office that today continues to service women's groups' interests within the Ministry of Culture and Social Services.

---

has received significant attention. It can be argued that these groups have their foundations in the tradition of mutual aid, and Barbara Thomas notes that the age-old custom of self-assistance was practiced by groups in most parts of Kenya. But the tradition of self-help has changed considerably over the years. New needs and complex community problems have meant that the spirit adapts. Thus groups can be found operating income-generating activities and performing highly structured activities in addition to continuing with merry-go-round routine activities.

In addition, the Harambee framework of local development has induced the growth of women's groups. The ideology of self-help gave women a legitimacy and recognized the purpose for forming self-help groups. It established the bases on which women could find means for solving their problems.

Over the years, disillusioned with disbursement of aid through governmental institutions, many donors identified self-help groups as conduits of aid. This led to an increase in the number of groups at the local level. The source of funding for many groups is mainly external—state and donors. Through the Women's Bureau Department in the Ministry of Culture and Social Services, some groups in Kenya receive financial support and others are given support in form of materials for their projects. Further, many donors and NGOs work in collaboration with the groups. Their aid for rural activities is directed through women's groups. In some instances, both the donors and NGOs not only give aid to the groups but also collaborate on projects.

There is ample evidence in other parts of Africa of the role played by traditional forms of collective action. For example, in Ghana and Nigeria several patterns are seen. First, there is the traditional pattern of mobilizing people to do communal work for the benefit of the community. People are mobilized in the field of environmental cleanliness and maintenance—cleaning of marketplaces, draining pools, clearing bushes, and so on. One day a week is set aside for such communal labor, and every able-bodied person is supposed to participate. The churches mobilize people to do this kind of work. This pattern is found particularly in Ghana. Second, in order to help each other financially, market women form groups to facilitate trading.

In Francophone West Africa, particularly in Senegal, Mali, Gambia, Mauritania, and the Guineas, some Muslim religious movements play an essential role in collective action. During the colonial times, Islam appeared as a shield behind which local people could organize resistance to colonial rule and cultural alienation. The first religious movement that developed at that time was the Khadria movement from the Iraqian inspiration. It took root in Mali and spread westward. The second was the Tidjan movement from Morrocan inspiration. It started in northern and eastern Senegal and spread from there. The third and most recent one (around 1915) is the Mourad movement. This is an indigenous one, born in the center of Senegal and flourishing there and throughout the neighboring region. It now mobilizes people easily for any collective action, including voting. It can get people to vote against a law if it is seen to undermine the interests of the citizens. It has contributed to two crucial areas: the development of intercity transport and the promotion of peanut agriculture, especially in Senegal.

In Nigeria, the phenomenon of "launching," the equivalent of Harambee phenomenon in Kenya, is prevalent. Through local initiatives, fund-raising is organized to achieve common goals such as the building of schools, roads, clinics, and water pumps. This process involves citizens of a given locality in their own development. They do this with the approval of the government.

Finally, the social clubs within cities that consist of people from the same localities are organized to help members in times of crisis, such as funerals. Regular contributions by members become a resource to be used for such needs. It is such initiative in looking toward a common goal that has in some cases crystallized into more structured local NGOs fostering self-help among people.

An outstanding example of the use of the traditional voluntary approach for contemporary problems is the NAAM groups in Burkina Faso. This movement was started as a challenge to the methods borrowed from western models of development, which were a failure. Naam is a traditional body composed of young people who voluntarily undertake various activities in the communities.

Due to lack of registration, most of the indigenous organizations remain unfunded. Most of their activities do not require capital inputs but labor. Those that have evolved into farmers' unions or cooperatives get outside funding for programs. The traditional women's clubs are mainly funded on a project approach by outside donors, local service organizations, or government community development programs.

Voluntary organizations have been able to raise their funds from membership subscriptions. These are usually banked and the interest gained is used to support administrative structures. The savings and credit movement has been opened up with the creation of apex bodies that impart modern techniques to the membership. These bodies are usually financed by outside donors, such as those from Canada, Ireland, and Germany, that have an interest in credit unions. Others survive mainly through public appeals, home-based fundraising events such as flag days, dinner dances, and so on. External churches and other charity trusts also fund these groups.

Trade unions have been raising money from their members through membership fees and check-off system. They have also developed links with donors to support their training programs. And the government gives them funding in terms of tax exemption on importation of certain items, such as computers for use in their work.

Cooperatives raise money from the members through membership fees and the shares that they buy. They have collaborative initiatives with donors who fund some of their programs, especially in training, marketing, and equipment. Similarly, consumer councils raise money from membership fees and some from donor funding. Last, the social justice campaign groups depend on donor funding to carry out their programs.

Apart from cases where an indigenous or voluntary citizen association is specifically targeted at a certain community, the institutions in this category have significantly opened up to allow broader participation of other groups. The interaction with service organizations has resulted in networking and/or affiliation by different groups to a wider body. For example, saving and credit unions are affiliated to ACCOSCA through their national umbrellas. Women's clubs and small income-generating groups have also been linked to different service organizations that they work with. Burial societies, on the other hand, remain closed and membership is restricted to the particular community.

Where grassroots institutions and voluntary associations have grown big in terms of membership and geographic coverage, and when they need external donor support, most of these institutions have sought government registration as welfare organizations or cooperatives (depending on the appropriate legislation in that country). Smaller groups, such as women's clubs, receive technical and financial assistance from government. In most cases they do not require registration. However, all formal voluntary associations such as cooperatives and welfare institutions must be registered with the government's department of social welfare or its equivalent. The government takes on a supervisory role and inspects facilities. This registration also allows them to make public appeals for funding.

Most of the money generated by these institutions has until recent years been deposited in convenient accounts that were not lucrative. Banks are beginning to be attracted to this sector, as it has great potential. For example, the Stockvels in South Africa command billions of rands and these are all channelled through the PERM bank. In return, the Stockvels use their power to determine the interest rates and other complementary services from the bank. These institutions see the private sector as a potential donor. Their relationship is therefore mainly donor-recipient. In cases where employment is part of the rehabilitation program, the private sector is encouraged to employ disabled people.

Overall, most of these institutions have little interaction with the private sector or with churches, except in cases where religious bodies are involved in providing technical and financial assistance to the sector.

Institutions in this sector are mostly very sector-oriented and deal with issues of survival. Strategic and long-term planning are not common. The biggest challenges facing them, particularly indigenous and voluntary associations, is growth and impact; for some groups, the challenge is sustainability and coping with a society that is no longer able to look after its own people. With the introduction of economic reforms and the attendant cost-sharing measures, these institutions find it difficult to cope. Natural disasters such as drought, economic hardships leading to unemployment, and epidemics such as AIDS are major issues for these institutions.

Trade unions will face more uncompromising situations with employers due to the economic recession, liberalization policies, and other World Bank policies adopted by the countries in the region. Each sector depends on one another, and the way issues are sorted out will be criticized.

161

If management is weak, cooperatives will face stiffer competition from more efficient businesses from other parts of the world. This will affect the profits generated and thus the viability of the sector. Social justice groups may constantly get into collision with governments as they advocate more rights for society than the governments are willing to yield. Privatization and liberalization brings in new challenges to consumer organizations. Community-based voluntary organizations, such as self-help groups, will be exposed to a multitude of unprecedented social-economic demands from beneficiaries. These demands will pose a challenge to the internal capacities and structures of such groups.

Trade unions are playing a more major role than in the past, especially in the democratization process. In Zambia, the trade union movement was at the forefront of the democratization process. In Zimbabwe, it has kept the government and employers alert to the impact of structural adjustment programs. In South Africa, this sector has been at the forefront of the liberation struggle and the dismantling of apartheid. Cooperatives and credit unions are providing alternative sources of credit and marketing opportunities, in view of the very competitive market situation.

Consumer councils are educating people on the effects of structural adjustment programs, albeit not aggressively, but the stage has been set. Social justice groups are sharing more and more practical cases and exposing some of the historical issues that were previously swept under the carpet. This is bringing about review of the laws in the light of changing global issues.

Nongovernmental Organizations

NGOs have different origins, diverse activities, and a multitude of interests. Two features outside Africa have affected the development of these groups there: the rise of Third World-oriented NGOs in the North and changes in donors' agendas.

NGOs in the North arose as a response to civil strifes caused by two world wars, and they expanded their activities to the Third World after Europe recuperated from the shocks of those wars. Initially, Northern NGOs in Africa were active in relief and welfare. But as it became clear that this did not attack the root causes of poverty, attention was increasingly focused on community development and institution-building. A link began to be made between the recurrence of these problems and the inadequacies of development policies followed by southern governments and bilateral donors.

The emerging critique of the linkages coincided with the wave of popular bilateral "aid fatigue" in the North, which stemmed from the poor results of official efforts to deal with droughts and famines. Demands arose for the mobilization of funds to directly reach the affected. This led to an influx of money to Northern voluntary organizations ready to "navigate" aid to developing countries, bypassing government institutions. Moreover, state institutions were blamed for failure to insulate the poor adequately from the consequences of natural disasters. The large-scale nature of governmental activities and their negligible returns to the poor led critics to seek alternative bases of sustainable development. This was identified as NGOs.

The second international factor, especially in the 1980s, was the transformation of donor agendas. The World Bank's prescribed structural adjustment measures underline the need for state institutions to withdraw gradually from micro-economic development activities, and the revitalization of institutional actors in the private sector to fill the resulting gaps.

These two influences led to the rise of Northern NGOs in the South and explains both the growth in numbers of NGOs in Africa and the change in their organizational aspects and activities. David Boyer has identified three stages of NGO involvement in the development process. These include relief and welfare, which entails NGOs meeting the immediate basic needs of people, especially in emergency situations, and providing for outsiders' intervention. Second, there is small-scale self-reliant development, in which NGOs shift their focus toward promotion of development activities. Third-stage development is defined in terms of empowerment, meaning that NGOs aim at empowering the community to meet their basic needs.

It is difficult to give an accurate figure of NGOs operating in Africa today. Most recent data suggest that there are more than 2,000 Northern NGOs in the Third World and that of this number, 1,800 are from Western Europe and Japan, 600 from the United States, and another 220 from Canada. Most difficult are figures on indigenous NGOs. Various directories focus attention on NGO operations in specific countries while others are built on a particular period of operations. In Kenya, for example, the Kenya National Council of Social Services has 288 NGOs (foreign and indigenous) while impressions from elsewhere show about 400 groups in Kenya. Similarly, the Voluntary Organisation in Community Enterprise in Zimbabwe documents about 243 organizations, but this includes also grassroots self-help groups. What is very evident in most directories is that NGOs operate in diverse fields. They are found in virtually all sectors, although notably in health, water, agriculture, environment, energy, and relief.

Documenting an accurate number for NGOs is hampered by the fact that many governments in Africa have not had the necessary NGO monitoring mechanisms. Some NGOs do not even register with relevant government ministries, while others, like the church development agencies, have exempted themselves from the exercise of notifying the government about their operations and the nature of their activities. Also, NGOs continued to filter into Africa throughout the 1980s, yet some governments had not set up mechanisms to record their growth.

The factors responsible for the unprecedented growth of NGOs in Africa include the donor fatigue and change of agenda just mentioned; droughts, famine, and floods; and increased donor aid. Between 1973 and 1985, matching grant contributions to NGOs from governmental aid agencies in Europe, Canada, and United States tripled from $331.9 million to $1.1 billion, constituting over one fourth of total resources channelled through the international NGO network. Alan Fowler has also estimated that NGOs receive more than $1.5 billion annually in official development assistance. Njuguna Ng'ethe further notes that NGOs raise as much as $3.3 billion per year from private sources. Michael Bratton has similarly noted that the European Community contributed more than $600 million annually through NGOs, and another $1 billion is thought to have reached Africa through combined channels.

NGOs constitute one of the major channels of finance from North to South. In 1989, NGOs transferred $6.4 billion to the South, about 12 percent of all western aid received, compared with less than $900 million in 1970. Moreover, members of the Development Assistance Committee of the Organisation for Economic Co-operation and Development give various kinds of grants to NGOs and collaborate with them to influence projects. For instance, in 1985, more than $4.5 billion was granted to NGOs in developing countries, and in 1986, another $5.3 billion was given to the voluntary sector. It may be argued, therefore, that funds available to NGOs have a direct bearing on the expansion of the sector. Acknowledging this contention, Samuel Kobia observes that it has become necessary to form NGOs to spend money that must be given out without delay, and certainly any group that registers as an NGO can find funds for its operations somewhere in the North.

On account of this, Ng'ethe and Karuti Kanyinga argue that numerous "hawking" NGOs exist in name only or are registered pending donor funding that is available through elaborate project proposals fine-tuned to the interest of the donor. The dramatized attention on NGOs by agencies like the World Bank and other international development institutions has also led to their growth. The World Bank, for instance, has recognized NGOs as a vital force in development activities and collaborates with them in implementing development projects.

Notwithstanding this, several factors have led to the emergence of local NGOs and the influx of foreign international voluntary organizations. One need add that governments' official recognition of and support for NGOs has been key to their growth. The following case studies of a few selected countries and subregions and of specific groups are used to examine the nature of the NGOs and to assess their contribution to human welfare and development.

In Central and Southern Africa, NGOs and private institutions for public services can be classified into three groups, based on their historical development:

- those started by religious organizations (33 in Zimbabwe, 5 in Botswana, and 11 in Zambia);
- those started independent of any religious affiliation (45 in Zimbabwe, 1 in Botswana, and 8 in Zambia); and
- those started as private national institutions for public work (165 in Zimbabwe, 37 in Botswana, and 42 in Zambia).

In the first category, religious organizations found themselves with more work than they could handle. It was therefore found necessary to establish independent NGOs to complement the mission work. Examples of these are Catholic Relief Services, which was started by the United States Catholic Conference; the Christian Children's Fund, started by U.S. Presbyterian churches; World Vision, started by some U.S. Protestant churches; and the Lutheran World Federation, started by the Lutheran Churches of Germany. Some of these have continued to be departments of churches, especially those supported by the Anglican churches and U.S. Episcopal churches. Several of them were started after World War II.

The second category includes Boy Scouts and Girl Guides, which emphasized good leadership and commitment to serve one's country. The Corporation of American Relief Everywhere (CARE) has also influenced the lives of the people with whom they have worked. As noted earlier, national NGOs and people's organizations have formed mainly to articulate their own concerns and mobilize people to start working for self-reliance.

The third category became more prominent after World War II. Their services became increasingly more noticeable with the first part of the independence era in many countries in the region. This was mainly in the 1960s to the 1980s, when most of the countries got their independence. After that, membership privileges were also extended to indigenous people whose social status was above average.

Many international NGOs are doing remarkable work within the region. Oxfam (UK and US), for example, has been working with the impoverished, especially women, to raise their status. Catholic Relief Services is working in small enterprise development and similar areas. And CARE has been supporting women in environment and sustainable development activities.

Subregional networks include IRED, which, although registered as an international NGO, has been actively involved in the region in leadership development programs, institutional capacity building, and small enterprise development. It has also been active in the collection, documentation, and dissemination of information. MWENGO, which was recently launched, will mainly focus on self-reflection, advocacy, and lobbying programs. SANDON focuses on networking and information sharing within the region.

With regard to national NGOs, there are some outstanding ones like Bricks Community Co-operative Alliance, involved in peoples empowerment in Namibia; Lesotho National Council of Women, involved in micro-enterprises for augmenting household income; and the General Union of Co-operatives in Mozambique.

In Zambia, there is the Village Industry Services, involved in agro-based enterprises; Village Development Network, involved in peoples' empowerment; and Malambo Development Foundation, working in similar program activities.

In Zimbabwe, the Organisation of Rural Associations for Progress (ORAP), is involved in integrated development program, leadership development, and total empowerment of the peasants. The Collective Self-Finance Scheme is involved in helping members get credit, and the Kajiwa Development and Coordinating Association promotes small business for its members and leadership development.

In Botswana, Co-operation for Research and Education has been involved in promotion for micro-enterprises, while the Rural Industries Innovation Centre is involved in promotion of rural industries. Some noteworthy groups outside this region are the Alliance of Women in Mauritius, which promotes women's issues in advocacy; the Association of Professional Fishermen of Mauritius, involved in empowerment; and the Mauritius Council of Social Services, involved in institutional development and information sharing.

South Africa is a special case. The history of the NGO sector there spans back about three decades. It started when the National Party that introduced apartheid rule came to power and when inferior education was introduced for

---

The National Society of the Crippled, Ghana

The National Society of the Crippled was founded in 1990. It has about 7,500 members and a budget of $30,000. This national organization of mentally and physically handicapped individuals and their families and supporters works for equal participation and opportunity for the disabled. Among its activities is the sponsorship of competitions and the bestowing of awards. It also operates a speakers' bureau and placement service, provides services for children and charitable programs, and organizes workshops and seminars. It is affiliated to Disabled People International

---

blacks in 1956. The country was subdivided into homelands, which led to the forced removal program. This was followed by the banning of people's political organizations and imprisonment of people's leaders. It became difficult to resist state oppression through political activity, and the only option left was for people to establish NGOs to further their cause.

The early 1970s in South Africa witnessed the uprisings of black people and the formations of community projects. The state clamped down on such developmental projects. With the 1976 uprising, there were massive school boycotts, detention, homelessness, further forced removals, killings, and several leaders forced into hiding. In response, NGOs were formed in large numbers to deal with the crisis. It is no surprise also that some of these NGOs were fronts of the banned liberation movements or those operating in exile.

In the mid-1980s, the state launched its total onslaught strategy to annihilate the black resistance in the country. The UDF and Azapo and their groups were banned. There were wild protests countrywide. Detention, massacres, and more forced removals followed. More NGOs were formed to resist state atrocity through campaigns and to provide relief and support to the victims of state atrocity. By 1988 there were more than 12,000 NGOs, most of which were not registered with the state. Prior to 1990, when the state lifted bans on political organizations, the major feature of the struggle against apartheid had been the emergence of a wide range of NGOs aiming at filling the gap left by apartheid laws in the provision of social services.

At present, it is estimated that there are 20,000 NGOs in South Africa. But the official number is 14,000, out of which only 4,000 are registered with the government. It is difficult to produce accurate figures, however. For example, some NGOs in independent homelands count themselves as part of the broader South Africa. In fact, all progressive NGOs do not recognize independent home-lands as states. The corporate sector and the NGO movement in South Africa have repeatedly been called on to play a role in development.

In West Africa, NGOS have flourished as a result of not only external factors but also internal conditions. These include the values of mutual support and collective responsibility, as illustrated by the following selected NGOs in Ghana and Nigeria (the Anglophone subregion) and in Mali and Senegal (the Francophone subregion).

Friends of the Earth in Ghana, which is affiliated to the Friends of the Earth International, was founded in 1986 and has about 2,000 members. Its membership is drawn from individuals and organizations concerned with environmental protection. It participates in direct efforts to revitalize the environment by collecting, analyzing, and disseminating environmental information.

Another Ghanaian group is the Bible Society. This was founded in 1966 when individual churches were having difficulty getting Bibles. In 1968 it was affiliated to the United Bible Societies. The society was formed to facilitate easy access to the Bible in terms of both ownership and availability in a native language. Thus its activities entail translation, production, supply, and distribution of biblical scriptures in various formats.

Other than the concern of availing the scriptures, the society is also trying to grapple with issues besetting the civil society. Its Youth Department each year celebrates Bible Week. During this session, they address themselves to the social issues in the community and try out solutions to these problems. One such issue is AIDS, which the society tries to find solutions for in the Bible too. In 1992, the week's theme was "The Bible and Social Transformation" and in 1994, which the United Nations designated as the Year of the Family, the program prepared a booklet on "The Family Under Stress." The society also runs a monthly newsletter called Link.

The funding of the society is based on donations from, among others, member countries of the United Bible societies who are self-supporting and can afford to share resources. Their donations are given not in cash but in kind, mostly in the form of scriptures. Income from the resale of these is then used locally. Funds are also raised through membership subscription drives.

In Nigeria, Sheriff Guards was founded in 1965 and has about 300,000 members. Its budget is about 30,000,000 Nigerian naira ($1.4 million, at government exchange rate). It is a national organization of Nigerian youth aged between 6 and 18 years of age, with older instructors and engineers. The group

---

Voluntary Workcamps Association of Nigeria

This association was founded in 1963 and has about 1,000 members. Its budget is about naira 100,000 ($4,500). It is a national association with groups at both the state and local level. It seeks to foster the development of voluntary work in Nigeria through workcamps that carry out community and rural development projects. It promotes the importance of voluntary service and strives to imbue manual labor with dignity and pride.

Among the completed projects are the construction of community, medical, and maternity centres, of youth hostels and schools, and of town halls and market stalls. It coordinates volunteer exchange programs, and organizes leadership training courses as well as seminars and symposia on rural development topics. It is affiliated with the Coordinating Committee for International Voluntary Service and UNICEF.

---

seeks to promote physical, mental, spiritual, and social development of youth. It encourages participants to follow the principles of justice, peace, cooperation, and voluntarism. It also seeks to instill qualities of self-restraint, bravery, self-sacrifice, and tolerance. And it fosters community service through work camps at which members help build public roads, bridges, wells, and drains.

The association operates a Regional Resources Corps that creates self-employment and that provides vocational training centers and helps local agricultural programs. It also operates Community Development Corps that increases public awareness of available voluntary services and assists local community service projects. And its Professional/Technical Corps coordinates the activities of professionals and technical personnel working on Sheriff Guards of Nigeria projects. The organization also participates in relief activities and helps other agricultural and athletic programs for young people. It bestows awards on youths who successfully complete training programs in community service, camping, hobbies, vocational skills, and athletics.

It plans to make land available to young people wishing to undertake agricultural and animal husbandry and small-scale industrial projects. The group maintains a mechanical workshop to provide vocational training to youths interested in industrial areas. It is affiliated to Sheriff Guards International.

The Women's Centre of Nigeria was founded in 1980 and has 190 members and five regional groups. The membership is drawn from low- and middle-

169

income women, concerned men, and volunteer organizations that seek to campaign against female circumcision, AIDS, and sexually transmitted diseases. It offers shelter and care to abused women, abandoned and orphaned children, the aged, and the homeless. It tries to increase public awareness of factors affecting the health of women and children in Africa through research and educational programs. It provides counselling on women's health and sexuality. The Centre has a library of about 1,000 volumes, organizational committees such as Research and Documentation, and newsletters.

Ahmadiyya Muslim Jama'at in Nigeria was founded in 1916 and has about 10,000 members, 137 local groups, and a budget of about $200,000. It is a national association that promotes Islamic teaching, disseminates information and runs educational programs, builds schools and hospitals, runs a missionary college, and provides nursery education.

The Light of Salvation Women's Fellowship in Nigeria was founded in 1982 and has about 320 members. It is a national association involved in missionary work. It encourages religious unity among women in Nigeria, and provides charitable assistance to orphanages and underprivileged individuals. It organizes training programs for women on preaching methods and offers placement services.

Three groups in Mali can be mentioned. The Group for Research Action for Economic and Social Promotion (GRAPES) was created in 1990 in Bamako. Its objectives include the creation of "cereal banks" for food security, the improvement of the management of natural resources, the promotion of women's involvement in development programs, and the promotion of education for girls.

To meet this objective, GRAPES organizes activities in agriculture, water and sanitation, environmental issues, women and gender issues, and education and training for girls and adults. Presently they have a vast program of gardening and food production and one for the popularization of posho mills, which facilitates womens' daily chores.

Second, Tam-Tam to Secure Dogon Plateau Populations was created in 1991 by young people who were committed to the improvement of the harsh conditions of the life of Dogon Plateau people. The association aims to help control the exodus of the Dogon people from their ancestral plateau home to Bamako and even to neighboring Burkina Faso. Activities include agriculture, water and sanitation, cultural events, and adult education and training. They also have programs aimed particularly at improving the conditions of rural women.

Table 1: NGOs in Kenya, 1978-88

Sector	1978			1988		
	Local	Foreign	Total	Local	Foreign	Total
Social Wel.	37	6	43	53	40	93
Relief	5	5	10	10	27	37
Social Devel.	72	57	129	184	219	403
Prod./						
Econ. Dev.	5	17	22	35	77	112
Women	9	6	15	11	15	26
Envir.	4	4	08	23	25	48
Devel. Ser.	3	3	06	14	21	35
Total	135	98	233	330	424	754

Source: Alan Fowler, "New Scrambles for Africa: NGOs and Their Donors in Kenya," *Africa Rural and Urban Development*, Michigan.

The Mali Association for Environmental Protection and Development in the Sahel was formed in 1992 by a group of people concerned with the development of villages and small towns in the Sahel region of Mali. It aims to raise the standard of living of the people in the Sahel desert area, promoting development through environmental programs, resource management programs, and cultural programs.

In Senegal, the Senegalese Confederation of Scouting is affiliated to the scouting movement of 35 African countries south of the Sahara, with headquarters in Nairobi, Kenya. In Senegal, the movement started in 1940. It consists of Scouts and *Eclaireurs*, with a membership of 45,000 young people from 6 to 35 years of age. In addition to education, the group is involved in health and hygiene, child survival programs, and family life education. These are run through sponsorship from relevant U.N. bodies such as UNICEF, UNFPA, UNESCO, and UNHCR.

The National Association for Literacy and Adult Education in Senegal was founded in 1990 in Dakar as part of the network of the African Association of Literacy and Adult Education, the secretariat of which is also in Nairobi. Its activities revolve around the broad areas of literacy, community development, and sociocultural affairs.

Also in Senegal, the Federation of Fouta Associations for Development was founded in 1986 to coordinate the work of the various grassroots organizations in the Fouta region of northern Senegal. It manages more than 135 village associations that are involved in education, food production programs, environmental programs, income-generating projects, and leadership training. The federation depends on funds raised locally but the bulk of the seed money comes from northern NGOs and from Senegalese people working abroad.

The NGO scene in Kenya is not very different from elsewhere in the region except that the country has the largest number of groups in the continent and therefore merits more extensive discussion. The NGO community in Kenya has been influenced by several factors, including the Harambee spirit of communalism. Some scholars have observed that Harambee activities are the main institutions through which NGOs have access to the grassroots. These scholars and the local voluntary groups are the main constituencies of NGOs, and the self-help voluntary environment has led to not only the evolution of many indigenous community-based organizations but also to the influx of many foreign NGOs.

During colonization, a majority of NGOs in Kenya were charitable organizations; others were religious bodies combining evangelical work with activities like education and social welfare. With independence, events changed a great deal as many organizations with social welfare as their principal objectives evolved. The flaws of the early 1960s became a center of focus and an entry point for many relief organizations.

Secular NGOs emerged in the 1960s and 1970s with a focus on development. Some of these groups slowly started shifting their focus from relief to development. Notable examples of early NGOs include the National Council of Churches of Kenya, the Child Welfare Society of Kenya, and Maendeleo Ya Wanawake. Notable foreign organizations included CARE Kenya and Catholic Relief Services. The growth of NGOs in the country has been fairly well documented. Various sources show that Kenya has well over 400 NGOs. The annual growth rate was 9 percent for indigenous NGOs and 11 percent for foreign NGOs during the 1978-88 period. This excludes some 23,000 women's groups and other traditional community organizations.

NGOs in Kenya have had substantial inputs to national socioeconomic development in many sectors. Some are also known to have come up with specific innovations in development, thus offering opportunities for government to adopt new and proven approaches. NGOs also offer employment to many school graduates, both in the rural and urban areas. They attract a significant amount of resources (foreign exchange), estimated to be between $150-200 million a year. The amount of resources they invest in their projects is estimated to be well over Kenyan shillings 6.9 billion ($115 million) per year.

Information on NGO budgets is hard to come by. The InterAction directory shows that out of 73 U.S. NGOs operating in Kenya in 1985, 28 undertook projects worth $2,530,943 in 1983. In 1984, the total value of these same 28 organizations had increased to $5,554,889, and in 1985 it was $9,484,239. The figures would undoubtedly have been higher had all NGOs provided the necessary data.

The Ministry of Economic Planning notes that between 30-40 percent of Kenya's development is provided by NGOs. Assistance in the field of education, for example, is remarkable, with more than 173 NGOs undertaking various programs such as school feeding, equipment schemes, school constructions, and education. The youth polytechnics have also received substantial support from NGOs in terms of financial, material and technical input, and personnel. NGOs have continuously complemented the government efforts in delivering health services to the poor, and provide up to 40 percent of Kenya's health care requirements. The Ministry indicates that NGOs provide 40-45 percent of family planning services in Kenya.

In the energy and environment sectors, Kenyan NGOs have made various contributions both to conservation of environment and providing affordable energy equipment. Self-help women's groups similarly receive enormous support from NGOs in terms of grants and interest-free revolving loan funds. They use these to operate their projects, particularly income-generating ones. Many water projects in rural areas are staffed by NGOs, either alone or in partnership with the government and donors.

In addition to this, recent studies in Kenya have shown that NGOs contribute enormously toward the creation of local capacity for sustainable development. They impart development skills and knowledge to their beneficiaries, and these are likely to be passed on to the indirect beneficiaries of NGO activities. These and other, more indirect contributions by NGOs support the view that NGO contributions to national development should not be underestimated.

Interaction with Other Sectors

Northern voluntary and nonprofit organizations—with their vast resources—have developed a paternalistic relationship with their southern counterparts. Initially they were active in relief and welfare, but as a result of unique situations, attention was focused on community development and institutional building. As a result, northern voluntary organizations constitute one of the major channels for the transfer of finance from north to south.

The relationship has not been smooth all the way. This has been occasioned by differences in priority. Northern organizations have been interested in specific outcomes that may not have long-term benefits. This approach has been narrow and superficial, according to various leaders and analysts of the voluntary sector.

The mechanism involved in releasing funds from northern to southern organizations has also had some weak points. The funding is on a project-by-project basis, which does not cover nonproject costs such as administrative and overhead expenses. African voluntary organizations have bitterly complained about this weakness. This kind of funding also perpetually ties the African nonprofits to the donors. In some cases, if the donors withdrew their support, the organizations would collapse. Energy is therefore spent on survival strategies rather than long-term strategic planning and management. And there is a lack of autonomy for deciding on-the-spot priorities. This has led to some resentment of northern organizations by African ones that see conditions placed on them as neocolonization and that dislike enforcement of some stringent measures and demands by donor organizations.

Some northern voluntary organizations use the well-established and participatory institutions of their southern counterparts, which proves to be cost-effective, while others establish their own operational institutions. The latter sometimes create conflict with southern institutions, which see this as an encroachment on their territory.

What therefore emerges from this picture is mutual distrust between northern and southern voluntary and nonprofit organizations. Groups in the south that do not have similar ideological orientations, project management styles, and target groups as their northern counterparts do not receive support.

NGOs also have complex relationships with the governments of their own countries. There are many examples to show that African governments and the third sector have collaborated to bring about rapid developments in education, health, and other sectors. Although this is not in doubt and must be appreciated and encouraged, some problematic issues need to be addressed if quicker progress is to be achieved.

The third sector has not been a comfortable bedfellow with African governments. This has been the case especially from the beginning of the 1980s, when the relationship between the two began worsening as totalitarian regimes became preoccupied with their survival in the face of democratization.

Foundations in Southern Africa

A new form of foundation evolved in many countries of the sub-region during the liberation struggle and in the early 1990s. Trusts and foundations were set up specifically to promote development activities. The oldest of these is the Cold Comfort Trust set up in Zimbabwe as a haven for those fighting for liberation in the 1960s. Examples of post-independence Foundations are the Zimbabwe Trust, Zimbabwe Project Trust, Legal Resources Foundation, and Foundation for Education with Production. These were set up to address specific development challenges that faced the country.

Toward the end of the 1980s and in the early 1990s, people's foundations were set up. In Mozambique, a Community Development Foundation was established to provide funds and technical assistance to communities and other organizations working to improve living conditions.

In Zimbabwe, the Organisation of Rural Associations for Progress set up the Qogelela Foundation, which was a graduation from peasant savings and credit movements. ORAP hopes to pool people's resources together with those from donors and the private sector in Zimbabwe to create a full-fledged foundation.

The people who started NGOs and other similar institutions at this time in Africa were those dissatisfied with the governments' efforts, and thus the governments naturally looked at them skeptically.

As noted earlier, two of the major influences on the relationship between the third sector and African governments were the transformation of donors' agendas and the wave of bilateral aid fatigue in the north. These two brought change in the organizational aspects of the sector and its activities, and even a rise in the number of actors.

The governments have been unhappy with the presence of voluntary and nonprofit organizations because they realized that donor funds were being channelled away from them due to inefficiency and corruption. The governments were unhappy about the third sector being "the darling" of donors and about the strong grassroots links that NGOs had forged with local communities.

175

The governments' claim that they were the only institutions that initiated development activities was being proved false. NGOs also targeted the marginalized poor and the needs that governments were either unable to give priority to or did not have funds for.

Many governments became wary and alarmed at the increasing autonomy and number of NGOs, and thus took measures to control them by imposing strict registration demands. Thus relations soured. In South Africa, NGOS had to register as voluntary organizations because they were viewed suspiciously, especially those aiding the oppressed black communities.

The political turmoil in Africa has not spared the voluntary sector. The central governments in crisis-prone areas have banned the operations of groups in areas they think are hostile to them or those with different religious or ideological orientations or working with ethnic groupings viewed suspiciously by central governments. Outright civil wars have made operations difficult or impossible.

The NGOs have also been wary of the governments. Some believe the very term NGO is negative and inadequate. Voluntary organizations would like to define themselves without reference to the governments.

These many suspicions have led some governments to attempt to put NGOs under the state machinery, or to require that all development assistance be channelled through government machinery. Sometimes outright coercion and threats of deregistration have been used against NGOs and the voluntary sector.

These elements of misunderstanding and distrust have had a deadening effect on the activities and programs of the voluntary sector. Energies that would otherwise have been expended on forward-looking programs have instead been diverted to overcoming misunderstandings. As a survival mechanism, the voluntary sector has at times opted for "safer" projects and programs, which might not be most pertinent to communities' pressing needs.

The control of the third sector by governments and co-optation of some voluntary and nonprofit-making organizations seems to have a negative effect not only on the sector itself, but also on the entire development process.

The third major area of interaction for NGOs is the philanthropic and foundation community. The origins of local foundations vary and depend on the initiator, as in other parts of the world. Most foundations therefore derive from legacies of individuals who leave sums of money for a particular cause. The region includes foundations for law, health, research medicine, education, wildlife, and sports.

In Southern Africa, for example, the earliest foundations were set up by people who participated in colonization. Notably, there is the Rhodes Trust and the Beit Trust, named after Cecil Rhodes and Alfred Beit respectively. These were set up from the estate of the two colonialists to promote education. Even today a number of schools in the subregion have Beit Halls that were built from money in these trusts. And South Africa has a Rhodes University.

Influence from Europe and America has helped create and increase corporate philanthropy in the region. As early as 1900, colonialists set up corporations mainly for mining and agriculture. The most prominent were Lonrho and Anglo-American. Brewers, tobacco, and soft drink companies, for example, are well known for sponsoring sporting activities as a way of advertising. Smaller companies have followed suit since this is a good way of boosting their public image. As the native people pressed for better working conditions through unions and nationalist movements, corporations put up departments of social welfare to partly meet their needs.

Charity organizations also made appeals to companies for donations. Some governments made charitable donations tax-deductible as an incentive for corporations to subsidize the government's welfare budget. This has influenced the nature of corporate philanthropy. Another form of corporate philanthropy is that given in kind as opposed to cash. Most companies donate their products to the needy. This is mainly directed to charity institutions. Since the motive of corporate philanthropy is publicity and a good image with the customers, almost all established private companies give some form of donations to a public cause.

Many foundations give scholarships for education and study in specified disciplines. Newer ones support specific areas of development such as community development, education of youth, cooperatives, environment and development, and legal education. Corporate philanthropy tends to focus on donations to sports and other high-profile causes, such as famine due to drought.

The role and contribution of northern philanthropic foundations in the region is typified by the Rockefeller and Ford Foundations.

The Rockefeller Foundation is one of the most conspicuous philanthropic organizations that has participated significantly in Africa. In pursuit of its broad objectives, the foundation addresses itself to such areas of concern as agricultural science and research, health science, global environment, development of arts and humanities in the academic world, the search of equality and equal opportunity, and international security.

Its main objective therefore has been to identify and address the sources and underlying causes of human suffering. To achieve these, the foundation gives grants and fellowships to researchers to conduct research and assist institutions whose programs are in line with the objectives of the foundation. In 1992, the grants appropriations, programming-related investments, and fellowships totalled $103,283,497. The foundation contributed in that year to research in its various areas of concern in West Africa, including Nigeria and Ghana.

The foundation collaborates with other international and national organizations on common concerns in Africa, such as:

- Networking with African Leadership Foundation, New York—this received $25,000 in support of the Obasanjo-Deny Peace initiative in Sudan.
- Committee for South African Development—this received $368,000 to support work in exploring ways the international community can promote the economic, educational, and social opportunities required in a post-apartheid South Africa.
- Donor to Africa Education—this group works on female participation in Africa; Rockefeller is one of the multi- and bilateral funding agencies that support this work.
- African Forum for Children's Literacy in Science—this forum also receives grants from Rockefeller.

The Ford Foundation is a private, nonprofit organization established in 1936 by Henry Ford, the American industrialist, and his son Edsel. To date it has made commitments totally $7 billion to more than 9,000 institutions and 1 million individuals in the United States, Asia, Africa, the Middle East, and Latin America.

Among the foundation's objectives that relate to Africa are the alleviation of rural poverty and the improved management of land and water resources that sustain agriculture. The focus here is on increasing small farmer productivity, promoting agroforestry, expanding non-farm income and employment opportunities, assessing the potential of small-scale immigration, and analyzing agricultural policy. In its support of the alleviation of urban poverty, the foundation helps local communities to provide basic services where public institutions have been unable to, and to develop low-cost mechanisms for housing construction.

The foundation's target groups include women, because they play a central role in African agriculture; the urban and rural poor; the underprivileged in society; and government and nongovernmental institutions for research, training, experimentation, and development efforts that show promise of producing significant advances in the fields of its program interests.

The philanthropic and foundation sector as a whole is private. It does not interact or network with one another. People relate to the sector by seeking donations. Even government institutions may seek donations. Because of the motives of the sector, media coverage is very important. Substantial donations are featured on local television with big publicity and checks displayed on a billboard.

The sector is usually nonpolitical, but if they need to seek favors from government, they will use the donations as a stepping stone. This is usually the source of corruption. Multinational corporations may decide to give donations to various countries where they are operating. Corporate bodies may decide to support groups by underwriting a specific campaign, such as environment. New foundations interact more with the NGO sector.

South Africa is a good subregional example of the contribution of corporate and private institutions. Corporate social investment is as diverse as the corporations themselves. Local and foreign, large and small, and direct company donations (with a few exceptions) were all jolted from their present mode of operations by the 1976 student uprising. It is estimated that there were more than 500 active corporate social investment programs, with a total volume of 840 million rand (equivalent to about $233 million) in 1991. Recently, 14 leading South African companies formed a private-sector initiative that would fund the newly created Joint Education Trust to finance vocational training. The 1980s also witnessed the creation of at least 20 independent grantmaking trusts by mostly U.S. corporations such as Union Carbide, Mobil, and Rank Xerox, most of which were run as an element in the disinvestment from South Africa.

Looking to the Future

As noted throughout this chapter, African traditional society thrived on an acute awareness of corporate existence and a strong sense of sharing a common destiny among people who lived in the same community. The contemporary voluntary citizens' associations emerged from the traditional recognition of the need to lean on and help one another in order to survive.

The need now is to foster mutual understanding between African governments and the voluntary sector, and also between the donors in the north and the voluntary sector in the south. Development and sustenance of a philanthropic culture is also important, with emphasis on the value of giving and not the quantity given. Participation by all, including the government, NGOs, and so on, should be encouraged for the devleopment of the sector.

African governments should involve the voluntary sector in policy formulation, and northern NGOs should avoid patronizing attitudes. Northern groups should also be aware of the priorities of the African region, which may not necessarily be the same as their priorities. These changes will improve the environment in which the sector can undertake its activities.

Outside factors that affect the sector must also be addressed. For instance, these groups have been severely affected by civil strife. The need for peace initiatives, with the voluntary sector being a major player, ought to be pursued so as to improve the working environment of the sector.

The dependence on northern donors for funds must be assessed for the long-term development and sustainability of the sector. In the light of increasing poverty, comprehensive economic initiatives are needed that would lead to more autonomy of the sector. These will enable Africa to carry out programs considered high priority, such as displacement of people due to civil strife and famine, and so on.

Although the voluntary sector has been preoccupied with the alleviation of poverty and economic development, its contribution to the democratization process can not be minimized. The sector has given support at grassroots as well as at national levels. At the grassroots level especially, the inevitable education of the people about their rights and about what to expect as meaningful democracy has been done by this sector.

As this history reveals at individual as well as at the communal level, the sector has always stood on great determination and commitment. It is hoped that this cornerstone will surmount the problems that seem to be a natural accompaniment of altruistic endeavors and will continue propelling the voluntary and nonprofit sector on the road to the creation of a civil society in Africa.

Bibliography

AAPAM. "Mobilising the Informal Sector and Non-Governmental Organisations for Recovery and Development: Policy and Management Issues." Presented in Abuja, Nigeria, 1990.

AACC Refugees and Emergency Services Report 1992-1993.

Adams, Michael. *Voluntary Service Overseas: The First Ten Years*. London: Faber & Faber, 1968.

African Association For Literacy and Adult Education. "The Spider," Information Newsletter, October 1992.

All African Conference of Churches. *Research and Development Consultancy Services 1990 & 1991.*

All African Conference of Churches. "Emerging Power of Civil Society: Report of workshop on approaches and skills in advocacy for development" (mimeographed).

ANEN. "African NGOs Environmental Network: An Institutional Approach." Nairobi, 1985.

ANGOC and ELCI (1989): *People's Participation and Environmentally Sustainable Development*. Manila: Asian NGO Coalition for Agrarian Reform and Rural Development, 1989.

Antrobus, Peggy, "Funding For NGOs: Issues and Options," *World Development*. Vol. 15, 1987.

Askwirth, Thomas G. *Progress Through Self-Help; Principles and Practice in Community Development*. Nairobi: Eagles Press, 1960. .

Baldwin, George B., "Non-Governmental Organizations and African Development," An Inquiry in *World Bank: The Long Term Perspective Study of Sub-Saharan Africa*. Background Papers Vol. 111, Washington, 1990.

Barkan, J.D., D. Gachuki et al. "Is Small Beautiful? The Organizational Conditions For Effective Small-Scale, Self-Help Development Projects in Rural Kenya," Working Paper No. 364, IDS, University of Nairobi, 1980.

Barkan, Joel D. and Frank Holmguist, "Peasant State Relations and Social Base of Self-help in Kenya," *World Politics*, Vol. 41, 1989.

Bedard, Guy et al. "The Importance of Savings for Fighting Against Poverty by Self-Help." German Foundation for International Development. Berlin, 1987.

Botswana Technology Centre. "Small Scale Management of Beef Biltong in Botswana," *Appropriate Technology*, April 1987.

Boyer, David. "The role of Northern NGOs in the promotion of sustainable development in Africa." Msc. Thesis in Faculty of Sciences, University of Edinburgh, CAS, 1990.

Bratton, Micheal. "The Politics of Government-NGO Relations in Africa." Working paper No. 456, IDS, University of Nairobi. 1987.

Brett E.A. "Voluntary organisation as development agencies. The benefits and costs of cooperation in service delivery system." IDS Sussex, 1990.

Brodhead, Tim. "NGOs: In One Year: Out the Other," *World Development*, Supplement Vol. 15, 1987.

Brodhead, Tim and B. Herbert Copley, *Bridges of Hope? Canadian Voluntary Agencies and Third World*. Ottawa: North-South Institute, 1988.

Brown, L. David. "Bridging Organizations and Sustainable Development," Working Paper No. 8. Boston: Institute for Development Research and Boston School of Management, 1990.

Cain, A. "Development Workshop on Building and Planning in the Third World." Presented at a workshop in Luanda, Angola, 1986.

Canadian Council for International Co-operation. "Mind if I cut in?" Report of the CCIC Task Force on CIDA-NGO Funding Relationships.

CDTF. "Multi-Donor Basket Funding as an Alternative Funding Policy." Presented at the Conference held in Dar-es-Salaam, Tanzania, April 1-4, 1992.

Chepkwony, Agnes. "The role of Non-Governmental in Development: A study of National Christian Council of Churches of Kenya, 1963-1978." Ph.D. Thesis, University of Uppsala, 1987.

Clark, John. *Democratising Development: The Role of Voluntary Organisations*. London: Earthscan, 1991.

CREA. "The Experience of NGOs in African Countries after Structural Adjustment Programmes in Ghana" (mimeographed). September 1992.

Department of Sociology, University of Nairobi, and International Development Studies, Roskilde University Center, Denmark. "Towards Integrated Development in Kitui—A Socio-economic Situational Analysis of Selected Sub-locations in Kitui Districts," Kenya, Vol. Two. 1992.

Development Dialogue. "The record of change in Southern Africa." July/August 1993.

Devereux, S. et al. *Credit and Savings for Development*. London: OXFAM, 1989.

Dijik, Van Miene Pieler. "Collaboration Between Governments and NGOs." *Development: Seeds of Change*. No. 4, 1987.

Drabek, A Gordon, ed. "Development Alternatives: The Challenges for NGOs—An Overview of Issues." *World Development*, Vol. 15, 1987.

ELCSA News. "Church and Liberation," report on the consultation held in Bulawayo, Zimbabwe, November 10-13, 1987.

Else J.F. "A Training Handbook for conducting feasibility studies" (planning income generating projects).

Environment Liaison Centre. *Directory of NGOs Working on Renewable Energy and Fuelwood Projects in Africa*. Nairobi: 1982.

FAO. "Attacking Rural Poverty." The FAO/ Netherlands cooperative programme.

Food and Agricultural Organization and Freedom From Hunger Campaign (1987): "NGOs in Latin America: Their contributions to Participatory Democracy" in Development, Seeds of Change, 1987.4

Ford Foundation. *Newsletter*. November 1989.

Fowler, Alan. "The Role of NGOs in Changing State-Society Relations: Perspectives from Eastern and Southern Africa." *Development Policy Review*. Vol. 9, No. 1, 1991.

Fowler, Alan. "New Scrambles for Africa: NGOs and their Donors in Kenya." Africa Rural and Urban Development 1//1 Michigan, 1990.

Fowler, Alan. "NGOS in Africa: Achieving Comparative Advantages in Relief and Micro-development." Discussion Paper No. 249, IDS Sussex, 1988.

Fowler, Alan F. "NGOS in Africa: Naming Them By What They Are," Occasional paper No. 50, IDS, University of Nairobi, 1985.

Gathaka, Kamau and Kabiru Kinyanjui. "In Search of People-Oriented— Alternatives to the Debt Crises. The Role of Grassroots Movements in Africa." Presented in a conference on Alternative Development Strategies for Africa, Institute of Development Studies, University of Dar-es-salaam, December 12-14, 1989.

Global Coalition for Africa. "Governance and Democracy in Sub-Saharan Africa." Paper presented at the First Advisory Committee Meeting, September 9-10, 1991.

Hay, Jean and Sharon Stitcher. *African Women: South of the Sahara*. Longman, 1984.

Heussen, Hejo et al. "Promotion of Self-help by Savings Banks." Economic and Social Development Centre; Bonn, 1987.

Hivos. "Rural Transformation, Social Movements and Non-Governmental Organisations." Report on workshop held in Kadoma, Zimbabwe, November 8-10, 1989.

Hulme, David. "Social Development." *Development: Seeds of Change*, No. 4, 1987.

Hyden, Goren. *No Shortcuts to Progress: African Development Management in Perspective*. London: Heinemann, 1983.

ICSW. "Strengthening Project Africa." June 1987.

ICVA, "Guidelines for Improving the Quality of Projects in The World Funded by NGOs." A Standing Policy Document. Geneva: 1984.

ICVA. "NGO Management Development and Training: Recent Experience and Future Priorities." Presented on Seminar in Geneva, February 25-28, 1986.

ICVA. "Consultation on uprooted peoples in Southern Africa."

IDS, University of Nairobi, and KNCS, A Preliminary Workshop Report on "Facing the Nineties: NGOs Participation in National Development." Nairobi, 1989.

IIED. "NGO Training for Institutional Development: Using Existing Resources More Effectively." A proposal by the Southern Networks Programme for funding to support the pilot phase of an NGO training initiative in Africa.

ILO. *Towards Action Against Child Labour in Zimbabwe*. Geneva: 1992.

IRED ASIA. "Foreign Development Agencies in Sri Lanka: A political Historical Perspective." Occasional Paper.

IRED/ESA. "The Role of Women's Organisations in Social Upliftment." Presented at a Seminar organised by IRED and the Mauritius Council of Women, Mauritius, April 13-14, 1989.

IRED/ESA. "Alternative Financing for Development Projects." Presented at the IRED/CUSA workshop in Lusaka, Zambia, April 26, 1986.

IRED/ESA. "Report on Access to Credit." Presented at Regional Seminar in Dar-es-Salaam, Tanzania, March 26-31, 1990.

IRED/ESA. "NGO Relations with SADC." Ppresented at the NGO-SADC Conference, Harare, Zimbabwe, January 25-30, 1993.

IRED/ESA. "Cooperative Partners Consultation Meeting Report." September 19, 1990.

IRED/ESA. "Resources for Women in Zimbabwe a Directory." Harare, September 1992.

Kajese, Kingston. "An Agenda of Future Tasks for International and Indigenous NGOs: Views From the South." *World Development*. Vol. 15, 1987.

Kanyinga, Karuti. "The Social-Political Context of Non-Governmental Organizations (NGOs) in Kenya." Political and Social Context of Structural Adjustment in Sub-Saharan Africa, Harare, Zimbabwe, March 3-6, 1991.

Kanyinga, Karuti. "Non-Governmental Organisations in Kenya: NGO-State Relations in a Changing Society." Presented in Festival Images of Africa, Copenhagen, Denmark, June 12-July 3, 1993.

Kanyinga, Karuti. "The Social Political Context of the Growth of Non-Governmental Organisations in Kenya." Uppsala, SAS, 1983.

Kanyinga, Karuti. "The Role of Non-Governmental Organisations (NGOs) in Creating Local Capacity of Development." MA Thesis, Department of Government, University of Nairobi, 1990.

Kanyinga, Karuti. "The Role of Non-Governmental Organization (NGOs) In Creating Local Capacity for Development: The Case of Meru District, Kenya: Research Notes," Presented at Workshop on Into the Nineties: Non-Governmental Organization During the Current Development Plan and Beyond, Nairobi, August 14-16, 1989.

Khatibu, M. "Report on Biogas for water pumping in Botswana." Rural Industries Promotion of Botswana. October 1983.

Kigozi, David. "A Popular View of Education for All." AALAE, Nairobi, 1992.

Kinyanjui, Kabiru, ed. "Non-Governmental Organizations Contribution to Development." Occassional Paper No. 50, IDS, Unversity of Nairobi, 1985.

Kinyanjui, Kabiru, "The African NGOS in context." Prepared for Presentation at NGOMEA WORKSHOP on The African NGO phenomenon: A Reflection for Action, Gaborone, Botswana, May 15-19, 1989.

Kisare, M. "A guide to rethinking African Churches involved in Development." 1990.

Kjelberg, E. and P. Mbithi. "The Role of Voluntary Agencies Operating Youth Programmes in Kenya." Working Paper No. 64, IDS, University of Nairobi, 1972.

KNCSS. "Directory of Voluntary Organisations in Kenya." Nairobi, 1978.

KNCSS, "Directory of (Non-Governmental) Voluntary Organisations in Kenya," Nairobi, 1988.

Kobia, Samuel. "New and Old NGOs: Approaches to Development." In Kabiru Kinyanjui, ed., *NGOs Contributions to Development*, Occassional Paper No., 40.50, Institute for Development Studies, University of Nairobi, 1985.

Konrad-Adenauer-Stiftung. "Economic symposium: Regional economic integration and national development." May 5-8, 1991.

Kooy. R.J.W. "Development in Southern Africa: An Assessment and Directory." *Prodder's Annual 1989-90: (Proda) Programme for Development Research.* 1991.

Korten, David and Rudi Klauss, "People-Centred Development; Contributions Towards Theory and Planning Framework," Connecticut: Kumarian Press, 1984.

Limuru Conference Centre. "Report of the workshop on promotion of NGOs participating development approaches and integration of their programme into national development efforts." March 11-12, 1987.

Lopezilera, Lus, "Social Co-operation and Alternative Autonomous Organisations: Grassroots Movements and Strategy Outlines." *Development: Seeds of Change.* No. 4, 1987.

M'Mwereria. "Promoting Grassroots Human and Development Rights In Africa." Southern Networks for Development (SONED) Africa Region, Nairobi, 1991.

Masoni, Vitorrio. "Non-Governmental Organisations and Development." *Finance and Development.* Vol. 22, No. 3, 1985.

Matla K. "Grassroots Cooperative Leaders," Workshop held in Maseru, Lesotho, December 15-19, 1986.

Matla K. "Post Exchange Programme Report Between Lesotho Handicrafts and Industrial Cooperatives Union Limited and Botswana Cooperative Movement," held July 2-7, 1990.

Mauritius Council of Social Services. "Directory of Organisations in Mauritius." 1993.

Mavimbela T. "South Africa challenges and issues in the transition to democracy." Presented in Bulawayo, Zimbabwe, August 29-September 2, 1991.

Mazingira Institute, "Directory of Women's Organizations in Kenya," Nairobi: 1984.

Mazingira Institute. "Women and Development." A Kenya Guide, Nairobi: 1992.

Mbithi, P. and R. Rasmusson. "Self-Reliance in Kenya: The Case of Harambee." Uppsala, Sweden: Scandinavian Institute of African Studies, 1977.

Micou, A.M. "Project Funding by Foreign Embassies within South Africa." South Africa Information Exchange Working Paper No 13. June 1990.

Minear, Larry. "NGOs Today: Practitioners of Development Strategies and Advocates for the Poem." *Development: Seeds of Change*, No. 4, 1987.

Minear, Larry. "The Roles of Non-Governmental Organizations in Development," in E. Clay and J. Shaw, eds. *Poverty, Development and Food.* London: MacMillan, 1987.

Mirii, Ngugi, ed. "Community Based Theatre Skills." Report of Bulawayo Workshop Organised by ZIMFEP, July 19-20, 1986.

Monstead, Mette. "Women's Groups in Rural Kenya and Their Role in Development." CDR Paper A. 78.2 Centre for Development Research, Copenhagen, 1978.

Morris, C.R. *Overseas Volunteer Programmes: The Evolution and Role of Governments in Their Support.* Massachusets: Heath and Company.

Muchira, Simon. "The Role of NGOs as a Tool for Change." *Development: Seeds of Change*, No. 4, 1987.

Mukasa, B. "The Role of NGO's and the Challenges They Face in the Development Process: Non-Governmental Perspective." Presented by Ranche House College, May 27, 1986.

Mupawaenda. A. "Report on UN-NGO Workshop on Debt, Adjustment and the Needs of the Poor." Presented at workshop, Oxford, UK, September, 19-22, 1987.

Mutere, Gilian. "Energy and Environment Agencies." A Directory For Sub-Sahara Africa. Regional Wood Energy programme For Africa, Nairobi.

Mutiso, Cyrus. "Research Agenda: NGOs Contribution to Development." in K. Kinyanjui, ed., *Non-Governmental Organisations Contributions to Developments*, Occasional Paper No. 50, Institute for Development Studies, University of Nairobi, 1985.

NANGO. *Directory of Non-Governmental Organisations in Zimbabwe.* Harare: 1992.

Ng'ethe, Njuguna J. "Harambee and Development Participation in Kenya: The Politics of Peasants and Elites Interaction with Particular Reference to Harambee Projects in Kiambu District." PhD Thesis, Carleton University, Ottawa, Ontario, 1979.

Ng'ethe, Njuguna. "In search of NGOs: Towards funding strategy to create NGO research capacity in Eastern and Southern Africa." IDS Occasional Paper No. 58, 1989.

Ng'ethe, Njuguna and Karuti Kanyinga. "The politics of development space. The State and NGO in delivery of basic services in Kenya." Working Paper No. 486, IDS, University of Nairobi, 1992.

Ng'ethe, Mitullah and Ngunyi. "NGOs local capacity building and community mobilisation." Working Paper No. 469, 1990.

Ng'ethe, Njuguna, W. Mitullah, and M. Ngunyi. "Government NGO Relationship in the Context of Alternative Development Strategies in Kenya," in *Critical Choices For the NGO Community: African Development in the 1990s.* Center of African studies, University of Edinburgh, 1990.

Ngoma Ya Mano. *AALAE Newsletter.* April 1993.

NGO Network. "The NGO Network report of proceedings -the sixth National Workshop - Silver Spring Hotel, Nairobi, 2nd July, 1992." IDS University of Nairobi, 1992.

NORAD. "A Directory of Non-Governmental Organisations in Botswana." 1989-93 and 1985.

Organisation for Economic Co-operation and Development. "Voluntary AID for development. The role of NGOs." 1988.

Oxfam. "Final statement of the UN/NGO workshop on Debt Adjustment and the needs of the poor." September 19-22, 1987.

Pradvervand, Pierre. *Listening to Africa*. New York: Praeger, 1990.

Queshi, M.A. "From Cold War to Cooperation: Dynamic of a New World Order." Presented at the 1991 International Development Conference, January 24, 1991.

RAFAD. "Access to Credit for Small Businesses." Workshop held in Nairobi, December 2-6, 1991.

RAFAD. "Narrative Report on Access to Credit." Presented by RAFAD Kadoma, Zimbabawe, October 16-20, 1989.

Ranche House College. "Development Technologies for Zimbabwe for the 1990s." Presented in Harare, November 12-16, 1990.

Ranche House College. "Linking for Development." National Seminar Series held in Bulawayo, Zimbabwe, March 23-26, 1993.

Ranche House College. "Towards a Better Tomorrow." National Seminar Series held in Harare, Zimbabwe, April 27-30, 1992.

Ranche House College. "Needs Assessment Workshop for Zimbabwe NGOs." Report, March 1985.

Ranche House College. "Urban Informal Sector Workshop Series." Report of Workshop held in Harare, Zimbabwe, August-September 1991.

RAP et al. "African NGOs Strategic Reflection." Background Document presented at workshop, August 29-September 2, 1991.

Research and Advocacy Agenda for African NGOs in Eastern and Southern Africa. The PVO/NGO initiatives project. Background papers for the PIP-funded Mwengo Seminar, September 1992.

Reverend, Chipenda. J.B. "All Africa Conference of Churches." Paper on the 6th General Assembly held in Harare, Zimbabwe, October 25-29, 1992.

SADCC. "Support to Women Entrepreneurs." Presented on Seminar held in Harare, Zimbabwe, October 9-13, 1989.

Shwari. "Newsletter for AALAE Peace Education, Peoples' and Human Rights Programme." March 1993.

Situma, F.D. "Some Legal Aspects of the Harambee Institution in Kenya." A Dissertation submitted in partial fulfilment of the requirements for the Bachelor of Laws (LL.B.) Degree of the University of Nairobi. 1987.

Somabhulani, C., et al. "ORAP Model in Building Coalitions to Strengthen Civil Society's Contribution to Development." Presented at the Coalition's Workshop, Bulawayo, Zimbabwe, April 26-30, 1993.

South-North Development Initiative. "A new resource for emerging foundations in the South." October 1992.

South-North Development Initiative. "New models of financial and organisational support for community development." Presented at the Coalition's Workshop, Bulawayo, Zimbabwe, April 26-30, 1993.

South-South NGOs Co-operation Conference March 1987. In A. Gordon Drabeck.

Streeten, Paul. "The Contribution of Non-governmental Organizations to Development." *Development: Seeds of Changes.* No. 4, 1987.

Stremlan, Carolyn. "NGO Co-ordinating Bodies in Africa, Asia, and Latin America," *World Development*, Vol. 15, 1987.

Thomas, Barbara, P. "Development through Harambee; Who wins and who lose, Rural Self-help Projects in Kenya." *World Development.* Vol. 15, No. 4, 1987.

Tototo Home Industry. "Partnerships in Development." Presented at the International workshop held in Mombasa, July 25-29, 1988.

UNESCO. "African Development Sourcebook." Paris: 1991.

United Nations Economic Commission for Africa et al.: "Information Kit for Machineries on the Integration of Women in Development in Africa." Addis Ababa.

United Nations Non-Governmental Liaison Service. "United Nations System and Sub-Saharan Africa. Profiles of United Nations System Agencies, Funds, Programmes and Services and Their Work for the Development of Sub-Saharan Africa." UNCTAD/NGLS/16. Geneva. 1989.

UNICEF. *Annual Report 1984.*

United Nations Food and Agriculture Organization. "Fighting Rural Poverty. FAO's action programme for agrarian reform and rural development." Rome: 1983.

USAID. "Constraints/challenges facing PVOs in Kenya. A report of a survey of PVOs resource persons." 1992.

Vincent, F. "A new concept for financing development to increase the Autonomy of People's Organisations and Non-Governmental Organisations (PO/NGO)" capital funds.

Voice. "Consultancy in Organisation Development." Paper on Team Building workshop, Harare. Zimbabwe, October 16-28, 1988.

Vukasin, L. H. "We carry a heavy load rural women in Zimbabwe speak out," Part 2 of "Ten Years Later 1981-1991" for Zimbabwe Women's Bureau, 1992.

Wangoola, Paul. "Proceedings of a Round-table on Strategic Issues in Development Management." Learning from Successful Experiences. Livingstone, Zambia, May 9-13, 1988.

Wangoola, Paul. "Promoting Indigenous NGOs As Instruments of Popular participation." UN Economic Commission for Africa. International Conference on Popular Participation in the Recovery and Development Process in Africa, Arusha, Tanzania, 1990.

Wangoola, Paul. On "The African Crisis: People's popular Participation and the 'Recovery' and Development". AALAE, Nairobi. 1991.

WILDAF. "Women, Law and Development Africa Program." Harare, Zimbabwe, April 1-3, 1993.

Wipper, Andrey. "The Maendeleo Ya Wanawake Movement in the Colonial Period: The Canadian Connection; Mau Mau; Embroidery and Agriculture" *Rural Africana*. Vol. 29: 195-214, 1975-76.

Working in Groups Co-op Education Series. "The co-op guide to Poultry Management." Harare: Training Aids Development Group, 1990.

6

EUROPE'S EMERGING THIRD SECTOR: EAST AND WEST

Because of the different patterns of development of the nonprofit sectors in East-Central Europe and Western Europe, this chapter was formulated through the preparation of separate preliminary sub-regional reports. The first half of the chapter, written by Ewa Les , will describe nonprofit organizations in East-Central Europe. The second half of the chapter, describing the complexity of the sector in Western Europe, was prepared by Alain Anciaux, Amaury Nardone, Dirk Jarré, and Sylvie Tsyboula.

THE VOLUNTARY SECTOR IN POST-COMMUNIST EAST CENTRAL EUROPE:

FROM SMALL CIRCLES OF FREEDOM TO CIVIL SOCIETY

Ewa Les

Although Eastern and Central Europe has been clarified from a geographical viewpoint, in political and cultural terms it is not yet clearly defined. Consequently, there is no common agreement about which countries belong to this region and which do not. While the Czech and Slovak Republics, Hungary, and Poland are generally recognized as Central and Eastern European states, Belarus, Moldova, Russia, and Ukraine are less frequently identified with the region.

This chapter presents the current situation and prospects of the voluntary sector in 11 countries in the region:

- Bulgaria (with 9 million people),
- Croatia (4.7 million),
- Czech Republic (10.4 million),
- Estonia (1.6 million),
- Hungary (10.2 million),
- Lithuania (3.7 million),
- Poland (38.4 million),
- Romania (22.7 million),
- Russia (148.4 million),
- Slovak Republic (5.2 million), and
- Slovenia (1.9 million).

The transition of 1989-90 allowed the re-emergence of an entire spectrum of voluntary organizations, groupings, and movements in the public life of East European societies. The voluntary sector varies significantly from country to country in terms of its scope, institutional types, and mission. After almost a half-century of "forced unity," the countries of Central and Eastern Europe are in the process of a "return to diversity."

Thus, the monolithic approach to the voluntary sector in the former Soviet bloc countries is being replaced by a multidimensional one that accommodates regional differences in development, traditions, local circumstances, and the current state of systemic transformation.

From Croatia, where the civil war is under way and where voluntary organizations are mainly involved in humanitarian relief, through Slovenia and the Baltic Republics, where the sector is in the process of being set up, to Bulgaria, Hungary, the Czech and Slovak Republics, Poland, and Romania, where voluntary organizations have attained certain legal and fiscal status, the voluntary sector is experiencing dynamic growth. Despite all the political, economic, and social differences, all voluntary organizations in the region are in the process of transition from state socialism to pluralism, seeking a place in the new institutional order. They have several characteristics and problems in common and often face similar challenges.

Most of the countries in question are heterogenous in their ethnic and religious composition. In Bulgaria, for instance, about 1 million of the 9 million inhabitants are Turks; Romanies account for some 700,000, and another 400,000 are Muslims. In addition to the prevailing Bulgarian denomination—

the Eastern Orthodox Church—the second largest religion is Islam, with the Roman Catholic and Protestant churches following.

The countries of East Central Europe vary considerably in their movement toward pluralistic, free-market democracies. According to Zbigniew Brzezinski, the former U.S. National Security Advisor, it will take at least 10 years for Central European countries to become pluralistic, free-market democracies while some, such as Russia, Ukraine, and Belarus, may not come anywhere near western standards in the foreseeable future. Reginald Dale, writing in the *International Herald Tribune*, notes that "As of now, politically and economically successful liberal democracy is not a foreordained outcome, except perhaps for five countries (Poland, the Czech Republic, Hungary, Slovenia and Estonia) out of the 27 post-Communist states."

Under the most optimistic scenarios, it is estimated that closing the gap between Central Europe and the West in gross national product per capita will take 20 years for the Czechs and 30 years for other Central Europeans. Other socioeconomic indicators such as low average salary, a high percentage of the population below a minimum standard of living, high unemployment, and high inflation rate situate most of the East European countries behind western levels of social development.

In Poland, for example, the inflation rate is only two digits yearly, but the high unemployment rate of 15 percent gives it the leading position in Eastern Europe, and third place in Europe (after Ireland and Spain) for this economic indicator. According to the Institute of Comparative Economic studies in Vienna, in 1994 the unemployment rate will stabilize in Hungary at 12-13 pecent while it will reach up to 20 percent in Croatia; 18 percent in Poland, the Slovak Republic, Slovenia, and Bulgaria; 7 percent in the Czech Republic; and 12 percent in Romania.

In Belarus, the monthly inflation rate is about 50 percent; in Lithuania, it is about 80 percent. In Russia, the 1993 year-end inflation rate was expected to be around 900 percent, while the unemployment rate in November 1993 edged up to just over 1 percent of the work force. According to the Russian Federal Labor Service, however, in reality the number of jobless was much higher—probably closer to 5 million rather than the 728,400 officially reported.

Thus, the "by-products" of the transition period in post-communist states of Eastern Europe such as unemployment, poverty, increasing violence, and a rapidly growing crime rate have contributed greatly to turning a good part of the initial enthusiasm and hope associated with the overthrow of the communist regime into disappointment, apathy, and political fatigue.

Such a social climate has been additionally fueled by a growing political distrust of the new elites in most post-communist states. It is commonly perceived that they have failed to keep their promise of economic reform and, instead, have allowed the communist nomenclature to transform national ownership into their own private businesses. In addition, a modernized system of social welfare has not been put into place, leaving many East Europeans grappling individually with the problems of increasing poverty.

According to a recent Hungarian survey, the number of those in favor of a market economy dropped 10 percent between 1991 and 1993. Although some 75 percent questioned agreed that privatization of the national economy is the main method of transforming the socialist economy into a market one, most of the respondents (46 percent) favored some kind of a "mixture between market economy and socialist economy."

A growing part of the populace does not share the optimism of some prominent economists and politicians of Eastern Europe who predicted economic growth after "transformational depression." More frequently they vote in favor of post-communist parties, as happened in recent parliamentarian elections in Bulgaria, Lithuania, and Poland; this is also likely to happen in forthcoming elections in other countries. A critical issue facing the region is the possible impact of this political reconfiguration on the position and prospects of its voluntary sector.

Jadwiga Staniszkis, a Polish analyst, maintains that "talking about the come back of communism is a mistake. It is rather a return to a certain scenario of overcoming communism." This scenario makes room for different interest groups, including voluntary associations, which together with Chambers of Commerce and other economic and insurance organizations can stimulate the birth of a neo-corporate order. Other Polish analysts, however, are less optimistic, seeing the newly emerging political status quo closer in the style of the South American model, where the economic and political power would be in the hands of a newly emerging capital oligarchy.

In post-communist Poland of 1994, the locus of political and economic power is being reconfigured and a new political way of life is being built based on an emerging "entente" between post-communists and the former opposition. Despite official statements underlining the importance of state welfare obligations and citizens' rights, it is quite likely that this newly developing corporate state may use the voluntary sector as a "shunting yard" for social problems, allowing itself to be rid of the problems while claiming that the issues are being addressed by voluntary organizations.

A Brief History of the Voluntary Sector

Despite common opinion, the voluntary sector in Central and Eastern Europe is not a product of the breakthroughs of 1989. Foundations and associations have a long history in the region.

In Poland and Hungary, the history of foundations and associations dates back to the thirteenth century, when both religious and nonreligious organizations were established. Their role was of utmost importance for Poland when its sovereignty was lost in 1772 for almost 150 years. During this period, foundations and associations (both officially registered and operating in conspiracy) took over the roles of nonexistent Polish public institutions, bolstering the national spirit and preserving Polish culture.

Prior to World War II, voluntary organizations played an important role in the First Czech Republic, Hungary, Poland, and Romania, although the sector's size and fields of activity varied significantly by country.

In Poland, prewar voluntary organizations complemented the government by playing a predominantly service delivery role in social assistance, education, and health, while in Hungary, voluntary associations were important in culture and politics at that time, but their role of providing service was much less important.

In comparision with the period 1918-39, the communist era after World War II was unfavorable for voluntary organizations in Central and Eastern Europe: their activities were under strict political and administrative control, particularly where the communist state claimed for itself the mission of creating reality and where the legal framework limited groups to only one allowable type of association. Consequently, the number of voluntary organizations drastically decreased after the early 1950s.

In the communist period, voluntary organizations existed mainly as quasi-independent agencies and were deprived of their greatest strength of defining and meeting public needs independently from government. Thus this period was marked by a lack of political and legal opportunities for truly independent civic initiatives. According to Russian economist Lev I. Jakobson, "the regime was incomparably more tolerant of the shadow economy and the black market than of attempts to establish really independent educational, cultural, religious or other organizations."

The authoritarian character of the regime based on the ideologies of state socialism and the "vanguard party" created a climate in which the interests and demands of certain segments of society were viewed by the state as "relics of past regimes," creating obstacles to "progress" and the realization of "national interests."

The state socialism and paternalism under which social needs were defined and organizational structures established to meet them resulted in a low tolerance for pluralism. Therefore, foundations, associations, and citizen initiatives were seen by the authorities as "suspicious" and were banned in the early 1950s. Any remaining voluntary organizations were either nationalized, incorporated into a state infrastructure in whole or in part, or subjected to tight administrative control.

Despite the fact that voluntary organizations were to varying degrees not the same as state and party organizations, in real terms their autonomy was heavily tested. The interference of government in the functioning of voluntary organizations took different forms, from the imposition of articles of organization and bylaws to direct and indirect restrictions and prohibitions. Political authorities in East Central Europe, under the principle of "ideological and organizational unity," exacted tight control over staffing decisions and monopolized the distribution of financial resources. Quite often, the state administration appointed its own people (the so-called nomenclature) to key positions in an organization, a phenomenon known as "interlocking directorates."

With these governing bodies under the control of the state, various groups were prevented from articulating their needs. In addition, the communist states' monopoly in the distribution of financial resources helped channel the articulation of interests of various population groups into ideologically legitimized voluntary organizations. Thus the funding mechanism that was established prevented civic initiatives from being institutionalized outside the ruling political system.

Since the early 1950s the activities of these quasi-nongovernmental organizations (NGOs) were heavily politicized, aimed at legitimating the political system. Their primary role was a political one, with service delivery a secondary function.

This paradox enabled the communist governments to publicly proclaim citizen involvement in addressing public issues, while at the same time exerting total control over the quality and extent of that involvement. Allowable forms of public activity were strictly defined, discouraging citizens' initiative and involvement. While truly independent civic initiatives were drastically limited in Central and Eastern European societies, various quasi-NGOs and movements were allowed and even forced to exist. Called "social organizations" and "social actions," they basically promoted the objectives of the communist state and legitimated it through massive, often coerced membership

---

Voluntary Organizations During the Communist Period

Despite constitutional guarantees, the communist period of Central and Eastern Europe resulted in the systemic violation of the fundamental principles that underpin voluntary organizations—freedom of association and freedom of expression. Consequently, voluntary organizations could not be formed by voluntary acts of decision and were limited to varying degrees in their ability to decide a course of action independently of the government.

However, there were considerable differences as to the extent of the communist state interference in the functioning of voluntary organizations among the countries in question. In Romania, even quasi non-governmental professional associations were banned in 1970s, while in Hungary and Poland self-help networks and other circles of voluntary groupings were allowed to exist.

Nevertheless, as Polish sociologist Stefan Nowak has noted: "Over the whole period of 1956-1979, there were untapped reserves of genuine, participatory motivation in Polish society while, at the same time, the imposed and ostensibly named public initiatives kept spontaneous citizen initiatives from actualization." The Polish experience was shared to a high degree by other countries in the region.

---

and volunteerism. The National Front in Bulgaria, the National Front in Czechoslovakia, and The Democracy and Social Unity Front in Romania serve as examples.

Thus between 1950 and 1989, intermediary bodies were not autonomous players in public initiatives and served as "transmission belts" of communist state policies. Despite the official slogans, during nearly a half-century of state monopoly and paternalism, the centralized and formalized model of public life arbitrarily defined the scope and direction of citizen initiative, and led to the preselection of social purposes as well as the means of their implementation.

Nevertheless, the recent growth of the voluntary sector in East European societies cannot be attributed solely to the political and economic changes following the overthrow of the communist governments. The renaissance of voluntary organizations in the region is also due to the deterioration of the socialist welfare state, the crisis of real socialism, and "pressures for occupational autonomy" exerted by middle-class professionals.

The model of the socialist welfare state has been eroding in Hungary and Poland since the late 1970s. The symptoms of this erosion include reduced subsidies of goods and services, modification of state social policies, and the increasing number of organized groups addressing issues independently of state control. The communist governments were forced to reform social welfare systems and to tolerate and recognize sectarian and nonsectarian voluntary organizations in this field. In order to increase the role of the voluntary sector, the governments of Poland and Hungary re-enacted the law on foundations in 1984 and 1987, respectively.

The recent rise of the voluntary sector in Central and East European societies is also explained by the very limited scope in which the so-called social organizations articulated and realized the various needs, concerns, and rights of different population groups during the communist era.

The crisis of real socialism was another fundamental impetus for the re-emergence of the voluntary sector in these countries. Over a period of time, countries of the former Soviet bloc manifested a growing dissatisfaction with the communist system that could not keep the promise of social justice and economic plenty. Political disappointment with the commmunist regime gradually led to the creation of the "alternative," "parallel," or "second" society, which expressed itself through voluntary groupings and informal networks concerned with public and economic life in several Eastern European countries during the late 1970s and the 1980s.

A good example of this is the Polish Workers' Defense Committee (KOR) established in 1976 by a group of Polish oppositionists and intellectuals to help the workers repressed by the communist regime after the strikes and manifestations in Radom and Ursus that year. In Hungary, according to Eva Kuti, "in the 1980s many of the newly emerging non-profit organizations were substitutes for political parties."

Thus, it is no exaggeration to claim that the voluntary sector prior to 1989 constituted one of the principal mechanisms of breaking citizens' apathy and setting up "small circles of freedom." As the cradle for multiparty politics, organizations such as the Workers' Defense Committee and Solidarnosc trade union in Poland, the Fund for Poverty Relief Szeta in Hungary, Charter 77 in the former Czechoslovakia, and the Popular Front in Estonia provided the institutional and moral basis for the peaceful democratization process in the region.

The rapid growth of the voluntary sector in Central and Eastern Europe was influenced as well by the moves toward autonomy by some professions.

Memorial

Memorial was set up in Moscow in August 1992 in order to provide services to the victims of political repression in the former Soviet Union. The organization has its roots in the group Moscow Memorial. According to its records, Moscow alone has about 10,000 victims of political repression who have been either incarcerated in prison, concentration camps, or clinics for the "insane" or have been excluded from higher education and certain types of work, curtailed of civic rights, or falsely incriminated of criminal charges.

Their needs range from socioeconomic to psychological help and legal aid. According to Memorial activists, the organization started to work among the victims of the communist terror and repressions after realizing that "the structure of state social security lacks the financial and organizational capability to ensure comprehensive help for these people."

Memorial is an example of a civic organization still rare in the region. It combines the functions of social assistance, medical aid, psychological and moral support, and legal aid to the victims of political repression with educational programs aimed at "breaking down the totalitarian way of thinking in the national consciousness."

Thus, Memorial is an example of the "filling the gap" function of the voluntary sector in providing personal social services, advocacy, and consciousness-raising groups.

These groups pressed for the formation of alternative, independent, professional outlets such as centers specializing in preventive and therapeutic services for children.

The remarkable upsurge in the formation of foundations, associations, and spontaneous citizen movements after 1989 is evidence of the pent-up interest in public participation by the citizens of Eastern and Central Europe and contradicts the widespread view of the so-called dependency culture and "learned helplessness"—behaviors supposedly developed by East Europeans during the communist period. Proparticipatory motivation indeed existed in these societies, a legacy of historical tradition and the accumulated potential of social energy.

In Poland, pre-Solidarity informal networks and the Solidarity movement exemplify this social energy at the grassroots level. The pressures from below helped form the Danube Circle in Hungary, Arche in the former East Germany, and the Green Movement in Estonia—all environmental organizations protesting such issues as the siting of a hydroelectric plant on the Danube, acid rain, and phosphorite mines.

Additional sources of inspiration for the renaissance of the East European voluntary sector are rooted in religious, philosophical, cultural, and legal traditions.

In both Eastern and Western Europe, the Roman Catholic and Protestant churches supported the development of voluntary organizations in the nineteenth and early twentieth centuries. Social and educational movements in Eastern Europe dating from the eighteenth century, such as the village and small town settlement house movements, the cooperative movements, and educational workers movements, were another important source of inspiration.

The legal tradition that regulates foundations and associations in Hungary and Poland, for example, dates back to the eighteenth and nineteenth centuries respectively. In other countries of the region, laws regulating the status of the voluntary sector were established in the 1920s and 1930s, providing a good foundation for the re-emergence of the voluntary sector after 1989.

More recently, the Catholic Church in Poland, the Lutheran Church in former East Germany, and the Orthodox Church of Russia played crucial roles. A turning point in breaking social apathy and enlivening self-organization in Poland came with the election of the Polish Pope, John Paul II. This provided a strong ideological and political alternative to the communist system, encouraging the struggle for democracy that gave rise to the Solidarity trade union movement. The Solidarity movement is commonly perceived as the turning point that changed the course of history in the entire region, and Solidarnosc itself came into being in close connection with the Church.

In Bulgaria, general moral and philosophical values ("sharing the problems of the fellow citizen") rather than religious values have been an important source of inspiration for the re-emergence of voluntary organizations. In Estonia, the tradition of citizens' expression in cultural associations, which preserved national identity and provided a sense of independence, stimulated the rebirth of the voluntary sector when the nation re-emerged as a sovereign state. The loosening of the economic system in Hungary in the mid-1960s opened the door to a civil society there. Networks of a mostly secular nature there provided the basis for a re-emergence of the voluntary sector.

Volunteer Services for Refugees in Slovenia

Between World War II and 1989-90, the problem of refugees was unknown in Eastern Europe, and consequently no institutions were established to assist displaced populations. The breakup of Yugoslavia and the ensuing civil wars have generated about 3 million refugees, with some 70,000 arriving in Slovenia from Bosnia and Herzegovina. Some 50,000 of them have the status of "temporary refugees," while the others are illegal refugees who entered the country after August 1992 when the Slovenian government closed its borders.

In addition to government help, the refugees have received basic supplies from the Catholic Church and voluntary organizations, andseveral hundred volunteers have started visiting the camps, focusing their efforts particularly on children and youth. Anica Mikus Kos, a Slovenian child psychiatrist and a volunteer herself, has described their work as "animating and tutoring different activities such as sport, theater, music, foreign language courses, sewing and taking care of children in kindergartens."

The work of the volunteers represents individual civic incentive based on solidarity, compassion, and philanthropic ethos. It is aimed at individual psychosocial assistance and softens the policies of the "big systems." It has been an indispensible contribution to "the development of more efficient mechanisms of help to refugees," complementing both the Slovenian government effort and those of big organizations such as the Red Cross.

An added benefit is that the work of volunteers helps the refugees, deprived of their families, homes, and a basic sense of security, to believe that human solidarity and compassion is real even under the extreme circumstances of war.

Interestingly, the recent growth of the voluntary sector is sometimes associated with motivations for economic profit and political influence. As Russian analyst Jakobson states: "Some basic motives for their creation were the desire of the nomenclature to participate in entrepreneurship without formally being considered entrepreneurs."

Foreign and international agencies, increasingly present in the region following the 1989-90 systemic transformations, have also supported and inspired the regrowth of the voluntary sector. For some countries, such as Albania, Bulgaria, Lithuania, Romania, and Russia, this international support has been critical for reinstituting the voluntary sector. International support has greatly encouraged and fostered the processes of self-organization of East European voluntary organizations, helped to identify new fields of activities (such as child abuse, family violence, and women's issues), and often introduced innovative forms of activities.

The Sector's Scope and Field of Action

At first glance, the Eastern European voluntary sector is a terminological jungle where several terms coexist and no one single term describes the complex nature of the sector. The existence of this "nomenclature chaos" makes defining the sector particularly difficult. Among the terms most frequently used are the nonprofit sector, the nongovernmental sector, the third sector, the independent sector, the charitable sector, and the voluntary sector. Even identification with the term "sector" is not yet very strong in the region.

None of the terms used have been coined locally, inside the region. The only one widely used in Central and Eastern Europe prior to 1989—"social organizations"—has been almost completely rejected due to its negative connotation symbolizing the structural dependence on government. The new (indigenous) vocabulary is still in formation, as is the sector's mission and status.

Among the diversity of terms, the "imported" terms nonprofit sector and nongovernmental sector are probably the most widely used in Central and Eastern Europe. The term voluntary sector is used here as it seems to better fit the role of these groups in ensuring a truly democratic transformation and setting up the basis for a civil society.

Although the voluntary sector is not the result of the breakthroughs of 1989, its remarkable upsurge is without question one of the most valuable assets of the transition period in Eastern Europe. The only exception is Croatia, where the war caused an overall decline in the sector.

The numbers of voluntary organizations should be viewed with reservation because of the sector's fluctuating character, the lack of information, and difficulties in obtaining solid data on their scope. For example, organizations may treat their local affiliates either as separate units or include them as part of the parent organization.

It is estimated that at least 80,000 registered voluntary organizations exist in the entire region. Based on available data, the breakdown is as follows:

- less than 50 in Albania;
- less than 100 in Lithuania;
- approximately 300 in Bulgaria;
- 4,700 in Romania;
- 13,347 in the Czech Republic;
- 3,906 in the Slovak Republic;
- 13,000 in Croatia (compared with 32,659 before the outbreak of the war in 1991);
- 17,000 in Poland; and
- 31,172 in Hungary.

Despite common opinion often identifying the voluntary organizations' activities with relief work, the main fields of endeavor of member-serving and public-serving voluntary organizations in Bulgaria, Croatia, Estonia, Hungary, Poland, and Slovenia are cultural, social welfare, education, leisure, and sport activities.

Culture as the main field of activity does not necessarily reflect a basic social need of post-communist societies, but rather should be viewed as an institutional legacy of the "ancient regime" and a "guide" to the best organized groups of professionals where pressures for occupational autonomy is the highest.

A Bulgarian analyst notes that the excess of organizations in the field of culture and art is a sign of deviation of the Bulgarian voluntary sector, where 80 percent of the population lives on the brink of poverty and where charitable organizations represent only 11 percent of the sector's structure.

Other components of the sector's scope are economic and community development organizations, advocacy and lobbying organizations, and legal service agencies. The two latter groups constitute the smallest part of the sector's scope, although in Hungary the number of advocacy groups is growing rapidly.

Among voluntary organizations, operating foundations (for example, grant-seeking and unendowed) constitute an important category, especially in Bulgaria, Hungary, and Poland, and definitely outdistance the number of grant-making foundations. The proliferation of grant-seeking (fundraising) foundations is a product of special tax law incentives issued to foster the rebirth of foundations. This type of foundation comes closest to resembling the U.S. concept of charities: nonprofits that serve the public good and need money to accomplish their goals.

What is not represented in the sector's scope are health care organizations. The health system in these countries has not yet been reformed and health institutions are still predominatly state-run. In some countries, like Bulgaria, Hungary, and Poland, there are foundations, associations, and centers that deliver fee-based health services whose revenues support state-run medical institutions. These organizations fall into the grant-seeking category.

In addition, many grassroot networks and informal groups are not formally registered, such as environmental protection clubs in schools, clubs of mutual support, and programs housed in public schools or psychotherapy centers that support the expenses of these efforts either entirely or in part. While the number of such networks is almost impossible to establish, their existence constitutes another set of vitally important citizens' initiatives; if these various local groups were included, the voluntary sector in Eastern Europe would be much larger.

Four main institutional types can be identified: social organizations (being in existence during communism), voluntary citizens' associations, NGOs, and foundations (established in the 1980s both by private individuals and legal entities).

Traditional charities that survived the communist period are almost exclusively church-run institutions. The NGOs and grant-seeking foundations are the most numerous institutional types. Their activities are mainly aimed at delivering public goods and services.

Voluntary citizens' associations were numerous at the beginning of the transition period. As Hungarian analyst Miklós Marschall has noted: "There are indications that this segment of the third sector (e.g. foundations, civic associations and mutual benefit societies) has grown more rapidly than social service, welfare oriented organizations." During the early stage of the political changes in Eastern Europe, voluntary citizens' organizations were widely believed to have a role to play as a vehicle for political, economic, and social reforms and to be an actor in the formation of civil society. Since then, however, such an understanding of the role of voluntary organizations in public life has become less popular among political elites in some countries. In Poland, for example, after several years of political, economic, and social changes, the idea of civil society has clearly lost its appeal for the political elites and, therefore, their support.

The function of voluntary organizations is no longer given broad interpretation. One recent example was the Polish Parliament's disregard of a campaign organized by voluntary committees for a referendum on the proposed anti-abortion bill. The law passed without a referendum. During a televised

---

Family of Hope Foundation

This initiative started in 1990 in Gdansk, Poland, with the goals of supporting families having problems arising and educating their children; supporting neglected children by organizing afterschool activities, summer holidays, and special educational centers; and providing in- kind and financial assistance to the most needy families. The Foundation runs two emergency round-the-clock residences and one after-school center for about 100 needy and neglected children. It dedicated its 1993 summer therapeutic camps to children from alcoholic families to promote the idea "Children—The Hope of Europe."

Through a wide variety of activites, ranging from learning about history, geography, culture, monuments, national dishes, and costumes to discovering national dances and national fables of some 18 different European countries, the organizers have focused on developing in children the values of tolerance and respect for other nations, cultures, and customs.

While running summer camps for needy children, the Foundation of Hope has helped children with psychological problems by improving their level of sociopsychological functioning and has provided medical therapy services as well as occupational therapy.

---

press conference, a deputy to the Parliament stated: "We cannot allow an adventitious society to decide a question of public morality."

Voluntary citizens' associations are a small part of the Bulgarian sector and are at a very early stage of their formation, being either professional associations or highly politicized groups (such as Eco-glasnost or Democratic Women's Union) serving as a specific branch and tool of certain political forces, according to Stephan Nikolov.

Private institutions for public services, corporate philanthropy, and private foundations still represent a small share of the voluntary sector in Eastern Europe. Private institutions for public services exist in Bulgaria, Hungary, and Poland but they are mostly for-profit ventures—private kindergartens, primary and secondary schools, and institutions of higher education. As Eva Kuti observed in Hungary: "The initiatives...are either disguised for-profits or the attempts of enthusiastic professionals...lacking both managerial skills and sufficient money to operate."

Little is known about corporate philanthropy in Eastern Europe after 1989. Prior to this period, corporate giving existed in the form of support by nationalized enterprises to selected "social organizations" in all the East European countries. Presently, due to the weak economic condition of most of these state-owned companies, their role in giving has declined, while private corporate giving mainly takes the form of spontaneous and ad hoc support.

Hungary is the only country in the region where information on corporate giving is available. Corporate donations constituted 10.6 percent of foundations' revenue sources and 7.5 percent of associations' sources as of 1991. In Bulgaria, where emerging private ventures are small and weak, corporate philanthropy takes the form of "occasional sponsorships, gifts, covering expenses of medical treatment for individuals, etc.," according to Nikolov.

In Poland, where the exact numbers of corporate giving are unknown, a recent study revealed that as of 1991, private companies were one of the four major funding sources for nonprofit social service organizations, along with government, state-owned ventures, and individual donors.

Private grant-making foundations currently constitute only a very small fraction of the East European voluntary sector.

As for organizational types, the East European voluntary sector varies significantly: from single purpose to multipurpose organizations, from direct service providers to intermediaries, from a simple organizational structure ("one desk office") to extensive office support, and from one-person operations to more than a dozen staff members.

The sector's clients are mainly from urban areas. In most countries of the region, including Russia, voluntary organizations operate predominantly in metropolitan areas and large cities. In Hungary, about 28 percent of the voluntary organizations (39 percent of foundations and 23 percent of associations) are located in Budapest. In Bulgaria, three fourths of the foundations and associations are located in Sofia, and the rest in other larger cities. Although almost all voluntary organizations are registered as national in scope, only very few, in the words of a Bulgarian researcher, "dispose of a network throughout the country or of chapters in at least the main regional centres."

Target populations cover all demographic groups from children, young people, and middle-aged groups to the elderly. Members and founders of voluntary organizations are often themselves clients or beneficiaries of the organizations they establish in Bulgaria, Croatia, Estonia, Hungary, Poland, and Slovenia. For Hungarian and Polish voluntary organizations, people in need represent a dominant client group.

In recent years, many East European voluntary organizations became "first-line soldiers," acting in the field of homelessness, child abuse, teenage maternity, and women's issues. Beyond that, the sector also plays an active role in mobilizing citizens to participate in public life in other areas.

Equally important are the roles of public educator; facilitator of everyday participation in civic life; advocate for public good causes; promotor of values of social justice, solidarity, mutual aid, compassion and brotherhood; and "watchdog" of democratic transformations.

A recent Polish survey revealed that approximately 50 percent of social workers cooperated with voluntary organizations in addressing such pressing social problems as poverty and homelessness, and in providing assistance to needy mothers, large families, and persons with physical or mental disabilities. In another Polish study, the activities of voluntary welfare organizations were primarily directed at providing financial aid, health-related services, rehabilitation, and nonmedical assistance.

Curiously, very little is known about the staff of the voluntary sector in Eastern Europe. Bearing in mind the scarce data available, it seems that the dominant group working and/or volunteering for the sector is mid-level career professionals.

A recent Polish study on social welfare organizations revealed that foundations had the highest number of paid staff as compared with other voluntary groups such as associations and church-related organizations. Needless to say, the status of its staff is unclear and often uncertain as the voluntary sector in Eastern Europe has only recently been developing its capacity as an employer.

In comparison with its service delivery role, the economic role is difficult to assess due to an almost complete lack of data. For the first time in the last 50 years, the Polish Statistical Year Book of 1992 explicitly highlighted the economic role of the voluntary sector in Poland by listing foundations among the new private-sector employers.

Based on available information, it appears that expenditures of the voluntary sector in Hungary (at current prices) rose very sharply from 3.4 billion Hungarian forints (HUF) in 1982 to 51.6 billion HUF in 1991 (from $32.7 million to $496 million, at June 1994 rates), and accounted for close to 3 percent of the country's gross national product in 1992.

It is not possible, however, to discern between the operating and nonoperating expenses of the sector from these figures. This issue became quite sensitive in recent years in Hungary and Poland, where some foundations have abused the not-for-profit status by either paying high salaries to some of its staff or by providing some executives with luxury "in-kind ser-

211

vices," such as paying for holidays abroad. In light of the report of the Polish Chief Board of Supervision on public foundations, several foundations spent almost half their operating costs on salaries. The Polish report and similar information about fraudulent voluntary sector operations in other countries dampened the spontaneous support that foundations and associations had at the beginning of the transition period.

Well-known examples of fraudulent activities include foundations established to provide health services without paying taxes, or those set up to import oil, spirits, and cigarettes to avoid paying taxes and import duties. These fake foundations have appeared in all the countries except Romania, where the law forbids foundations and associations to engage in solely fundraising purposes. The Romanian law permits, however, the creation of "a for-profit subsidiary" to run business activities, but it is subject to taxes relevant to such entities.

In Bulgaria, voluntary organizations and foundations in particular have often been used as "handy" profit-making entities and vehicles of political influence for the elites, while being much less vocal about citizens' concerns. In the words of Stephan Nikolov, "Ordinary people do not have the feeling that foundations are something good for them."

It is clear that beyond the altruistic motivations that have led to the re-emergence of the voluntary sector in Central and Eastern Europe, there have also been selfish and profit-oriented motivations as well. This threatens the very existence of the voluntary sector as it allows the various for-profit businesses to use the legal forms of voluntary organizations and the tax benefits granted to them to generate unfair profit for private use.

Fake organizations of the voluntary sector have provided unfair competition with for-profit companies who are burdened with a higher tax rate, and have opened the door to business practices that, if not stopped, will likely provoke an anti-voluntary sector reaction from the legitimate business sector. The business sector, in turn, may reduce its commitment to policies of corporate citizenship for the medium- and long-term future. There is a real danger that the East European voluntary sector may be accused of facilitating the continuation of the "second economy" or the "grey zone" in a new institutional form. The problem is even more serious for the East European voluntary sector because part of sector's executives themselves are interested in maintaining such a status quo.

Legal Issues and Treatment in Tax Laws

Between 1948 and 1984, the only allowable legal form for voluntary organizations in the former Soviet bloc countries was an association. Since the mid-1980s, the legal situation in the region has gradually improved.

Unlike previous regulations, the new legislation of the mid-1980s was conducive to the development of voluntary organizations, and enabled a process of restoring and creating the legal and fiscal structures for the voluntary sector, first in Poland and Hungary. This process was further strengthened after the breakthrough of 1989, when the fundamental principles underpinning voluntary organizations—freedom of expression and freedom of association—have been generally guaranteed and enforced in East European countries by the Constitutions and Charters of Human Rights and Freedoms.

In Poland and Hungary, a legal form of the foundation was reenacted in the Civil Code in 1984 and 1987, respectively, and a new Association Law was introduced in both countries in 1989. Both private individuals and legal entities can set up a foundation. Previously, in order to be considered a legal entity, a foundation had to receive approval from a supervisory ministry (or from a local government, in the case of Hungary), which had jurisdiction over the subject matter with which the foundation was concerned.

Under the Laws on Associations of 1989, the role of administrative authorities has changed from an oppressive control mechanism to oversight ensuring that associations operate in a legal manner. An association must register in a court but, unlike in previous regulations, it does not need the permission of administrative authorities before registering. The new regulations require fewer conditions to be fulfilled to register an association, such as having a minimum number of members, a declaration of articles, and bylaws.

The Hungarian voluntary sector enjoys the most progressive legislation in the region. Modifications of the Civil Code made in November 1993 expand the existing legal forms of voluntary organizations and allow for "the introduction of new legal types of nonprofit organizations, such as the service providing nonprofit company, public law foundation and public law association."

The Czech and Slovak Republics, unlike Poland and Hungary, have not had a separate law on foundations. In both, the Civic Code regulates the status of voluntary organizations. The Law on Associations that came into force in 1990 only generally regulates the rights of citizens to associate and does not distinguish between public-serving and member-serving organizations. In the Czech and Slovak Republics the existing law allows for two forms of voluntary organizations: civic organizations and foundations.

In the Czech Republic a legal reform aimed at expanding the notion of the voluntary organizations is being discussed. It is an attempt to denationalize the budgetary sector (that is, schools, hospitals, and research institutes). The main goal of this reform effort is to introduce a new type of voluntary organization: the "nonprofit" (legal enity) that would allow schools, hospitals, and research institutes to be included as part of the voluntary sector.

In Russia, the law "About Voluntary Associations" introduced in 1991 limits the voluntary sector to membership organizations. This regulation does not allow for the establishment of a nonmembership-based trust or endowment. In establishing these, the trust or endowment must either register as an association or as a for-profit enterprise. Nationwide voluntary organizations register in the Russian Ministry of Justice, while local organizations register in the Department of Justice according to their area of work. Voluntary organizations such as housing associations or professional clubs register in the Registration Chamber, while other voluntary organizations such as philanthropic funds or libraries register in the Interdepartmental Commission of Non-profit Organizations and Mass Media in the Moscow City Council.

In Lithuania, the law regulating charities ("The Law on Charities and Sponsorship") came into force in June 1993. It defines the legal status of voluntary organizations and provides them with two legal forms: association and foundation. In Bulgaria, the legal status of voluntary organizations is regulated by the Legal Persons and Families Act of 1949, which allows both associations and foundations.

In Romania, the voluntary sector is governed by Law No. 21 of 1924 and a regulation from the communist rule (Decree of 1954). While the law provides for the existence of associations and foundations, associations still need the approval of a relevant ministry before registering in a court, and foundations require a dedicated fund in order to register. In Estonia, the legal foundation for the voluntary sector dates to the commmunist period. A new law regulating activities of voluntary organizations is being developed.

In summary, except for Russia, the existing laws of East Central European countries allow voluntary organizations to exist in two legal forms, associations and foundations, even though among the countries in question only Hungary, Poland, and Lithuania have a new, separate law on foundations and associations. In the other countries, the status of the sector is either regulated by laws passed during the communist rule or by the Civic Code and the law on charities/associations. In Russia, there is no separate law on associations. The Russian law on Voluntary Organizations regulates the activities of both associations and other organizations such as trade unions and political parties.

In most of the countries in question, both associations and foundations are permitted to undertake economic activities and are eligible for certain tax exemptions and deductions either overall or on a case-by-case basis. For example, voluntary organizations in Romania are allowed to engage in economic activities only if such ventures are compatible with their nonprofit purpose, while in Bulgaria, Czechoslovakia, Hungary, and Poland, the initial laws were not as strict.

A legal issue not yet satisfactory elaborated in some tax laws is a clear definition of "public-serving organizations" and "public good purpose." In Bulgaria, public good purpose has not been defined yet in the tax law, and tax treatment of voluntary organizations is subject to the general Trade Act regulating activities of commercial ventures.

In Russia, according to Russian economist Lev Jakobson, "there were no clear criteria stipulating a right for tax exemptions and other privileges. In many cases the privileges were given to those organizations which had managed to get patrons among influential politicians." Currently tax benefits are granted by tax laws to charitable organizations but, again, there is no definition of charitable organization yet elaborated. As "the legitimate status of nonprofit organizations is not defined," a case-by-case tax policy continues. This situation creates "ample ground for abuse and genuine non-profit organizations are often forced out by pseudo-nonprofit organizations."

Another important issue, especially for foundations, is the regulation of the income tax laws that does not allow for the establishment of a nonmembership-based trust or endowment, or, as in Poland, where foundations are subjected to 40 percent income tax if they do not spend the funds initially at their disposal within two years.

A legal issue that merits attention is the generally more favorable tax benefits granted to foundations than to associations. This was done mainly to enhance the rebirth of foundations and has resulted in a proliferation of grant-seeking foundations in some countries in the region that otherwise would prefer to take the legal form of an association. This is especially the case of Bulgaria, Hungary, and Poland. By contrast, in Romania where the treatment of foundations in the tax law was not as generous, there is no significant difference in tax treatment between foundations and associations.

Until 1992, in Hungary and Bulgaria treatment of foundations in the tax laws provided no restrictions on business activities, tax exemption on business income, or eligibility for tax deductions. These regulations have allowed foundations to engage in economic activities—either in furtherance of their not-for-profit purposes or solely for fundraising activities. While tax-exempt profits have subsidized the aims of many foundations and were the only way to ensure funds for organizational activity, some groups have misused this tax-exempt status and served as "profit distributing tax shelters."

In comparison with foundations, associations received less favorable tax treatment although, gradually, tax advantages for foundations and associations in some countries, such as Hungary and Poland, equalized.

Another legal issue not yet satisfactorily elaborated on in the existing tax laws is the regulation of deductions for charitable contributions. The process of changing the rules regulating the sector's activities and tax benefits is under way. It seems to be the most advanced in Hungary.

Before the reforms, business activities for associations in Hungary were restricted and only associations engaged in scientific and technical research, culture, environmental protection, sports, health care, social assistance, child care, and youth welfare could earn tax-exempt profits to subsidize their statutory purposes.

In contrast with foundations, Hungarian associations were also not eligible by law for tax deductions of membership fees and donations; these tax benefits could be granted on an individual basis by government authorities. Then with the Hungarian tax laws of 1992, associations were made equal with foundations in regard to business income benefits.

The Hungarian tax laws of 1992 changed earlier regulations on granting foundations tax exemption or tax deductibility benefits. According to the current legislation, a foundation may be exempt from tax on business income only "if it does not exceed 10 percent of total income or HUF 10 million per year."

The legislature also introduced tax deductibility status (permitting the tax deduction of donations) for foundations working in these areas of the public good: preventive medicine, health care, scientific or technical research, environmental protection, protection of cultural heritage, education, sport, religion, public security, and care for the elderly, the poor, national and ethnic minorities, refugees, and Hungarian minorities in foreign countries.

By contrast, in Bulgaria, the fraudulent activities of some foundations "have made the government introduce in February 1992 by special decree severe restrictions, which in practice deprive nonprofits in general of any exemption and discouraged any possible interest in donating," according to Nikolov.

In Poland, the steps undertaken to solve the problems of abuse of tax-exempt status by parts of the voluntary sector is somewhat in between the Hungarian and Bulgarian approaches. The revised Law on Foundations of 1991 adopted certain regulations on the economic activities of foundations. It

Central Versus Local Government Funding

Central government is still the major source of income of Hungarian organizations and significantly exceeds local government input. In Hungary, state support to voluntary organizations increased by 434 percent between 1990 and 1993.

Polish organizations rely on both central and local government funds in equal proportions. In Slovenia, Estonia, and Croatia, the input of central and local governments to voluntary organizations funding base is the same. Compared with Poland and Hungary, however, central government support is at a much lower level.

The local government contribution to the voluntary sector funding base is highest in Poland, where, during decentralization, local authorities have been assigned the compulsory tasks of financing and providing social assistance services and soon will be responsible for financing the school system. The lowest input from central and local governments to voluntary organizations' funding base seems to be in Bulgaria.

states that foundations may engage in economic activities but only within the limits and in compliance with the rules stated in the statute. The law permits foundations to engage in economic activities that further their purposes but prohibits them from engaging in solely fundraising activities. Unlike Hungary, Polish tax laws are still quite liberal, and restrict neither business activities nor tax benefits granted to foundations.

The Romanian income tax law of 1991 permits a deduction of contributions to certain voluntary organizations of up to 2 percent of profits but it is limited to businesses. In the former Czechoslovakia, corporate donations were nondeductible. The deductions for charitable contributions were only available to individual entrepreneurs and imposed a ceiling of 10 percent deductions on their tax basis. According to Jiri Janda, a Czech analyst, in light of the new tax laws that were to come into force by the end of 1993, corporate donors "will most probably have the possibility to deduct a maximum of 2 to 3 percent from their tax basis."

In relation to individual charitable contributions, it is noteworthy that while in Romania, Bulgaria, Estonia, and Croatia, charitable contributions made by individuals are nondeductible, the tax laws of Hungary, Poland, the Czech

Republic, the Slovak Republic, and Slovenia permit deductions for individual contributions. It is not clear whether individual contributions to voluntary organizations are deductible in Russia, but businesses can obtain a deduction of up to 3 percent of their taxable income, except for banks and insurance companies, which can deduct up to 1 percent. In Slovenia, the tax advantages for business contributions can be up to 0.1 percent of their annual income. In Estonia, those in business can obtain a deduction of up to 15 percent of their net income.

In Poland, both individuals and corporations are eligible for deductions of up to 10 percent of taxable income if the contributions support scientific, educational, cultural, religious, sporting, environmental, charitable, health, or social assistance activities, rehabilitation of the disabled, or municipality housing.

To promote corporate philanthropy, some East European countries need to reform their tax laws. For the development of civil society, not only must tax benefits for voluntary organizations be ensured, but these groups must also be eligible to receive tax-deductible gifts.

In short, in Hungary, Poland, and the Czech Republic, where the systemic transformations started earlier, the process of setting rules for voluntary organizations is much more advanced, while in other countries it is at a rather embryonic stage. It would be unrealistic to expect, however, that this Herculean task, requiring both updating the prewar laws where relevant and setting up new regulations, would promulgate a consistent legal and fiscal framework in only a few years.

Funding Base

In 1989-93 the sources of funding for voluntary organizations in East Central Europe changed significantly. During the period of real socialism, state sponsorship was the major source, with additional funding from other sources holding just a minor position in organizations' total incomes. After 1989, the sources of funding became more diversified. Hungarian voluntary associations and foundations, for example, rely mainly on government support, private donations, and earned income, while the main funding of Bulgarian voluntary organizations consists of unrelated business income, international support, and private donations. In Lithuania, foreign aid and private donations (especially corporate giving) are the prevailing sources of funding.

One of the characteristics of funding sources for voluntary organizations in post-communist countries is the changing role of the central government.

Unlike the commmunist period, when either public agencies financed by the government provided social welfare services or so-called general government donations were granted to social organizations, for some years now the government agencies in Poland and Hungary have started to participate in a new form of financing—contracting out or purchasing selected services.

The process of "contract culture" first started in Hungary, where both the government and the voluntary sector itself contributed to the parliamentary decision of 1990 that voluntary organizations delivering basic social, educational, and cultural services were equal with state-run agencies in terms of being entitled to per capita government subsidies.

To receive the subsidies and to acquire funding through contracts with the government, Hungarian voluntary organizations must meet several quality requirements. By August 1993, two major subsectors of the Hungarian voluntary organizations were listed among the institutions entitled to the per capita subsidies: certain kinds of social and educational services.

In contrast to Hungary, equal access and subsidies entitlement are not legislatively regulated in Poland. However, the Polish Council of Ministers issued a resolution in 1992 that listed specific services in 10 categories eligible for purchase from voluntary organizations: education, culture and arts, health, social assistance, sport, recreation, public safety, environment, consumer goods, and other activities as such protection of the rights of children.

In Russia, Lena Young notes that "in the provinces, it is common for charities to have contractual arrangements with the state. Usually voluntary efforts are seen as cheaper than direct state efforts to address social problems." In other countries of the region "the contract culture" is at an embryonic stage of formation, impeding the voluntary sector from becoming a more stable and mature service provider.

Purchase of services by government is traditionally an important source of financing for the voluntary sector. Thus despite obstacles, the first step has been made and "the contract culture" has been introduced as an important funding source for East European voluntary organizations. It also is slowly moving the voluntary sector away from "being entirely independent from government" to seeking government funds, and even pressing for government money.

One of the crucial issues for the successful implementation of "the contract culture" in Eastern Europe is to elaborate the standards, requirements, and effective supervision mechanisms that would restrain both sides of the contract from inappropriate behavior.

But the major and most pervasive obstacles toward integrating the "contract culture" as a funding mechanism of voluntary associations in Eastern Europe include high budget deficits in all countries, a lack of consistent social policies that clearly define the responsibilities of the public and private sectors, and distinctly determined policies of the state vis-à-vis the voluntary sector.

While the process of working out a new funding relationship between the government and the voluntary sector is a long-lasting endeavor for the sector's survival, it is indispensible to have the government cofinancing the service delivery function in the period of transition.

In some countries, the shrinking role of central government as a revenue source for the voluntary sector is partly balanced by the growing financial input from local governments.

It is noteworthy that in recent years a significant proportion of total funding for voluntary organizations has come from private donations through the appearance of an entirely new funding source—foreign and domestic grantmaking foundations. Earned income, including first of all the earnings from for-profit activities and, to a much lesser degree, endowments are also important sources of funding.

Although the voluntary organizations vary considerably in terms of the importance of these various funding sources, domestic grantmaking foundations and endowments play a marginal role in funding the sector's activities and will not be an important funding source for many years to come. In the long run, however, individual and corporate donors may have a significant role if the expected growth of the middle class in Eastern Europe is realized. Much depends also on the public perception of the sector's trustworthiness, and the maintenance of legislation supporting private giving.

In this context, it is critical to conduct research on the attitudes of East European societies and businesses toward private giving to voluntary organizations. Although exact numbers are not available, corporate donations dominate over individual giving in Croatia, Estonia, and Poland, while individual donors' contributions have the highest position in Bulgaria and Slovenia. In Hungary, the number of private donors more than doubled, and the size of average donations more than quadrupled between 1988 and 1990.

Although individual giving is an important and particularly precious funding source, as it expresses citizens' support for the common good, alone it is insufficient to ensure a financial basis for the East European voluntary sector. This view is widely shared by analysts and activists of the voluntary sector in Eastern Europe, and is hardly surprising considering the low income levels in these countries. This argument again points to the need for an active government role in providing part of the funding base for voluntary organizations.

Foreign and international governmental and nongovernmental agencies have contributed significantly to the income of East European voluntary organizations. In the words of a Lithuanian voluntary sector representative, Algirdas Lipstas, "foreign aid was a push to start the Lithuanian voluntary sector running."

In some countries, the impact of international support to the voluntary sector is now lower than just after the breakthroughs of 1989. There is growing concern about how to substitute international financial aid for domestic revenues, but this international input still constitutes a significant part of voluntary sector revenues in Eastern Europe. International agencies have been also crucial in helping the sector to stabilize, in shaping its professional and ethical standards, and in expanding its fields of action.

The existing diversity of funding sources of voluntary organizations in East European countries does not automatically mean that these organizations have a stable financial position. Except for foundations set up by government institutions that have received large grants from their budgets or received formerly public funds and turned part of them into endowments or business activities, and with the additional exception of foreign foundations, the majority of the sector is financially unstable. For instance, according to Bulgarian data, five foundations have funds of $100,000 or more and these are entirely funded by foreign agencies, while 90 percent of the units of the sector have very modest resources of at most $10,000.

Insufficient or nonexistent financial resources is a serious problem that has accompanied the rebirth of the East European voluntary sector from the very beginning. In Poland, it is generally estimated that one third of newly formed voluntary organizations do not survive, mostly because of the lack of financial means. This phenomenon partly explains why economic activities of voluntary organizations are often not tied to their statutory purposes, are quite often actually conducted at the expense of it, and are a commonly used mechanism to ensure income throughout Eastern Europe.

These unrelated, for-profit activities are, undoubtedly, one of the burning issues for East European voluntary organizations that must find a just solution in forthcoming regulations. The problem cannot be solved, however, by simply introducing restrictive regulations that would forbid the organizations to undertake for-profit activities, as this would be disastrous to many civic initiatives that otherwise would not be able to perform their mission.

Interactions With Others

East European voluntary organizations have developed several links and networks on both the local and national levels that are represented by the formation of unions, federations, centers, forums, or chambers. The Union of Bulgarian Foundations, the Information Centre for Foundations and Other Nonprofit Organizations in the Czech Republic, the Hungarian Foundation Centre, the Polish Forum of Foundations, and the Information Centre for the Nonprofit Organizations in the Slovak Republic are just a few examples of such nationwide organizations serving as a source of information for voluntary organizations and a channel for networking.

These entities are also aimed at building up the relationship of confidence and cooperation within and outside the sector, promoting professional standards, and ensuring internal democratic accountability. In reality, however, their impact is not yet strong enough to promote the sector's mission among the general public, to strengthen its legitimacy, or to discourage the dishonest practices and misconduct of part of the sector.

The Union of Bulgarian Foundations has managed to gather only a small fraction of the organizations under its umbrella, while most of the others remain autonomous and independent. The same is true for relevant organizations in other Central and East European countries. This is a sign that most voluntary organizations still do not identify themselves as being part of a "third sector" and have not perceived the need for self-regulating procedures. It might also be a sign of fear of being subsumed by umbrella groups.

There are, however, encouraging examples of the activities undertaken by these organizations, such as the initiative in 1992 of the Polish Forum of Foundations aimed at providing an overview of the existing legal framework and submitting proposals for legal reform. There are also various umbrella organizations acting in specific fields, such as the Federation of Foundations Serving Children and Young People in Hungary or the Union of Christian Youth Polish YMCA.

The voluntary sector newspapers and periodicals are another instrument that promotes the sector's objectives by providing current information and references to existing laws, as well as presenting the history of charity and voluntary activities in other countries. The Hungarian *Kurazsi* and *Sansz*, the Polish *Pomost*, and the Russian *Vestnik Blagotvoritelnosti* newspapers and magazines are examples. In addition, in Hungary, there is a weekly radio program, and every two weeks a television program focuses exclusively on the nonprofit sector.

The interactions within the sector have evolved from being spontaneous, friendly, ad hoc relations at the beginning of the transition period to being more cooperation-based as well as more conflict-fueled and competitive in recent years.

Among the challenges facing the voluntary sector as a whole are how to expand its activities and resources beyond major urban centers, how to support locally based organizations and self-help groups that often run out of energy and resources, and how to provide the sector's activists with knowledge and skills.

A specific feature of East and Central European societies is still the largely untapped potential of pro-social motivation. Individual citizens are harnessing the social energy accumulated during the past regime and using it to address serious societal problems. The sector should incorporate this valuable resource into its ranks by increasing links with local community residents and tapping the reserves of citizens' participatory energy.

Consequently, a critical issue for the voluntary sector is to develop opportunities for volunteerism—that is, everyday, regular citizen involvement—and to build legitimacy through public information and education. It is the responsibility of the voluntary sector to rebuild a sense of community, of belonging, and to take the next step toward creating a civil society.

Some analysts and managers of the East European voluntary sector put strong emphasis on creating new leadership in order to rebuild the intellectual potential the sector had prior to the breakthroughs of 1989. This leadership was often "absorbed" by the emerging democratic institutions. Their position has received the active support of some experts, educational centers, and foundations from the United States and Western Europe.

In summary, the sector's interactions with itself are limited. While partly due to the lack of appropriate communication channels, insufficient funds, lack of experience, and an instinctive resistance to any attempt at "organized unity" inherited from the "ancien regime," it is also tied to the neo-politization of the voluntary sector in Central and Eastern Europe. A recent example of this can be seen in Poland, where a number of voluntary organizations campaigned actively for certain segments of the political spectrum. And in Hungary, the relations within the sector have become fragmented, with several interactional patterns emerging, such as a "sector-minded" camp and "politically oriented groups."

In terms of relations with government, even though the systemic transformations of the region eliminated the state monopoly of the voluntary sector, it is too early to typify the current interactions. Almost all the possible patterns are now present, from the polar approach of paternalism and mutual neglect on the one hand to partnership and cooperation on the other hand. There are also examples of competition, rivalry, tensions, and conflicts between the state-run and voluntary agencies. This particular interaction often occurs in the environmental and human rights arenas but is also present in human services.

Thus several issues need to be addressed in regard to NGO interactions with government:

- Charting new relations with government involves both maintaining the sector's autonomy from government (and partisan political groupings) and developing the regulatory and funding functions of government.
- Two major concerns of the voluntary sector are how to ensure the right balance between autonomy and support from government and how to rebuild appropriate and partnership-based interactions with government.
- The communist practices based on state monopoly and paternalism vis-à-vis social organizations proved unsuccessful as they did not lead to a greater use of resources and did not effectively address important public issues despite the fact that these organizations received substantial funding from the state. The absence of autonomy of voluntary organizations proved to be disasterous to fulfilling their missions.
- How can the voluntary sector meet the priorities of both government and other funders while maintaining its own mission?

These challenges also still face many nonprofit executives in western democracies with a long history of balancing funding needs with program integrity. It is a particularly timely issue in Eastern Europe as voluntary organizations desperately seeking funds may fail to be sensitive to potential problems generated by the expectations of their funding sources.

The relationship between the government and the voluntary sector in Hungary, Poland, and the Czech Republic is at the point of breaking down mutual prejudices and building up a climate of confidence. In other countries, the levels of distrust, ignorance, and paternalism remain high. However, even in such countries as Slovenia, where the government is not aware of the sector's existence, or Croatia, where the relationship is more paternalistic, or Estonia, where the sector itself is advocating legislation regulating its legal and fiscal structure, there are various attempts—often initiated by the voluntary sector itself—to bridge the gap in communication with the government. In this context, one of the issues often mentioned is how to educate government about the sector's functions, capacities, and competence as well as its limits.

The advancement of this process and the level and quality of dialogue and cooperation between voluntary organizations and governments (at their different levels) vary significantly from country to country. In Hungary, the former Czechoslovakia, and Poland, the move toward cooperation and partnership, although not without controversy, seems to be the most advanced. Recent Polish research results indicate that the extent and quality of cooperation between the voluntary sector and government increases in proportion to the level of decentralization: the lower the level of government administration, the better are the indicators of cooperation and support.

In general, the governments of Hungary, Poland, and the Czech Republic have gradually assumed a funding function and, albeit to a lesser degree, a regulatory function. Jiri Janda, a Czech activist, has pointed out "the government itself has been recognizing its role and, in spite of economic difficulties, substantial government grants have been made to numerous organizations by the relevant ministries, although better coordination and evaluation would be desirable." In Hungary, the state increased its financial support to voluntary organizations by 174 percent between 1990 and 1992. An official of the Polish Ministry of Labour and Social Policy noted: "From our stand point, we see our financial participation in the form of purchase of services and coordination of service delivery."

As noted earlier, government funding—although not the sole funding source it used to be—still constitutes an important, and in many cases, a decisive source of income for voluntary organizations in Central and Eastern Europe. Government funding is essential to guarantee the most underprivileged groups of society access to basic goods and services. It can help overcome the four major deficits embodied in the very nature of voluntary organizations—insufficient resources, paternalism, particularism, and lack of professionalism. Government funding is crucial for the very survival of the sector and it is, therefore, of utmost importance that the government continue to be one of the major funding sources for the voluntary agencies in Eastern Europe. Distribution of these funds must be done in a transparent and just manner, however.

NGOs and the Private Sector

According to the scarce information available, relations with the private sector are not institutionalized and are based on informal contacts, networks, and sympathies. In Hungary, the Czech Republic, and Poland, where the privatization of the economy is more advanced, corporate giving is becoming an additional source of revenues for the voluntary sector.

In 1991, Hungarian corporate giving was the source of at least 10 percent of the revenues for foundations and 7.5 percent for associations. In Bulgaria, Croatia, Estonia, and Slovenia, where the privatization of the economy has just started, the role of corporate giving is "poor and occasional."

Despite local differences in the advance of the market economy, East European voluntary organizations need to learn strategies to target corporate donors in order to promote corporate giving and corporate citizenship among the newly created private companies.

Sound government policies for funding voluntary organizations have not been yet developed in most of the countries in question. What Lena Young observed for the large cities of Russia also proves true for most of the region: "the state chooses to support either big, long established funds...or concentrate on `people they know' rather than on organizations."

While part of the voluntary sector in Central and Eastern Europe wants to maintain its independence from government and does not accept any government funding, another segment builds its future upon government funding.

As already stated, there is an urgent need in Eastern Europe to develop transparent procedures for contracting for services, which would include standards of practice, application requirements, reporting, auditing, and evaluation mechanisms.

There is a growing awareness among some representatives of the voluntary sector of the need for a level of regulation and the institutionalization of mutual relations between itself and government. In practice, however, "the combat culture" prevails and hampers the establishment of institutional relations that would permit voluntary leaders to interact formally with government representatives. This is reflected by informal alliances and agreements between voluntary organizations and political leaders (who themselves often came from the voluntary sector). The existing bilateral frameworks, such as the Bulgarian Trilateral Commission on Social Issues, are often not effective in addressing these issues, nor are the ad hoc contacts between government and the voluntary sector.

Relations with three other key groups in society—religious institutions, the scientific community, and the media—are also mixed. Currently the Church plays an important role as a founder, a sponsor, and a partner of the East European voluntary sector, although its impact varies from country to country. In some countries, such as in Poland, the Catholic Church has been a critical actor in the rebirth of the voluntary sector. In others, such as Bulgaria, the dominant religious group (the Eastern Orthodox Church) has played a much less significant role. But other religious denominations in Bulgaria, such as the Muslim, Catholic, and Evangelic churches, were active in promoting community activity during the transition period.

The active involvement in the voluntary sector of religious institutions whose operations are partly financed by foreign sources has generated certain tensions. For example, financial aid from Saudi Arabia in support of Bulgarian voluntary organizations based on Islamic values generated some resentment among the people.

In Hungary, a country that is 66 percent Catholic, the relations between sectarian and nonsectarian organizations can be characterized as both cooperative and competitive. In order to work out ways of cooperation with the Church, local "social round tables" have been created.

In Poland, the relations between the Catholic Church and the voluntary sector are cooperative in the field of service delivery, while tensions exist in such areas as the abortion issue. According to recent Polish findings, the Church was cited by social service organizations as the primary institution that provided cooperation and support, and was listed before other institutions such as local government, local community, and the private sector.

A mixture of altruism and self-interest has been built into the considerable support offered by the scientific community in Central and Eastern Europe to its voluntary sector since the very beginning of the systemic transformation. The scientific community, supported by researchers from the U.S. and Western Europe, actively participates in setting up new organizations and serving on their boards, consults and organizes training for voluntary organization leaders, and promotes research on voluntary activities.

The Informal Sector

One example of the bridging efforts of the voluntary sector is the Borderline Foundation of Sejny (a small town in northeastern Poland). For several years now, the Foundation has successfully brought together children and youth of Polish, Belarussan, Ukrainian, Lithuanian, Transylvanian, and Romany origin to promote ethnically sensitive educational programs.

Another effort is seen in the Stefan Batory Foundation in Poland, which is part of the Soros Foundation network in Eastern Europe. In addition to supporting other programs, Batory promotes research projects and exchanges in the region aimed at breaking down historically based antagonisms among neighboring countries and assisting with systemic transformations.

In most countries, both training programs and research projects are at an early stage. The exceptions are Hungary and Poland, where courses on the voluntary sector have been introduced at some colleges and universities. In general, the relations between the scientific community and the voluntary sector can be described as cooperative and professionally supportive.

Relations with the media and its contribution to portraying a positive image of the voluntary sector vary from country to country. In Hungary and Poland, voluntary organizations and the media have sought each other out. There are good examples from the print media, television, and radio of reports about organizations' engagement in addressing the needs of homeless people, neglected children, and vulnerable elderly persons. But in Bulgaria, the media has concentrated on fraudent activities of foundations. Nikolov points out that "there are very few examples of successful cooperation between the various media and groups from the voluntary sector. Articles and broadcasts which positively depict its activity are rare."

In all the countries in question, it is still rare to find examples of cooperation between the media and the voluntary sector aimed at explaining to the public the notions of a foundation and an association, their functions in the contemporary society, and the laws on tax deductions for donors.

Not only have many voluntary groups given birth to democratic institutions during the early stage of the systemic transformation in Central and Eastern Europe, but social and political movements have given rise to voluntary organizations. Today, voluntary organizations differ greatly in their position on "how political" the sector should be, as do their political sympathies and interests.

Being pluralistic in nature, and often as divided as the political scene in a particular country might be, the sector can mobilize resources and act as a force to alleviate crisis situations and to support the democratization process. This is especially the case in Croatia, where politically diversified voluntary organizations and movements, such as The AntiWar Campaign Croatia, have created a unified front against the ongoing civil war.

The past experience in regard to the relations between political organizations and movements and the voluntary sector points to the need of some regulations that would make the sector less vulnerable vis-à-vis political groupings and better protected against being used by different political forces.

In some countries, voluntary sector traditions go back to the informal and underground networks of the 1970s, when these organizations themselves were part of the informal sector. Very little is known about present links between the voluntary sector, self-help groups, and other informal networks. There are examples of support from formal voluntary organizations to informal networks, such as the Polish Society of the Friends of Children, which supports self-help groups of parents with handicapped children by offering them access to the organization's facilities and financial resources.

East European voluntary organizations have also undertaken bridging efforts, often indigenous, locally based initiatives. Their aim is often to alleviate historically and politically based antagonisms between nations and cultures, and to initiate multiculturally sensitive educational efforts with school children and youth.

There are numerous examples of the sector's activities that promote not only "the widening of the citizen's choices" but that also open up possibilities for a citizen to meet his or her own needs. Preservation of the cultural heritage and protection of the cultural rights of minorities (often forbidden under communism) serves as one example. Another is welfare organizations aimed at assisting the homeless, AIDS victims, and the disabled.

Many examples point to the sector's role in widening choices of citizen involvement in public life. Numerous initiatives are aimed at mainstreaming disabled children and youth into society through the founding of integrative kindergarten projects (for disabled and able-bodied children).

Several voluntary initiatives offer children and youngsters active participation in their communities through ecology projects. These initiatives are often supported by domestic and international sources.

The Sector's Internationalization

The extent of the sector's internationalization varies among the countries of Central and Eastern Europe. It depends on the state of advance of the democratic transition as well as reflecting the particular interests of the western democracies in specific countries. As a result, the pace of the sector's internationalization is uneven, and not all countries benefit equally from international support. Stephan Nikolov notes that "the sector...in Bulgaria is very eager and open toward such cooperation, but a lack of interest prevails from the potential international partners."

Internationalization occurs in two directions: through the initiatives of international relief and development organizations and multinational government structures, and through the efforts of indigenous structures to set up links with international networks.

A number of international nonprofit institutions operate in the region, including the European Foundation Centre, Independent Sector, the U.S. Peace Corps, United Way, International Federation of Social Workers, Medicins sans Frontier, and Save the Children. Most recently, funders of local voluntary organizations have become more involved in the region. Examples of this are the International Youth Foundation, which established the Polish Foundation for Children and Youth, and Fondation de France, which set up Fondation de Pologne.

Some national voluntary organizations (such as professional associations, ecological organizations, and family planning societies) have become part of international networks. There also exist private voluntary organizations that constitute part of an international network, such as the Soros Foundations or the Helsinki Committee network.

International bodies, such as U.N. agencies and international humanitarian organizations, have increased their activity in the region after having operated here prior to 1989-90. The worldwide U.N. organizations, such as UNICEF and UNESCO, have offices in all the countries of the region, but they have not established relationships with the recently created voluntary organizations. Sometimes, international humanitarian organizations do not cooperate with the local voluntary groups in offering assistance. This has been the experience in Croatia.

The sector's internationalization also consists of links with western universities, especially in the United States, in the provision of technical assistance, consultation services, and research.

Beyond these private initiatives, multinational institutions supplement and subsidize the development of the voluntary sector in Eastern Europe. A major project of support and cooperation is the Phare program of the European Community. The Civic Dialogue Fund of Phare in Poland and the Civil Society Development Fund of Phare in the Czech and Slovak Republics were launched in 1992. The Civic Dialogue Fund supports a number of voluntary sector activities—information, education, and training programs for voluntary organizations, as well as funding legal services and projects run by formal and informal voluntary groups.

In regard to international funding and cooperation, one of the sector's main concerns is how to obtain more-appropriate support that would better address its needs for the skills of community organizing, development of organizational capacities, and long-term commitment of organizational support. International support, however, should be undertaken on a collaborative basis, in close cooperation with indigenous organizations.

One way donor countries may contribute to the development of civil society institutions in Eastern Europe is to better coordinate their support efforts and to expand assistance beyond organizations founded by the political elite.

Another dimension of the sector's internationalization is the future inclusion of several East European countries into the European Union. Although there will be opportunities for information and the diffusion of innovations between the West and East European voluntary sectors, there might also be adverse consequences, such as a competition between nonprofits in the two regions.

Major Issues and Challenges

The majority of organizations declare their political neutrality or nonpolitical character, even if in practice some of them relate closely to certain segments of the political spectrum. In some countries the level of politization of voluntary organizations is unacceptably high, as in Bulgaria, where "there is a common pattern of interaction..., if the government is `theirs,' voluntary organizations support it verbally, if it is not, they fight against it and blame it for all kinds of shortages and evils," notes Nikolov.

The most recent example of this "neo-politization" of part of voluntary organizations comes from Poland, where political involvement of some foundations and associations either through support of certain political parties or through entering their own candidates in parliamentarian elections challenges the notion of political neutrality.

231

While the answer to the question of how political the sector should be needs further discussion, the argument presently raised in some countries is that the sector should keep a certain distance from the political sphere and should influence the political system from the outside. The argument points to the need for the sector's political independence and its avoidance of the charge of being used by certain political forces as "a clearly political tool." In this view, the role of voluntary organizations is to be a guardian of the democratic transformation process and an advocate, not a policymaker.

Even these latter roles, however, are sometimes questioned. A recent study of the voluntary sector in Bulgaria found that 49 percent of respondents were against the advocacy role of voluntary organizations, while some 28 percent found advocacy acceptable as part of an organization's mission. This results from the recent shift of a good part of the sector's human and organizational resources into politics after 1989 (for example, Eco-glasnost in Bulgaria, the Green movement in Lithuania, the Solidarnosc union in Poland), which fostered controversies and disappointment when "diving into politics" resulted in the loss of focus on the organizations' missions. As Stephan Nikolov has remarked, "Eco-glasnost, the first opposition movement during the communist regime, was created with a specific anti-pollution program. As it split into several factions and is most frequently identified now with issues seen as `pro' or `contra' the President, it has almost forgotten about resolving environmental problems."

A pressing legal issue for the voluntary sector in East Central Europe is the weakness of state regulatory and monitoring mechanisms over voluntary organizations and the internal regulating procedures of the organizations themselves. Government regulation is still a very sensitive issue as the memories of detailed oversight by the communist governments are still fresh among activists. Nevertheless, public control and "compulsory accountability" are indispensible to ensure that the voluntary sector operates in a legal manner in all respects and is trustworthy.

East European analysts and executives of the voluntary sector believe that organizations should concentrate on the following issues in response to its major challenges:

- Develop standards of accountability, both service and financial.
- Increase skills in organizational development and management.
- Develop more varied opportunities for voluntarism.
- Facilitate opportunities and the proper conditions for networking, federating, and joint projects.

- Maintain liaisons with politicians, educating and participating (when relevant) in policy determination (social, economic, environmental, and so on) on the local and national levels without leaving the sector and becoming politicians themselves.

In the view of East European practitioners and researchers at a seminar in July 1993, the sector's role and, at the same time, its challenge will be to act as a social safety net providing services to neglected and abused children, at-risk youth, youth in general (who view the future negatively and lacking opportunities), large and low-income families, elderly and handicapped persons, the unemployed, the poor, former convicts, refugees and displaced populations, and the victims of war and violence.

Moreover, the sector will also be challenged with the role of accommodating the increased stress on society of coping with the problems of economic dislocation and displacement of social status that is taking place on a large scale in Eastern Europe. Also stressed during the seminar was the need to expand voluntary sector activities and resources beyond major urban centers to rural areas.

Another major issue is "fake" foundations. Although they are a minority among those in operation, their fraudulent activities have created suspicion and have cast doubt on the reputation of all foundations in the region. In Bulgaria, Hungary, and Poland, this issue has mobilized both government authorities and voluntary organizations' representatives toward a legal reform effort.

The continued growth of East European voluntary organizations should not be taken for granted. In a politically still-fragile environment—where the number of countries breaking up almost equals those that remain intact, where the democratic systemic transformations are endangered in some countries, where economic crises are a daily occurrence, and where fundamental changes of societal value systems are under way—there is a need for internal and external constancy in efforts to support East European voluntary organizations.

Having been a guardian of a democratic and peaceful transformation, the voluntary sector is already a significant force for change in most countries of the region. Its power lies not only in an adherence to a socially useful cause, but also in its role as a "watchdog" of democratic transformation and as a restorer of a sense of belonging and of individual and community empowerment—values suppressed under communism.

Thus, voluntary organizations in post-communist countries, where modernization is yet unfinished, serve as mediators between the demands for individual freedom and rights and the obligations of community responsibility. Contributing to the compromise between individual rights and community responsibility for fellow citizens, the East European voluntary sector strengthens the process of shaping a civil society.

Bibliography

Anheier, Helmut K. and Eckhard Priller, "The Non-profit Sector in East Germany: Before and After Unification." *Voluntas.* Vol. II, No. 1, 1991.

Barath, Arpad. "The Nonprofit and Voluntary Sector in Croatia: Critical Reflections on History, Present and Future." Unpublished Paper. 1992.

Bibo, Istvan. Quoted in Daniel Siegel and Jenny Yancey, *The Rebirth of Civil Society: The Development of the Nonprofit Sector in East Central Europe and the Role of Western Assistance.* New York: The Rockefeller Brothers Fund, 1992.

Bichniewicz, Michal and Piotr M. Rudnicki. *Time for Change, Interview with Jaroslaw Kaczynski.* Warsaw: Editions Spotkania, 1993.

Boczon, Jerzy, Witold Toczyski, and Anna Zielinska. *A Nature and Question of the Poverty.* Gdansk-Warsaw: 1991.

Dale, Reginald. "A Little Help for East Europe, Please: Thinking Ahead." *International Herald Tribune.* December 8, 1993.

Darendorf, Ralf. *Reflection on the Revolution in Europe.* New York: Random House, 1990. Quoted in Miroslav Ruzica, "Transition, Civil Society, Voluntary Sector: Focus on East Central Europe and Yugoslavia," Prepared for delivery at the Third International Conference of Research on Voluntary and Nonprofit Organizations, Indianapolis, March 11-13, 1992.

DiMaggio, Paul J. and Walter Powell. "The Iron Cage Revisited: Institutional Isomorphism and Collective Rationality in Organizational Fields." *American Sociological Review,* Vol. 48, 1983.

Ilczuk, Dorota. "Public Purpose Institutions in the Polish Tradition." Prepared for the Conference on the Polish Nonprofit Sector in Culture, Radziejowice, December 17-18, 1993.

Jakobson, Lev. "The Emergence of the Third Sector in Russia." Paper delivered at the International Conference on Well-Being in Europe by Strengthening the Third Sector, Barcelona, May 27-29, 1993.

Janda, Jiri. "An Enabling Environment in Czechoslovakia." In Ann McKinstry Micou and Birgit Lindsnaes, eds. *The Role of Voluntary Organizations in Emerging Democracies: Experience and Strategies in Eastern and Central Europe and in South Africa.* Copenhagen: The Danish Centre for Human Rights, 1993.

Kietlinska, Krystyna. "Comment on Stephen M. Wunker, The Promise of Nonprofits in Poland and Hungary: An Analysis of Third Sector Renaissance." *Voluntas.* Vol. III, No. 3, 1992.

Klon Database of Self-Help Social Service Initiatives in Poland. Warsaw: 1993.

Kontek, Ted. *Foreign Aid to Russia and the Newly Independent States: Lessons Learned from Poland and Other Former Bloc Countries.* Warsaw: Peace Corps Poland, 1993.

Kos, Anica Mikus. "The Psychosocial Help of Volunteers to Young Refugees in Slovenia." Prepared for the Spring Research Forum on Transmitting the Tradition of a Caring Society to Future Generation. San Antonio, Texas, March 18-19, 1993.

Kuti, Eva. "The Beginnings of a Contract Culture in Hungary." Prepared for the Conference on Contracting, Selling or Shrinking? Voluntary and Non-Profit Organizations and the Enabling State in International Perspective. London, July 20-22, 1993.

Kuti, Eva. Information given during the Civicus International Expert Meeting on The Third Sector in Post-Communist East Central Europe. Warsaw, July 26-27, 1993.

Kuti, Eva. "Defining the Nonprofit Sector: Hungary." Working Paper No. 13, Johns Hopkins Comparative Nonprofit Sector Project. Baltimore: The Johns Hopkins University Institute for Policy Studies, 1993.

Kuti, Eva. "Social, Political and Economic Roles of the Nonprofit Sector in Hungary in the Period of Transition." Paper, 1993.

Les, Ewa. "Social Benefits for Poverty Stricken Groups." In Andrzej Piekara and Jolanta Supinska, *Social Policy in Poland in the Period of Change.* Warsaw: Economic Publishing House, 1985.

Les, Ewa. "Polish Voluntary Organizations in the Period of Real Socialism: An Untapped Potential." Prepared for *Voluntas*, 1993.

Les, Ewa. "The Non-profit Sector in Poland in a Period of Political, Economic and Social Changes." Prepared for the Johns Hopkins University Institute for Policy Studies on Non-profit Managment Training Workshop. Jachranka, Poland, April 25-29, 1993.

Lipstas, Algirdas. Executive Director, Open Society Foundation. Interview. Warsaw, July 1993.

Marschall, Miklos. "The Nonprofit Sector in a Centrally Planned Economy." In Helmut K. Anheier and Wolfgang Seibel, eds. *The Third Sector Comparative Studies of Nonprofit Organizations.* Berlin, New York: de Gruyter, 1990.

Nikolov, Stephan E. "The Emerging Third Sector in Post-Communist Bulgaria." Unpublished Research Report. Sofia: Institute of Sociology, 1993.

Nikolov, Stephan and Kapka Panayotova. Analysts of Bulgarian voluntary sector. Interview. Warsaw, July 25, 1993.

Nowak, Stefan. "Postawy, Wartosci i Aspiracje Spoleczenstwa Polskiego." In *Polskie Systemy Wartosci i Modele Konsumpcji.* Warsaw: Warsaw University Press, 1984.

Perri 6 and Eva Kuti. "Into the European Community: Impacts of Future Membership on Hungary's Non-profit Sector." Prepared for the ARNOVA Conference, New Haven, October 31-November 1, 1992.

Polish Council of Ministers, Resolution No 76, July 9, 1992.

Salamon, Lester M. "Partners in Public Service: The Scope and Theory of Government—Nonprofit Relations." In Walter Powell, ed. *The Nonprofit Sector: A Research Handbook.* New Haven: Yale University Press, 1987.

Salamon, Lester M. "The Global Associational Revolution: The Rise of the Third Sector on the World Scene." Occasional Paper. Baltimore: The Johns Hopkins Institute for Policy Studies, 1993.

Simon, Karla W. and Leon E. Irish. *Report of Romanian Assessment Visit.* Washington, D.C.: International Center for Not for-Profit Law, 1993.

Sokolowski, Wojciech S. "Beneath The Veil of the Corporate State: The Normative Influences on Organizational Behaviour in Eastern Europe." Prepared for the 1993 Annual Meeting of the Eastern Sociological Society, Boston, April, 1993.

Staniszkis, Jadwiga. "Ideology in Contempt." *Rzeczpospolita.* December 23, 1993.

Wojnarowski, Jacek. Deputy Director, The Stefan Batory Foundation. Interview. Warsaw, July 1993.

Wyrwicka, Krystyna. Deputy Director, Department of Social Welfare, Ministry of Labour and Social Policy. Interview. Warsaw, May 1993.

Young, Lena. *Charities in Russia.* Tonbridge: Charities Aid Foundation, April 1993.

The Third Sector in Western Europe

Alain Anciaux, Amaury Nardone, Dirk Jarré, and Sylvie Tsyboula

The third sector is a very ancient tradition and a very vivid reality in Europe, where one adult out of two is reputed to be a member of at least one association. But the term "third sector" appeared only recently in Anglo-American literature, and the concept of such a sector is actually alien to Europe. Various terms are used to refer to very diverse European realities, deeply rooted in different religious and political influences.

This section considers the countries which form the extreme Western part of the Indo-European continent, and which have globally been referred to as "Western Europe" since the end of World War II. This is to differentiate them from the other European nations locked behind the Iron Curtain until the fall of the Berlin Wall in November, 1989.

In Western Europe, the terms "voluntary sector," "private sector," "social economy," "citizen movement," "charitable sector," and "associations" are the most commonly used. Collectively, these terms refer to the myriad number of self help groups, mutual assistance and solidarity organizations, citizen associations, cooperatives, voluntary initiatives, charitable trusts, philanthropic foundations, and other groups that exist in the region. These organizations are involved in or influence nearly every aspect of European life.

But this massive and growing phenomenon, ancient and widely spread around Europe (the existence of foundations can be traced back to the Greek golden age, five centuries before the birth of Jesus Christ) has hardly been viewed as a sector until recent years. Those who consider it a sector still have some conceptual difficulties defining its borders. However, the core definition of the sector is that it is private, nongovernmental, and nonprofit, with a social objective aimed at public good.

Nonprofit status does allow third sector organizations to carry out for-profit activities in order to fulfill the social objectives of the organization, as long as this profit-making activity is not the organization's main purpose and does not personally benefit the board members. For example, the ONCE Foundation in Spain runs a large lottery which provides jobs, facilities, and assistance to Spanish blind people, but does not financially benefit the Foundation's board.

Cross-Cutting Activities

Some groups are moving toward activities that defy simple categorization—"transcategory" activities that result in a breakdown of age, ethnic, and regional barriers.

In the case of intergenerational focus, the Entr'Ages association in Belgium is developing activities that break down barriers between young people, adults and the elderly.

Several programs have been launched in interethnic issues such as the Immigrants' Advisory Council in Dresden, Germany, and S.O.S. Racisme in France. This is more of a genuine mass movement than a simple association trend. It is the result of efforts to make people aware of the problems of racism and xenophobia.

While the sector encompasses many aspects of life, its activities show particular concern for certain categories of the population, such as children, women, the underprivileged, young people, and the elderly.

Initiatives by or for women can be found in various countries. In France, the Coeur de Femmes association helps women in very difficult situations (homeless, jobless, alcohol-dependent, or drug addicted) by developing hostels, assistance, and work integration, handicraft programs, and so on. In Germany, the Women's Teaching, Research and Information Centre (FFBIZ) in Berlin has spent the last 10 years gathering information on women; the Women's Health and Self-Help Movement is an information center; and the Feminist Health Centre for Women (FFGZ) offers women training on matters relating to nutrition, contraception, pregnancy, AIDS, cancer testing, and so on. The first Danish association on women's issues appeared in 1871 (Dansk Kvindesamfund). And in Greece, the XEN movement was set up in 1923 by Greek women from Asia Minor to establish rural schools.

The underprivileged—the poor, homeless, unemployed, HIV-positive, and AIDS victims—are also a major objective for the third sector. In recent years, the number of associations concerned about these groups has grown significantly. The main fields are prevention, assistance, and treatment. For example, in the Netherlands, Junkiebonden (associations of drug users) developed educational programs to combat syringe sharing. In Sweden, Noah's Ark is a private voluntary program providing prevention, education, counselling, and assistance programs with funding from the Swedish Red Cross and state subsidies.

The Third Sector in the Former Yugoslavia

One of the most remarkable examples of third sector activity in recent years is its involvement in the former Yugoslavia. Several projects and programs were launched with a total lack of organization (such as sending food, clothes, medical personnel, and so on).

Furthermore, the sector has a role (consciously or unconsciously) of making up for the lack of support from local or international authorities that are unable to find a solution to the conflict. The activities of the third sector have become the conscience of the evident failures of the public sector. In this instance, the third sector in Western Europe may have become a hostage to the authorities.

Results vary from one country to another. In the Netherlands, the spread of HIV within the drug addict community was curbed. But this was not the case in Italy and Spain.

Another large group within the third sector comprises the thousands of people involved in cultural and recreational activities, such as choirs, music schools, birdwatching associations, bicycle leagues, and county football clubs. These organizations are entirely run and supported by volunteers who dedicate most of their free time to enable others to enjoy an art or sport.

Inspiration and Historical Background

As a general rule, the influence of the Catholic and Protestant churches has been the underlying force in the creation of the association movement, although the growing trend toward secular movements in the nineteenth and twentieth centuries cannot be ignored.

The influence of the Catholic Church has been and remains important in aid and mutual assistance in Western Europe, especially around the Mediterranean basin. However, intervention became a matter for the secular authorities relatively early. Two different trends influenced the action of Catholics in civil society: liberal Catholicism, with Lammenais in France and Cavour in Italy; and social Catholicism, defending corporations, families, and communities.

In the nineteenth century, Protestant churches saw increasing activities by deacons. Many social and charity organizations were created to help children, the poor, the handicapped, and the homeless. Others were born in the follow-up to the evangelical renewal. In the first part of the nineteenth century, Protestant churches created an umbrella organization, Innere Mission.

For a long time the churches dominated the development of organizations forming the civil society in Europe. The countries of southern Europe and the Mediterranean basin were influenced more by the Catholic Church, while the northern Anglo-Saxon and Scandinavian countries were influenced by the Protestant religions. Southern countries in Europe have felt more impact from churches and, in some degree, from grassroots organizations than their Northern neighbors. For example, the Portuguese "misericordias" launched by local priests and parishes have been active in the social field for more than five centuries, taking care of invalids, educating children, assisting the poor. In the last decades, these groups have become more independent from the Church and are in vivid renewal today. In Italy, the Church-affiliated "Opere Pie" have resisted numerous attempts from the state to bring them under its control.

Beginning in the eighteenth and continuing through the nineteenth century, new needs and new secular initiatives arose from the workers (cooperatives, trade unions, housing societies, and so on). Civil society was profoundly affected by secular ideas inherited from the eighteenth century Enlightenment period. Its birth was initiated by ideas from different historical and theoretical sources: the influence of Montesquieu (the principle of devolution), Locke (liberal philosophy putting the stress on citizenship), and the Freemasons (the secularist and women's rights defense). Influenced by Taine and Fustel de Coulanges (ideas coming from the old regime) and opposed to absolutism, Alexis de Tocqueville showed the importance of the association in the United States. He recognized the advocacy power of those groups.

Other sources which should not be ignored are the "pre-Marxist" socialists such as Utopian socialists and libertarians; Charles Fourier was one of the leading figures of these trends. The intention of the Utopians was to improve society: the dominant factors in the new community, whether socialist, communist, or democratic in their widest sense, would be humans and the human personality. Another pre-Marxist socialist, Cabet, anonymously published a philosophical novel, *Le Voyage en Icarie*, which propounds egalitarian and pacifist communism. Wilhelm Weitling's approach was more subtle. He founded a communist colony under the name of Communia, which quickly failed (although it does have the merit of having existed).

Other alternative secular sources of inspiration appeared also in Scandinavia. In Norway, for example, Marcus Thrane (1817-90) was a disciple of Louis Blanc and Proudhon. He attracted public attention to the most deprived in Norway. A Thrane follower, Eilert Sundt founded in 1864 the second workers' union. August Palm played the same role in Sweden as Thrane did in Norway, spreading socialist ideas in the workers' world.

In France, Charles Gide continued the Utopians' thinking when he established the Nîmes school, which amalgamated the most dynamic schools of thinking just mentioned, such as Fourierism, the heritage of the Rochdale pioneers, and the English cooperative school. His friend Lavergne outlined the (modern) history of cooperatives by putting the establishment of the world's first consumer cooperative (Rochdale) in its proper context.

The advent of the association movement in Europe was preceded by a series of organizational attempts and social movements such as the college, the millenarian movement, organized benevolent actions, guilds, corporations, compagnonnage (a craftsmen's guild peculiar to France), mutual assistance societies, cooperatives, and communities.

Colleges of craftsmen in the Roman empire date from the fifth century BC. The members of these colleges had certain advantages such as exemption from civic duties, from torture, and from military service. The first formal guilds date from the eighth and ninth centuries in England, when mutual protection guilds, trade guilds, and craft guilds were created.

The corporation dates from the eleventh century in France. Its objectives were to divide all craftsmen into three classes: apprentices, valets, and master craftsmen, with each category having its own rights and obligations. Compagnonnage is the umbrella term for associations that sprang up in the sixteenth century in France, when the working class first took form. They survived the Le Chapelier law against associations and were very active until 1848.

Mutual assistance societies were first formed in the seventeenth century, while professional mutuals were established in cities in France from the beginning of the nineteenth century. The famous pioneers opened the first modern form of a cooperative shop in Rochdale near Manchester in 1844. The influence of the Rochdale form of cooperative was felt throughout the world.

The community is another form of organization that predates the association movement. Robert Owen, for example, devised a plan to reform society and found a new commonwealth (New Harmony) in 1825. Cabet's disciples went to America in 1848 to found a colony initially in Nauvoo (Texas). The case of Godin is also significant. A Fourierist, he succeeded in implementing what Charles Fourier never had the opportunity to do for lack of financial means: a phalanstery (a Fourierist cooperative community), in which attempts were made to make workers responsible for their actions.

Financing

The third sector in Western Europe is predominantly financed by public money, either through government subsidies to organizations or through indirect payments, such as welfare reimbursements to individuals or education allowances to families. A recent survey coordinated by the Institute for Policy Studies at the Johns Hopkins University (U.S.) revealed that governments of France, Germany, Italy, and the United Kingdom provide an average of 40% of the direct funding to the sector. This figure is representative of goverment assistance to nonprofit organizations in Western Europe. The amount would be less in such southern European countries as Spain or Greece, where the lower tax rate reduces the money available for social programs. The government funding of the third sector would also be lower in Scandinavian countries, despite a high tax rate, where national and local authorities provide more direct services to individuals rather than rely on the nonprofit organizations for service delivery.

The proportion of earned income by the sector, which ranks from around 30% in Germany and France to approximately 50% in the United Kingdom and Italy, may also largely consist of public money, depending on the country and field of interest. For example, education tuitions in France are private earnings, although part of it is provided by family allowances, but this would not be true in the United Kingdom. Generally speaking, welfare states such as Germany, Belgium, France, the Netherlands, and Luxembourg grant their citizens a very encompassing social security system, which enables the citizens to pay or be reimbursed for services provided by third sector organizations.

Not surprisingly, private giving for voluntary organizations is very low, with a high in the United Kingdom (12% of the funding sources) and a low in Germany (4%). In France and Germany, private giving as a share of personal income is less than 0.2%. Donations made by individuals in Western Europe are also determined by authorized tax deductions for payments made to charity or humanitarian associations (for example, deductions are authorized for all donations in Germany, whereas in Belgium, only donations exceeding BFr. 1,000 [approximately $30] are deductible). Though marginal, individual giving seems to be growing under the influence of a new feeling of solidarity, reinforced by the lasting economic crisis affecting Europe. Media campaigns for such causes as assistance to the disabled or AIDS patients are raising more and more money.

Corporate giving, although at a relatively high level in countries like France, Italy, and the United Kingdom (about 10% of total private giving) has a limited impact, but has raised new concerns about management and strategy, and is helping the sector to become more professional. Corporate giving largely remains focused on cultural and environmental issues.

Private grantmaking foundations tend to be more socially oriented than the corporations, and tackle such burning issues as AIDS, homelessness, and unemployment. Although the financial weight of private foundations is not much higher than that of the corporations, their impact comes more from their moral authority and their innovative capacity.

Overall, the third sector in Europe relies heavily on government support. This large and growing sector, predominantly funded by public money, contradicts the commonly accepted stereotype of state versus voluntary efforts. In fact, looking at the high level of government support reveals how much the sector serves the state.

Subsidizing used to be the common way of funding associations by national and local governments, but contracts are becoming increasingly favored by public authorities who use the contracts as tools for monitoring costs and policies. The so-called "contract culture" has been initiated by the British government as a way of reducing the excessive weight of the health care system by allowing commercial and voluntary private organizations to compete for contracting home care delivery.

Contracting is still a fairly recent development and needs to be explored further. Although the concept contains seeds for innovative relationships and organizational creativity, it still raises suspicions. Nonprofit organizations are afraid of becoming constrained by prescriptive regulations inspired by governmental financial limitations and/or political liberal visions. But the emerging "contract culture" does offer one of the most tangible evidences of the changing relationship between Western European democracies and their citizens: the latter is being granted more responsibility, and the former is more aware of its own limitations.

Other means of financing come from supranational institutions, as is the case with resources redistributed to European Union member-states through the intermediary of various mechanisms and funds that are distributed to the association system either directly or indirectly (national, regional, or local authorities). The following are pertinent examples: the European Social Fund, the European Fund for Regional Development, and the European Fund for Agricultural Orientation and Security (General Directorates XVI and VI).

Scope and Main Themes

The scope of the third sector in the European Union is estimated at more than 2 million organizations, although this figure may be well below reality. As it is impossible to get homogeneous data, because the legal definitions for non-profit organizations vary from country to country, one can only rely on approximations: 800,000 nonprofit organizations in Germany, including 6,000 foundations; 600,000 in France, with only 500 foundations; 300,000 charities and charitable trusts in the United Kingdom; 200,000 nonprofit organizations in Italy; 60,000 in Spain, including about 10,000 foundations; 30,000 organizations in Portugal; 100,000 in Belgium and the Netherlands; and 3,000 in Luxembourg.

The third sector may be classified by the structure of organizations. Most are statutory (de jure) groups, such as associations or cooperatives. Their main feature is their egalitarian system, based on the principle of collective responsibility combined with the democratic segregation of power and sometimes a distribution or division of tasks aimed at enhancing new relations between people based on solidarity and consensus (as opposed to competition and hierarchy).

Another important attribute of the sector is the existence of secondary-level organizations. These are federations, networks, or complexes of organizations with common aims covered by an umbrella status at the national level (compared with a simple association or cooperative). One example is the Economic Alternatives Network in Belgium, whose members are organizations that consider themselves adherents to the philosophy of the tertiary sector.

Other larger groups exist at the European level, such as the European Community Coordinating Committee for Cooperative Associations (Comité de Coordination des Associations de Coopératives de la Communauté Européenne); the European Red Cross Liaison Committee, which is the representative body for the national Red Cross associations throughout Europe; and the European Committee on General Interest Associations (Comité Européen des Associations d'Intérêt Général), whose specific and interesting feature is its transsectoral nature. Some of these are tertiary level organizations—that is, umbrella movements for secondary-level organizations.

An additional point determines the shape of the third sector in Western Europe: the existence of a spectrum of organizations orbiting around two economic sectors—the public, and the private, profit-making sector. This is the case, for example, of NGOs that receive money from the authorities and are often labelled QUANGOS (quasi-autonomous, nongovernmental organizations), such as the Krankenkassen in Switzerland, which operate on a mixed private and public system. It must, however, be noted that some groups in the tertiary sector in Western Europe exceed their "social objective" by diverting funds or goods to assist the Third World. This is the case in 1988 of the Tvind-Humana association, which had shops in Copenhagen, London, Marseilles, Brussels, Hamburg, Utrecht, and Amsterdam.

A main feature of the third sector in Western Europe is the wide range of themes that are addressed, with an emphasis on social programs. They fall into the following categories:

- *aspects of the economic sector:* unions, workers' associations, consumer associations (for example, the CIRAT, which defends workers' associations in French-speaking Belgium);

- *protection of family values:* family associations, feminist associations (for example, XEN in Greece, a section of the Women's Christian Union);

- *ecology promotion:* ecological associations (for example, Greenpeace), but political parties are not included in this classification;

- *protection of democratic rights:* Amnesty International, the League of Human Rights, Democratic Lawyers ("Juristes Démocrates"), peace associations in Finland;

- *teaching and educational programs*: promoting active methods in teaching children (for example, in Austria, where there is a series of pre-and post-school activities) and the action of cultural associations (for example, the Aimé Maeght Fondation in France);

- *health promotion*: the objective of certain associations is to promote public health in general, for example the Groupe d'Etude pour la Réforme de la Médecine (Study Group to reform medical practices, in Belgium) and sports associations;

- *the struggle against social marginalization*: these activities address specific questions (housing, food, health, action, law, and so on), for example, the ENKA association in Turkey, which helps Bosnian refugees;

- *aid for development and the Third World*: many organizations operate in this field, either in overall development or on a specific form of cooperation or development help, such as the Christian Solidarity association in Greece;

- *economic growth*: intermediary enterprises (France), profes- sional apprenticeship enterprises (Belgium), local job creation initiatives (in countries dependent on the European Community), cooperatives;

- *social work, assistance, and social self-help*: mutual assistance societies, mutualities, Caritas, and so on.

The third sector spans society and has the image of a safeguard of democ- racy: it contributes to the cultural development of individuals and the struggle against injustice in life, and provides the population with the means of being heard (pressure groups). It also contributes to economic growth, either in the form of the jobs it creates in the association sector or through the action of cooperatives.

The European third sector tends to emphasize its democratic component more than its charitable one, as its representatives consider this organizational feature as its most remarkable and more precious. Nevertheless, the sector is primarily active in the social services (dominant activity in France and Italy), health (dominant in Germany), and education (dominant in the United King- dom). These three trends perfectly reflect the traditional welfare state con- cerns for people, and confirm the high financial support the sector receives from governments.

Few organizations are dedicated to civic and human rights and advocacy in general, even though the most famous of this type of organization—Am- nesty International—is European born. This probably is an indication of how any societal dissatisfaction tends to be addressed through political representation or trade unions, more than through third sector organizations.

Third-sector organizations address limited fields and rarely have multiple activities to cover varying aspects of the same issue. For example, the main objective of benevolent societies in Ireland is social help and not—to cite just one other possible goal—assimilation into the professional world. This is why the sector's analysis of leading themes gives the impression of being a "fragmented universe," a feeling that is strengthened by the small number of joint actions that involve several organizations. When a common issue arises, action is not always supported by coordinated effort.

The Legal Position of Associations

It is difficult to describe the law of associations in Western Europe, given the widely varying forms in existence, sometimes even within the same country. There is, however, one notion about which all agree: that the association (here meaning an organization with non-profit-making objectives) is characterized by the "universitas personarum," because it amounts to a grouping of individuals, as opposed to a "universitas rerum," which is the distinguishing feature of a foundation.

Many countries—Greece, the Netherlands, Italy, Portugal, Germany, and Switzerland—have set aside space in their civil codes for the rules governing association. France, whose Napoleonic Code is the ancestor of European civil codes, does not provide for any rules relating to associations in its own civil code. It will, however, be recalled that governments have treated them with suspicion.

Belgium, Spain, France, and Luxembourg have all chosen to promulgate statutes regulating associations with non-profit-making objectives. In Ireland, the United Kingdom, and Denmark, the law of associations is based on case law, even if certain statutes have been passed concerning, for example, certain associations in Denmark, "friendly societies" in Ireland, or charities in England.

Legal personality is an important distinguishing mark in the laws of Western Europe. Obtaining such a personality enables a distinction to be made between the association and its members, and confers legal capacity to a greater or lesser degree, depending on the situation.

Associations without legal personality have no legal capacity, as in Germany, or extremely limited capacity, as in France, where associations that have not been declared to the authorities have the right to take part in legal

---

Immigrant Associations

Following massive immigration to Western Europe either from poorer European areas or from developing countries, associations of immigrants were created in considerable numbers during the last 20-30 years. They offer immigrants a secure social and cultural framework in which they can maintain their national, ethnic, religious, and linguistic identity.

West European governments do not always welcome these organizations, as they often also pursue, openly or secretly, nationalistic or political goals, and consequently are sometimes considered as troublemakers or even subversive elements in the host country.

---

proceedings as defendant, or in the Netherlands, where they may receive donations.

In various countries, associations having legal personality have restricted capacity. They may only benefit from substantial bequests following authorization from the government, and may not acquire real estate except for that necessary for carrying out their objectives (as in Belgium, Spain, France, and Luxembourg). In Italy, even the acquisition of real estate by publicly recognized associations is subject to official authorization.

The method of obtaining legal personality varies considerably from one country to another, depending on how much the authorities intervene. The two most liberal countries in that regard are Switzerland and Denmark, where the signature of the memorandum and articles of association is alone sufficient to confer separate legal personality on an association. In Denmark, however, associations that comply with the conditions laid down by the statute of 1984 must apply for registration at the Registrar of Foundations.

Portugal and the Netherlands already involve the authorities at that stage, because separate legal personality is only granted to associations in those two countries when their memorandum and articles are drawn up in authenticated form—that is, before a Notary. The most restrictive system is the Italian, where associations may only acquire legal personality under a decree issued by the President of the Republic.

The level of intervention by the authorities required to obtain separate legal personality may involve requiring publication of a notice in an official

---

The United Nations in Europe

The substantial presence of the United Nations in Western Europe (particularly in Geneva and Paris) has always been important for international NGOs, particularly those dealing with human rights issues, development matters, culture, social affairs, and health care.

Their particular relationship with the UN specialized agencies not only allows them to be closely associated with the UN agenda but also permits them to meet each other frequently, to discover their common interests, and to cooperate internationally in matters of mutual concern.

Without any doubt, the United Nations declarations of International Years and Decades on constitute an important unifying factor for NGOs working in the same or in similar fields and promote a spirit of solidarity and cooperation among them.

---

journal, preceded by a declaration to the authorities (in France) or followed by the formality of filing (in Belgium and Luxembourg) or of registration on a public register (in Germany). Sometimes such registration is preceded by a review by public authorities, which may take the form of review by the court (in Greece) or by a government body (in Spain). In all cases, the review is to check legal compliance, not suitability.

In the "common law" systems, the distinction between structures with legal personality and those without it is particularly relevant. Certain types of companies in the form of associations have separate legal personality from their members (such as the industrial and provident societies, or companies limited by guarantee), whereas others do not (such as friendly societies or members' clubs).

Finally, whereas in some countries the courts have held that associations may arise as a matter of fact, elsewhere they are recognized by statute. This is the position in France regarding associations that have not been the subject of a declaration to the authorities, and in Italy regarding those that are not officially recognized, along with committees. In fact, in Italy most associations wishing to avoid any control by the state opt to not be officially recognized.

Some countries grant to associations fulfilling certain conditions a sort of public benefit or public interest label, with both notions being closely linked and resulting in all kinds of advantages (such as wider legal capacity and tax exemptions). The English and Irish charities are examples of this, and they occupy a dominant position in the associations of those countries. To obtain this status, an organization must have a charitable (public benefit) objective—such as relief of poverty, advancement of education or religion, or any other activity benefitting the community—and must be approved by a public authority, the Charities Commission. It will then be entered into the Charities Register.

Associations' industrial or commercial activity is permitted to varying degrees in Western Europe. In fact, although all the countries allow economic activity, it must as a rule be incidental or occasional, and must be for the purpose of pursuing the association's objectives without any profit motive. Some countries (such as the Netherlands and Switzerland) have a more liberal approach and allow associations to be included in the Trade Registry.

Nonprofit organizations pursuing objectives in the public interest or of public benefit are generally exempt from corporation tax. This is the case of charities in the United Kingdom, for example. But certain countries (Germany and Luxembourg) also exempt other activities, such as religious ones. It may be necessary to obtain prior approval in order to benefit from these exemptions, as in Portugal.

To obtain an exemption, one condition must be complied with even by approved organizations—the commercial activity must not compete with commercial companies. In France, this criterion has been defined by the courts and the tax authorities as any activity that has a social utility by satisfying needs that are not met, or are met insufficiently, by the local commercial market.

The Legal Position of Foundations

Foundations have existed in Western Europe since antiquity. An oft-quoted but perfectly representative example is Plato's Academy, founded by Theophrast, who devised his garden on the basis that his descendants should allow the disciples of his school of thought to use it. It lasted eight centuries.

Roman law developed the concept of "universitas rerum," the universal ownership of goods, which remains one of the essential characteristics of foundations. Nowadays, foundations are the usual prerogative of great industrialists or governments (for example, the Max Planck Institute); the annual cultural expenditure of the Portuguese Gulbenkian Foundation, for instance, is the equivalent of one third the annual cultural budget of Portugal.

In general, a foundation may be defined as the irrevocable endowment of property by one or more persons for a defined purpose. Depending on the

251

circumstances, this purpose may be to the public benefit or for private purposes.

Certain legal systems—in Belgium, Spain, France, Luxembourg, and Portugal—only recognize foundations for the public benefit. Others recognize foundations for private purposes. In Denmark, foundations with profit-making objectives are subject to a specific statute. In Greece, the provisions relating to foundations are found in the civil code, which provides that they do not need to be for the benefit of the public. In Italy, family foundations are permitted.

In the Netherlands, the statute of 1956, which was incorporated in the civil code in 1976, only provides for the need to have a "specific" objective; this allows foundations to pursue private or even economic objectives. In Germany and Switzerland, foundations for the benefit of public or private objectives are allowed without any restrictions. In the United Kingdom and Ireland, "trusts" may pursue objectives for the benefit of the public and obtain the status of "charities."

The authorities are more involved with foundations than with associations. The very vocation of a foundation is to perpetuate the will of its founder by means of the property endowed, so this requires that the aims are not betrayed or the property diverted from its proper purpose. For this reason, the organization and activities of foundations are placed under the protection of authorities almost everywhere. Except for the British or Irish "trust," which does not have legal personality and requires no official permission or registration, it is necessary to obtain official authorization to create a foundation or to follow certain registration formalities.

The extent of protection varies from country to country. It may take the form of an audit of accounts (Belgium and Luxembourg, for example) or of prior authorization for gifts made to the foundation (France). As a general rule, however, protection will be limited to authorizing sales or other disposition of property that materially affects the property of the foundation, or to supervising the managing organs of the group. Above all, protection extends to the alteration of the objectives of the foundation or its dissolution, whereby the pursuance of its objectives would be affected or made impossible. The authorities would then be obliged to allocate the property of the foundation to organizations pursuing identical or similar goals.

NGOs in Third World Development

In the early 1970s, national development NGOs realized that the Commission of the European Community had come to the painful conclusion that its direct interventions in the former colonies were for the most part not very successful. And that they had to find, in addition to purely economic actors, societal voluntary organizations as partners to carry out developmental projects and public opinion campaigns.

National development NGOs organized themselves on a European Community basis and created a formal Liaison Committee of Development NGOs to the European Community to facilitate their cooperation with the Commission and the other organs of the Community. Believing that they could maintain their independence from the Commission through the necessity and the quality of their work, they accepted that the functioning of this structure was financed by Community funds.

In general terms this assumption proved to be right, and the cooperation between the national NGOs and their European intergovernmental partners developed well. Cofinancing from the Commis-

---

The Sector's Internationalization

The two decades after 1945 witnessed for the first time in modern European history very strong associations that were organized transnationally and promoting the idea of European unity. These were partly the expression of people's desire to see a fast and effective European integration process, and therefore to stimulate public debate about the issue. They were also the result of progress in European integration policies. As such, they played an important educational role.

At the same time, two other new and significant transnational types of associations began to play an important role in international relations. The first type was trans-Atlantic organizations basically imported from the United States to extend networks and activities to West European countries. These groups became rapidly accepted agents of the "American way of life" and effectively promoted North American convictions, values, and standards, particularly in educational and professional matters, in culture and leisure, in volunteer work and active participation in public matters, in consumer affairs, in the environment, and in human rights.

The other national and European associations oriented toward the rest of the world were those concerned with "underdeveloped countries" and particularly with issues of human aid and political solidarity. Many originated from church organizations that had vested interests in these countries; others had more political-ideological backgrounds. As they were aware of the changing geopolitical conditions, they promoted a new moral consciousness toward countries throwing off colonialism. They played an important role first in the process of decolonization, and later in the support for survival and the implementation of development strategies in what eventually became known as the Third World.

With the sudden breakdown of the socialist-communist regimes in the late 1980s, NGO leaders with experience in international cooperation were aware of both the extreme needs of Eastern Europe in respect to civil society and the new opportunities offered for the development of their own organizations. Considerable government funding from national as well as from European Community sources became available for developmental projects in the former East European communist states, and West European NGOs could obtain a substantial part of it.

Their main advantages in comparison with market forces were that they could use already existing personal or institutional contacts in these countries, they could operate with flexible structures, they could provide appropriate concepts for small or medium-sized projects, and they had proven services to offer. In comparison with commercial actors such as consulting firms, they have been created by citizens for citizens, and thus command a much higher degree of confidence. Still, NGOs do not always act without self-interest and out of pure altruism; often their programs in Central and Eastern Europe were for them instruments to gain more visibility, recognition, financial support back home, and thus entry and influence in international cooperation.

The intervention of West European NGOs in the Eastern part of the continent has been and still is particularly significant and valuable in terms of quick humanitarian aid for the victims of the ongoing military conflicts. Their provision of social services for those badly affected by the disastrous effects of the changes in the economic and administrative systems in Central and Eastern Europe and their efforts to cover basic survival needs of the large, newly marginalized groups in these countries should not be underestimated. At the same time, they have a lot of indirect political merit in trying to keep the public aware of the fundamental reasons behind the tensions and problems in

---

The European Citizen Action Service

Most local, regional, and national NGOs—and even the international ones—cannot afford full-time representation in Brussels, but they still need to be properly informed about the Community's intervention in their field of activities and about how to lobby where. The European Citizen Action Service (ECAS), based in Brussels, provides them with appropriate data and advice on the basis of service-oriented fees. ECAS itself takes certain initiatives by raising European issues of common interest to NGOs, such as Community budgeting matters, the need for transnational training for NGO leaders, and problems in data protection matters. It also creates temporary NGO coalitions in order to promote awareness of and action in up-coming important questions.

---

this area by organizing relief campaigns and public demonstrations and by using the media.

Many national organizations engaged in the various fields of international relations and cooperation made substantial efforts to identify appropriate partners in other West European countries with which they could cooperate. But there were, and still are, many obstacles to this. The first one is that West European associations are predominantly local, at best with some efficient national structuring. The culture has hardly developed any consciousness of the advantage of and the need for transnational cooperation.

Second, the traditional legal basis of associations in Europe does not at all promote, or perhaps even permit, an international dimension of the organizations' networks and activities. International NGOs had—and still have—enormous difficulties being accepted. Basically, West European states do not recognize international NGOs and, consequently, only permit them to be registered as a national NGO, which is obviously in contradiction to their nature and requirements. At the same time, transfrontier cooperation of NGOs also encounters many problems and obstacles and is much more difficult than the international establishment of business enterprises.

The only West European state explicitly open to international NGOs was, at an early stage, Belgium, which adopted in 1919 a very appropriate law on international associations. It easily allows the constitution of such bodies and

The European Council for Voluntary Organizations

Stimulated by the first European Conference on Social Economy in Paris in 1989, French associations with international interests took the initiative, together with partners in other Community member-states, to create the European Council for Voluntary Organizations (CEDAG, the Comité Européen des Associations d'Intérêt Général). Its aim is to defend at the Community level the common interests of the whole nonprofit association sector and to promote the recognition of and measures for associations pursuing goals in the general interest of society and contributing to social and cultural development.

As a nonsectorial European membership organization, CEDAG strives for the recognition of associations on all levels: constitutional; legal, by applying specific European legislation; fiscal, through taxation measures; and structural, through institutional cooperation. CEDAG has become the major recognized dialogue partner of the Community's institutions—the European Parliament, the Commission, the Council of Ministers, and the Economic and Social Committee—in matters of the statute for European associations, in fiscal matters, and in the issue of developing a suitable Community policy for consultation and harmonization.

permits them to be composed of Belgians and foreigners, with the only condition in respect to nationality being that the board of the international association must include at least one Belgian national. Furthermore, it accepts that international associations that have their legal seat in a foreign country may exercise in Belgium the rights given to them by their national statute provided they conform to certain Belgian laws and do not act against public order. The issue of the legal basis of international NGOs and their international recognition by states is important as it determines their political position and their opportunities for taking action.

Despite persisting legal difficulties mentioned, West European society at large and politicians in particular have accepted the role of associations as powerful and even indispensable actors in international relations. Because of their courageous actions and the interested support of the media, organizations like Greenpeace, Médecins sans Frontières, and Amnesty International have globally become quite influential and highly respected or even feared.

Nowadays, many national administrations and intergovernmental bodies seek in various areas of intervention close cooperation not only with domestic NGOs but also with international ones, thus recognizing that states by themselves are no longer in a position to provide solutions to all problems and accepting that other actors of a nonpublic nature, such as market forces and voluntary nonprofit organizations, have a complementary transnational role to play in an ever more internationalized world context.

The Council of Europe is the oldest Western European political intergovernmental organization. Created in 1949 by 11 European governments, it currently unites 32 member states. The Council's aim is "to achieve a greater unity between its members for the purpose of safeguarding and realizing the ideals and principles which are their common heritage and facilitating their economic and social progress. This aim shall be pursued through the organs of the Council by discussion of questions of common concern and by agreements and common action in economic, social, cultural, scientific, legal and administrative matters and in the maintenance and further realization of human rights and fundamental freedoms."

On the one hand, the objectives and the activities of the Council of Europe in vastly different areas are of great relevance for NGOs. On the other hand, NGO expertise in the various sectors is needed and their initiatives are highly welcomed by the Council. For this reason, the Council of Europe established rules for the consultative status of international NGOs that define their rights and obligations in the framework of mutual cooperation. Today, more than 350 international European NGOs hold consultative status with the Council. While actively supporting the organization's aims and goals, these NGOs can participate in a wide range of activities of the Council of Europe and contribute to its policies and programs.

A rather unique feature of this international cooperation between governmental and nongovernmental structures is the existence of a Joint Committee composed of an equal number of members of the Parliamentary Assembly of the Council of Europe and of representatives of European NGOs. It is considered as a subcommittee of a parliamentary commission and it was, curiously enough, even on one occasion chaired by an NGO representative.

Together with the General Secretariat and the Parliamentary Assembly of the Council of Europe, the European NGOs in consultative status have organized significant conferences on present conditions of European society and its future perspectives. They have dealt with important issues such as "interest groups: a help or a hinderance to parliamentary democracy?," "new poverty in

---

The Red Cross

The Red Cross covers more than 6.5 million individual members in its national societies in the 12 member-states of the European Community. Their importance can partly be measured by the fact that they have more than 80,000 employees and far more than 1 million volunteers.

In order to negotiate with the Commission of the European Community on assistance and cooperation in matters of disaster relief and other emergency intervention in member-states or in the Third World on sociomedical services and many other domains, these European national societies have created their own permanent Liaison Bureau Red Cross-European Community in Brussels. The same is true for other broadly oriented NGOs of a similar kind, such as Caritas Europe.

Europe," "voluntary effort in social welfare," and "politics and citizens—politics serving the citizen and citizen's participation in politics."

The Assembly of the Council of Europe has always been aware of problems and obstacles encountered by NGOs on the national as well as the international level. It has appealed repeatedly to political parties, the media, and legislators in the member-states to give more attention, consideration, and support to these groups. The Council recognized the need to create an international legal instrument aimed at facilitating NGO programs, cooperation, and mobility at the international level.

To help overcome inadequate provisions, the Council drafted and adopted in the mid-1980s a European Convention on the Recognition of the Legal Personality of International Non-Governmental Organizations, which was opened for signature by member-states in April 1986. Although this represents a rather timid and minimal approach to the problem, it took almost five years before the convention came into force through the required minimum ratification of three member-states.

The European Convention is a major breakthrough. It gives clear evidence of an important shift in the perception of these bodies by West European governments. In the meantime, it has provided the conceptual basis for other, more progressive projects of international legislation to promote the development of European associations.

The real influence of NGOs on the establishment and the implementation of pan-European policies in the various areas of life through the Council of Europe is clearly limited. This is mainly because NGOs, despite their uncontested importance and responsibilities in a democratic and pluralist society, have in general not sufficiently developed political attitudes and strategic skills. Consequently, they are used by governmental structures as valuable transmitters to and from the citizen or as useful service providers, but they are not highly ranked as politically relevant actors.

The European supranational institution that has most attracted the interest of national and European NGOs during the last two decades and particularly during the last four to five years is undoubtedly the European Community (known as the European Union since the Maastricht Treaty of November 1993). Its actual power has been growing constantly and the direct impact of its decisions is much greater, although different, than that of the United Nations organizations or the Council of Europe. Community legislation has immediate consequences in the member-states and thus increasingly affects most areas in which associations are active.

The Treaty of Rome of 1958, the legal basis of the European Communities, is essentially centered around issues of European economic cooperation and neither mentions the role of citizens' associations nor refers to NGOs. For almost three decades, their existence and vital role in European society was largely ignored despite the fact that citizens' organizations such as the European Movement, founded in 1948, and many other pan-European associations had considerably contributed to the discussion about and the promotion of European integration.

Certain specific types of NGOs, representing the partners in industrial relations (employers' organizations and trade unions) and some other economic forces (consumers' associations), have been given an institutional representation only in the European Economic and Social Committee of the European Community, which has merely a consultative role.

Still, since the early seventies certain mechanisms of cooperation have been developed between the Commission of the European Community and sectorial national NGOs in member-states. This occurred mainly because the organs of the Community realized that collaboration with nongovernmental structures was in their own best interest. Formal structures of collaboration were established in the field of development aid—an important domain because the Community has, by the Treaties of Lomé, special obligations toward the African, Caribbean, and Pacific states, the former colonies of the member-states.

The Community started in 1977 to cofinance NGO activity programs in the Third World. The European Community Council of Ministers, responsible for development aid, stated in May 1991: "The Community has found in NGOs efficient and reliable partners to carry out programs and projects aiming to improve living conditions and the perspectives of development of populations in the receiving countries. Thus the Community responds to the commitment and to the support which the European public gives to the solidarity actions on the non-governmental level."

Other fields of collaboration between the Community's institutions and NGOs are the various programs to combat poverty and to address certain environmental issues, consumer affairs, and youth exchange, just to mention a few sectors. While the contacts mainly started with initiatives from national NGOs, these groups soon felt the need to seek contacts in other member-states and later realized the advantages of organizing themselves on a European basis so that they could express and defend their needs and interests vis-à-vis their intergovernmental European partners, increasing their credibility and influence.

A somewhat different European collaboration is represented by structures created on the direct initiative of Community institutions, particularly the Commission, to deal with important or even burning issues on the European level and to support Community programs. This is the case of, for example, the European Anti-Poverty Network and the Youth Forum of the European Community, both of which have a touch of a QUANGO as they are largely financed by Community funds. It is, in fact, difficult to evaluate the degree of independence and autonomy of action they enjoy.

In the second half of the eighties, three factors contributed to a drastic change in the perception of NGOs by the Community. The first was the Single European Act of 1986, which extended the Community's field of action to new policies concerned with economic and social conditions. At the same time, the negotiations on the revision of the Community treaties leading to the European Union started and turned Community policies progressively into a matter of public debate. The second influence was the development of a clearer vision of a citizens' Europe as one of the goals of European integration. The third one was the sudden discovery of the importance of NGOs in economic terms—their impressive turnover, their function as service providers, and their role as employers. This was obviously a result of fundamental ideological and economic changes in West European society in general.

On the initiative of the French government, the Commission of the European Community created in the late 1980s a new working unit on Économie Sociale (the so-called social economy), the economic sector of nonprofit organizations consisting of cooperatives, mutuals (friendly societies), associations, and foundations. In December 1989, the Commission submitted a report on the situation of the enterprises of the social economy in relation to the achievements of the Single Market in 1993. It argued that these types of enterprises are properly part of the economic sector, as they carry out productive activities and produce negotiable goods and services. At the same time, it gave impressive evidence of the economic importance of the sector. The report showed the direction and measures to be taken in order to give these economic actors access to the opportunities of the new Single Market by eliminating all discrimination in comparison with commercial enterprises.

Furthermore, the Commission strongly suggested the creation of specific European legal statutes for each of the three components of the social economy (associations, voluntary organizations, and NGOs). With the support of the Economic and Social Committee, the relevant article of the Treaty of Rome that explicitly excludes non-profit-making bodies from the scope of Community action would be reinterpreted so that these groups in fact produce internal profits and thus act like any other economic performer. According to their philosophy and their statutes, however, they do not distribute these benefits (as companies do, for example, to their shareholders) but reinvest them internally into activities to attain their goals and objectives.

The Commission continues to explore and document the problems and the economic as well as the social potential of associations in the member-states of the Union. It works closely with the European Foundation Centre in Brussels, set up by European foundations with the support of some U.S. foundations to document and provide information on that sector and to do some lobbying. The working unit on Économie Sociale is preparing a White Book an associations in Europe based on an intensive data collection campaign done through questionnaires to public authorities and literally thousands of important associations, and followed up by direct interviews. The Commission hopes that the presentation of hard facts will convince national governments to recognize the relevance of the sector in a Single Market perspective as well as in terms of the construction of European civic society, and that they will consequently agree with the appropriate legislative measures (European statute and fiscal strategies) and provide material support through a European Fund for the promotion of the voluntary sector at the European level.

The Commission already provides some financial support to the activities of European associations. In addition, it promotes research on the Économie Sociale throughout the Union and cofinances a major conference of the sector every other year. These European Conferences on Social Economy have played a significant role in establishing some degree of identity and public recognition of the European dimension of this sector and have helped organizations identify their common features and interests.

An important issue raised by the sector since the first European Conference on Social Economy in 1989 in Paris is the need for appropriate methods and structures for consultation and harmonization, which it strongly requests the Commission to provide.

The public debate about the Treaty of Maastricht, the political European Union, and particularly crucial issues such as the "democratic deficit" of the European institutions and the vision of a Europe of the Citizen has recently driven the Commission to a more constructive and cooperative relationship. The Commission has asked the sector to come up with a single proposal for a consultative committee that will guarantee balanced representation and easy cooperation.

An appropriate Union policy for consultation and harmonization would not only advance groups' political and economic recognition but also give them more direct access to decision-making procedures within the Commission. This would greatly enhance their influence in all matters pertaining to their own existence and activities. However, the sector itself has great difficulty identifying common denominators and formulating a common strategy.

There can be no doubt that the importance of the relationship between the Community institutions and associations in Europe will grow rapidly. As the Treaty of Maastricht has extended the power of the European Union and even opened substantial new areas to its competence—such as social policy, environmental matters, education, vocational training and youth, culture, public health, and consumer protection—the Commission will need partners to implement European policies successfully. This represents a great opportunity for European NGOs, whether they are national or transnational. The same is true for the development of European citizenship, another complex issue of highest importance for the Union.

Visions For Tomorrow

Government efforts to transform the economic European Communities into the political and monetary European Union and the potential growth of membership of this integrated structure have been, during recent years, of considerable interest to NGOs already operating on transnational lines in Europe. They are aware that the political and economic integration process in Europe will, in the long run, have substantial evolutionary effects on European society and, consequently, affect people and their voluntary organizations. However, the rather remote government decision-making processes that led from the Single Act to a more precise approach to the European Union through the Treaty of Maastricht—even though judged as necessary by a majority—were largely perceived as dangerously lacking citizens' participation and therefore indicative of an acute "democratic deficit" in the integration process of Western Europe.

A good number of European and national NGOs, keen to actively articulate their convictions and interests in the matter, became strongly involved in the rather polarized public dispute about the future direction and the contents of the Union. On the whole, this provoked the renewal of an old dispute among NGOs as well as in the government spheres about whether and how much nongovernmental organizations should voice their opinions on political issues.

The ongoing debate on the application of the principle of subsidiarity in Western Europe gives NGOs an interesting position in the future design of sociopolitical structures. On the level of the European Union, subsidiarity means that the European political and administrative organs should not deal with matters that are better and more efficiently dealt with at the national level. But in the national context, it means that the state or regional and local public administrations should abstain from handling problems and demands that people are able and willing to solve adequately themselves. Nowadays there is a clear trend that questions or even denies increasingly the state's supreme responsibility for extended areas of human existence and that emphasizes more and more the need for and the advantages of individual responsibility, self-help, and actions by citizens' voluntary organizations.

Unfortunately only a relatively small number of NGOs in Europe—and for obvious reasons, mostly "European" ones—have fully understood this crucial issue thus far and its importance for their own relevance in society. Even fewer try to participate actively in the political debate in order to influence it—not only to defend their sectorial or client-oriented interests but also to contribute to the general promotion of civil society in Europe and not leave it all to the politicians.

Another major set of changes in Western Europe that nongovernmental organizations now observe with great attention and to which they try to react are the consequences of the crisis of the welfare state combined with the effects of the present sustained economic depression. In this context, NGOs have to deal with a variety of rather fundamental problems touching the very heart of their existence.

The welfare state is being called into question for two different reasons: political and structural. The political debate is obviously centered around the issue of the relationship between the state and the individual, and particularly the question of how much responsibility the state should have—even to the point of monopoly, perhaps—in providing social security and personal services. After the Great Depression of the 1930s, comprehensive social policies with very strong public involvement were considered the appropriate answer to the strongly felt need for individual and collective security. But experience shows that governments may have inherent problems providing adequately the whole range of goods and services required in this area.

In addition, structural changes in Western Europe have put tremendous strain on governments during the last two decades. The problems of an aging population, the urgent need for more long-term-care facilities, the tensions caused by massive immigration and multicultural coexistence, the rising cost of medical services, the consequences of the growing risk of unemployment—just to mention some major issues of structural changes—have led to the conclusion that government is no longer able to solve these generalized societal problems by itself. Budgetary breakdown and organizational exhaustion are unavoidable. Apart from that, additional public investment in this domain clearly conflicts both with peoples' willingness and capacity to pay more taxes and with the need for government investments in infrastructure and productive areas.

What started in the 1970s as a rather academic debate about the need and the advantages of a "welfare mix"—a cooperative arrangement between public and private providers of welfare—seems to have evolved in favor of the open market option and personal self-reliance. This leads to a high degree of competitiveness and to more individual choices, which opens up opportunities as well as risks. On these grounds, governments try to desocialize public social security systems as well as health and welfare services by deregulation and privatization in order to attract and strengthen private providers.

With the rising acceptance of the overwhelming importance and "moral value" of economic success by individuals and anonymous company structures, which is actively promoted by public authorities, there seems to be less and less common agreement on humanistic societal visions in European society. Competing individual and corporate self-centered egos act clearly against the concept of solidarition and financing system, their management, and their corporate identity and public image. But those that have realized and understood the recent changes in European society and politics and are aware of the pressing needs for their own change and reorientation are still a minority. Most NGOs continue to be convinced of their moral superiority and to expect external help (mostly from governments or other public structures) when encountering difficulties or responding to new demands.

The expected diminishing role of the nation-state in Western Europe due both to the already mentioned crisis of state and to the rapidly developing importance of the bureaucracy of the European Union will lead to a growing need to strengthen existing intermediary structures or even to invent and create new ones. Otherwise the central administrations of "integrated Europe," which are—understandably or even necessarily—so remote from the realities of people will not be able to perceive and understand people's desires, problems, aspirations, needs, hopes, and fears. Their inevitable structural distance may render them less and less capable of grasping the economic behavior of individuals and groups determined by different cultural and social backgrounds.

Yet the central European democratic institutions, which are at the same time a result and a decisive driving force of European integration, need to be strengthened politically and supported by citizens' organizations in order to be able to exercise their responsibilities toward all citizens and to fight nationalistic preferences and centrifugal tendencies of member-states. In the framework of the European Union, mutual recognition of the respective organizational capacities and limitations of public institutions and NGOs are as necessary as the respectful and supportive cooperation between these two natural partners in a pan-European integration process.

Despite or rather because of the process of centralization in the European Union, the regional structures, the political or administrative units in the member-states, have recently successfully imposed their claim to become, in at least a formal consultative capacity, part of European decision-making institutions. Unavoidably, the same will happen step by step, though at a much slower pace, with nongovernmental and noncommercial organizations: they will become one of the essential tools of transmission between the central political and administrative structures and the individual citizen in both directions—from top to bottom and from bottom to top.

The actual crisis of European democracy—with growing doubts as to the integrity of politicians and the adequacy of existing institutional arrangements—will lead to a profound rethinking about the values and orientation of European society. There is good reason to believe that the concept of true civil society may, after all, determine the future of Europe. The association sector will then become a politically fully integrated structural element of modern European participatory democracy as an appropriate instrument to express the diversity of citizens' wills and needs in a specific complementary fashion. In this way, the sector will contribute to the legitimization of state at different levels.

Perhaps the most challenging issue for nongovernmental, nonprofit organizations in the future will be a clear definition of their distinctive nature and their particular value for society in comparison with public institutions and commercial market forces. Ideological reasoning will definitely not be enough—nor will economic or structural arguments. The public will have to be convinced by visionary participatory concepts in which each person occupies the central place as subject and object of association contribution to and intervention in civil society.

There is absolutely no doubt that West European society has by and large developed during the last century a perfectly democratic political system with democratic institutions. What seems still somewhat lacking is the true democratization of the system and its institutions so that the vision of civil society becomes lived reality. To consciously struggle hard and unerringly for this end may become the most noble objective of NGOS in Europe in the future.

At the same time, the sector will have to understand that its actual European concept and forms of association and voluntary organizations may no longer serve as the guide to others in different cultural contexts. There is a growing awareness in other sociocultural surroundings that different approaches are actually adequate and desirable. Europeans should be ready and eager to re-evaluate their current solutions and develop new visions.

Bibliography

Actes du Colloque. "Institutions Sanitaires et Sociales France-Espagne." Toulouse: Les Cahiers de l'Isard, 1989.

Alternatives Wallonnes. "Reconnaissance juridique des entreprises à but social, d'intérêt social, d'insertion: quelques lueurs dans l'obscurité" (Legal recognition of enterprises pertaining to social aims and interests and assimilation - a glimmer of light in the darkness), No. 88, September 15, 1993.

Archibault, Aline. "Rencontre Européenne sur les perspectives de l'économie alternative et solidaire." *Alternatives Wallonnes*, No. 75, p. 25, 1991.

Behrend, Erik et al. *Handboek Maatschappelijk Werk, Ontwikkelingen in Het Beroep*. Samson, Alphen An der Rijn, 1986.

Bravo, G.M. *Les Socialistes d'avant Marx*, FM, Petite Collection Maspéro, Vol. 2, p. 126, 1970.

Chancel, J. and P.E. Tixier. "Le désir d'entreprendre." *Autrement*, September 1979, p. 9. (Signalons cependant qu'il n'existe pas de traduction directe en allemand de l'expression "nonprofit sector" ou "Tiers Secteur").

de Combrugghe, Dominique, "Les Associations en Europe." *Alternatives Wallonnes*, Nos. 73-74, p. 40, 1991.

Delespesse, M. "Le Tiers-Secteur." CUNIC, Centre Universitaire de Charleroi, November 1981, p. 2.

Delors, J. "Le Troisième Secteur: Le Travail au-delà de l'Emploi." *Autrement*, No. 20, pp. 151-152, September 1979.

DeSanti, D. *Les Socialistes de l'Utopie*. Paris: Payot, pp. 310 and 314, 1970.

Documents submitted during the Third International Conference on Research in the voluntary and non-profit making sector, Indiana University, Center on Philanthropy, Indianapolis, March 11-13, 1992.

EEC, *Cooperative, Mutualist and Associative Organisations in the European Community Candidate Nations*, Vols. 2 and 3, Brussels, 1984.

European Symposium on Voluntary Associations, Voluntary Associations in East and West Europe, Report, Leiden, Netherlands, October 9-14, 1990.

Fabre, Christine, Michel Autes, and Jacques Eloy. *Agir sur le Lien Social en Europe*. Editions APASE, Maubeuge, 1990.

Fol, Jean-Jacques. *Les Pays Nordiques aux XIXe et XXe Siècles*. Paris: Presses Universitaires de France, 1978.

Gide, Charles, *Le Familistère de Guise et la Verrerie Ouvrière, Trois Leçons du Cours sur la Coopération au Collège de France*. Paris, pp. 3-4, May 1923.

Godin, J.B. *Solutions Sociales*. Paris-Brussels: A. Le Chevalier, Guillaumin & Cie, Office de la Publicité, 1871.

Horman, Denis. "Le financement des coopératives de production et des entreprises alternatives." *Alternatives Wallonnes*, Nos. 49-50, pp. 8-14, 1987.

Lavergne, B. *L'Ordre Coopératif I. Les Faits*. Paris: Librairie Félix Alcan, pp. 82-83, 1926.

Mabille, Xavier. "Pourquoi les associations?" in Fondation Marcel Hicter, *Des Associations, Espaces Pour une Citoyenneté Européenne*. Brussels: Vie Ouvrière/PAC, p. 12, 1987.

Meister, A. *Vers une Sociologie des Associations*. Paris: Les Editions Ouvrières, 1972.

Ragot, Alain and Hughes Robert. *Ethical Investments*. Fondation de France, August 1990.

Rocard, M. "Le Tiers Secteur, c'est la primauté de l'individu sur l'argent." *Autrement*, No. 34, p. 11.

Salamon, L. and H.K. Anheier. "In Search of the Non-profit Sector. II: The Problem of Classification." Johns Hopkins Comparative Nonprofit Sector Project, Institute for Policy Studies, Johns Hopkins University, Baltimore, Working Paper No. 3, October 1992.

Salamon, L. and H. K. Anheier. "The Emerging Sector: The Nonprofit Sector in Comparative Perspective—An Overview." Johns Hopkins Comparative Nonprofit Sector Project, Institute for Policy Studies, Johns Hopkins University, Baltimore, 1994.

Salberg, J.F. and S. Welsh-Bonnard. *Community Action*. Paris: Les Editions Ouvrières, p. 19, 1970.

Tillette, B. "Des Entreprises à quatre dimensions." *Autrement*, No. 34, p. 6, October 1981.

Weisbrod, N. *The Non-profit Economy*. Cambridge, Mass.: Harvard University Press, 1988.

7

CIVIL SOCIETY IN THE ASIA-PACIFIC REGION

Isagani R. Serrano

From the Margins to the Mainstream

A large number of citizens are active players in the unfolding Asian drama. Many belong to citizens' movements that challenge dominant structures and processes, aspiring to build a future for the region different from that envisioned by the elite.

Major events of the past two decades indicate that these movements have emerged from the margins to the mainstream of social, political, economic, and cultural life. An accounting of the movements' achievements as well as their failures reveals a net progress in the struggles to broaden the centers of power.

From 1970 to 1990, authoritarian regimes in Asia fell one after the other. The toppling of the Marcos regime in the Philippines in 1986 is an archetype of people power. The feats of the people of Iran, South Korea, Thailand, Bangladesh, and Nepal in deposing dictators are comparable. The democratic challenges in countries like China, Taiwan, Myanmar (Burma), and elsewhere are equally noteworthy.

In all these transitions, citizens' movements played a central role. Citizens, through their voluntary associations or spontaneous participation, have demonstrated how much their collective strength can do. They can do more than just help themselves: they can also resist and bring their power to bear on the state and even bring down unaccountable governments.

Civil society is a concept alien to Asia. It refers to self-organization of citizens in contrast to state or government, and is rooted in western rational tradition and political culture. The concept of citizenship, which suggests who is included and who is excluded in public affairs, is also a modern one.

Voluntary action is deeply rooted in Asian communities. It is directed toward common concerns that cannot be adequately addressed by individual families and extended kinship support systems: production, exchange, rituals from birth to death, and collective security, all of which maintain community consensus and cohesion.

The most common form of organization is the self-help and mutual-exchange group. In Indonesia, the *gotong royong* or mutual help is equivalent to *bayanihan* in the Philippines. Funeral associations, of which there are thousands in Thailand, are also mutual-benefit societies.

The present generation has inherited the rich tradition of indigenous organizations and principles of natural-resources management. One principle is sovereignty. Communities that live off a natural resource base have the greatest stake in its conservation. They reserve the basic right to control, exploit, manage, and benefit from it. Conversely, abuse of the right either by the local inhabitants themselves or by outsiders often results in overexploitation of resources at the expense of the community and the ecological system.

Ecosystem is another essential organizing principle in natural resources management. Indigenous peoples and local communities have proved their capacity to live in accordance with the limits of their environment. They retain a reverence for nature; trees, rivers, stones, and animals have spiritual value. In their holistic animistic view, as opposed to the anthropocentric, nature is not subordinated to human desire.

The growth of voluntary organizations and movements can be traced through the last 200 years, from colonial times to independence and after. Colonialism and modernization undermined indigenous social relations and philanthropy. Colonialism wrested from peoples their sovereign right over natural resources and vested it in the state. It linked far-flung rural villages to the global centers of economic and political power. Modernization built on colonial domination and pushed globalization to the limit.

During colonialism and modernization, certain patterns shaped civil society. The first was the stubborn assertion of precolonial forms of social organizations against those western. The second was the assertion of autonomy of social voluntary action against a hegemonic state agenda represented by governments-in-waiting or by the political parties or instruments for state power and governance.

What follows from the dynamic interplay of these historical patterns will have a profound impact on the solution to global problems. The raging development-versus-environment debate has highlighted the need to establish institutions that will create a sustainable global order. It has also started a return

Citizens Resist the Greens

In April 1993, in Malaysia, three Asia-based citizens' networks came together to form the Global Anti-Golf Movement (GAGM). The new movement was born out of the Conference on Golf Course and Resort Development organized by the Global Network for Anti-Golf Course Action, the Asia-Pacific Peoples Environment Network, and the Asian Tourism Action Network and attended by delegates from Hawaii, Hong Kong, India, Indonesia, Japan, Malaysia, the Philippines, and Thailand.

GAGM was a response to the increasing outcry of many local communities against the expansion of golf courses everywhere. The new movement calls attention to the adverse social and ecological impacts of an ever expanding space for an elitist sport, which powerful business interests are lobbying for inclusion in the Olympic Games. The golf industry is a multibillion-dollar enterprise involving transnational corporations in agribusiness, construction, consultancy, sports equipment manufacturing, airlines and hotels, real estate, advertising and public relations, and high finance. Memberships in golf courses are expensive. Most of the foreign-exchange earnings generated does not stay in the local economy.

The most significant campaigns perhaps have been the anti-golf activities in Indonesia. A long-standing struggle of farmers in Citeureup supported by students, lawyers, and local media against the conversion of vital paddy fields into a golf course by a private company resulted in a temporary ban on new golf-course development issued by Java authorities. In October 1993, several protesting farmers were imprisoned, underlining the human-rights dimension of the golf issue.

In Malaysia, citizen opposition has temporarily stalled the construction of a golf resort by raising the issue of environmental impact. The citizen protestors demanded an environmental impact assessment of the project because of its anticipated effects, such as severe soil erosion, siltation, and river pollution.

Continued on next page

273

Continued from previous page

In Hong Kong, environmentalist groups went to court to challenge the developers of the Gary Player-designed Sha Lo Tung Golf Course.The project was stopped on the ground of heritage protection: the golf course would have been built on a parkland.

Inspired by these initial successes, the Global Anti-Golf Movement has set its eyes on other parts of Asia. China, Vietnam, Laos, and Cambodia are current targets of greens development.

---

to the wisdom of premodern societies and sparked a rethinking of the myriad forms of social organization in furthering the common good.

Social movements emerged before and after the two world wars. Although well-rooted in local conditions and oppression, these were to a great extent western-inspired. The ideals and symbols came directly from the Enlightenment and the Jeffersonian tradition, expressed in slogans like democracy, liberty, freedom, and equality. The institutional forms were derived from western democracy, like political parties, trade unions, peasant organizations, the women's emancipation movement, suffrage groups, free-thinkers societies, mutual aid societies, academic-freedom associations, and so on. As is typical in highly stratified societies, an institution corresponded to almost every social concern. Western civil society was transplanted to Asia.

And yet tradition died hard. Native symbols and forms suffused the borrowed ones, integrating all external influences. Asians embraced the symbols and ideals as their own and turned them into powerful instruments against their oppressors. States and governments that arose out of the independence struggles became both the new targets of social mobilization and voluntary action and the new symbols of oppression, perpetuating the colonial legacy of poverty and inequality.

Instead of becoming a region of peace and prosperity, postwar Asia-Pacific became a center of cold war conflict much like Africa and Latin America. The decades following World War II saw political turmoil and revolutionary upheavals rooted in unresolved issues of landlessness and poverty. In the 1960s, it became clear that authoritarian development would be the typical elite response to social unrest. By the 1970s, most countries were under dictatorship.

For four decades Asians were torn between authoritarian development and revolution. Social movements and citizen action galvanized by this contradiction chose revolution. The Vietnam War was a watershed. Powerful peace movements flowered and a whole generation of young people demanded an end to the war. Many leaders of today's social movements trace their initiation into activism to that period.

In Asia-Pacific, many nongovernmental organizations (NGOs) have grown out of peoples' organizations. Some of them owed their beginnings to social action inspired by Christian churches, Catholic as well as Protestant. Others have been formed by like-minded citizens wanting to respond to some human welfare issues affecting themselves or the public at large.

Many NGOs work in partnership with grassroots organizations, offering a package of political, technical, material, and spiritual support. This type of group stresses empowerment of the poor and marginalized. Their involvement in social awareness-raising, community organizing, livelihood, health, and other projects enhances popular power. Other NGOs limit their activities to advocacy for or against certain state policies that affect the citizens. The positive outcomes of their work complement the bottom-up empowerment process.

The size of the thousands of Asian-Pacific NGOs in terms of staff, budget, and scale of operations varies from small (such as Participatory Research in Asia of Dr. Rajesh Tandon), to medium (such as AWARE of P.K.S. Madhavan, and PROSHIKA of Faruque Ahmed), to the truly big, like Sarvodaya and the Bangladesh Rural Advancement Committee (BRAC). The last two examples stand out as the largest NGOs in Asia, and probably in the world.

Founded in the late 1950s by the charismatic A.T. Ariyaratne, the Sarvodaya Sharamadana Movement (SSM) has more than 7,700 staffers and covers 8,000 villages—a third of Sri Lanka's total—in both the Singhalese and Tamil regions of the country. SSM is inspired by Buddhism and the works of Ghandi. Its long-term goal is to build democracy from below. It focuses on low-caste families, hoping that they can be integrated into the mainstream of public life.

SSM runs a variety of economic projects, including batik and sewing shops, machine shops and carpentry, printing presses, and other income-generating activities for the farmers. Its welfare programs address the needs of the deaf and disabled, preschool children, and victims of ethnic conflicts. It helps people mobilize their own resources, especially their labor, through forms of participation and self-reliance attuned to the country's cultural traditions.

In recent years, Sarvodaya has taken a high profile in national affairs, with Ariyaratne on the lead. It has openly challenged official development policies and reached out to the other sectors such as lawyers, the police, the judiciary, the media, and various action groups. Ariyaratne and Sarvodaya have become important players in Sri Lankan politics.

NGOs in China

Until recently, the NGO concept barely existed in the Chinese psyche. To some Chinese, it comes closest to the definition of the Communist Party. The civic voluntary tradition in China was broken when the communists took over in 1949. What used to be nongovernmental formations challenging the feudal lords and the Kuomintang government were later transformed wholesale into organs of the new government.

China, however, has opened the door to NGO revival. A consortium of European NGOs has operated in China since 1986.

Called the NGO China Group, it involves Oxfam (United Kingdom), NOVIB (Netherlands), and German Agro-Action (Germany), and assists the Chinese government in reaching out to the poor.

China has one of the best records in social levelling and food security. But 70 million of its 870 million rural population still remain under the poverty line. They are mostly minorities who live harsh lives in the barer regions of China. Moving these poor millions out of absolute poverty will require the participation of private voluntary societies. Recognizing this, the Chinese government allowed the formation of the Foundation for Underdeveloped Regions in China (FURC) in March 1989.

The antipoverty focus of FURC is quite clear. Its NGO character, however, is a bit fuzzy. The people who compose it are a mix of government and party officials and private citizens, which indicates how far NGOs in China (and there are only three to speak of as of now) have gone toward genuine autonomy from government. Private enterpreneurship has been having a field day since the start of reform in 1978, and the NGO seems like a halfway house, not influencing policy until recently. China has nearly completely given up on the commune. Cooperatives could have been revived and allowed to develop alongside and in spite of full-scale privatization. This could have provided a solid basis for the NGO resurrection. Apparently, these options were not taken into account by the policymakers.

The development process in China is so complex as to make judgment difficult. But a bold guess is that government has been omnipresent and overbearing for four decades and has virtually left no room for private voluntary organizations.

> For having assumed absolute responsibility over more than a billion people, the government has no one to blame but itself for all the problems that later grew out of such a closed system and the choking sociopolitical climate that it breeds. The recent Tienanmen tragedy, just like those that preceded it, may simply be symptomatic of a fundamental problem attending every revolution that forgets its ownbeginnings upon victory.
>
> The communist party and its organized constituency were but an alternative NGO system before coming to power. As in other socialist countries, this tradition in China seems to have the misfortune of falling victim to short memory from the moment of victory onward.

The Bangladesh Rural Advancement Committee is almost as big as Sarvodaya, with about 6,000 staffers and activities covering around 15,000 of the total 68,000 villages of Bangladesh. This is a tremendous achievement from its modest beginnings from February 1972, when a small group of committed people organized BRAC and started work among the refugees in the Sulla district following the country's war of liberation.

From relief and rehabilitation, BRAC soon turned to concerns and activities of a more structural nature. These cover institution building, nonformal and functional education, primary education, health education, family planning, the development of some basic clinical health services through paramedics at the village level, legal awareness, savings and credit, around which are woven several other activities.

By 1992, BRAC's integrated rural development program, which is being carried out through its 217 area offices covering 14,974 villages, had produced 22,361 village organizations with a total membership of nearly 800,000, of which women account for 65 percent. Credit disbursement amounted to $47 million with repayment rates of 97-98 percent. BRAC had set up nine training centers and 8,666 ongoing schools run by 7,708 teachers for 262,980 students. Its oral rehydration therapy teaching program has reached 13 million households nationwide after 10 years, a feat in a country where 250,000 children die of dehydration from diarrhea every year.

The need to scale up NGO impact is probably the single biggest justification for the emergence of the large NGOs like these. Now in the center stage of NGO discourse, the question of impact has yet to put to rest the issue of appropriate size, since a number of other strategic options for achieving the same purpose have entered the debate.

As voluntary associations of citizens with a stake in development, NGOs have the same right to exist as any other organization. But as with any organization, they often face repressive legal obstacles. The situation in Malaysia and Indonesia illustrates the problems often faced by NGOs.

The Societies Act of Malaysia requires all social organizations to be registered with the Registrar of the Ministry of Home Affairs. Answerable only to the Minister, the Registrar exercises almost unlimited powers, including that of dissolving organizations and searches without warrant. A judge cannot intervene with the Registrar's acts, and appeals can be raised only to the Minister of Home Affairs. More than 14,000 organizations are covered by this act. These range from sporting clubs and Chinese trade guilds to consumers associations.

The Societies Act forms part of the all-embracing Internal Security Act, a draconian law enacted by the Malaysian government following the social and political unrest of the 1960s. This was meant to tighten government control over social and political organizations, whether or not they were linked with the communist movement.

In 1981, new amendments further tightened government control and sparked a massive protest against the Societies Act. Led by a broad coalition of social organizations called the Conference of Societies, the protests challenged the government's definition of political and nonpolitical organizations and the unlimited powers vested in the Registrar. The government considered political all organizations trying to influence government policy. These were forbidden to have any contact with foreign groups or to receive money from abroad.

As a result of these protests, the amendment bill was put aside but reappeared later in a form that was eventually passed by the Parliament. The amended Societies Act no longer makes any distinction between political and nonpolitical organizations, which are now allowed to enter into contract with foreign organizations without having prior permission from the Registrar. But they have to inform the Registrar of all their foreign financial and organizational transactions. Also, the Registrar reserves both the right to forbid such contracts and transactions and the right to carry out searches of the organization's premises without warrant, to remove an organization's board, and to amend relevant statutes as he deems necessary. Yet the voluntary associations of citizens in Malaysia have continued to grow in spite of these repressive laws.

Similarly in Indonesia, despite stirrings from different Islamic leaders and organizations and NGOs, in 1985 the Parliament passed the Undang Organisasi Kemasyakaratan, or Law on Social Organizations. Within two years the government required all social organizations to comply with the stipulated terms. So far, everyone seems to have done so.

An outstanding feature of the Law on Social Organizations, which caused protests, was the obligation to adopt the *Pancasila* as the sole principle for all social organizations. *Pancasila* is the declared state philosophy, which has five pillars: the One and Almighty God; just and civilized Humanity; The Unity of Indonesia; Democracy or Kerakyatan, guided by wise policy through consultation and representation; and Social Justice for all the Indonesian people. It is the guiding state ideology.

In addition to the Pancasila, the law also provides for the compulsory registration of all social organizations, obligatory membership of these organizations in umbrella organizations, the right of the Government to guide and dissolve social organizations, and Government control of the flow of funds from foreign donor organizations to Indonesian partners.

Compulsory registration and reporting was not part of the 1945 Indonesian Constitution. Only organizations opting for legality, such as the *Yayasan* (Foundations), have to register as required by the Court and by the Ministry of Justice. Under the Law on Social Organizations, virtually no organizations are spared from such obligation.

Social organizations can be suspended, dissolved, and declared illegal for activities the government considers to be disturbing of general security and order. These activities include spreading of hostility among ethnic groups, religions, races, and groups; destroying the unity and integrity of the nation; undermining the authority and/or discrediting the Government hindering the implementation of the development programmes; and other activities that may disturb political stability and security.

Similar sanctions also apply to getting aid from foreign parties without the Central Government's consent and/or rendering assistance to foreign parties detrimental to the interests of the State and Nation. Assistance from foreign parties includes finances, equipment, personnel, and facilities. Assistance to foreign parties detrimental to the interests of state and nation include any that may harm the relations between Indonesia and other countries; may give rise to threats, challenges, hindrances and disturbances directed against the security of the state; may disturb national stability; or are detrimental to foreign policy.

The Indonesian Law on Social Organizations has much in common with the Societies Act and Internal Security Act of Malaysia. Indeed, all three are classic examples of repressive laws informed by the national security doctrine that guided authoritarian governments in Asia, Africa and Latin America, including part of the western world, in the 1960s and 1970s.

Changing Social Movement Paradigms

In Asia as in other parts of the so-called Third World, social and voluntary action have been most powerfully influenced by the idea of revolution. Inspired by the struggles of Asian peoples against colonialism, explicitly revolutionary mass movements have swept across the region for a great part of the twentieth century. Their ideological roots are western and predominantly Marxist or socialist.

If the collapse of socialism in Eastern Europe and the former Soviet Union has weakened orthodox revolutionary projects, the idea of socialism has not ceased to inspire revolution. The reason is simple: social reforms continue to fall short of expectations, and problems of rights, development, and environment continue to fester while the means to solve them remain inadequate.

Both successful and failed revolutions in the Asia-Pacific region have been based on alliances of peasants, workers, and youth, usually led by a proletarian party. Peasants produced the mass membership and most of the guerillas who together mobilized the rural masses. Workers, considered by revolutionary orthodoxy as the advanced forces of production, were the leading class. Youth and students, because of their special position in society, sparked the revolutionary prairie fire.

The paradigm holds sway to this day. Even the more recent form of voluntary organization, the NGO, cannot quite part from tradition, and continues to support grassroots movements of peasants, workers, and communities.

Peasant movements include organizations of farmers, fishers, indigenous peoples, rural women, and peoples' cooperatives, all generated and sustained endogenously or by urban-based institutions. The movements address a wide range of issues, including land tenure, inequalities in income and income distribution, public policy biases against the rural sector, social service delivery, trading and marketing, usury, and deterioration of the environment.

The most potent peasant movements have been those associated with revolutionary projects, as in China and Indochina. In both failed and still-thriving revolutions—for example, in Indonesia, Thailand, Malaysia, the Philippines—peasant movements have been the base of national movements. Even in countries where national revolution is nowhere on the horizon, peasant movements still constitute the largest movements of the oppressed.

In the more industrialized countries like Japan and the newly industrializing countries (NICs) of South Korea and Taiwan, farmers' movements continue to be a significant although gradually diminishing force. Japan's 3 million farmers, represented by major farmers federations linked to mainstream political parties, still greatly influence government policy formation.

In South Korea, the *Saemul Undong* or New Village Movement was created by the authoritarian elite to serve as its rural base for industrial takeoff. In Taiwan, the Kuomintang formed the Farmers' Associations, patterned after Mao's peasant movement, to link the government to the countryside. In both cases, the farmers' movements were the most powerful of the forces that shaped agricultural development.

In the Philippines, a major part of the peasant movement is communist-led and constitutes the main rural base of the New People's Army. There are many independent peasant organizations that are influenced by other ideologies. Independent peasant organizing in the country has also been assisted by many rural development NGOs. To counter both types of peasant movements, former President Marcos rapidly formed more than 20,000 farmers' cooperatives by using subsidized credit from the World Bank.

In South Asia, peasant movements and rural cooperativism are the single biggest force in the local economy and self-governance. South Asian NGOs, which are the largest in the world, are mostly rural development-oriented and benefit mainly peasants and the rural poor. Together, the peasant movements and the NGOs form the basis of grassroots democracy.

Fishers' organizations are organically linked to peasant movements because they also address agricultural problems. They are also linked to trade unionism by big commercial fishing, large-scale aquaculture, and fishery-based industries. However, they are emerging as a distinct grassroots movement. Fisherfolk have long fought for control over coastal and marine resources, and against overexploitative fishing giants, illegal fishing methods, industrial and human pollution, and the destruction of fish habitats.

Fishers' groups lead in advocating aquatic reform and in negotiating the Law of the Sea Treaty. Migratory fishstocks straddling territorial boundaries in the high seas is also an outstanding issue.

Ethnicity is a stranger to the traditional revolutionary paradigm, where indigenous peoples are no more than a mass of diminishing tribes to be won over lest they become enemies of the revolution. But now, indigenous peoples, oppressed by centuries of colonialism and marginalized by modernization, are central to the environment versus development debate.

Today, indigenous peoples are high on governments' and NGOs' list of priorities. They are held to have the same rights as the enfranchised lowland citizens. They are the main protectors of the forests and upland ecosystems and other primary resources that are relentlessly overexploited by corporate interests. Their disappearing cultures seem to harbor the solution to the environment and development crisis confronting humanity.

Indigenous peoples have a long tradition of asserting their right to self-determination and of resistance against domination. Beyond the issue of sovereignty is the question of sustainable development itself. Advocates of sustainable development claim that we need to reexamine our view of what makes an enduring society and that we must become ecocentric, as opposed to anthropocentric. Our new world view should include the key role of indigenous cultures and beliefs in social transformation.

The struggles for the rights of indigenous peoples strike at the heart of globalization from above, a process that concentrates resources and decisions in the hands of the major powers. The aboriginal movements in Australia, the Maori peoples struggle in Aotearoa (New Zealand), the nuclear-free and independence movements in the South Pacific island states, and the struggle for nationhood of the Kanaks and the East Timorese are all examples of movements for self-determination. Like the American Indians, indigenous peoples in Asia-Pacific have been pushed to near extinction by genocide, colonization, resettlement, population control, and destruction of their homelands and cultures.

Through years of resistance, indigenous peoples have preserved their tradition, culture, language, religion—their way of life—against relentless attempts to assimilate them and other oppressive policies of settlers and states. Their resistance teaches useful lessons in protecting diversity of cultures in face of homogenization and massive violation of human rights. In the mid-1970s, for example, the Cordillera peoples of northern Philippines showed how a united struggle could stop construction of a multimillion-dollar dam project funded by the World Bank.

The role of trade unions is also being rethought. Workers have always been a major force in modern history·and in the most significant transformations in the Asia-Pacific region. Agenda 21 cites them and trade unions as one of the nine groups with a major role in implementing the global plan.

Industrial workers are but a small fraction of the nearly 3 billion people in Asia, but they wield power disproportionate to their number. They are the

The Australian Aborigines

In Australia, the world's biggest inhabited island and the smallest continent, there existed a culture rich and diverse in its customs, language, and religion, preceding by several centuries the civilizations in the Middle East, China, and Europe. For at least 40,000 years before Captain Cook set foot on The Great South Land in 1770, more than 300,000 Aborigines inhabited the river systems, coastal plains, mountains, tropical rainforests, drylands, and deserts of this continent. They spoke 500 languages grouped into 31 related language families that were as rich and complex as the modern European languages.

The white colonizers found Australia's environment largely as it was 400 centuries before, thanks to the Aborigines' way of life. The Aboriginal traditions were built in harmony and close spiritual bond with every living thing and even with inanimate things such as rocks, rivers, and the wind. The Aborigines regard themselves, nature, and the land as inseparably bound and interdependent. It is this culture of integrity with nature that probably kept environmental degradation to a minimum.

The Aborigines are natural conservationists. Their economy, based on the hunting activities of the men and the fishing and gathering of the women, was attuned to the regenerative capacity of the environment. For example, a good hunter who knew intimately the habits of his game and understood the changes of the seasons took only what was needed to feed his people, thereby keeping the balance with natural reproduction. Starvation was unknown in their fragile but complex land.

The Aborigines' relationship with the land was so intimate and complex that to uproot them from the land meant spiritual death. Anthropologist W.E.H. Stanner had this to say of the Aborigines' land relationship: "No English words are good enough to give a sense of the links between an Aboriginal group and its homeland. Our word home...does not match the Aboriginal word that may mean camp, hearth, country, everlasting home, totem place, life source, spirit centre

Continued on next page

> Continued from previous page
>
> and much else all in one....When we took what we call land we took
> what to them meant hearth, home, the source and locus of life, and
> everlastingness of spirit."
>   Without this perspective, it is difficult to understand the Aborigi-
> nal movement in Australia, or, for that matter, the cause of the Maoris
> in Aotearoa (New Zealand), the South Pacific peoples, and the indig-
> enous peoples' movements elsewhere.

main builders of the industrial societies of Japan, Australia, and New Zealand.
They helped to realize the economic miracles of the NICs. They are the principal modernizing sector of the emerging economies of the basically agrarian
countries of the Asia-Pacific region.

Workers' movements, found in most Asian-Pacific countries, are the most
highly organized and, as a rule, a major part of social movements. In the traditional revolutionary model, they lead other mass movements. But they are
also more subject than others to the influences of political parties and their
state agenda. Their inclination toward self-governance stops at the factory
premises. Outside the factory lies the world of politics and the struggle for
state power. Here, trade unions tend to be adjuncts of political parties, whether
in power or waiting for electoral victory.

Following the European socialist tradition, many Asian trade unions started
as cooperative societies before plunging into the politics of collective bargain-
ing, first at the factory and then at the industry level. Factory unions grew into
federations and then into trade-union centers that linked Asian labor movements to each other and to global unions.

Trade unions and workers' parties in the Asia-Pacific have always led
movements for social and national change. They were at the vanguard of revolutions in China, North Korea, Vietnam, Laos, and Cambodia. They forced
regimes out of power in Japan, Australia, New Zealand, and parts of India.
Worker-based citizens' movements felled dictators in the Philippines,
Bangladesh, and Nepal. Even where less successful, they continue to challenge state and corporate systems.

The biggest resistance to the authoritarian elite of South Korea was initiated by workers, thousands of whom confronted the power structures beginning in 1987 and led the long drawn-out strike in the strategic Hyundai ship-

yard in April 1989. The middle class joined the struggle, forming a powerful national movement that toppled the Chun dictatorship.

But times are changing fast, more so since the collapse of socialism in Central Europe and the former Soviet Union. The historic changes have a far-reaching and profound impact on the role of workers and the trade union movements in social and national transformation. Social movements are now thoroughly re-examining, if not rejecting completely, the revolutionary model that revered workers.

Three other trends might explain the dwindling influence of workers, trade unions, and their political parties. One, key countries that still adhere to the socialist vision, like China and Vietnam, are rapidly turning from the state-dominated economy to the free-market system, undermining constitutionally guaranteed wages and benefits that workers have enjoyed for decades. The role and position of workers and trade unions have been downgraded and subordinated to that of the emergent entrepreneurial class.

Two, many now see industrialism, which gave the workers their honored role, as responsible for many of the troubles confronting humanity. While the economic miracles of the NICs have not lost their allure for governments and big business, their viability and desirability are being questioned by citizens' movements.

Three, the regime changes and challenges to dominant paradigms have given birth to a new type of social movement that is no longer worker-dominated but that cuts across social classes. In these emergent broad citizens' movements, hegemony belongs to those who can challenge and offer alternatives to orthodoxies. Working-class vanguardism is out; dynamic plurality is in.

Environmental issues were of marginal interest to Asian-Pacific social movements until the 1980s. Perhaps this is because the ecological space in the region remains wide; its source and sink capacity have yet to be exhausted. Human rights and development were the focus of voluntary action from the 1960s to the 1980s, the decades of authoritarian development that saw many countries, led by South Korea and Taiwan, fall under dictatorships.

Human rights were propelled mainly by the middle classes. In the 1980s, human rights movements took on development and environmental concerns. The meeting of 202 Asian human rights organizations in 1993, in advance of the June World Conference on Human Rights in Vienna, attested not only to the comprehensive nature of human rights advocacy but also to the strength of human rights organizations in the region.

Environmentalism in Asia has been greatly influenced by western ecological movements. The "hippie" generation of the 1960s inspired similar back-to-nature movements in Asia, which drew many young people toward greater concern for environmental protection and traditional cultures and religion, especially Indian spiritualism.

Asian social movements linked environment and development only in the late 1980s. Earlier, citizen action on environmental issues was sporadic and isolated. There was little public awareness of the extent and potential threat of rainforest destruction, chemical agriculture, overfishing, and industrial pollution until just before the U.N. Conference on Environment and Development (UNCED) meetings, after which environmentalism took giant strides forward.

Meanwhile, the consumers movement has gained headway, especially in Malaysia, the Philippines, and Japan. Where it once focused on prices and product quality, it has now taken up environmental safety and consumption patterns that stress ecosystems. Since colonial times, the region has seen major conflicts among the global powers. Now citizens' movements against militarization and nuclear proliferation are part of the broad movement whose long-term goals are peace and security.

The Rise of Citizens' Movements

Civic responses to the endemic crisis of participation cross class boundaries. Traditional categories are proving inadequate for identifying friend and enemies who, many now realize, can come from any class or institution and may switch roles so unexpectedly that the fixed lines of old are blurred.

Although rooted in the earlier conventional mode of social mobilization, citizens' movements that rose in the 1970s and 1980s were multiclass or supraclass in membership and leadership. Previous revolutions were also multiclass, but the mass of participants came mainly from peasants and workers, and leadership was usually assumed by workers' political parties. In contrast, the citizen uprisings in Iran in 1979, in the Philippines in 1986, and in South Korea in 1990, plus the democratic upsurge in China in 1989 and the citizen revolutions in Eastern Europe and former Soviet Union that began in 1989, drew mass support from the entire citizenry and a leadership not distinctly proletarian.

The struggles for participation are common to both capitalist and socialist systems. Indeed, citizen responses are not particularly motivated by the ideological basis of either system but by the elite's monopoly of power. The endemic crisis of poverty and environment has closed the traditional ideological divide. Rights, development, and environment have ceased to be class issues and are now issues for every citizen demanding a more equitable and sustainable society.

Although peasants and workers continue to provide the base of voluntary movements, women's emancipation movements have recently emerged as a powerful force. The strongest feminist organizations are found in Australia, India, and the Philippines. Their numbers are difficult to ascertain, but their collective voice and influence penetrate all classes and sectors of society. There are women's organizations among the workers, peasants, and indigenous people, in the urban poor communities, among consumers, in the so-called NGO community, in the academic and professional community, in government and business, and among the middle class and the rich.

Cooperativism among poor women is strong. In South Asia, savings and credit organizations of peasant women are the best example of how the poor can mobilize resources and build and manage alternative systems for financing their own development projects. Indigenous women's groups are among the most outspoken critics of the model of development that they believe undermines their rights and destroys their fragile habitats.

Women are prominent in some Asian trade unions. In South Korea, for example, women workers, who account for more than half the labor force, were in the forefront of thousands of strikes and street marches from 1987 to 1990. Organizations of women workers have also been formed in the Philippines and other countries.

Women are in the thick of other citizens' movements for consumerism, environmentalism, peace and security, population, and health. Women's emancipation movements might even one day replace workers' parties as the vanguard and lead other social movements with a new perspective and vision of development.

Youth and children are also gradually taking responsibility for the future of the region. Thousands of associations of youth and children are found in schools, workplaces, cities, and villages. Most NGOs are run by people who were once involved in youth and student movements.

Feared by elites and governments, youth movements have always added fire and spirit to mass movements and great social upheavals all over the world. Youth associations mobilized massively during the Vietnam war. More recently, they led the Tiananmen uprising. Idealism and dynamism—and, negatively, the prospect of an uncertain future—drive the youth to voluntary action.

Japanese Housewives in Environmental Activism

An estimated 3,000 active grass-roots conservation organizations exist throughout Japan. For example, a loose network of recycling groups formed the Japan Recycling Citizens Center with about 40,000 supporters. Several consumers' organizations and consumers' cooperatives are also involved in a wide range of environmental issues.

The most striking feature of this array of small organizations, says Mary Goebel Noguchi of Ritsumeikan University in Kyoto, "is that so many are run not out of offices by paid professionals but out of homes by volunteer housewives."

Noguchi interviewed six of these women and came up with an interesting profile of the leadership of the grass-roots environmental movement. These highly educated mothers ranged from 37 to 70 years old and became involved in environmental activism at different times, one as early as 1960.

One writer, Takie Sugiyama, asserts that a professional housewife has some time to offer for volunteer work and that her responsibility for monitoring the family health may induce her to be alert to health hazards like industrial pollution, food poisoning, medical malpractices, which may involve her in consumer movements and ultimately in politics.

Jonathan Holliman suggests that Japanese men have defaulted on social ining two or three hours a day and spending long hours at the office or factory, most working people have little time or energy for community affairs. In this situation, it is mainly housewives who have both the free time and the concern for environmental health.

Whatever the reasons, and there are many, nobody can deny that Japanese women are breaking new ground in social activism. The political changes sweeping across Japan since the mid-1980s have seen the rise of women political leaders such as Takako Doi, the passage of the Equal Employment Opportunity Law, and the so-called Madonna movement in the late 1980s through which Japanese women voters helped deliver the ruling Liberal Democratic Party its first major electoral loss since 1955. These events, among

> other things, have given the Japanese women what Noguchi calls a new-found sense of freedom and power, while making local governments more responsive to their demands.
>
> Japanese women are definitely a growing force for change in Japan. The emergence of the housewife activist leaders of environmental movements adds more color to this phenomenon.

The citizens' movements that have brought about some of the most dramatic changes in twentieth-century Asia-Pacific are yet to be fully understood. Explanations from purely social, economic, political, and cultural perspectives are inadequate.

One missing link is the spiritual and ethical dimension of struggle. The issues around which millions of citizens mobilize and risk their lives have a moral value. These people see their struggles as a moral cause, a fight between good and evil. Being on the side of the good gives people spiritual strength. This invisible inspiring element also serves to cement the solidarity among the actors.

The spiritual dimension is an integral part of the struggles of indigenous people and minorities in Asia-Pacific. They invoke the power of the spirits whenever they defend a tree against commercial loggers or a river against a dam project. This holds true for the Australian aborigines, the Maoris of New Zealand, the Polynesians, and all indigenous peoples and tribes in Asia-Pacific.

The influence of Islam, Hinduism, Buddhism, Christianity, and other religions also runs deep. It affects rulers and ruled alike. Religions can be a stabilizing or destabilizing force. Their intervention or nonintervention makes and unmakes political regimes or, at the very least, influences social changes.

The Iranian peoples' revolution that overthrew the Shah in 1979 is an outstanding example of the power of religion. Islamic values inspired the revolution from its beginning until the climactic fall of the government and after.

In South Korea, an August 1993 mobilization called the South-North Human Chain for Peace and Reunification Rally was initiated and organized by the Korean churches. Some 60,000 men and women linked arms to form a 50-kilometer-long human chain to symbolize their long-standing desire for reunification of their divided country. The human chain started from the Independence Park in Seoul and went up to the dividing line at Panmunjom. It was a modern form of *Kang-kang-su-wul-le*, which is derived from a traditional

Seikatsu Club Cooperative Movement

Among the cooperative movements in Asia-Pacific, the Seikatsu Club Consumers Cooperative (SCCC) in Japan is probably one of the biggest and most successful. By 1991, it had expanded to 12 prefectures, enlisted 200,000 member households or about 800,000 individuals, and was running an alternative domestic economy valued at 600 billion yen.

The SCCC was started in 1965 by a Tokyo housewife who initiated bulk buying to get cheaper milk. From this modest beginning, it has grown into an economic giant distributing 400 products, all produced according to strict environmental and social standards, to 20,000 local groups of some eight-member-families each. The Club also uses its multimillion-dollar member-investment to produce its own goods when other producers do not meet the Club's standards for product quality.

Other activities of the SCCC include the formation of worker collectives to generate employment for its members; campaigns around human rights, peace, and environmental issues; and participation in elections. In the May 1991 unified local election, as many as 52 Seikatsu Club candidates won assembly seats.

In its struggle for social, political, and economic reforms, the Seikatsu Club Cooperative Movement advocates what it calls citizens' seikatsusha social participation model. Held up as an alternative paradigm to capitalism and socialism, this envisions a social system based on people's participation, cooperation, decentralization of authority, and self-government.

Korean play where women held hands forming a circle, singing, dancing, and wishing upon the moon. It has been adopted by peace and environmental movements in other parts of the world.

Since 1945, reunification has been a running theme in the activities of various citizens' groups and churches in South Korea. Although muffled for a long time, the aspiration for reunification has resonated in recent years following the successes of citizens' mobilizations against the authoritarian order. Many Korean churches have consistently supported people empowerment activities, ranging from organizing trade unions and campaigns for democratic constitution and elections to environmental protection and national reunification. Forty-nine denominations are now involved in the reunification movement led by the National Council of Churches of Korea, which itself has only six member churches.

In the Philippines, the citizens' revolution that toppled the Marcos regime drew support from the churches, both spiritually and materially. Church-inspired social action has long been part of the social movement in the country; words of support from church heirarchies even lent legitimacy to extra-legal initiatives of the citizens.

Democratization of information is another big factor in the growth and success of citizens' movements. Although the ownership and modes for using information continue to be monopolized by a few, modern communications technologies have made information more accessible to a great number of people.

Grassroots organizations and NGOs in Asia-Pacific relate to each other face to face and indirectly through a variety of communications media. Telephones, faxes, modems, VCRs, radios, and printed media complement and sometimes substitute for direct communication.

Suppression of information always accompanies authoritarian regimes. Yet even under the strictest of conditions, people are able to find ways to get the information flowing. The authorities themselves, whose legitimacy is under question, help create the forces that one day will topple them. They have to provide better education to produce a highly educated work force needed for economic takeoff. In the process, they produce educated citizens who demand more freedoms. This irony was vividly illustrated in the case of the Asian economic miracles. In South Korea and Taiwan, for example, the citizens' movements that challenged authoritarian governments included highly educated individuals.

The value and impact of the media may be difficult to determine. But it is safe to say that television, radio, newspapers, and other forms of media have been important in shaping mass behavior and in deciding the outcomes of dramatic social changes in Asia-Pacific. Certainly, media played a role in galvanizing people's responses, in deterring dictators from engaging in mass slaughters in the Philippines, South Korea, Nepal, Bangladesh, Thailand, and elswhere, and even in just letting people know what is happening in a faraway forest.

Local Development and Self-Governance

Democracy from below has two key elements: voluntary action and the organized participation of citizens, and community-centeredness and horizontal spread of popular centers of power.

Voluntary action involving masses of people democratizes society. The more inclusive the participation, the more democratic the outcome. The spread of decision-making power across sectors countervails the monopoly of power by government and corporations.

But plurality in decision-making does not necessarily lead to local development and self-governance. Social movements, especially workers and trade union movements and trade union-influenced sectoral movements, for example, have followed a vertical path of organization.

Local development and self-governance require deliberate reorientation of voluntary action. Creating a favorable national climate is essential to expand the space for local initiatives. But for democratization to be thoroughgoing, decision-making has to be pulled down to the lowest possible level at which small groups and even individuals can exercise control.

Democratization at the subnational level is happening not only in isolated communities; NGO-supported grassroots movements are working everywhere to transform local communities and their environments through a holistic area development strategy.

The concept of integrated area development has evolved over time. In the 1970s, it was promoted by bilateral and multilateral agencies such as the U.S. Agency for International Development and the World Bank. The integrated area development strategy required concentration of development assistance in areas such as agricultural basins to build a geophysical framework for local government development efforts directed by a central authority.

Integrated area development varies from country to country. Where the ecosystem is the defining factor in development, as it is in the upland indigenous communities or lowland agricultural basins, the area is designed around the watershed. Where geopolitics is the prime consideration, the area follows political boundaries.

Area scope likewise varies greatly, depending on geophysical, demographic, political, and economic factors and, most important, the scale of an area. In some countries, areas are only as big as a district or province. In others, they are no less than a bioregion spanning several districts or provinces, such as the desert of Rajasthan in India.

The challenge of making an impact on the local economy and micro-ecosystems has been taken up by many NGOs and grassroots organizations across Asia-Pacific. The Convergence for Community-Centered Area Development (CONVERGENCE) in the Philippines is a network founded precisely for this purpose.

CONVERGENCE was formed in 1990 by about 20 Philippine NGOs with many years of experience in organizing local communities. These groups believed that by pooling their capacities and resources they could heighten their impact and bring about local transformation even without immediate dramatic changes at the macro level.

The group defined their scale of impact and sustainability according to sociopolitical, economic, and ecological factors. An area usually consists of a small district or province of more than 1,000 square kilometers with around 400,000 inhabitants whose everyday life is woven around a local economic system linked to a major natural resource base such as, for example, an agricultural basin or a fishing bay area.

By 1993, members of CONVERGENCE had experimented in area development in the uplands, lowlands, and coastal ecosystems throughout the archipelago. Results are measured by increased local capacities in resource access and mobilization, poverty alleviation and sustainable livelihoods, and restoration of damaged micro-ecosystems.

A sustainable area-development process hinges on the regaining of sovereignty by local communities, which must dictate the substance and direction of their own development and end the net resource outflow. Thousands of grassroots and development support organizations are striving to regain their sovereignty by promoting integrated area development. Their activities include awareness raising, organization and leadership building, land and asset reform, management training, natural resources management, livelihood systems development, savings and credit and alternative development financing, sustainable agriculture, micro-enterprises, alternative trading and marketing, and improved service delivery systems.

Through consciousness-raising programs, local communities become aware of their own realities as well as of greater society's, of the development-versus-environment debate and of the imperative of voluntary action. NGOs help local communities acquire skills in scale management and organization. Primary peoples' institutions, such as sectoral associations, cooperatives, and community organizations, eventually grow into area-level structures of self-governance. They also launch local and national campaigns against poverty and for welfare, reform, and environmental protection.

The Ting Hsien Experiment

In the late 1920s, Dr. Y.C. James Yen began an experiment in Northern China in a district called Ting Hsien. It was based on his experience in the battlefields of France during World War II, when he realized the power of bringing literacy to the thousands of coolies he was an interpreter for. In a county of 480 square miles, 472 villages, and about 400,000 inhabitants, he tested his vision of rural reconstruction, which he alternately called human reconstruction.

The experiment began with a literacy program. It used the "Peoples Thousand Character Texts" prepared by Dr. Yen on the basis of the spoken language of the people. The module could be mastered by the average illiterate in four months, working only an hour a day. A complete system of education evolved, covering organization, teacher training, and supervision. The emphasis later shifted from extensive promotion of literacy to intensive study of life in the rural districts. All this took the character of a massive movement. The Ting Hsien project was complemented by mobilization of citizens from the upper and middle classes. A leading Peking daily reported at that time: "It was the most magnificent exodus of the intelligentsia into the country that has taken place in Chinese history to date. Holders of old imperial degrees, professors of national universities, a college president and former member of the National Assembly, and a number of PhDs and MDs from leading American universities left their positions and comfortable homes in the cities to go to the backwoods of Ting Hsien, to find ways and means to revitalize the life of an ancient, backward people, and to build democracy from the bottom up."

Education for self-governance was the central theme of Yen's project. He said, "What good is it to fatten a man's purse, teach him to read and write, and help him toward better health, if he remains dependent on government and others? He must be taught the responsibility of citizenship in a democratic society, shown how to band with his neighbors to run community affairs. Education in citizenship is at the very core of rural reconstruction. Self-government is not a gift from above; it's an achievement by the people."

The Ting Hsien experiment was replicated in many parts of China. The results, matched or surpassed only by Mao's revolution, were amazing. Pearl S. Buck had this to say of Dr. Yen and his movement: "He taught many millions of his countrymen to read and established hundreds of rural centers to combat poverty and disease, to reform land tenure and to develop self-government. What he accomplished history will record as one of the great constructive achievements of our time."

The rural reconstruction movement in China spread to other parts of the world after World War II. The first to follow China was the Philippine Rural Reconstruction Movement begun in 1952, with active participation by Dr. Yen himself. In the course of seven decades, beginning from the 1920s, the rural reconstruction movement has gained a foothold in Asia, Latin America, and Africa.

These local communities engage in livelihood activities designed to build a community-centered economy attuned to the carrying capacity of the environment and based on sustainable agriculture and rural development. Alternative financial systems, from micro-savings and credit schemes to people's banks, mobilize the funds.

The poor, indeed the poorest among them, have demonstrated often and in many parts of Asia that they can set up, own, and run their own banks to finance their livelihood projects and other activities. The most outstanding example so far is the world-renowned Grameen Bank in Bangladesh. It is one of the most successful experiments in extending credit to the landless poor.

The Grameen Bank was conceived and developed by Professor Muhammad Yunus of Chittagong University in Bangladesh. It started in 1976 as an action-research pilot project in the village of Jobra. The first beneficiaries were the poor women weavers who were being exploited by moneylenders. Professor Yunus initially guaranteed bank loans to those who had no collateral. This first try proved successful, as indicated by above 99 percent repayment rates.

The Grameen Bank Project (GBP) became a full-fledged bank in 1983. The Bangladesh government shouldered 60 percent of the initial paid-up capital, with the borrowers providing the rest out of their savings. Foreign subsidy has been considerable but dependence on this has declined from 83 percent to 60 percent.

By 1991, the Bank's services had reached 23,000 of the 68,000 villages of Bangladesh through its more than 800 local branches. Some 1 million households have received credit. Intended principally for working capital, the loans have generated a great deal of employment, especially for rural women.

The elements of this successful innovation are organization, close relationship between bank and borrowers, deliberate intention to reach the poorest, and the unhurried process of group formation itself. People are organized into groups of five, and each member has to guarantee the repayment of a loan to any of the other four members.

The project struggled through many years to be what it is now—a bank largely owned by the poor for the poor. Seventy-five percent of the shares are owned by the landless borrowers and the rest by the Bangladesh government. As of 1992, the Grameen Bank had more than 400,000 borrowers, 82 percent of whom were women. It lends out $2.5 million every month in tiny loans averaging $67, with a high recovery rate of 98 percent. Borrowers have accumulated a savings fund of $7 million out of the negligible required savings of one taka per week for each borrower.

Alternative trading and marketing reduce and eventually eliminate the exploitative monopoly traders and directly link rural producers to urban consumers. The more successful communities now trade globally. A new experiment, the local exchange and trading system in Australia and other countries, seeks to cut the local economy off from the global system by localizing currencies. Patterned after Robert Owen's labor exchange in England in the nineteenth century and similar efforts in Austria, the United States, and Canada, the system is successful only in small areas. Whether it will work elsewhere on a larger scale remains to be seen.

Restoring damaged ecosystems is a tall order. Activities and funding for environmental protection, restoration, and management have increased visibly. Local communities and NGOs are mobilizing massively for conservation and development of the integrated protected areas systems, community-based agroforestry, watershed protection and management, and coastal and marine resources management.

The most popular campaigns to save the forests have been mounted by indigenous peoples and local communities in Sarawak, Thailand, Indonesia, the Philippines, and India. These campaigns target governments, the multilateral development banks, and the timber companies.

Despite significant advances in environmental protection, controversies remain: the subordination of indigenous peoples and local communities to external profit-seeking groups in the conservation and management of the forests; persistent logging; inadequate state policies and laws; poor enforcement of laws; intervention by foreign NGOs; and funding by the World Bank and the Asian Development Bank of projects that undermine conservation, such as the construction of big dams in forests. High consumption in rich countries such as Japan also sets back environmental protection because it is one of the causes of poverty and misery in less developed countries.

Official development assistance for area development is sorely inadequate. Not only does it fail to reverse the net outflow of resources from communities, it has been used to promote globalization that undermines local autonomous development. In contrast, donor NGOs in the North, such as NOVIB (Netherlands), support local efforts at integrated area development in different parts of Asia, although the impact of funds and other forms of assistance on local self-reliance is yet to be fully evaluated.

Because local development and self-governance need a supportive national policy, grassroots movements and NGOs lobby to influence public policy. Advocacy themes vary from country to country. The concerns of citizens' movements in industrial countries, such as Japan, Australia, New Zealand and the NICs, differ from those in poor countries, such as Bangladesh. Issues also differ from one country to another. China, for example, confronts problems different from those of India. But no matter how different priorities are, these countries have much in common. Every issue they address is linked to the environment-versus-development debate, to disparities in and among countries, and to the right of citizens to demand public accountability and respect for human rights.

Equity is the most prominent policy advocacy theme. Central to sustainable development, the resolution of inequality between and within nations, between men and women, and between the present and future generations will remove the main stumbling block that divides societies.

Two out of 10 Asians are members of the elite. Nationality matters little. Twenty percent of the population earns more than US$20,000 a year and produces over 20,000 kilograms of waste annually. In contrast, five to seven of 10 Asians, depending on their country, are poor and powerless. They live on US$2 a day at most. They probably produce less than 1,500 kilograms of waste per person annually—a level that U.N. scientists say will enable humanity to sustain itself through to the twenty-first century, assuming constant population and no deforestation.

Progressive citizens are aware of the dangers of ignoring equity for the sake of growth. Land reform, as part of asset reform, is a popular cause in poor as well as middle-income countries of Asia because skewed landownership

Village Institutions in India

By Anil Agarwal and Sunita Narain
Centre for Science and Environment

Government programs have over the years created a feeling of total dependence within people. Today, villagers expect the government to not only build roads and schools and give them employment but also plant trees and grasses and look after their local water sources like ponds and tanks.

This has been self-defeating. The natural resource base of a village can only be managed by the villagers themselves. Villagers have to ensure that animals do not graze in their protected commons, that the catchments of their local water bodies are conserved and properly used, and that the common produce from these lands is equitably distributed within the village. Environmental regeneration is a task the people must undertake themselves.

They can do all this and more only if there is an effective village-level institution to energize and involve them in controlling and managing their environment, and to resolve any disputes that may arise amongst them.

Voluntary agencies are often cited as effective agents for ensuring people's participation in rural development programes. We have found that all good cases of environmental regeneration undertaken by voluntary agencies have invariably involved the establishment of an effective institution at the village level. The creation of a village level institution brings the people together, spurs them into action, and ensures the protection and the development of the natural resource base.

The village of Sukhomajri near Chandigarh, for example, has been widely hailed for its pioneering efforts in micro-watershed development. The inhabitants have protected the heavily degraded forest land that lies within the catchment of their minor irrigation tank. The tank has helped to increase their crop production nearly three times and the protection of the forest area has greatly increased grass and fodder availability. This in turn has greatly increased milk production.

In just about five years, annual household incomes have increased by an estimated Rs. 2000 to 3000—a stupendous achievement by any count—and all of it has been achieved through the improvement of the village natural resource base and self-reliance. Few government schemes can boast of such results.

The crucial role in this entire exercise was played by a village-level institution that was specifically created in Sukhomajri for the purpose. Called the Hill Resources Management Society, it consists of one member from each household in the village. Its job is to provide a forum for the villagers to discuss their problems, mobilize them to take control of their environment, and ensure discipline among the members. The society makes sure that no household grazes its animals in the watershed, and in return it has created a framework for a fair distribution of the resources so generated—water, wood, and grass—among all the households in the village. Today the entire catchment of the tank is green and the village is prosperous, capable of withstanding drought.

A second example of the power of village institutions is the Chipko Movement. Nowhere in the world has a more successful community afforestation programe been organized than this one, formed under the leadership of the Dasholi Gram Swarajya Mandal in Gopeshwar. The Mandal has organized an informal village-level institution in each of the villages it is working. This institution—a Mahila Mangal Dal—consists of a woman member from each household in the village.

The village dals have slowly taken control of the community lands surrounding their villages. They protect these lands, plant trees on them, and ensure fair distribution of the grass and fodder that becomes available in increased quantities from the land. The forum of the Mahila Mangal Dal gives the women of these villages an opportunity to get together, discuss their problems, seek their solutions, and assert their priorities. And they are steadily moving toward articulating other needs and activities beyond afforestation, such as the provision of drinking water, schools for their children, and primary health care facilities.

symbolizes the great disparities in resource and power distribution. Citizens' movements also address problems of foreign debt, trade and investment, and aid, seeking debt relief, fairer trade terms, and the reversal of resource flows.

Citizens' movements work for the basic right of every person to demand good and responsive governance, inclusive participation, and equal electoral opportunities. Citizens' electoral movements have a long tradition in countries such as the Philippines—back to the 1950s and earlier. The National Movement for Free Elections (NAMFREL) was the first to mobilize thousands of volunteers around nonpartisan activities, such as voters' education, campaigns for clean and fair elections, poll watching, and ballot counting.

The tradition continues to this day as even more groups take part in protecting the ballot. The 1984 and 1986 elections called by former President Marcos saw tens of thousands of citizens risk their lives and limbs to ensure that voters could exercise their free choice and that every vote was counted. Those events are captured by photographs of ordinary citizens on 24-hour vigils and of nuns, priests, and high-society women in a tug-of-war with armed men and escorting ballot boxes to their destinations. In Thailand, Myanmar (Burma), Cambodia, South Korea, Nepal, and other countries that have recently undergone transitions to democracy, citizens banded together into movements to press for new constitutions and free elections.

Policy advocacy and integrated area development are complementary dimensions of a holistic strategy for transforming the substance and process of development. Policy advocacy creates the climate for expanding area development, and area development shapes policy advocacy. Lack of appreciation of this dynamic can create tension within the voluntary sector. True enough, policy advocacy that is not well rooted in local community-based initiatives lacks substance and will most likely run out of steam in the long haul.

But to reduce everything to local empowerment and community development is one type of fundamentalism; it may be called area determinism or ecoanarchism. It can foster the illusion that area development can be sealed off from external influences and mature entirely on its own.

Local areas are the ultimate site of development projects—state, corporate, or otherwise—although the benefits may be destined for someone else. There are centers and institutions of decision-making detached from but affecting the local communities. The local area is but one of the arenas or spaces of engagement for development activists and voluntary organizations. The others are the nation-state; interstate systems at the subregional, Asian, and global levels; multilateral institutions; and global corporate structures.

To be effective, voluntary action should take place in all these arenas. Some voluntary organizations operate at all levels simultaneously. Others confine themselves to one arena. But if all voluntary organizations share the same development vision and values, their efforts will converge and achieve their common goals.

Transnational Democracy

Over the last three decades, democratization from below has crossed local and national frontiers and spread throughout Asia-Pacific. Peoples' movements and other voluntary organizations are now linked regionally by structures and processes they have created over the years.

Before, Asian peoples were linked mainly through structures and mechanisms created from above. People-to-people linkages, mediated by states and interstate systems, were centered on trade, education, culture, and sports. They were, and still are, largely bilateral or subregional, such as the Southeast Asia Treaty Organization and its successor, the Association of Southeast Asian Nations. Except for the Asian Games, Asia-wide state-mandated people-to-people contacts are almost nonexistent.

Citizens' groups and movements are more closely linked to their Northern counterparts than they are to one another. One reason is globalization that accompanied colonialism and modernization. Another is the vastness of the region, with distances between countries magnified by poor communication technology. For instance, it is much easier to communicate or travel between the Philippines and Europe than between the Philippines and India, even though English is widely used in these two countries in official as well as personal communication.

Colonialism, imperialism, and wars have a way of bringing people closer to one another. They have triggered the feeling of "Asian-ness" among Asians. Unfortunately for the Japanese people, World War II moved Asians toward solidarity against them and their country. The Indochina War gave birth to powerful anti-U.S. peoples' solidarity movements across the Asia-Pacific. The wounds of war take time to heal and the healing has not been hastened by the behavior of either the United States or Japan, whose continuing hegemony brings Asian peoples closer together.

The consensus among Asian elites that economic growth should be pursued at any cost has been consolidated by the success of the NICs. Governments and big business justify their position by pointing to the economic stagnation and the endemic and rising poverty in the region. The elites' idea of

First Asian Indigenous Women's Conference

Indigenous women's groups from various parts of the Asia-Pacific region gathered for a pioneering meeting in January 1993 in Baguio City, in the Cordillera highland region of the Philippines. Representatives from indigenous women's groups from Bangladesh, Myanmar (Burma), India, Indonesia, Japan, Korea, Malaysia, Nagaland, the Philippines, Taiwan, Thailand, West Papua, and Vietnam (as well as Guatemala, Germany, and the Netherlands) came to share their situations, issues and concerns, values, visions, strategies, and programs and to add their voices to the cause of indigenous peoples in the region and all around the world.

The conference took up the plight of women belonging to different ethnic communities. Presentations covered a wide range of issues affecting indigenous groups: the Karens of Burma; the Dalits and Naga people in India; the Jummas in Bangladesh; the Dayaks of Indonesia; the Ainus and Buraku of Japan; the Dusuns, Bajau, Muruts, Rungus, Paitan, Minokok, Lun Dayeh, Kadayan, Sungai, and Suluk of Sabah; the Sengoi (Orang Asli) of Peninsular Malaysia; the Amis, Puyuma, and Yami of Taiwan; the Karen, Hmong, Mien, Lahu, Akha, and Lisu in Thailand; the 54 ethnic groups in Vietnam; and the indigenous peoples of the Philippines. A Guatemalan Mayan delivered a message from 1992 Nobel Peace Prize winner Rigoberta Menchu.

The conference also featured songs, poetry, and dances by the different groups. The message of the First Asian Indigenous Women's Conference may be captured in the refrain of the song written by Joji Cariqo, Judy Cariqo, and Nancy Jouwe:

We are the women of Asia/We are the people of the land
We are the women of Asia/We stand together hand in hand
We work on our native soil/Feel the sweat—from our toil
With the power of our hand/We feed the people of the land.

growth will likely be the dominant influence in the development processes that will take Asia-Pacific into the next century.

Grassroots movements and voluntary organizations are challenging the new growth orthodoxy with their own vision and strategies. They are not anti-growth; their alternative development agenda promotes equitable and ecologically sound development for the whole region.

In 1988, a Japanese peoples' alliance proposed a brilliant, forward-looking and innovative idea: People's Plan for the 21st Century. The idea is now an Asia-Pacific, if not global, citizens' movement. It was originally proposed by the Pacific-Asia Resource Center, an action-oriented research, education, and documentation center established in 1973 to promote people-to-people solidarity mainly in Asia-Pacific. The movement is now known as PP21.

PP21 grew out of the need to "produce a vision of the future society which is worth winning together." It counterposes a people-based, people-centered vision of an alternative Asian future to regional economic, political, and cultural integration by transnational corporations and international power elites. It proposes a model of development that measures social progress by the degree of equality, justice, dignity, and conviviality with nature.

By 1989, PP21 had linked largely autonomous activities of grassroots and citizens' movements throughout Japan and Asia-Pacific. Farmers and fishers, indigenous peoples and ethnic minorities, workers, women working outside the home, housewives, consumers, and activists in the cooperative, alternative trade, alternative aid, anti-nuclear, peace, human rights, environmental, and NGO movements all began to go beyond criticism of society to the assertion of a positive vision of the future. In 1992, Thai groups replicated PP21. Some groups in the Philippines are doing the same.

From 1989 to 1992, several gatherings of Asian voluntary organizations took place. Women, indigenous peoples, NGOs, and adult and popular educators were the most active. They forged sectoral, national, and subregional positions on development and environment, but no common Asian position.

During the last three decades, events that had transboundary impact or that affected large masses of people brought citizens' organizations together. War, war-related famine, gross violation of human rights, massive rainforest destruction, and large-scale natural disasters were caused or worsened by states, multilateral institutions (such as the World Bank and the Asian Development Bank), and transnational corporations.

Peace movements born during the Vietnam war, far from being exhausted, continue to fuel voluntary citizen action despite the end of the so-called Cold War era. Citizens are mobilizing and pressuring governments to establish a nuclear-weapons-free and demilitarized zone of peace and security. They are particularly worried by the remilitarization of Japan, the continuing military presence of the United States in South Korea and elsewhere in the Pacific, and the rising tension resulting from intense economic competition between the United States and Japan.

A Nuclear-Free Pacific

An alternative security system for the region would build on successful limited initiatives at the subregional level during the 1980s, which were propelled by unorthodox alliances between governments, NGOs, and mass movements in the context of favorable public opinion.

Most notable have been the creation of the South Nuclear-Free Zone by 11 states; the banning of nuclear-armed and nuclear-powered vessels from New Zealand ports; and the Philippines' decision to terminate the U.S. lease to Subic Naval Base. So strong, in fact, is the popular mood in favor of arms control in the region that even Indonesia and Malaysia, two conservative U.S. allies, have proposed making Southeast Asia a nuclear-free zone.

The 1971 war in Bangladesh was another important transboundary issue. It inspired a sense of common humanity and gave rise to citizens' movements inside and outside the country in support of war victims. Most of the big NGOs in Bangladesh were born during this period. International assistance created a great sense of people-to-people solidarity.

Transnational democracy movements in the Asia-Pacific region are fuelled by massive human rights violations in countries that follow the path of authoritarian development. Asians have been moved by atrocities in Indonesia in the 1960s and, more recently, in the Philippines, Thailand, South Korea, Taiwan, Singapore, Kampuchea under the Pol Pot regime, Bangladesh, Nepal, Myanmar (Burma), and Tiananmen.

Human rights movements are also at the vanguard of struggles for democracy because development and environment are fundamentally issues of rights and, therefore, linked to almost every human concern that moves every citizen to voluntary action.

The 1993 U.N. World Conference on Human Rights in Vienna brought human rights groups from all over Asia together. Before the meeting they agreed on a common position. In Vienna, they engaged Asian government delegations in sharp debates, indicating that they can pressure governments into changing their policies. Later, human rights groups made their presence felt at the meeting of government ministers hosted by the Singapore government, a clear sign that states are forced to respond to pressures from below.

A Permanent Peoples Tribunal established in Rome by the International League for the Rights of Peoples has responded to 17 complaints. The Asian cases it has taken up include self-determination for Tibet, gross violations of human rights during martial rule in the Philippines, Soviet aggression against Afghanistan, and industrial disasters, such as the massive chemical poisoning in Bhopal and mercury poisoning in Minamata.

In July 1993, Japanese citizens' groups organized the Tokyo Tribunal to judge the Group of Seven. It was modelled after the 1988 Berlin Permanent Peoples Tribunal, which charged the International Monetary Fund and World Bank with acting as agents of global capital and with imposing a variety of intolerable economic burdens on countries of the South. The Tokyo Tribunal charged the United States, Japan, Germany, Canada, the United Kingdom, France, and Italy with causing poverty and inequality and with destroying the environment.

In keeping with the spirit of transnational democracy from below, the Tokyo Tribunal deliberately refrained from rendering a judgment. Asserting that the privilege was reserved for the peoples of the world, it indicted the G-7 countries based on oral and written testimonies and the knowledge and experience of its panelists.

Citizens' environmental movements strengthen regional democratization from below. Some of the best recent examples are the campaigns to save the Sarawak rainforests and to stop the Narmada dam project in India, the Pak Mun dam in Thailand, the Three Gorges Dam in China, and the nuclear testing and dumping of hazardous, toxic, and nuclear wastes in the South Pacific. The considerable impact of these campaigns evokes in citizens' movements across and beyond the Asia-Pacific a sense of urgency to act and to demonstrate their solidarity with the millions of people affected.

Broad movements found that they needed institutional structures to link their activities. Different groups formed a string of Asia-wide coalitions, networks, forums, and coordinating committees.

The nature of the structures depends on the reasons for forming them, the kind of groups that gravitate toward each other, and the groups' goals, activity cycle, resource requirements, and resource availability. Some structures are permanent; many last only as long as the project.

Long-term groups include the Asian Coalition for Agrarian Reform and Rural Development (ANGOC), the Third World Network, the Asia-Pacific Bureau on Adult Education (ASPBAE), Asia-Pacific Peoples Environmental Network, Asian Alliance of Human Rights Organizations, and the Asian Students Associations. Examples of temporary and more fluid groups include the

UNCED coordinating committees, the Asian Development Bank lobby group, the South-North Project for Sustainable Development in Asia, and Sustainable Agriculture Network.

ASPBAE stands out among NGOs because its main focus is education. Founded in 1964 in Sydney, Australia, following a UNESCO seminar, ASPBAE is recognized internationally for its contribution to nonformal adult education. Its membership base includes national associations of adult education, individuals, and institutions. By 1988, it counted among its members 14 national associations, 35 institutions, and 75 individuals. At its First General Assembly in 1991, hundreds of delegates came representing around 35 countries. ASPBAE is also affiliated to the International Council of Adult Education (ICAE).

Regional and national activities of ASPBAE and its members cover a wide range of concerns: peace and human rights, trade union education, environment, women, youth education, education of indigenous peoples, social awareness, curriculum and pedagogy development, participatory methodologies, and many others, including health and drug abuse.

Many other groups in the Asia-Pacific are training and developing an increasing number of popular educators who can galvanize citizen action around development, environment, and human rights issues. Not only do they deliver a basic service to the millions who continue to suffer government neglect, they use education as a means to people empowerment.

In many cases, centralized structures are not necessary to establish Asia-wide links among organizations and movements. Bilateral relationships are sometimes favored over multilateral. Multiple bilateral arrangements and flexible multilateral structures avoid bureaucratization and promote a wider latitude for direct voluntary action.

Supranational integration of economic and political power is the biggest impediment to democratization from below. As markets and ecological space diminish, resources and decisions are concentrated in fewer and fewer institutions dominated by the most powerful states and transnational corporations. The result is regionalization. While regionalization can move power away from the traditional international elite, it can also mean hegemony of Japan or more intense Japanese competition with the United States, which is not about to give up its hold on Asia-Pacific.

The elite consensus that growth should be achieved at any cost means that the social and ecological problems of this century will be magnified severalfold in the next. Rapid economic growth will undermine the commitment of Asia-Pacific states to carry out UNCED agreements. NIC-type industrialization, together with Japanese-type modernization, will further stress the ecological capacity of the region. Asia is still rich in biodiversity and minable resources but will not be able to sustain high-speed growth for long. The region's sink capacity, which remains comparatively large, will not last long either once industrialization goes full steam ahead.

The international power elites have a decided edge over grassroots and citizens' movements in the battle for Asian hearts and minds. The media and all instruments of educating and informing the masses are under elite control. The superhyping campaigns for NIC development in schools, newspapers, television, and radio—not to mention the voluminous literature churned out by official development institutions—highlight the citizens' movements disadvantage.

Citizens' movements, especially at the grassroots, are handicapped by channels for information exchange that are not only limited but expensive. As noted earlier, access to information has improved a great deal in the past few years due to electronic technology and computer-based communication systems. But while some voluntary organizations are already hooked up to these systems, many more are not, especially grassroots groups that cannot afford installation fees or whose remote location does not allow them easy access to the systems.

The feverish pace of globalization of development and environment problems underlines the need for more effective communication in order to pool together and organize the scattered responses of different citizens' groups. The policies and activities of regional institutions, such as the Asian Development Bank (ADB), the World Bank, transnational corporations, and interstate bodies must be monitored.

As a major development institution, the ADB has become a focus of lobby activities of a growing number of NGOs and peoples' organizations within and outside the Asia-Pacific region. Since its founding in 1966, the bank has financed development investments in its developing member countries (DMCs) amounting to US$43 billion—a total of 1,180 projects in agriculture and agroindustry, energy, industry, transport and communications, social infrastructure, finance, and the private sector. Its annual lending increased from US$1.7 billion in 1981 to US$5.3 billion in 1993.

An ADB NGO lobby began in 1989 through the initiative of two U.S. NGOs—Friends of the Earth and Environmental Policy Institute—and ANGOC. All three have also been involved in the World Bank NGO lobby network. Since then, there has been a dramatic increase in the number of lobby groups demanding reforms in ADB policies and activities.

307

The twenty-fifth ADB Annual Meeting in May 1992 in Hong Kong saw a significant expansion of the lobby network with the participation of the South-North Project for Sustainable Development in Asia. This was organized in 1990 to do research and lobbying around the themes of agriculture, forestry, and micro-ecosystems. It was originally composed of six Asian organizations—AWARE (India), Project for Ecological Recovery (Thailand), PRRM (Philippines), PROSHIKA (Bangladesh), SAM (Malaysia), WALHI (Indonesia)—and a donor-partner in the North, NOVIB (Netherlands). During the lobby phase, two more groups were enlisted into the network—Japan Tropical Forest Action Network and the Bank Information Center-USA—because of their track record in lobby work with multilateral development banks.

Participation in the lobby campaigns increased to over 30 organizations between the 1992 and 1993 ADB annual meetings. Aside from members of the major networks, these included AID Watch (Australia), Greenpeace International, Sustainable Agriculture Network, Philippine Development Forum (from the United States), Freedom from Debt Coalition (Philippines), Environmental Defense Fund (U.S.), and Thailand Rural Reconstruction Movement, among others.

The NGO lobby has raised a variety of issues and concerns over the social and environmental impacts of Bank policies and projects. These issues have been forcefully backed up by case studies conducted by the NGOs in partnership with affected local communities.

ADB has been responding positively to NGO pressure for changes. Apart from liberal use of trendy sustainable development rhetoric, ADB has recently issued new guidelines incorporating environment and social dimensions in policy formation and program and project cycles. ADB has also opened some space for NGO and local community participation in project implementation, monitoring, and evaluation.

But these reforms are considered by NGOs and local communities as too little and too slow in coming. A budget analysis reveals that the bulk of ADB's money still goes to traditional growth projects that produce adverse social and ecological effects. Justifiably, the lobbyists continue to doubt if ADB is capable of making a fundamental shift in its strategic orientation, policies, and activities.

One problem confronting the voluntary sector is its dependence on development assistance from the North. Some grassroots movements and development support organizations are totally dependent on foreign funding. Their dependency gives rise to a number of problems, the most important of which is the loss of autonomy of the recipient organizations. Many donor organizations impose their own views on how development should proceed in the South. Local organizations' dependence draws them away from opportunities that are available within the country, limiting the possibilities for local resource mobilization. The decline or cutback of foreign assistance will surely magnify this problem.

Civil society flourishes in pluralism and diversity. Conflicts of agenda and multiple strategies and approaches add color and fire to citizens' movements. As long as groups can demonstrate a fairly high threshold of tolerance for differences, they will overcome dependence and other problems, and eventually converge toward a common higher goal.

Looking to the Future

The evolving scenario for transnational democracy in the Asia-Pacific region is difficult to paint. It is certain that there is no stopping the growth roller-coaster and that advocates of an equitable and sustainable Asian future will be hard put to redirect the growth trajectory. Yet Asian citizens can convert problems into opportunities and assert an alternative vision for a twenty-first-century Asia-Pacific.

One opportunity for citizens' movements is the commitment made by Asian states and governments to carry out all UNCED agreements. Monitoring compliance by governments at the national and regional levels is a crucial task that can complement grassroots initiatives to promote a just and ecologically sound development.

Citizens' movements increase the pressure on governments to draw up a common regional or subregional plan to calibrate modernization to the limits of the region's natural environment. Appropriate scaling of development requires a shared definition of industrial and trading niches; a common but differentiated responsibility for curbing transboundary pollution and dumping of hazardous, toxic, and nuclear wastes; and a plan for protecting and restoring biodiversity and the health of the upland, lowland, coastal, and marine ecosystems. The growing ecological agriculture movements should play a key role in pressuring business corporations and governments because rapid industrialization is killing agriculture.

Citizens must press for structural adjustment that will harmonize comparative advantages, offset relative resource scarcities and correct inequalities and imbalances within and among nations. A cut-and-share arrangement in production and consumption should be worked out among the haves and the have-nots of Asia-Pacific.

As subregional trading blocs will eventually consolidate at the regional level, citizens' movements must vigorously advocate better trade terms for the time being and an alternative trading system strategically.

Although difficult to build, an alternative trading system that is linked to grassroots activities must be established to provide citizens' movements' perspective and vision in current and future negotiations among the Asian states. A people-oriented "altertrade" system not only promotes fair trade but ensures that communities and countries trade only their surpluses after meeting basic needs and services. Today, countries and transnational corporations are trading goods and services at the expense of local communities and their life-support systems. This weakens the capacity of local communities for self-determination and destroys the ecosystems on which these communities depend for their living.

People-to-people trade is a direct counterpoint to the global trading system. The International Federation for Alternative Trade has significant achievements in promoting people-to-people trade. Some Japanese citizens' groups trade in organically grown bananas, linking producers in the Philippines directly to Japanese consumers in an equitable and environment-friendly relationship. These successes suggest what is possible within the limits of an unequal global trading system.

Trade wars in Asia-Pacific among the rich and powerful can be tamed by citizen action up to a point. They cannot be prevented by simple recourse to the package of liberal policies that aim to pry open the economies of Asian countries, as proposed by the International Monetary Fund, World Bank, Asian Development Bank, and transnational corporations.

Several Asian voluntary groups are lobbying directly against the policies and activities of multilateral development institutions and transnational corporations. The lobby group on the Uruguay Round of the General Agreement on Tariffs and Trade is an outstanding example. As noted earlier, Asian groups have mounted a similar campaign to take on the Asian Development Bank.

Citizens' movements led by human rights, peace, and anti-nuclear weapons movements go beyond trade issues and are pressuring governments to establish a regional zone of peace, security, neutrality, and prosperity. Their activities can be effective not only against the intensification of trade wars but also against the eruption of open military conflicts.

Asia-Pacific can be transformed from a region of instability to a zone of peace and security based on demilitarization, respect for the sovereignty and dignity of people, and environmental sustainability. The change will happen only if citizens' movements use their collective voice and power to define new terms of engagement with states, interstate systems, and business corporations.

The world that favored the rise of the Asian economic miracles is no more. What confronts the citizens of Asia-Pacific is a planet whose economic and ecological space may soon disappear. Citizens must continue to engage in voluntary action and strive for an alternative path to a common Asian future.

Bibliography

The American Council for Voluntary International Action. *1991 InterAction: Member Profiles*. New York: 1991.

Ampo: Japan-Asia Quarterly Review. Vol. 18, Nos. 2-3, 1986; Vol. 19, No. 1, 1987; Vol. 19, No. 2, 1987; Vol. 19, No. 3, 1987; Vol. 20, No. 3 (series no. 77); Vol. 22, Nos. 2 & 3 (series nos. 84, 85); Vol. 23, No. 2 (series no. 87); Vol. 24, No. 1, 1993; Vol. 24, No. 2, 1993.

Asia Monitor Resource Center. *Min-Ju No-Jo: South Koreas New Trade Unions*. Hong Kong: 1988.

Asian Development Bank. *Annual Report*. Manila: 1992.

Asiaweek. May 19, 1993.

Arena Bulletin: Asian Exchange. May 1993.

Bello, Walden. *People & Power in the Pacific: The Struggle for the Post-Cold War Order*. San Francisco: Pluto Press/Institute for Food and Development Policy/Transnational Institute, 1992.

Bello, Walden, and Stephanie Rosenfeld. *Dragons in Distress: Asia's Miracle Economies in Crisis*. England: Clays Ltd, St Ives plc, 1992.

Bello, Walden. *Toward a Peoples Pacific*. New York: The People-Centered Development Forum, 1992.

Brown, Michael and John May. *The Greenpeace Story*. New York: Dorling Kindersley, 1991.

Clark, John. *Democratizing Development: The Role of Voluntary Organizations.* London: Earthscan, 1991.

Cordillera Womens Education and Resource Center, Inc. *Proceedings of the First Asian Indigenous Womens Conference.* Baguio: 1993.

Crawshaw, Josie. "Wallow in the Backwaters or Sink in the Mainstream? No! Navigate New Waters!" Presented at a conference organized by the Maori Womens Welfare League, Darwin, Australia, 1993.

Development Support Service of the IRED Partners in Asia. "The Colombo Statement of Asian NGOs & Peoples Organisations on Peoples Empowerment in Asia." Document No. 01. Colombo: 1992.

The Ecologist. July/August 1992; March/April 1993; May/June 1993.

Ekins, Paul. *A New World Order: Grassroots Movements for Global Change.* London, New York: Routledge, Chapman and Hall, Inc., 1992.

Fernandes, Rubem Cesar. *Back & Forward to Civil Society.* Written for the Working Group on Poverty, Economy and Environment of Unit III, World Council of Churches.

Food and Agriculture Organization of the United Nations. *Directory of Non-Governmental Organizations for Rural Development.* Rome: 1985.

Hill, Helen. "Non-Governmental Organizations in the South Pacific Region: Towards a Typology for Identifying Learning Needs." Presented to the Commonwealth Association for the Education and Training of Adults Conference, Nottingham, UK, 1993.

Hill, Helen. "Peoples Organization and International Issues, Towards a Typology for North and South." Presented to a conference of The Australian Sociological Association, Adelaide, Australia, 1992.

Hill, Helen. *Directory of Australian NGOs.* May 15, 1993.

Ho Shuet Ying. *Taiwan After a Long Silence.* Hong Kong: Asia Resource Center, 1990.

Hodgkinson, Virginia A., Richard W. Lyman et al. *The Future of the Nonprofit Sector.* San Francisco: Independent Sector, 1989.

Holloway, Richard. "Civil Society—the Non-profit Private Sector: Trying to Categorize It in Bangladesh." Presented to UNICEF, Dhaka, Bangladesh, April 1993.

Hongkong Trade Union Education Centre and Asia Monitor Resource Center Ltd. *At the Crossroads: Hong Kong Independent Trade Union Movement and the International Trade Secretariats (ITS): Report on the August 9-10, 1988 Conference.* Hong Kong: 1988.

Hunt, Janet, Russel Rollason et al. *One World or...None: Making the Difference.* Australia: Australian Council for Overseas Aid and Pluto Press Austria, 1989.

International Campaign for Ecological Justice in Indonesia. *Down to Earth.* June 1993.

The International Peoples Tribunal to Judge the G-7. "Indictment." Tokyo, Japan, July 3-4, 1993.

Japanese Working for A Better World: Grassroots Voices & Access Guide to Citizens Groups in Japan. San Francisco: Honnoki USA, 1992.

Korten, David. *Getting to the 21st Century-Voluntary Action and the Global Agenda.* Connecticut: Kumarian Press, 1990.

Leung Wing-yue. *Smashing the Iron Rice Pot.* Hong Kong: Asia Monitor Resource Center Ltd, 1988.

Lippmann, Lorna. *Generations of Resistance: Aborigines Demand Justice.* Australia: Longman Cheshire Pty Ltd, 1992.

Lokayan Bulletin. Delhi. November-December 1991.

Lu Ping. *China: A Moment of Truth.* Hong Kong: Asia Monitor Resource Center Ltd, 1990.

McCarthy, Kathleen D., Virginia A. Hodgkinson and Russy D. Sumariwalla. *The Nonprofit Sector in the Global Community: Voices from Many Nations*. San Francisco: Jossey-Bass, Inc., 1991.

Morales, Horacio Jr. *A Call for Peoples Development*. Manila: National Council of Churches in the Philippines, 1990.

Mukul. *Against the Stream: India's Economic Crisis and Workers' Alternatives*. New Delhi: Charu, 1992.

National Campaign for Housing Rights (NCHR). *Sapping India Sapping the Indian People: The Impact of the IMF Structural Adjustment Package on Housing and Living Conditions in India*. Bombay: NCHR, 1992.

National Geographic. May 1993.

Noguchi, Mary Goebel. "The Rise of the Housewife Activist." *Japan Quarterly*. July-September 1992, pp. 339-51.

de Oliveira, Rosiska Darcy and Fatima Vianna Thais. *Population Danger: Sex, Lies and Misconceptions*. Rio de Janeiro, 1993.

Organisation for Economic Co-operation and Development. *Directory of Non-Governmental Environment and Development Organisations in OECD Member Countries*. Paris: 1992.

O'Connell, Brian, ed. *America's Voluntary Spirit: A Book of Readings*. New York: The Foundation Center, 1983.

The Organizing Committee for Peoples Plan for the 21st Century (PP21). *From Hope to Action: The Alliance of People*. Bangkok: 1992.

Philippine Rural Reconstruction Movement. *Bataan: A Case on Ecosystem Approach to Sustainable Development in the Philippines*. Quezon City: 1992.

Project for Ecological Recovery. *The Future of People and Forests in Thailand After the Logging Ban*. Bangkok: 1992.

Sahabat Alam Malaysia. *Directory of Environmental NGOs in the Asia Pacific Region*. Kuala Lumpur: APPEN, 1983.

Samaj Parivartana Samudaya, Federation of Voluntary Organisations for Rural Development - Karnataka (FEVORD-K), Action Committee for Protection of Common Lands (ACPCL), Citizens for Democracy - Karnataka and Jana Vikas Andolan. *Janaaranya: Peoples Participation in the Management of Natural Resources*. Dharwad and Karnataka (JVA-K)Blore. Bangalore: Samaj Parivartana Samudaya, Federation of Voluntary Organisations for Rural Development - Karnataka (FEVORD-K), Action Committee for Protection of Common Lands (ACPCL), Citizens for Democracy - Karnataka and Jana Vikas Andolan, 1991.

Saunders, Malcolm and Ralph Summy. *The Australian Peace Movement: A Short History*. Canberra: Peace Research Centre, Australian National University, 1986.

Serrano, Isagani R. *On Civil Society*. A Monograph Series. Quezon City: Philippine Rural Reconstruction Movement, 1993.

Society for Participatory Research in Asia. *Holding Together: Collaborations and Partnerships in the Real World*. New Delhi: 1991.

Tandon, Rajesh. "Citizen Action: Future Challenges." Presented at Managing Change Asian Workshop of Ashoka Foundation, Calcutta, India, March 31-April 2, 1993.

Tandon, Rajesh. "Civil Society, The State and Roles of NGOs." New Delhi, August 1991.

Tandon, Rajesh. "General Reflections on the Status and Issues of Civil Society in South Asia."

Tandon, Rajesh. "Adult Education, Cultural Development and Social Movements: The Contemporary Challenge." Presented at International Seminar on Educational and Cultural Development in Local Communities, Aranjuez, Spain, April 27-30, 1993.

Tandon, Rajesh. "The Role of Voluntary Action in Contemporary Context: Implications for Institutional Development." Presented at the seminar on the above theme held in Orissa, India, May 18-19, 1993.

Third World Resurgence. December 1991; November 1992; May 1993.

Transnational Institute. *A Directory of Non-Governmental Organizations in Developing Asia and Pacific.* Amsterdam, The Netherlands. 1991.

United Nations. *Earth Summit Agenda 21: The United Nations Programme of Action from Rio.* New York: United Nations Department of Public Information, 1992.

United Nations. *In Our Hands: Directory of Non-Governmental Organisations Accredited to the United Nations Conference on Environment and Development.* New York: The UNCED Secretariat-NGO Unit, 1992.

United Nations. *Earth Summit: Convention on Climate Change.* New York: United Nations Conference on Environment and Development, 1992.

United Nations. *Earth Summit: Convention on Biological Diversity.* New York: United Nations Conference on Environment and Development, 1992.

United Nations Development Programme. *Human Development Report 1993.* Delhi: Oxford University Press, 1993.

Walker, Ranginui and William Sutherland, eds. *The Pacific: Peace, Security and the Nuclear Issue.* Tokyo: Zed Books Ltd. and The United Nations University, 1988.

WALHI. *Mistaking Plantations for the Indonesias Tropical Forest.* Jakarta: 1992.

Weerackody, Chamindra. *An Attempt at NGO-PO Networking: A Sri Lankan Experience.* Document No. 10. Colombo: Development Support Service of the IRED Partners in Asia, December 1992.

World Bank. *World Development Report 1992: Development and the Environment.* New York: Oxford University Press, 1992.

World Bank. *World Development Report 1993: Investing in Health.* New York: Oxford University Press, 1993.

Yamamoto, Tadashi. "The Survey on Non-Governmental Underpinnings of the Emerging Asia-Pacific Regional Community" (draft proposal). Presented to Japan Center for International Exchange, Tokyo, Japan, February 15, 1993.

Yamamoto, Tadashi. "Cooperative Activities and Networks of Non-Profit Organizations in the Asia-Pacific Region." Research paper, Seoul, Korea, 1993.

Yamamoto, Tadashi. "Preliminary List of Basic Reference: The Survey on Non-governmental Underpinnings of the Emerging Asia-Pacific Regional Community."

Yokota, Katsumi. *I, Among Others.* Yokohama: Seikatsu Club Seikyo, 1991.

Zivetz, Laurie et al. *Doing Good: The Australian NGO Community.* Sydney: Allen & Unwin Pty Ltd, 1991.

8

THREADS OF
PLANETARY CITIZENSHIP

Rubem César Fernandes

Citizen participation is the leading idea for CIVICUS and for this book. Histories and cultures abound, dramatic and puzzling as they are, and yet the regional chapters show a genuine common thread woven around those two words—a kind of "participation" that implies "citizenship," and vice versa.

The idea has been, or is being, universalized. No matter how far or how deep you go, the notion should still make sense and be relevant to people's lives. Be it in the innumerable Pacific islands, the Himalayan heights, the African deserts, the Siberian plains, or the Amazonian river banks, soon no village will be found that has not somehow been touched by citizenship claims.

Extensive traveling has deeply transformed the notion of citizen participation. Meanings have expanded and multiplied—not beyond recognition, or at least not necessarily so, but certainly in unexpected ways. The regional chapters express these transformations, showing how dense, diverse, and troublesome universalization can be. The boring repetition of the same key words—citizen participation—gives way to a rich scenario of multiple and often conflicting histories.

It should be noted, therefore, that in spite of standing as building blocks for CIVICUS' world alliance, the regional reports do not constitute a new religion claiming the one right path. Brought together in this volume, they carry a sense of gravity that springs from a fundamentally doubtful condition. The common thread may well be broken. "Participation" is becoming a universal value, but it may be spread so thin that it loses collective substance. Individualistic claims, by people themselves and their families or by particular groups with a specific agenda, may bring it to a condition that is better described as "fragmentation." Claiming the rights of citizenship on a worldwide scale in a background of appalling inequality, deeply injured historical memory, ecological threats, and highly diverse hierarchies of values may be too much to handle for common wisdom. The language of rights, as we know so well, can provide the rationale for group resentment, anarchy, civil war, exploitation, foreign aggression.

No objective analysis can lessen this insecurity, and yet the signs are plentiful, from every region, that a positive disposition is available, actively seeking to prove itself. The mood changes, with good reasons, from one continent or country to another. But the signs of solidarity, beyond narrow self-interest, can be found crossing the most difficult borders.

Looking for such signs and spelling out their case, CIVICUS' regional reports demonstrate that valuable alliances, with a universalistic intent, are possible indeed from the local to the world levels. Furthermore, they seriously suggest that the time is right for the growth of such a planetarian sense of citizenship. Past the years of global confrontations, the opportunity beckons for new lines of solidarity, less exclusivist in nature and more open to the variety of existing possibilities. Beyond the stiff polarity between state and market mechanisms, attention can be given to the growing significance of citizen participation in the public arena. This chapter reviews some of its main features as shown in the regional reports.

Democratic Transitions

In the midst of so many erratic episodes, one trend may be distinguished: for the last twenty years, political change has mostly been inclined toward democratic forms of government. Results are various and uncertain, but the pattern is there, opening a new chapter in contemporary history.

The decades following World War II carried over the warrior's spirit as the ultimate source of resolution in political dilemmas. The division of the world guaranteed by military presence, wars of liberation in Asia and Africa, guerrilla warfare in Latin America, military coups, tactical confrontations between the superpowers, revolutions and counter-revolutions, and the horizon of a nuclear holocaust were all taken to express the profound nature of politics. Clausewitz's understanding of war as a natural follow-up of political disputes was widely assimilated and even heightened by an almost messianic vision of the issues at stake.

In hindsight, however, we see now that by the mid-seventies, the "war for the war" started to fade out, losing power to get people and things moving. Violence is still very much there—indeed, even more so as it spreads through a series of critical situations—but it is no longer perceived as the key to heaven or hell. It has moved, so to speak, to the margins of our imagination, as a sympton of political and societal failures. In contrast, the ability to negotiate social and political differences is seen as a better concept. Despite the countercurrents, which are also there, the democratic ideal has gained worldwide significance in the last decades.

The events of this new period are easily recalled. Political changes labelled as "democratic transitions" have consistently claimed, among other things, the citizen's right to participate in free and fair multiparty elections. They started in Europe with the fall of the last dictators from before the war—Salazar (1975) and Franco (1977)—and the military in Greece (1974). South America followed suit, moving out of the authoritarian 1970s through a hard-won series of multiparty presidential and legislative elections—Bolivia (1982), Brazil (1982), Argentina (1983), Uruguay (1984), Paraguay (1989), and Chile (1990), to name but a few. Central America, torn by cold war confrontations, struggled through a similar path in the following years—Honduras (1985), Guatemala (1986), Nicaragua (1991), El Salvador (1991), and even the long one-party rule in Mexico came under unprecedented pressure to allow opposition into the center stage.

On the other side of Europe, east of Berlin from the Baltic through the Adriatic and on to the Black Sea, expanding east toward Siberia, south to the Caucasus, and further through the Asiatic steppes, the amazing collapse of state socialism was followed by fast-organized multiparty elections in just about every old and new state in the region. Between 1989 and 1992, hundreds of millions of voters were called for this kind of political participation in the former socialist states of Eurasia, often for the first time in their country's history.

Asia has not moved at the same tempo. The success of the four newly industrializing economies under authoritarian regimes, the gradualist approach taken by the Chinese communists, and a stronger hierarchical tradition all combined to slow down the electoral expansion. Still, even in the Far East, the trend has been clearly noticed in the late 1980s and early 1990s. Popular pressure brought dictators down in several countries, starting democratic transitions with elections and the call for new constitutions in the Philipines (1986), South Korea (1992), Thailand (1979), Bangladesh (1978), and Sri Lanka (1989).

Sub-Saharan Africa has experienced a frightening economic and institutional crisis during this period. In line with the historical trend, however, development failures have often turned into a demoralization of the former military and personalized patterns of government. In every subregion, the pluralistic electoral avenue is being claimed and formally affirmed as an alternative. The presidential election in Senegal (1983), legislative elections in Cameroun (1992), and approval of a multiparty system in Kenya (1991) are examples to that effect. Despite the uncertainties involved, Africa does offer a most impressive historical case: after so many years of struggle, it was an electoral procedure, closely monitored by international observers, that finally defeated apartheid and brought Nelson Mandela to power supported by a broad coalition.

Southern Europe
    1970-1979   • • •
    1980-1989
    1990-1994

Eastern and Central Europe
    1970-1979
    1980-1989
    1990-1994   • • • • • • • • • • • • • • • • •

Latin America
    1970-1979   • •
    1980-1989   • • • • • • • •
    1990-1994   • • • •

Asia
    1970-1979   •
    1980-1989   • •
    1990-1994   • • • • • • • •

Africa
    1970-1979
    1980-1989   • • •
    1990-1994   • • • • • • •

Transitions toward multiparty elections per region by decade of first election.
• — one country.

In the Middle East, peace negotiations between Israel, the Palestinians, and other surrounding states can be counted as major steps in a similar direction.

Another aspect should be remembered. The tendency has been to expand the categories of people allowed to take part in the elections—young people, women, indigenous peoples, migrants, illiterates—putting pressure on the limits to citizen participation. Take the case of Brazil, for instance, a country with a liberal tradition that, however troublesome, dates back to the first half of the nineteenth century. In the last presidential election before the authoritarian period (1960), there were 16 million voters in Brazil; by the constitutional election that sealed the end to dictatorship in 1989, this had become 80 million. Voters amounted to less than one fourth of the population in Brazil in 1960, but they were more than half in 1989. Adding the new categories of voters to the generations that grew up under dictatorship and to the many countries with no previous democratic tradition, it becomes clear that for a vast chunk of people in the world, these have been the years of a first contact with the practices of liberal democracy.

This is not the place to discuss "democratic transitions." Questions of sustainability and of local variations must be left untouched here. Four general points need to be made, however, as we explore CIVICUS' common thread.

Most mass movements rely on symbols and organizations inducing collective identity; multiparty elections promote, instead, individualization. The approach of election day, the disputes, the promises and interpretations, the fashioning of party identities, the research of public opinion, the emotional appeal, the solemnity of gestures, the secret of the ballot, the celebration of victory—all this ritual enchantment is ultimately addressed to the individual, who is supposed to decide the collective ways of the future. The sociological content of such practices vary, but the element of choice, placed within the individual's consciousness, is a constant.

"Choosing" is certainly a complex affair, conditioned by multiple loyalties, but it does imply a moment when the individual is called to think and act as a sovereign self. To that extent, the multiplication of elections around the world is associated with the expansion of a sense of individual identity, which is appropriate to full-fledged "citizens."

On the other hand, this process applies to the most diverse categories of people. Whatever their age, sex, class, caste, nationality, tribe, native language, religious faith, or ideological belief, people are simply counted, one by one, as just one more voter in the ballot's list. It is a drastic egalitarian mechanism. Participation qualified through "citizenship" spreads the notion that at a certain fundamental level we are considered equals. It may go one step further and pretend to equalize all subjects, but that is a nightmarish perspective that is not implied by the electoral procedures.

In fact, unanimous decisions are viewed with suspicion, for elections are meant to express the differences of interest and opinion existing among voters. It does imply, however, that differences should be expressed according to a common and egalitarian set of rules that is voluntarily accepted by all concerned. "We should all be equals before the law" is the citizen's claim. Such is the tremendous contention at work in the multiple movements and initiatives captured by the regional reports in this book.

Clearly, public institutions become the target of awesome demands before citizens' claims. The choices available for election will only be considered fair to the extent that multiple interest groups find an appealing alternative in the ballots. Parties and other political institutions are supposed to give shape and structure to this diversity, but they can hardly accommodate all collective claims at any given time. That being the case, the system must be flexible enough to support the belief that over time the desired alternatives can be brought to bear. Furthermore, adverse results are only acceptable if they can be considered a temporary outcome, liable to be overturned on a next round.

In other words, electoral procedures need time to make sense and a careful effort at institutional engineering. Within that, preserving and improving the rules of the game should be more important than winning or losing at any given turn. Fragile, corrupt, rigid, or overbiased state institutions cannot stand the test and may soon demoralize the whole endeavor. Elections are so demanding that they may be easily considered an irrelevant fraud.

Just as trying, or even more so, are the relationships to be reached among citizens themselves, which is a crucial point to our argument here. Were they composed of a fairly homogeneous, well-off, well-educated and small group, as the ancient Greek philosophers thought fitting, the problem would not be so acute. Modernity, however, has universalized the concept of citizenship and it can no longer be sustained in the mode of exclusive clubs. Today it must encompass the most diverse ensemble of values and interests and still be experienced as a relevant component of each person's identity.

To develop such a democratic culture is a decisive challenge with consequences on a worldwide scale that are barely beginning to be explored. Nation building has often been accomplished through the unifying action of charismatic leaders, global identity symbols, and state integration. The bond of citizenship, however, in a multinational and multicultural context, amidst multiple instances of identity, cannot be assimilated unless it follows a different trajectory, growing through the social fabric, proving itself in daily intercourse. It needs to expand beyond and below the political sphere, penetrating both very large and very small levels of symbolic interaction, which seldom become the object of government decisions. In spite of their significance, elections and politics constitute but a limited (albeit central) element in the agenda implied by "citizen participation," as the following sections indicate.

Voluntary Associations

Voluntary associations are becoming a massive phenomenon worldwide. People get together, in small or large groups, to pursue a common goal. They do so voluntarily—not in response to an authority's command, not as a traditional obligation, and not with profit as the motive. They do it simply to accomplish something. Like elections, this kind of association, a product of individual choice, has boomed in the postwar years. The time coincidence (from the 1960s, in some cases, but mostly from the 1970s on) is quite obvious for some movements, such as of women, indigenous peoples, ethnic minorities, environment, gay rights, consumers, elderly, and the handicapped.

A new institutional form acquired substance in this period, introducing an odd new term now recognized in many languages: nongovernmental organizations, or NGOs, whose actions, according to a U.N. Development Programme estimate, benefit today about 250 million people in developing countries. But the phenomenon is much wider than these NGOs, for it covers the full range of goals that people may eventually find to be in their common interest to pursue. Sports, arts, recreation, community issues, education, health, security, identity, personal fulfillment, and so on may all provide an indefinite series of occasions for associations of multiple kinds.

Local circumstances introduce, of course, important variations. In Eastern Europe, in the 1970s and 1980s, the notion of "self-ruling" associations carried a heroic aura of defiance, opening "small circles of freedom" in the totalitarian environment. Organizations such as the Workers' Defense Committee and later Solidarnosc in Poland, the Fund for Poverty Relief Szeta in Hungary, Charter 77 in the former Czechoslovakia, the Popular Front in Estonia, and Mary and so many other "dissident" groups in Russia will see their names registered in history books. A few years after liberalization, estimates are of some 70,000 registered voluntary organizations in the region. Analysts suggest that many of these seem to provide an alternative to "private initiatives" lacking initial capital.

In Latin America, where traditional forms of participation (unions and parties) were blocked by authoritarian regimes in the 1970s, in a context of rapid urban growth, associations boomed at community level. An extensive survey conducted in Rio de Janeiro and São Paulo in 1987 found that more than 90 percent of the existing neighborhood associations had been created since 1970.

From Asia, we learn not only of numerical growth (for instance, 3,000 grassroots conservation associations in Japan), but also of very large and complex initiatives. In Sri Lanka, the Sarvodaya Sharamadana Movement has a staff of at least 7,700, serving 8,000 villages—a third of all villages in the country. In Bangladesh, BRAC has a staff of about 6,000 in 217 area offices working for 15,000 villages. PP21 (People's Plan 21) is a joint program involving thousands of organizations from the entire region in a concerted network.

NGOs have become a major kind of institution in Africa. That region's report quotes growth from 125 secular NGOs in Kenya in 1974 to more than 400 in 1988, from 376 in Zimbabwe in 1980 to 1,506 in 1985, and from 12,000 in South Africa in 1988 to some 20,000 today. Most telling in Africa is the combination of voluntary associations with traditional forms, such as burial societies multiplying in the cities, or women's clubs in the villages.

In the Arab region, autonomous secular associations are by and large inhibited by political culture and state regulations. But the numbers are most impressive when it comes to the voluntary services performed through religious centers. Even there, however, the trend is noticed in some countries: formally registered private voluntary organizations grew among the Palestinians in the West Bank and Gaza from 272 in 1987 to 444 in 1992, from 221 in Jordan in 1980 to 587 in 1992, and from 1,886 in Tunisia in 1988 to 5,186 in 1991.

In West Europe and North America, analysts debate a decrease in civil participation, possibly associated with a "post-modern" segmentation of social bonds. Although this process may be affecting massive forms of social and political involvement, researchers in the voluntary association field claim that this multiple and topic kind of social participation is, on the contrary, growing well. Lester Salamon notes: "A survey I conducted of nonprofit human service organizations in 16 America communities in 1982, for example, showed that 65% of the organizations then in existence had been created since 1960....The number of private associations has similarly skyrocketed in France. More than 54,000 such associations were formed in 1987 alone, compared to 10,000 to 12,000 per year in the 1960s. Between 1980 and 1986, the income of British charities increased an estimated 221%.... In Italy, recent research records a substantial surge of voluntary organization formation during the 1970s and early 1980s."

In short, while "democratic transitions" may be unstable and short-lived in many instances, the growth of voluntary associations cuts across the different regions, taking root under the most diverse political circumstances. In that manner, they show citizenship moving around the globe with a relative but consistent autonomy in terms of the conditions of the state.

The debate over the growth or decline in citizens' involvement in public issues in the northern industrial regions is interesting in that it seems to imply a significant change in the patterns of participation. While traditional forms, originating in the nineteenth century and composed mainly of workers and business associations, were geared toward the vertical axis from society to the state and vice versa, the associations mentioned in the regional reports tend to spread horizontally through society, many of them (if not most) never reaching a strictly political definition.

While the former pattern took shape in European history, the latter is typical of North American civic culture, and more so of the United States, a society known for the low level of political participation. Yet there are about 1.14 million registered nonprofit organizations there, largely dependent on private contributions, with up to 90 percent of nongovernmental funds coming from voluntary individual donations. Nowhere else does individual participation have such a significance. But the tendency to spread out through society rather than to cluster around political parties is probably becoming a dominant pattern. Variations on this point and their consequences are discussed in the regional reports, so the dicussion here is limited to a few general comments.

Self-reliance, rather than vertical loyalty, tends to become a key value in the practice of such associations. Voluntarily created, they may in principle be dismantled or left behind at the members' will, which places on them the burden of deciding on the association's fate. Assuming an independent legal existence, the members become formally responsible for what happens within the groups. State restrictions on the associations' legal autonomy become an object of regular resistance and criticism. Our regional reports relate many instances of this, as in Indonesia, Malaysia, China, several African countries, the Arab states, and Cuba.

Furthermore, being dispersed through so many objects of interest and organizational forms, the groups tend to deviate from the bureaucratic tendency to grow into ever more complex and heavy organizations. Most voluntary associations tend to stay relatively small, which means closer to the members' decision capacity. When cooperating among themselves, they often use a term borrowed from computer language, denoting connections that are compatible with independent performance: they form "networks." In short, voluntary associations take the value of individual freedom one step beyond the individuals themselves, giving shape to small but multiple clusters of independent judgment and initiative within society.

They associate for a common cause—to have fun, to preserve something, to further an objective, to support others; any differentiating link, any issue may give the occasion, provided some people come to see it as their common interest, worth the time and the effort. Associations promote sociability in an individualistic context. In their practice, collective ends and collective goods are perceived as the individual concern of those involved. Public life is inscribed in private initiatives. Citizenship is personalized.

Thus public life extends beyond the state and becomes an open-ended heterogeneous composition, as diverse as private initiatives can be. Decentralized, segmented, diffuse—the association pattern induces imagination to move from the micro connections around home to a wide landscape of possible social interactions. It matches well the communication possibilities created by the new technologies. As Waldemar Nielsen put it, "The landscape...is untidy but wonderfully exuberant. What counts is not the confusion, but the profusion. There is literally something in it for everyone."

The challenge, of course, is to find and to nurture the common thread binding such a pluralistic society together. One association may see another as a definite threat to its vocation, which is often the case. Neighborhood youth groups may be called to make war among themselves rather than have fun together; ethnic tensions may build up under the stimulation of voluntary militants; death squads have been conducted under the genuine belief in the value of individual initiative; the pleasures of hunting offend animal lovers, meat eating may be disgusting to vegetarians, and "pro-choice" women's groups face the opposition of "pro-life" movements.

The well-known answer to this problem calls upon common law: associations may be wonderfully profuse provided they function according to the law—which sends us back to the political dimension. Certainly, citizenship cannot subsist without agreeable state institutions and law enforcement. It depends on the fate of the "democratic transitions."

The political answer, however, is not sufficient for at least three good reasons: in the first place, ruling elites in most cases are not used to democratic forms of government—they must be forced by or at least find support in a democratically oriented civil society. The political solution, which makes citizenship possible in the long run, depends in turn on citizens' action. At some point, the two things must go together. Second, unbearable inequalities and the cultural confrontations implied by "development" make the ideal of a basic consensus an extremely difficult affair. The sense of a common origin (so common that it could be called "natural"), which made the notion of a social contract a reasonable concept in the West, does not apply here. Citizens worldwide cannot reasonably believe that they were born equals. Planetarian citizenship must, somehow, evolve as a new and worthwhile experience. And third, the decentralized, segmented, diffuse, small, and at the same time internationalized nature of voluntary associations make them rather difficult to control from outside. General Pinochet could not do it properly in Chile: local associations grew under his military rule, as they did generally in the 1970s, an authoritarian period in most regions.

Unless the common thread is reinforced and nurtured within society itself, penetrating people's consciousness, becoming a habit, generating spontaneous social cohesion and coercion, there is no chance for "citizen participation" on a world scale. Elections and new constitutions, welcome as they may be, will not be enough without the development of a democratic culture.

Social Movements

"Social movements" is another recurrent expression to describe citizen participation. It has been used as a broad category in political discourse since the 1970s, especially in Europe, Latin America, and Asia. The term "movements" is used because of the unstable nature of the groups, different from structures organized for the long haul; they are "social" because of the kind of issues involved, as well as the distance they usually keep from the state machinery.

They involve associations and have several features in common with them, but they are not formally circumscribed and move in waves of hot voluntary participation. They may have such wide expressions as the peace demonstrations in Western Europe in the 1980s, the protest movements in Eastern Europe in 1989, and the struggle against apartheid in South Africa. They are often rather small, however, emerging as a response to local issues. In every region, probably in most countries and in regions within countries, hardly a day goes by without something happening as a result of some social movement's action.

Like associations, social movements provide a framework for the assertion of legal and moral rights by independent subjects. They contribute, in that way, to the assimilation of modern notions of autonomy in the most diverse contexts. Women, youth, indigenous peoples, ethnic minorities, and so on have remarkably multiplied the circumstances in which respect is demanded for an equally valuable self. The common values of citizenship are unevenly distributed through the spectrum of human differences, which is perceived as unfair and provides the rationale for innumerable movements of protest. That, in fact, is another point to distinguish social movements from associations. While the latter tends to be proactive, gathering people to do something, the first carries a reactive connotation, mobilizing people around some kind of protest. The distinction is not sharp, of course, for people may associate to further a protest, but the militancy characteristic of social movements does seem to feed especially from the sources of contradiction.

Unlike associations, on the other hand, social movements have tended to underline collective identity, raising the demands and asserting the rights of collectively defined subjects. The People and the Nation were the typical expressions of such global identities in the last couple of centuries. Social movements, however, have segmented such grand holistic notions into a variety of actors. The collectivity that assimilated everything and everyone was substituted by a more specific scale of identification, giving visibility to a number of collective proper names. Ethnic groups, minorities, tribes, religions, local communities, sex, age, professional, and other categories added an unrestrained complexity to the use of the word "we" in the public scene.

The complexity is furthered because such transformations do not occur evenly throughout regions. "Nationhood" is very much an issue in Eastern Europe, for instance. In the southern hemisphere, the Popular Movements, class-based, are strong in the memory and in the horizon of relevant actors. The People's Plan for the next century articulated by NGOs and social movements in Asia has been described mostly in line with that region's popular traditions. Religion may spur a strong sense of identity cutting across national borders.

On the other hand, movements of a universalistic nature make themselves present in every context, the women's movement being probably the most obvious case to that effect. Without exception, the regional reports highlight the importance of women in the citizens' agenda, both in the numbers of people most actively involved and in the content of the issues entailed. Ecology introduces other references and scales. In short, social movements voice citizenship claims everywhere, but not in the same tempo; they give shape to a highly "asynchronic" world composition.

How can the common thread be woven through such a heterogeneous scenario? Our reports are sensible enough not to give clear-cut answers to this question. The edges of contradiction are exposed in too many points and shapes. The reports do express, however, a common inclination: an insistent questioning on how the channels can be kept open for the communication among the multiple collective claims. Contrary to the warrior style prevailing in the Cold War period, the case is made, time and again, that peaceful resolution of conflicts is not only desirable, but possible. This is not an objective statement derived from some kind of analytical certainty. It is the expression of a growing conviction that both individual and collective rights cannot be sustained, in the long run, except under the condition of a peaceful coexistence within and among societies.

Raising collective claims over contradictory issues, social movements pose a crucial testing case to the negotiating capacity within democratic transitions. The way they go about it, their style and their methods, and their approach to limiting situations should be consequential for the long-run chances of citizenship. The Chiapas case in Mexico, in 1993, offers a significant example in that respect: a movement that could turn into one more endemic source of well-founded local violence moved instead toward negotiations, with far-reaching consequences both for the social agenda and for democratization in Mexico. The concerted efforts of the local church, peasant associations, and several NGOs to keep communications open between the Chiapas leadership and the national government, playing a conscious mediating role, was certainly a crucial element in that situation.

Another challenging issue is raised by "participation" itself. Social movements are strong in voluntary content, but they are not formed through regular procedures of representation. Their leaders speak on behalf of entire collectivities, but they have not been formally elected to do so. Their weight and relevance must be evaluated through other means—the numbers they can mobilize, the pungency of the words they pronounce, the symbolic impact of their gestures. Escaping the formalities of representation, they open the doors for the participatory demands latent within society, and specially for those segments that cannot find a proper place for themselves within the established channels of communication.

Likewise, however, they may or may not value democratic constraints and opportunities. However pertinent, collective will can be quite threatening to others. Racism, for instance, has been a powerful source for voluntary mobilization. Thus, the dynamics relating social movements to the threads of citizenship are often subtle and critical. When a positive interaction occurs, walls and locks may fall for the general wonder; when, on the contrary, communication is broken, global confrontations send us back to the bipolar scenario of final wars.

NGOs

The expression nongovernmental organization comes originally from United Nations vocabulary to designate a special category of participants in the U.N. system. This original context explains the expression's awkward generality— it was supposed to include a wide spectrum of nongovernmental institutions deemed fitting to be a part of some U.N. body. The meaning has changed substantially, but the connection with the mechanisms of international cooperation remains a relevant component of the phenomenon we have come to call NGOs.

The term is well known in the Western areas of Europe, as well as in Asia, Africa, and Latin America. It is confused with other names in Eastern Europe, where the expression "foundations" indicates often a similar kind of institution; it is understood in a broader sense in North America, as an alternative name for what we shall be calling here the "third sector." At any rate, the word emerging out of development cooperation between West European and Third World countries in the last decades refers to a specific institutional type that deserves to be distinguished and discussed on its own.

In this limited sense, NGOs are independent institutions. They are not an organic part of larger structures. Thus while a church pastoral, a university department, a political party, or a business section may eventually do similar work, they would not count as NGOs. Furthermore, they are not representative of a wider constituency. Their value is derived from what they do, not whom they represent. Strictly, they are not entitled to speak on somebody else's behalf. Unions, neighborhood associations, and other member-serving organizations may belong to the same field of work, but they would not be counted as NGOs either. They are supposed to deliver social services that are not typically self-sustainable, so NGOs must seek funds elsewhere. And they are not funding agencies, which makes them different from foundations.

Thus a series of contrasting marks differentiates NGOs: nongovernmental, not-for-profit, not a part of larger structures, not representative, not funders. To be positive, however, their short but characteristic history needs to be remembered. In our limited sense, NGOs were born within the circuits of global cooperation. They provided unofficial channels for the international support of social projects typically carried on a local and micro level. They were not the only ones to do that (churches and unions, for instance, were also involved), but they became specialists at it. Their independence facilitated unofficial international connections and their small size was favorable for local immersion. Thus they were free to mediate between international and local agendas, specializing themselves in projects that made sense at both extreme ends of the "development" program.

Furthermore, unbound by the duties of representation, NGOs were not limited to a territorial or even to a functional definition. They could move from one place to another, one group to another, and even one subject to another, without formal constraints. If their services were welcome, they would stay and do their job. Once a project was finished, they would move to somewhere or something else. This mobility, of course, was quite functional for the intermediary role they were to play between global institutions and grassroots organizations.

Such origins gave shape to a characteristic institutional style. NGOs must produce projects that are interesting to available funders and carry them through successfully enough to justify a following round of projects and fundings. They must rely on performance to be sustained, which demands some kind of specific competence in a competitive environment. Albeit in a discreet fashion, NGOs are bound to compete for project funds. Thus, in local interactions, they distinguish themselves not only for their extended connections but also for a tendency to assume a professional approach to an otherwise nonprofit and often voluntary kind of activity. Thus, even unintentionally, they are led to introduce the pragmatic logics of institutional efficiency in the field of nongovernmental social actions.

The alleged efficiency of NGOs is a matter of dispute that should be judged through specific evaluations (and "evaluation" is indeed a growing concern in that field). But there is another point that is particularly relevant for our concerns here: NGOs, by their institutional features, have become a key element in the designs of planetarian citizenship. The double face (locally immersed and internationally connected), combined with the multitude of independent initiatives and instances, provides a timely and flexible tool for the weaving of the common threads of citizenship in a heterogeneous and segmented world. Bound by the limits inscribed in the language of projects, NGOs can move through all sorts of groups and issues, but they cannot afford to break loose from a minimum set of values and rules that are taken for granted in international cooperation. Through NGOs and their projects, in a loose, pluralistic, and dispersed fashion, local actions become globally linked.

Specific advantages bring with them specific problems. Our regional reports raise some crucial doubts concerning NGOs, which are related to the difficult balance between international and local involvements. Dependence on foreign funds may inhibit the search for local resources. Engagement in an international agenda may induce a "modernistic" bias that alienates NGOs from local traditions. In poorer countries, NGOs may become major institutions and move beyond their role as mediators within civil society. The African report, for example, mentions situations where NGOs seem to be more attractive to funds and to qualified personnel than the state itself is. In every instance, the challenge is clear: how to go further and deeper into local situations without losing international meaning, and vice versa—how to preserve the universalist intent without neglecting local resources and experiences.

Foundations

Independent, dispersed, and involved in multiple projects, like NGOs, foundations are funding institutions, putting private money to nonprofit uses. They are, in their origins, a typical expression of the civic culture in the United States. As the North American report points out, steel magnate Andrew Carnegie, oil baron John D. Rockefeller, and financier Andrew W. Mellon stand, among others, as emblematic founders of a kind of institution that proliferated in that country from the beginning of the twentieth century.

When he retired in 1901, Andrew Carnegie stated that the rich should give money to create "an ideal state in which the surplus wealth of the few will become, in the best sense, the property of the many." He endowed libraries in the United States and Canada, and donated more than $350 million to foundations. Carnegie said that libraries and agencies, such as the Carnegie Institute of Technology in Pittsburgh, were "ladders upon which the aspiring can rise."

In addition to private foundations, created by wealthy families, there arose "community foundations," designed for the benefit of a particular state, city, or even neighborhood. These usually raise funds from individuals and business for projects of a public interest in their area. Corporate foundations, on the other hand, were created as a result of tax incentives passed by a law of 1935.

Today, there are about 32,000 grant-making foundations in the United States, holding about $138 billion in assets and making about $8.3 billion a year in grants. In Europe, public investments were mainly conceived as a matter of political decision to be implemented by government, whereas in the United States the private sector was largely complementary to the state in that role. Business leaders, community organizations, and individuals became directly involved in the provision of funds, the creation of mechanisms, and the definition of the goals to be pursued. Individual giving to specific causes became a mass phenomenon. As a matter of fact, contributions by individuals amount to over $100 billion per year, accounting for about 90 percent of the nongovernmental funds donated to nonprofit groups in the country.

Besides giving money, individuals give time for such public purposes. In the United States, 51 percent of adults are volunteers, with 14 percent giving at least five hours a week; the value of this is estimated as at least $176 billion. This impressive activity has many causes, of course, but the underlying assumption stands out: individuals and business are encouraged to make direct social investments rather than going through the state.

A good many foundations work overseas. In fact, some of them are known today almost everywhere. The common threads of citizenship woven through the "projects" are often processed through their offices. More important to the purposes here, however, is another trend: the concept itself is expanding. All regional reports mention the emergence of indigenous private foundations, set up by local business or as a result of community efforts.

In Canada, foundations started to multiply in the 1960s. Elsewhere, the tendency became noticed in the 1980s and 1990s. In Latin America, the trend acquires a growing visibility in countries like Brazil and Mexico. In Eastern Europe, the issue is raised along with the rebirth of a private sector. Despite the sector's fragility in those countries, there are signs that social funding may take roots in the business culture of some post-socialist societies. In Hungary, in 1991, corporate donations constituted 10.6 percent of nonprofit associations' global income. And in Poland, a recent study revealed that as of 1991, private companies were one of the four major funding sources for nonprofit social service organizations along with government, state-owned ventures, and individual donors. In Japan, Thailand, and several other Asian countries, powerful foundations have been organized; and the African report speaks of similar initiatives in some countries, such as Tanzania and South Africa.

Furthermore, the creation of indigenous foundations is fast becoming a priority item for international funders, both private and multilateral. Funding for the formation of local private funders becomes an international concern. Internationalization is obviously an important component of this process. With exchanges of all kinds assuming a multinational dimension, social policies must in some measure transcend state borders. Instantaneous global communication transforms local dramas into international issues. Private initiatives, formalized through foundations or NGOs, can follow these processes at a relatively fast tempo, bypassing governments or eventually cooperating with them.

The search for resources in a context of social scarcity is another powerful stimulus to this trend. However rationalized, governments alone cannot cope with the tremendous load of social demands. Resources accumulated in private accounts around the globe must be tapped, somehow, and used in cooperation with rather in dispute with or sabotage of public investments.

Finally, and more important, the expansion of foundations may be a sign and a tool for the weaving of citizenship values within business circles. Taxes, the main instrument for the socialization of private benefits, are forcefully imposed by the state. Nonprofit funding, on the other hand, expresses the voluntary decision to invest in the social and cultural environment. Whatever the pragmatic calculus involved, the point is thereby clearly taken that public needs are an integral part of doing business.

The financial value of such donations are only a small fraction of what is due to the state through taxes, but the symbolic meaning is probably higher. It implies judgment and decision on collective needs; it demands personal and institutional involvement; it creates bonds of solidarity between business and communities in need; it enhances the public image of private donors; it shows up in marketing. Through social investments, business circles recover a sense of belonging to society at large, breaking the isolation that is induced by profit alone.

Traditional Forms

Associations, NGOs, and foundations are modern structures organizing the independent initiatives of individuals, groups, and institutions. Our regional reports, however—especially those from the East and the South—provide extensive information on other kinds of nongovernmental, nonprofit actions. They derive from traditional forms of social solidarity based on kinship and community ties. Every society knows them. Folklore, cultural studies, social history, anthropology have described them at length. And yet, they are not usually considered in development programs, for the common notion among developers is that traditional forms of mutual aid belong to the past.

CIVICUS' regional reports deliver, however, a different picture: traditions rarely die out; they are transformed and remain active under the new conditions, influencing and modifying the ways of development. Age groups and clan and tribal loyalties are key components, for instance, of social interaction in the cities of Africa. Migrants do not move at random but follow friends and kin, expanding local bonds to a vast network. Mutual gifts, borrowing and lending, personal exchanges, social clubs, festive celebrations, religious encounters, and so on feed those relationships with enough energy to keep them moving from the country to the city and further to the world at large. Hunting for jobs and opportunities in the market, for papers to accommodate bureaucracies, for help in times of need, for a sense of identity and continuity through turbulent life—migrants make sure to keep those networks alive.

Traditional religions, deeply embedded in communities, show a similar dynamism. The Latin American report quotes astonishing figures on the growth of mediumistic religions: about 1,200 new centers (including ones on Kardecism, Umbanda, and Candomblé) have been formally organized in metropolitan Rio de Janeiro in the last decade. That amounts to an average of 10 new centers per month, or one every three days, without counting the widespread informal mediumship activities. Here we have a tradition that is certainly not dying out.

This phenomenon is relevant here because in addition to the religious celebration, every such center provides a series of social services that constitute an integral part of people's resources to cope with life's afflictions. The same is true for Catholic parishes and for the fast-growing Evangelical and Pentecostal churches.

Most impressive in this respect is the report on the Arab region. Islamic shrines and Sufi orders are centers of multiple social services. "Wakfs" is a traditional concept of religious endowments to benefit the poor and the needy. Schools, hospitals, institutions for homeless children, the aged, and the disabled are typical beneficiaries. Tithes, or the notion of "zakat," is a major source of funding for nonprofit social projects in the region, which are usually collected and managed by zakat committees in the mosques. The positive interaction of this old concept with modern institutions is exemplified by the growing role of banks in the administration of zakat funds. In Egypt, about 3,000 mosques have annexed health centers to their premises, spreading the resources of modern medicine through the grassroots of community life.

The transformation of traditional charities into modern institutions is remarkably exemplified in the United States, where more than half the nation's 6,700 hospitals are organized as nonprofits, a trait that is also relevant for the educational history of that country.

Transformations of traditional forms, rather than their disappearance, introduce considerable complexity into our subject. They bring cultural and historical diversity to bear in the universalist claims of citizenship, giving prominence to the disturbing assertion of a "right to be different." The growing relevance of this principle, not only in the less developed regions but in the metropolitan areas as well, derives precisely from the vitality of traditional forms of social solidarity.

Bonds of an interpersonal nature, adjusted to urban conditions, give a specific quality to the ways of integration, or marginalization, in the modern environment. Traditional hierarchies are combined with egalitarian norms; complex group loyalties modify the processes of individualization, qualifying the individual's profile; conservative and progressive values mingle in various ways; formal rules are systematically conditioned by informal exchanges; the forest of symbols, to use Baudelaire's phrase, grows over the asphalt pavement of modern cities.

Ethnic discrimination and cultural fundamentalism are threatening responses to this situation, which are matched, as a counterpoint, by the modern bias orienting most development programs. Culture-blind projects, which abound not only in official but also in nongovernmental and even in human rights circles, end up stimulating conservative reactions. The foolish polarization between fundamentalism, on the one hand, and modernism, on the other, poses a major challenge to the growth of a democratic culture today. It takes a civilizational contour in the Islamic areas; it involves religions, communities, and nations in whole areas of Asia and Europe, as well as tribal and national identities in Africa; it combines with the marginalization of the poor majorities in several Latin American countries.

Reflecting on those issues, our regional reports welcome the challenges and opportunities posed by the diversity of cultures and histories at work inside the social environment and, moreover, inside a person's life. To avoid useless polarizations, the best hope we have lies in experiences that show a positive interaction between traditional and modern kinds of social solidarity. Instead of a search for systematic coherence, which goes along with exclusion, the taste for diversity is explored in a series of exemplary cases throughout the regional reports. Here, again, the dynamic aspect stands out, mixing hope with uncertainty. Creative interactions are clearly occurring both in very traditional and very modern environments, showing the positive connections that may be found in the contradictory signs of the time.

Civil Society

Is there a common name to capture so many different expressions of citizen participation? The East European report speaks of a "terminological jungle" and makes the significant point that none of the terms in use has been coined locally. This is also true, by the way, for the regions in the southern hemisphere. Indigenous expressions do exist, but they usually refer to traditional and diverse forms of social cooperation.

The modern universalist claims take us back to the North Atlantic cultural history and further, to Ancient Greek and Roman civilizations. Planetarian citizenship is bound to European and North American conceptual frameworks. The words have traveled, however, and our regional reports do provide genuine substance for a few general observations. In short, two expressions prevail—civil society and the third sector—one better known in Europe, the other in North America. Together, they are transformed and make room for a common field of discourse.

Civil society conjures up seventeenth and eighteenth century European philosophers, such as Hobbes and Rousseau, who established the contractualist vision of citizenship. The expression was coined in their writings to distinguish a society ruled by common law from a supposedly primitive condition where independent individuals were led by passions and needs. *Societas civilis* represented a break away from *societas naturalis*, instituting a political body where freedom and reason were to be, somehow, reconciled.

The notion has changed considerably, and yet, some continuities remain. When, by the late 1970s, the expression started to be retrieved from the history books by social activists in Eastern Europe, Latin America, or Asia, it was also perceived as a sign for a conceptual break. Within it, freely organized subjects claimed the right to participate in global political decisions. Expressions like "autonomy", "self-rule," or "independence" indicated the proper status of the elements (individuals, movements, institutions) composing civil society; the word "empowerment," widely used, expressed the claim for participation; and the outcome should be a democratic form of government, where differences could be argued and disputed according to universal and egalitarian rules. "Human rights," another key expression, summed up the lines of continuity with eighteenth century ideals.

The conceptual break, however, was deemed to take place not within "nature" but within "history." Most social activists inherited the notion through a revisionist branch of Marxist literature, bent by a Hegelian lineage. The writings from the 1930s of Antonio Gramsci, a heterodox Italian communist and a studious reader of B. Croce, who was then the most prolific interpreter of Hegel in Europe, made the connections. In that intellectual context, the transformations that were formally conceived as taking place between nature and society were assimilated into society's own internal processes. Thus "civil society" came to represent an intermediary level of socialization between the "natural" groupings around families and the fully rationalized rules of the state.

The "civil society" in Marxist-Hegelian circles meant the ensemble of individuals and private groups who are already actively involved in public life, but at a level outside and logically prior to the state. In that manner, it was both opposed to and complementary to the state. Further, containing all the contradictions distinguishing individual and class interests, "civil society" was conceived as the open field for power struggles that should be regulated in the laws and policies of the state. The key issues raised within "civil society" demanded political participation and could only be resolved at the global political level.

In line with Marxist and enlightenment traditions, reference to "civil society" in our regional reports usually implies a break with traditional forms and hierarchies. It is not simply a synonym of "society" but a way of thinking about it that carries both a sense of self-rule and equal rights. To be called so, civil society must be composed of independent individuals and institutions who are conscious of and zealous about their independence. Thus a paradoxical inversion occurs—what was a natural state for the early philosophers and a logical condition for modern politics in Hegel and Marx becomes a goal for our social activists: "civil society" should be "built," "reinforced," "consolidated," to overcome deeply ingrained habits of personal dependencies in public life.

The importance assumed by the notion of "consciousness raising" and the international role of educators such as Paulo Freire and Ivan Illich illustrate the point. Beyond pedagogy, however, and considering the fragility of such notions in most regions, emphasis was placed on group action. The standard reference has been to organized civil society, meaning associations that are particularly conscious of and fervent about their civic duties.

The assimilation of Hegelian Marxism was not passive, though, and inflicted a series of deep changes in the original conceptions of Hegel, Marx, and Gramsci. In the 1970s, the claim for civil society was raised in the context of authoritarian or even totalitarian regimes, and thereby acquired an extra emphasis on the autonomy of this realm. To put it in dialectical terms, the moment of opposition was overcherished. Some Marxists denounced so much attention to the "bases" and the "grassroots," but the main thrust was undoubtfully geared toward the values and actions that could be nurtured within civil society itself.

To open "small circles of freedom" within an authoritarian environment, many activists assumed the bold posture of "giving their backs to the state." That was a key move to bring, at least to some partners, the Central European categories of discourse closer to the North American spirit. Instead of counting on the state as the proper locus for the final resolution of conflicts, more and more attention was given to what could be done within and by society itself.

A deeper transformation occurred in the presumed relationship of that notion to the market. In Hegel, the rules of a market economy were central for the structuring of civil society. Private individuals and institutions behaved, in his model, according to the limited pragmatic reasons of self-interest, which was why a further step of socialization had to be accomplished in and by the state. Marx followed suit, identifying simply "civil society" with "bourgeois (bürgerlich) society," which, in his historical vision, had to be overcome and abolished, together with its complementary opposite, the state.

This crucial conceptual point was actually left behind after the concept's most recent dissemination. Asserted as the foundation for democratic transitions, "civil society" is called upon to stay, rather than to be dismissed. And further, articulating the multiple forms of social activism, it is understood in contrast not only to the state, but also to the market. Civil society, in the language captured by our regional reports, refers to a third dimension of public life, different from government, on the one hand, and from the market, on the other. Thus distinguished, the concept acquires a very different connotation. Instead of suggesting an arena for power struggles and selfish competitions, it is deemed to signify exactly the opposite: a field where values of social solidarity are learned and exercised.

In civil society, we hear now, the bonds of mutual cooperation are demonstrated through an astonishing variety of voluntary initiatives. Accordingly, the funds that make them possible flow in good measure through channels that have been named "international cooperation." At that stage, conceived in those terms, the notion of civil society comes closer to North American ideas concerning a consensus that is founded in society's basic grassroots experiences, rather than in government orchestration. And the triad scheme matches well the American concept of a nongovernmental, nonprofit, voluntary "third sector," the second comprehensive expression for what we are describing.

Third Sector

Ideas on this subject in North America date back to seventeenth century philosophers as well, in an even clearer line of continuity. John Locke's image of a first contract struck among settlers in the open spaces of a new territory provides a lasting model.

High school students in the United States learn to think of their own society as the result of a voluntary assent of its members. The famous "Book of Rules" is universally assimilated at an early age as a guide for fair and rational collective decisions, be it in private or in public. Government in that perspective is but a necessary instrument for individuals' association, which, of course, is far less than Hegel thought necessary to render the dignity and unity of the nation-state. Likewise, the typically American congregational conception of the church reduces the value of hierarchy to a functional device at the service of the real ecclesia, which is to be found amidst the brothers and sisters gathered at the local temple.

Thus the U.S. approach to our subject focuses on the individual's plight: to serve oneself and/or to serve others, to serve oneself while serving others, to serve others while serving oneself, and so forth. The idea of a "nonprofit sector" becomes then easily understood as a reference to all those circumstances in which individuals find themselves serving others rather than themselves; it contrasts with the market situation, where the same individuals work and produce socially relevant goods, but serving their own benefit in the first place. Egoism and altruism are complementary sides, both relevant and legitimate, for individuals interacting among themselves.

In the same vein, it sounds natural to say that while working for others, individuals perform a "public" service, for the public, in this context, is nothing but individuals associated together. That extra unifying quality that restricted the "public realm" to state functions in European parlance does not apply here. On the contrary, the same individualistic spirit, the "do it yourself" maxim that enhances competition in the market, stimulates private initiatives resulting in public benefits.

The idea of a third sector, therefore, comes out of this civic culture, proposing a simple scheme to distinguish between private and public dimensions of behavior. To put it in brief, the following four alternatives result:

AGENTS		ENDS		SECTOR
private	for	private	=	market
public	for	public	=	government
private	for	public	=	third sector
public	for	private	=	corruption

This is the concept's positive sense: private organizations and initiatives aimed at the production of public goods and services. The neighborhood association that calls on its members to plant trees along local streets is performing a public function well suited to its dimensions and its institutional mandate. Planting trees, in that example, is not a "substitute function" vis-à-vis the state; on the contrary, it is the sort of activity that justifies the existence of a neighborhood association.

Such goods and services are called public for a double reason: they respond to collective needs, and they are not supposed to generate profit. Collective needs may be universal, such as clean air, or specific to an area, as a neighborhood, or to a group, such as refugees. The ban on profit, on the other hand, means that eventual benefits must be reinvested to accomplish the organization's purposes. Equipment and income are to be kept apart from the staff's private patrimony.

The concept is surely broad and may be qualified in a number of ways. Variations occur and borderline cases elicit polemical disputes, as happens with any classification. The strong and common element, however, implies important transformations in the inherited ideas in most regions. The public sphere is expanded to include initiatives directly resulting from citizens' participation. This is the crucial point, which, as we have seen, has a good chance of entering the agenda that is being required of a "civil society."

The negative qualification (nongovernmental and nonprofit) of the elements composing the third sector deserve some further comments. The organizations and initiatives at stake are not a part of government now and are not supposed to become one in the future. They are different from political parties in this way, for the latter are meant to mediate the transition from society to the state and back. In the third sector, instead, organizations are presumed to provide collective services that do not involve the exercise of government power. This means, among other things, that these organizations cannot legitimately use violence in order to secure acceptance of their goals. Their policies are not compulsory. Their influence must rely on persuasion. In fact, they are often very persuasive, and consequently very influential, precisely because they do not speak from a position of coercive power.

Pictures of environmentalists chained to a tree under the threat of a chain saw, of mothers exposed to police brutality on Plaza de Mayo, of a solitary student standing before a line of tanks in Beijing, of a frail-looking Mother Teresa in Calcutta, of HIV-positive Betinho calling on citizens and governments in Brazil to fight hunger, of a crowd of young people dancing in a demonstration against racism in a poor Johannesburg neighborhood, of a millionaire providing for a huge donation in his will—these are all images that symbolize strength within the third sector.

On the other hand, private initiative finds within it other motivations than profit. The second negation, "nonprofit," refers to organizations and actions whose investments exceed their ultimate financial returns. What they do is simply too expensive for the available markets. Museums, artistic creation, religious worship, research, health care, education, community organizing, defense of minorities, support for the needy, mobilization of public opinion—all these require human and material resources that often exceed the interested parties' purchasing power. And yet collective wisdom suggests that they should still be provided.

If the state cannot or will not support all these activities, the remaining option is private donations. This point reintroduces a distinction already mentioned: whereas the services offered by the state are financed by compulsory taxation, those offered by the third sector depend on voluntary donations. The sector survives because at some point the search for profit gives way to free giving.

The sector's existence involves a triangular exchange in which some give that others may receive. To include someone else's expenses in your own budget is the economic expression of the moral thesis that stands behind the third sector: to care about others—neighbors, underprivileged people, distant foreigners, future generations, and so on—is an integral part of individual conscience. Such words as gratitude, loyalty, charity, love, compassion, responsibility, solidarity, truth, and beauty are the currency that make up the assets of the third sector. The more convincing they sound, the more resources will flow into its activities. The existence and performance of this sector offers an index of the social vitality of moral, aesthetic, and religious values.

Being nongovernmental and nonprofit does not imply, of course, being in another world, beyond the influences of the state and the market or immune to social conditioning. The third sector is not a realm of angels. Persuasion generates moral and ideological coercions whose power over individuals should not be underestimated. When it is effective, voluntary dedication generates resources and thus disputes over their distribution.

Third-sector institutions incorporate the need for self-reproduction and take the quirks of corporate bodies. They generate a specific labor market. They influence legislation in its most varied domains and condition government, company, and individual budgets. In short, they absorb the problems of interests and power. Nevertheless, they make up a distinct institutional sphere, with characteristics derived precisely from the negation of the profit motive and of state power. Subject to this dual constraint in their very statutory definition, third-sector organizations are characterized by their reliance on belief in values that transcend utility. To exercise and promote voluntary adherence to values as ends in themselves is their specific raison d'être. It is on the basis of these assumptions that the play of interests and power gain specific features within the third sector.

The Third, The Second, and the First

This triangular conception seems to gain a particular attraction as the memory of the Cold War recedes. If the market is here to stay and the state is apparently not going to wither away either, the global polarization of an earlier time turns into a contextual sort of questioning: What kind of market? What kind of state? What limits to profit? What limits to violence? How inclusive can this market be? How wide the scope of citizenship? How much investment for the future? How much room for participation? How much investment in human factors? How much recognition of human diversity? How much acceptable inequality? How accessible and effective the legal system? How wide the gap between regions? How centralized the state? How sensitive to the environment? How sensitive to the quality of life? How universal? How exclusive?

Away from the context of global judgment, market and state are exposed to so many specific questions that we can hardly formulate them without resorting to a third term of reference. The questions asked and the intensity of the questioning must clearly vary according to the values that are most deeply felt in each context. And the affirmation of values, as we have seen, is the distinctive characteristic of the third sector. In other words, the assimilation of this concept seems to help make us see that markets and states are not independent spheres, regulated by a rigid internal logic. Variations in the behavior of the third sector are likely to interfere in the ways of politics and the dynamics of the economy. The questions "What kind of market?" and "What kind of state?" are intrinsically related to the question "What kind of third sector?"

The answers to this question are, of course, a matter for future deeds whose contents cannot be deduced from the poor simplicity of conceptual schemes. The very idea of a third sector is far from clear in most contexts. To make it clear is both an intellectual and a practical task, for it will make no sense unless a significant number of those concerned come to think of it as a meaningful idea.

CIVICUS' regional reports make the case that the possibility is there and the time is right, but that is no more than a bet on the odds of the future. The approximation between European and North American concepts, exemplified here by the notions of civil society and third sector, is a positive sign in that direction, but will they take solid roots in other regions? Will they move beyond exclusive circles, skip blind confrontation with traditional forms of solidarity, and produce creative interactions that can expand and thus transform the ways of citizenship?

Much depends on the "first" and "second" sectors. Once three are involved, there is a tendency for two to ally against one. Will civil society be able to join with the state and put pressure on the market to assimilate at least the necessary minimum of social and environmental costs to make development sustainable? Will the third sector and the market develop enough ties to force state reforms that can render government both democratic and efficient? Will international cooperation be able to bridge the widening gaps provoked by technological progress? Will it be translated into regional, national, and local cooperation, thus multiplying the resources available to counter the current self-destructive tendencies? And how will such questions sound in different parts of this planet?

Even if we knew all the answers, we might not know how to implement them. CIVICUS' bet on planetary citizenship is not an objective statement derived from exact knowledge. It is a well-informed and careful attempt to join with those who can see that concept in the realm of possibilities, and who are doing their best to bring it closer to reality.

Reference

Salamon, Lester M. "The Global Associational Revolution: The Rise of the Third Sector on the World Scene." Baltimore: The Johns Hopkins University, Institute for Policy Studies, Occasional Paper No. 15, 1993.

9

HUMANITY IN TROUBLE BUT HOPEFUL

Isagani R. Serrano

Imagine there's no countries, nothing to kill or die for, imagine all the people sharing all the world, living life in peace. These stirring lyrics from "Imagine" by John Lennon caught the ears, hearts, and minds of millions around the world when the song first hit the airwaves in the early 1970s. John was a dreamer and certain he's not the only one; he hoped that someday we would join him, and the world will be as one.

In many ways John Lennon symbolizes the new citizen of the world. Much of his mature life was dedicated to civic activism sans frontieres. He wrote songs, addressed world leaders about world peace, and occasionally took to the streets as an activist. Through the medium in which he excelled—popular music—he communicated to millions of people across the globe ringing messages of love, caring, and humanity. These messages evoked a universal feeling of connectedness, of belonging to one world without racial, class, gender, religious, or other prejudice. His was a global dream every citizen should find worth building.

In 1980, John Lennon died a violent death—a sad testimony to the perils that confront citizens throughout the world. We all are dreamers, and we build our dreams mindful of all the risks along with the drama and excitement this endeavor would bring.

Looking to One World Without Illusion

On May 10, 1994, Nelson Mandela became the first black president of South Africa. Standing on the podium in the town hall of Johannesburg, he declared the fulfillment of a dream—the end of apartheid. It is a dream that he and many women and men inside South Africa and across the globe have labored for years to bring about. Mandela's message resonated throughout the world, thanks to global communications, and brought new hope to millions of freedom-loving citizens.

Elsewhere, in Somalia, in Rwanda, in Bosnia, in Haiti, thousands upon thousands of people were being killed and maimed in 1994, starved to death, thrown into prisons, or driven off their homelands as a result of intense civil and ethnic conflicts and violence. Like the events in South Africa before them, these attest to the unbelievable capacity of some groups of people to inflict harm on others.

These mixed images, brought to every corner of the world by global electronic media, give us a good picture of the present human drama. From one place, it would seem that the world is finally coming to peace with itself. From another view, however, it appears that humanity is being torn further apart. It is the classic dilemma of whether to view things from a half-full or a half-empty perspective.

Richard Barnet and John Cavanagh, in *Global Dreams*, pictured a world that is getting smaller and smaller but is not coming together. It feels nice to share the sweet and casual optimism of Disneyland's "It's a Small World After All." And yet we know that the so-called smallness of the present world is a product of love for humanity as well as the lack of it.

Globalization is now a buzz theme in today's world. Global forum, global village, global citizen, global workshop, global trade, global finance, global cultural bazaar, global shopping mall, global this, global that. Ideas, goods, and services are generated anywhere and get traded everywhere, linking together individuals, families, and nations like nothing we have seen before.

Likewise, the whirl of world-spanning changes is dizzying. How easily a person gets detached from his or her living space and natural affinities and becomes connected somewhere else before even having the time to think, much less decide about it. To get connected to the stream of events means to run faster each time. And yet we are never able to catch up. It seems happiness is ever elsewhere.

What does this new globalization trend hold in store for humanity? More caring and sharing, or more poverty and hunger? Less war and more peace? More cheating in between wars? More global harmony or, as some would say, just plain globaloney?

After 500 years of an ever-accelerating race to human progress, we are still faced with a distressing reality that four of five citizens of this planet have to struggle daily to regain control over their own lives. With the prospect of a widening rich-poor divide and collapsing natural systems, we can only wonder when and how every individual on earth will attain real human security and a better quality of life.

What happened to world development? Why has the promised human emancipation not arrived for the many? Will life in the twenty-first century be any better than what we have today? What will it take to build it? What are the trade-offs? What choices are available to every citizen, given the extreme uncertainties, myriad possibilities, and formidable challenges? Can each of us regain control over our lives, resist the pull of civic apathy, cynicism, and inertia, and contribute our level best to creating a more humane, livable, and enduring human future?

The very foundation of world development stands in question. It behooves the principal architects of this grand drama—the ideologues and politicians, the scientists and technicians, the corporate leaders, and all the institutions built in their image and visions—to explain why things happened the way they did. For their part, the billions of alienated ordinary citizens need also ask themselves why they let this happen and continue the way it is.

Humanity is in distress but not hopeless. The challenges are formidable but not insurmountable. Despite severe constraints, opportunities do exist to make fundamental shifts before it becomes too late. But we need to acquire a renewed confidence to make the right choices and move in the right direction.

Humanity confronts a very different turn of the century than previous generations did. Before, human history featured mainly the collapse of one empire and the emergence of another along the road to progress; today it still talks of such grand narratives but under dramatically-altered conditions. The nature of the human predicament is not just humanity needing to squeeze free from its own prejudices and follies, not simply humanity against itself, but also humanity having to find harmony with its living space.

What does it matter if a citizen of this world gains dominance over another citizen, or if a powerful country becomes dominant over the rest of humanity? Or we can take it from the positive side. Suppose the goal of human emancipation were attained in the 1990s and then a more egalitarian social order existed at the onset of the new millennium. At the end of the day, humanity will still have to square with the grim reality that the natural systems on which it depends for sustaining life on earth are coming apart massively and, perhaps, irreversibly.

Environment is where we live. Development is what we do to make our life better there. Until two decades ago, there had been almost no awareness of the connection between the two. Today, the realities of the world itself compel us to see that kind of connection. We may be able to better the present human order, but we must make sure we will continue to have a livable space to do it in. There is no escaping this interlocking challenge for every citizen of this planet.

The Growth Revolution

It has been said that God created the world but the Dutch made Holland, an obvious tribute to a people who were able to dike the sea and make a human living space out of it. The same tribute can be paid to the whole human civilization for radically transforming through its own inventions what was there only in natural, pristine form. Precious little has remained untouched and beyond the reach of human activity. It seems virtually nothing will remain forever unknowable and impossible to human beings driven by the obsession to grow and acquire more.

In the course of interaction with nature, human beings have created wealth and waste beyond measure. The size of the present stock is amazing enough. By 1990 the measured value of the world economy stood at $19 trillion, which, if spread equally to all citizens of this planet, should be able to feed, house, clothe, educate, lengthen the life, and enlarge the freedom of every man, woman, and child now living. There would probably also be more than enough left to clean up the mess.

Even more incredible is the doubling time that characterizes this wealth creation. It took all of human existence for the world economy to reach $600 billion in 1900, but this huge pie now grows by more than this amount every two years. On average, the additional economic output in each of the last four decades has equalled the total from the beginning of civilization until 1950. Within this century, the global economy has increased 20 times, and nearly five times since 1950, going from $4 trillion to $19 trillion.

The invention of the car typifies the growth revolution. Like the steam engine in the eighteenth century, the coming of the car had great industrial and social impact in the twentieth century. The same can be said about the ship and the airplane, but the car is probably the most illustrative.

The United States had 8,000 cars in 1900, a number that increased to 79,000 by 1908. Around the same time, Japan had only 62 cars. By 1921, 10 million Americans owned cars, a level not reached in Europe until the 1950s. Doubling roughly every 20 years, U.S. carownership rose to 26 million in 1930; the whole of Europe had just over 5 million cars during the same period. By mid-1970s there were 120 million car owners in the United States. In Europe, carownership boomed between 1950 and 1970, going from 2.5 million before World War II in the United Kingdom to 23 million by the 1980s. The world had 50 million cars and light vehicles in 1950 and more than 400 million by the 1980s, at which point some 33 million vehicles were being made every year.

Car production now consumes more resources than any other industry. It accounts for 20 percent of the world's steel production, 10 percent of its aluminum, 35 percent of its zinc, 50 percent of its lead, 60 percent of all natural rubber, and more than a third of the world's oil consumption. Connected with this are various subsidiary industries, such as roads and other infrastructures, gas (petrol) stations, service garages, and a string of productive and commercial activities of every description.

The car is the umbilical cord that connects the United States to the chief source of oil, the Middle East, about half of whose oil production output goes back to that country. In 1980, U.S. passenger cars and light trucks consumed about 6 million barrels of petroleum products every day.

The car has bridged great distances and brought about a level of human mobility never seen before. It has made mass tourism possible. According to the World Tourism Organization of the United Nations, 429 million people—almost 8 percent of world population—traveled from one country to another as tourists in 1990. That same year, consumers from industrial countries, where traveling for leisure ranks third in household expense after food and housing, spent $232 billion on tourism.

Mass tourism may now be the world's largest employer. Its network of hotels, restaurants, and transportation facilities is valued at about $3 trillion, almost one sixth of the measured value of the global economy. One in every 15 workers throughout the world makes a living by transporting, feeding, lodging, guiding, or entertaining tourists.

Tourism is no longer the preserve of a tiny leisure class and those who travel because it is part of their work, such as soldiers, sailors, traveling businesspeople, artists, and academics. It has become accessible to the mass of citizens, although many people will still probably die where they were born.

Much like other industries, tourism creates employment for millions and at the same throws other millions out of work. Devouring acres and acres of coastlines, agricultural areas, and habitats to pave the way for beaches, roads, buildings, golf courses, and all sorts of come-ons, tourism has brought dramatic changes in people's lives everywhere. It provides the means for global cultural encounters but it also causes the spread of drugs and dreaded diseases like AIDS, and of social maladies such as child abuse and prostitution. It has also put tremendous strains on the environment in different parts of the globe. Until it is made friendly to both people and the environment, through the practice of ecotourism, for example, global tourism will only induce further disintegration to the world it has otherwise brought closer together.

Like the global economy, world population has also been growing exponentially. It took 2 million years, until 1825, for world population to reach 1 billion. The second billion was added in 100 years, the third billion in 35 years (1925-60), the fourth billion in 15 years (1960-75), and the fifth billion in just 12 years (1975-late 1980s). The present population of 5.7 billion is projected to reach between a low of 8.1 billion and a high of 11.6 billion by 2025.

Just how far world resources can support a fast-growing economy and population has been a subject of intense debate. While there is a fairly wide consensus that serious environmental problems of global proportion do exist, positions tend to polarize with respect to root causes and approaches to their solution.

Has human activity passed the earth's carrying capacity? This concept is used to tackle questions about impact of population on an environment; it means the largest number of any given species that a habitat can support indefinitely. If this optimum level is breached, the natural resource base starts to decline and so does the population eventually.

Growth in Poverty, Misery, and Impacts

Perhaps human beings should be judged less in terms of their ability to expand the economic pie than in their capacity to share it among themselves. They are certainly a great success at the first, but a big failure in the second.

Despite the "lost decade," coined in Latin America to refer to the development reversals of the 1980s, the world economy continued to grow. Indeed, there have been significant achievements in human development during the past three decades. And yet, all these achievements in growth and human development have brought with them the reality of continuing exclusion.

The quintupling of global economic output and the doubling of world population in the past five decades are key driving forces that stress the earth's carrying capacity. But a third equally important factor, and often a discounted one in the growth narrative, is the widening divide in the distribution of wealth and income. The great imbalances are expressed in various levels: between nations, within nations and societies, between men and women, between majority and minority populations, between people in the cities and those in rural areas, and between today's and future generations.

Even more than our fear of the tragic Malthusian scenario, the reality of inequality in all its manifestations should rank highest in our priority list of global concerns. A more equal future world order will improve human relations and will be better able to deal with the negative impacts of all human action on the environment.

A dramatic change in the life-styles of the rich nations has never been more pressing. Accounting for only a fifth of the world's population, these nations command four-fifths of the world's income and consume 70 percent of the world's energy, 75 percent of its metals, and 85 percent of its wood. This high level of consumption can only be maintained at the expense of the rest of humanity and the global ecological space.

More than a billion of the world's people continue to live in absolute poverty, and the richest 20 percent earn 150 times more than the poorest 20 percent. In 1960, the richest 20 percent got 70 percent of the global income; by 1989 the wealthy's share increased to about 83 percent. The poorest 20 percent during that same period saw their share of global income drop from an already puny 2.3 percent to just 1.4 percent. The ever-increasing gap in the income share between the richest fifth and the poorest fifth thus grew from a ratio of 30 to 1 in 1960 to 59 to 1 in 1989, and it is even worse in 1993.

Women still earn only half as much as men and have little power to level the gap, although they constitute more than half the votes in probably every country and certainly globally. Rural people in developing countries still receive less than half the income opportunities and social services available to their urban counterparts. And many ethnic minorities and indigenous peoples still live like a separate nation within their own countries and continue to be marginalized and disadvantaged on all counts.

The great inequity between the world's richest and poorest has a differentiated but complementary negative impact on the environment, expressed in high consumption at the upper bracket of the income ladder and abject poverty on the opposite end. Neither the richest nor the poorest live environmentally friendly lives—the rich because of their overconsumption of energy, raw materials, and manufactured goods, and the poor because they have to eke out a daily existence by gathering fuelwood from receding forests, collecting water from dwindling and contaminated sources, growing crops or grazing animals on lands that are fast being degraded, and catching fish in overfished and polluted waters.

A few examples should illustrate this reality of inequity. Take the use of a critical resource—water—over which future wars and civil conflicts are quite likely to erupt. Families in the western United States often use as much as

3,000 liters of water a day, enough to fill a bathtub 20 times. Excessive use of water there has contributed to the depletion of rivers and aquifers, destroyed wetlands and fisheries, and, by creating an illusion of abundance, led to an unsupportable consumption level.

In contrast, nearly one out of every three people in the developing world—some 1.2 billion people in all—lack access to a safe supply of drinking water. This contributes to the spread of debilitating diseases and deaths, and forces women and children to walk many hours a day to collect enough water to meet their family's most basic needs.

Great disparities in food consumption is another glaring example. As many as 700 million people do not eat enough to live and work normally. The average African, for instance, consumes only 87 percent of the calories needed for a healthy and productive life. Meanwhile, people in rich countries feast daily on diets so full of animal fats that they cause increased rates of heart disease and cancers. Moreover, people consume a great deal of junk food that their bodies can do without to sustain a healthy life.

Correspondingly, there exist also great disparities in waste creation, and, by extension, in shouldering the costs of waste disposal and clean-up. Annual per capita carbon dioxide emissions in the United States run up to more than 20,000 kilograms in contrast to less than 200 kilograms in most African countries. Disposal of these wastes, especially the most toxic and hazardous ones, has already become a global concern. Given the fact that there have not been any dramatic reductions on waste emissions or increases in absorptive capacities of the countries where the wastes originate, we can reasonably say that somebody else's backyard is unduly being made to pay the costs.

Jobless Growth

Throughout the world a new phenomenon has arisen—jobless growth, as the U.N. Development Programme (UNDP) puts it. Loss of jobs following the invention of labor-saving machines has always accompanied civilization's march to progress. The difference in the present trend is the proportion that this has taken—it is now a world phenomenon.

Among members of the Organisation for Economic Co-operation and Development (OECD), unemployment stayed above 6 percent throughout the 1980s, reaching a peak of 6.9 percent in 1991, amounting in absolute terms to 30 million jobless. Unemployment in the European members of OECD increased threefold, from 3 percent in the mid-1970s to about 10 percent in 1992.

The picture in the developing countries is much worse. In sub-Saharan Africa, not a single country was able to bring down unemployment from double-digit figures during the same period. In Latin America, urban unemployment has been above 8 percent. In Asia, countries like India and Pakistan, despite respectable economic growth rates (more than 6 percent a year), registered unemployment rates above 15 percent. Only the East Asian countries, the so-called growth miracles, had low unemployment rates—below 3 percent.

The rise in economic growth rates in various regions of the world during 1960-73 and 1973-87 shows just the opposite trend from employment. This is a common situation in both industrial and developing countries.

The pattern is similar for transnational corporations with subsidiaries in developing countries: they have made substantial investments without creating significant job increases. In 1990, there were at least 35,000 transnational corporations with more than 150,000 foreign affiliates. Of the 22 million people they employ outside their home country, some 7 million are directly employed in developing countries—less than 1 percent of their total economically active population.

UNDP's *Human Development Report 1993* points to four major causes of this jobless-growth phenomenon. First, the search for labor-saving technology was encouraged by the demographic situation of industrial countries, where stagnating population growth often led to growing labor shortages in the 1960s. Second, it was enhanced by rising labor costs resulting from sustained activities and demands of trade union movements. Third, technological innovation in the civilian sphere often resulted as a by-product of military research and development, which usually has a preference for capital intensity. Finally, the prevalent technologies reflect the existing pattern of income distribution—20 percent of the world's population has 83 percent of the world's income and, hence, five times the purchasing power of the poorer 80 percent of humankind.

The outlook for balancing labor supply and demand is bleak. About 1 billion new jobs are required for the next decade to absorb the number of people currently unemployed and underemployed. More than 400 million entered the labor force in developing countries during 1960-90 due to rapid population growth (2.3 percent a year), an increase in the proportion of people of working age, and an increase in women job-seekers. The labor force in developing countries will continue to increase by 2.3 percent annually in the 1990s, requiring an additional 260 million jobs. Women's participation in the labor force is likely to increase. And there will be a steady migration to urban areas of people seeking job opportunities that are not likely to expand easily.

Additionally, job security is deteriorating. Enterprises have been reducing their reliance on a permanent labor force, hiring instead a highly skilled core group of workers surrounded by a periphery of temporary or casual workers. Even in Japan, the time-honored lifetime employment security is now giving in to the pressures of corporate competition.

Perhaps the most important upcoming threat to job security is a radical change involving the replacement of human beings in the factory by robots and automated machines. For more than two centuries, industry has been undergoing all sorts of transformation such as those connected with mass production, assembly system, or "just-in-time" production without losing the common key element in which human beings are brought together in a place of work. This time we are seeing a technology-driven revolution that hopes to achieve great improvements in efficiency and productivity but that in the process will make the services of many people unnecessary.

It is about time we begin rethinking the notion of employment in particular and of work in general. If indeed this world teems with problems, there is no reason why anyone with something to offer as service to the common good should be out of work, struggling to survive.

Nation-States Under Pressure

The role of the nation-state, this relatively modern but now pervasive form of organization to which citizens turn for protection and advancement of their interests, is under severe challenge from many who see in this institution some kind of functional and accountability failure. From one end we find global market forces demanding less government. From another end, there are people themselves, especially the alienated and impoverished masses, who are demanding that government deliver all the "goods" and discard all the "bads" attendant to governance.

The state system as we know it today is composed of all member countries of the United Nations—184 in all, as of mid-1994. Each of the modern nations that compose it has all the attributes of a sovereign entity recognized in international law and diplomacy. Each state controls definite territories whose boundaries are supervised by public servants such as customs officers, border police, and immigration authorities backstopped by armed forces with elaborate land, naval, and air services.

National allegiance is exacted from every citizen, either by force or through laws, symbols, practices, and rituals. A national flag, anthem, language, education, religion, historical figures and events, special holidays, and so on are used to generate consciousness of national identity, which causes citizens to rally, to die even, against external or internal belligerent forces, whether real or imagined.

As an institution, the nation-state is at the center of the life of the national community. It is a centralizing mechanism whose business is to govern and demand citizen allegiance by legal or forcible means, to command resources by taxing citizens, and to provide people with educational, health, and other types of social and economic services. The nation-state is the single biggest institution in any society that embodies national security.

Today, this so-called national security is disintegrating or transforming fast. For one, it means little except as a negative factor to global corporations spearheading borderless and unrestricted economic pursuits. For another, many citizens who should feel secure with it no longer do for various reasons, and hence are repulsed by the idea, or at best remain ambivalent about its usefulness in their everyday lives. People are demanding a new kind of governance.

The emerging global economic order is undermining the nation-state. It is led by a few hundred corporate giants from among some 35,000 transnational corporations, many of them bigger than sovereign nations. For example, Ford's economy is said to be larger than Saudi Arabia's and Norway's, and Phillip Morris' annual sales exceed New Zealand's gross domestic product. Unlike inflexible nation-states, these global business corporations have technological capacity and a long view unshackled by traditional concepts of national boundaries. With the most advanced technologies at their disposal, they have developed products that can be made and traded anywhere, built a global system for moving money at high speed, and control information that can breach physical boundaries and link individuals, villages, or neighborhoods anywhere in the world.

The power balance in world politics is shifting away from nation-states toward global corporations that cannot be bound easily by national regulations. As governments continue to be stuck to the narrow confines of their territories—and even there, they often fail to deliver on their promises—global corporations move at will around the world, occupying as much public space as they can and exerting influence that strikes deep into the lives of millions. Not a single nation-state, not even the United States or Japan, can remain impervious to the deep-penetrating and encompassing hegemony of these giant corporations. Indeed, even the most autocratic governments have either collapsed or are fast losing control over the lives of citizens under their sway due in large measure to the influence of these global corporations.

Today's global problems are exposing the inadequacies of nation-states.

World poverty, affecting more than a billion in developing countries and about 300 million in industrial ones, and global economic recession are beyond the capacity of any single state or even a combination of states to solve. The same goes for addressing what the *Human Development Report 1993* calls the "silent emergencies" of poverty (water pollution, land degradation, environmental diseases) as well as the "loud emergencies" (global warming, ozone depletion). At the very least, these problems need a multilateral approach involving the whole or a major part of the U.N. system.

The failure of command or state-directed economies in the former socialist Eastern Europe and Soviet Union and in other non-communist dictatorships elsewhere in the world is a big negative lesson for rethinking and reshaping the role of nation-states. Total control by government in these countries produced not only economic and environmental disasters but also widespread civic apathy and inertia, leading to eventual social disintegration.

On the other hand, leaving the field at the complete mercy of market forces is likewise no guarantee for solving development and environmental problems. Market competition can stimulate private enterpreneurship. But the playing field is not level to begin with. As in a state monopoly, power in the so-called free market tends to gravitate and get concentrated around a few big private corporations in the long run, creating the need, at least, for some anti-trust regulation to maintain an environment of fair competition.

Structural adjustment programs prescribed by the World Bank on heavily indebted developing countries during the 1970s and the 1980s emphasized deregulation and resulted in the further weakening of client states through cutbacks in public spending and reduction of government participation in economic activities. They also eliminated the social safety nets that cushioned people, especially the masses of poor people, from the negative impact of market competition, in the process eroding further the legitimacy of the government.

The conclusion of the Uruguay Round of negotiations for a new treaty on the General Agreement on Tariffs and Trade (GATT) signifies further liberalization and reduction in state control over how goods and services are going to be exchanged. On paper, the new treaty gives every nation-state a fair chance to compete with others. But reality speaks differently. In the first place, some nations are far stronger than many others. And until now, few developing countries have overcome the trade losses accumulated through years of engaging in an unfair global exchange. Coming from a weak base, these countries will most likely be clobbered by the big powers, fair rules notwithstanding.

Nation-states are facing severe challenges from above and from below, forcing a rethinking of their role in social transformation. Globalization from above, occasioned by boundless movement of capital and advances in information technology, has been undermining bounded state power. And yet, even where they are in a position to wield power, that is, within their own borders, nation-states are too trapped by their traditional role to be able to respond with flexibility. A new form of governance has to be fashioned together with the forces of civil society.

With three quarters of humanity now living under some kind of democratic set-up or in a process of transition to it, there is ample scope for state leadership in resolving outstanding governance issues. Some countries still suffer from colonialism and subjugation. In more than 100 countries, various forms of human rights violations persist, according to the 1993 report of the Amnesty International. A way should be found to put an end to all these forms of human oppression.

The concept of security has been undergoing a major shift. First, from an exclusive emphasis on territorial security to a much greater stress on people's security. Second, from arms security to security through sustainable human development. The shift entails addressing squarely all threats to economic, political, personal, community, and environmental security. Freedom from want and fear of any kind is the foundation of human security.

Humanity's problems can no longer be adequately addressed by national governments. A new form of global governance will be required to meet the present and future challenges. The convening of two world summits within a decade—the Earth Summit in Rio in 1992 and the Social Summit in Copenhagen in 1995—should be indication enough of an urgent need for new global institutions of governance guided by a new paradigm of human security and development.

The 1995 World Summit for Social Development offers an opportunity for governments to make a decisive step toward the resolution of humanity's problems. Toward this end, a six-point agenda has been offered by UNDP.

The first agenda item is a new world social charter that will establish the framework of equality of opportunity among nations and people. The second is a 20:20 compact for human development, under which 20 percent of developing-country budgets and 20 percent of industrial-country aid was allocated to achieving basic human development levels for all their people. The third is capturing the peace dividend resulting from an agreement on a targeted reduction of 3 percent in military spending in order to increase social spending. The fourth is a global human security fund pooled from the peace dividend, taxes on pollution and international currency speculation, and official development assistance—all to be used to address global issues.

The two other items concern major institutional changes. One is a strengthened United Nations umbrella for human development, which entails a rationalization of major U.N. institutions involved in development, such as UNDP, UNICEF, the U.N. Population Fund (known as UNFPA), the International Fund for Agricultural Development, and the World Food Programme. The final item is the setting up of an Economic Security Council, which would be given a mandate equivalent to that of the UN Security Council.

This six-point agenda is probably the minimum needed to transform the state system in ways that would make it more responsive to twenty-first century challenges. Short of this, states have few options left to meet pressures from every imaginable direction, especially those coming from the citizens.

The Swing to Markets

The collapse of the socialist system in the former Soviet Union and Eastern Europe has been viewed by many as a resounding vindication of the market. The easy judgment has been extended to cover all command systems or state-directed development. What has been lost in this euphoria is that state-led development had at least shown a mixed performance, combining failure, as in the case of former socialist Europe, and relative success, as in the case of the East Asian growth miracles. Besides, there is much more to the collapse of many socialist regimes than just failure of state. But more important, in real life—and notwithstanding the age of globalization featuring the dominance of global corporations—development has always been simultaneously influenced to a greater or lesser degree by both state and market.

Neither state nor market all by itself will do. Until the nation-state framework is tossed out of the window, which is unlikely to happen even in the distant future, the challenge will be to find the most appropriate balance between the two. State and market can feed on each other's strengths and can provide the mutual checks against excesses on either end. Both can be harmful or can enhance the pursuit of common good. But still, their best will not be enough without active participation by citizens.

Markets are equated with free enterprise, the virtue of which lies in giving free rein to human creativity and enterpreneurial ability. Free markets allow for impersonal matching of supply and demand, of employers and workers, and for constant correction of price distortions.

But the conventional wisdom that free markets provide the most efficient mechanism for the exchange of goods and services cannot be taken without

360

qualifications. Consider that the so-called free market is only relatively free in reality and not accessible to all people affected by it. And being neutral or blind to a host of "externalities," the free market is indifferent as to winners and losers, to its impact on income distribution and other development opportunities and benefits, and to its effects on the environment.

In the recent past, privatization has been one of the most important features of economic liberalization. Between 1980 and 1991, about 7,000 enterprises worldwide were privatized, some 1,450 of them in the developing world, mostly in Latin America. In theory, privatization should stimulate private enterpreneurship. But because state and market are in many cases dominated by interlocking interest groups and the market itself is not really free to begin with, the privatization process merely occasioned the shift from one kind of monopoly to another.

The *Human Development Report 1993* lists "seven sins of privatization": maximizing revenue without creating any competitive environment, replacing public monopolies with private ones, using nontransparent and arbitrary procedures, using proceeds to finance budget deficits, simultaneously crowding the financial markets with public borrowings, making false promises to labor, and privatizing without building a political consensus. These sins are typical, arising from a shortsighted and selfish profit motive and sheer lack of accountability. We should be reminded that the parties to the transaction, government and private sectors, have yet to reverse the pattern of increasing alienation between them and ordinary citizens.

Until now, markets have not proved that they can promote sustainable human development. Their demand for unrestricted operations in the name of efficiency and productivity has almost always led to more people getting thrown out of jobs, increasing inequality in income and wealth distribution, more poverty and misery, intensifying trade wars among nations and firms, and further depletion of natural resources.

The world economy is now dominated by a few hundred global corporations, originating in a handful of industrial countries, such as the United States, Japan, Germany, France, Switzerland, the Netherlands, and the United Kingdom. The top 300 corporations account for a combined asset that is roughly one quarter of the total productive assets in the world.

Those top corporations now spearhead a process of global integration never before achieved by great civilizations, much less by a single nation-state, no matter how powerful. They deal in all sorts of products and services that can link distant corners of this planet. They have made the world smaller for us by universalizing what to eat, drink, and wear and how we live and enjoy life.

Their products and services convey common global images that can shape popular dreams and pull people together. On the other hand, the same images and dreams can detach people and communities from their cultural roots.

Scarcely visible to ordinary citizens, but perhaps most powerful of all, is the global network of financial institutions involved in currency transactions, global securities, credit cards and plastic monies, swaps, buyouts, and a mind-boggling menu of speculative devices for repackaging and reselling money. Every day, $1 trillion flows through the world's major foreign-exchange markets as bits of data traveling across the globe through the computer networks. Yet no more than 10 percent of this staggering volume of money has to do with actual physical movement of goods and services.

Moving money around the world has become an end in itself, a highly profitable game for a few who can skirt state regulations almost at will. James Tobin, winner of the 1981 Nobel Prize for Economics, has proposed a tax on international currency transactions. The proposal may not be able to stop money speculation, but the proceeds from such a tax could raise some revenue to fund international undertakings.

The global corporate community is a complex system that employs only a few million people but touches the lives of billions. It creates some jobs but also make many jobs useless. The myriad products it churns out daily influence greatly the way we think and relate to each other. In the same instant, wherever we may be on this planet, we can be entranced by the gyrations of Michael Jackson while drinking Pepsi. Or, thanks to CNN, we can be transfixed by the space-age fireworks in Baghdad staged by the U.N. multinational force. We could also be as one with the South Africans as they cheered their victory over apartheid, and listened to the stirring messages of Nelson Mandela.

Together with the U.N. system and other supranational bodies, the global corporate system is leading the process of globalization from the top. As citizens across great distances create bonds of solidarity, the world's biggest corporations control the enormous energy, capital, and technology to make it possible. Yet at the same time that we are being pulled closer into one world, the same processes are tearing apart the ties that bind families, neighborhoods, village communities, and nations.

Markets can be made more accountable to people if nation-states and citizens choose to do so and are prepared to face some negative consequences. Even the most volatile resources of all, money and information, are ultimately grounded on hardware that requires physical sites. These sites are the domain of one or other type of sovereignty, whether state or local community. A physical plant, a product or service, even the movement of toxic wastes, for example, can be permitted or denied so long as nation-states and local communities are willing to exercise their sovereign right fully conscious of what this implies.

Markets can and must be a means to human development. But their built-in strengths in promoting private initiative, efficiency, and productivity need to be combined with equity and sustainability. Markets should serve people, rather than people serving markets. But can markets really be made friendly to people as well as to the environment? Doing this will require balancing the markets' positive strengths with measures that regulate their negative aspects, and correcting the distortions that they create in the process. Markets, as we know them in practice, give rise to a number of distorting factors.

One is inherent in their operations. Some distortions may be due to monopoly power combined with a drive by most businesses for short-term gain. Others are due to controlled prices, fiscal disincentives, and excessive government intervention. These make markets less competitive, less efficient, people-blind, and harmful to the environment.

Two, distortions arise out of the differing capacities among people who enter the market, implying that the playing field is not level in the first place. Many people wishing to compete lack the ability and means to do so. They lack the education, the skills, the assets, the credit to be competitive at all. In addition, many are from the beginning already excluded on gender, racial, or ethnic grounds.

Three, markets are blind to a lot of so-called externalities. They fail to reflect true costs and benefits, like pollution, an external cost, or the prevention of communicable diseases, an external benefit. Many things do not figure in market calculations, which account only for goods and services that are paid or monetized. For example, much of what happens in the household or neighborhood—things that make other visible, paid economic activities possible, like home management, backyard gardening, planting a tree, and a lot of the unpaid work by women, children, and the old—never show up in national income accounts. And a market accounting system does not cover the depreciation of natural capital.

Until all these distortions are corrected, markets will continue to be indifferent to the social and ecological costs of their operations. These corrections are a prerequisite for making markets more friendly to society and nature.

Citizen Participation

In light of the failure of both the state and the market, citizens—as individuals and, even better, organized—exerting efforts to democratize both state and market and doing things by themselves must occupy an ever expanding public space to influence the processes and outcomes of development at all levels.

As the *Human Development Report 1993* puts it, people's participation is becoming the central issue of our time. Ironically, it was also the rallying theme of social movements in the 1960s. Many things have happened since then. During the past three decades, authoritarian regimes have fallen one after the other. In all these regime changes and democratic transitions, movements of citizens cutting across social classes have played a major part. Indeed, we now see the worldwide emergence of people's organizations demanding on behalf of every citizen more and more say in shaping our own lives.

Many people are now fed up with the performance of both state and market and are impatient to see big changes happening without further delay. Aware of the weaknesses of state and market and refusing the continued domination by both, quite a few courageous citizens want to take control, with or without any clear alternative agenda of their own. There is so much human energy being generated; if it is not harnessed in a positive direction, it can result in a kind of polarizing civic energy and a scenario of anarchy equal to the worst achieved in wars among nations and market forces.

Participation goes beyond involvement in this or that project. Nor is it limited to people being able to pressure government for changes. In its full sense, participation means that people are able to control events and processes that shape their lives. By this definition, the extent and quality of participation by citizens in the economic, social, cultural, and political processes that affect their everyday existence is still far from the desired level. To reach this, much more will be required, and efforts in that direction will need the dynamic interplay of all parties—states, markets, and citizens.

When the *Human Development Report 1993* was released, UNDP noted in its press advisory that "90 percent of the world's people lack control over their own lives in spite of recent changes around the world favoring market economies, multiparty democracies and grassroots activites." This may sound exaggerated, but a close examination of the nature of control that people have over their lives, using the essential meaning of participation, will probably bear UNDP's estimate out.

In today's world of 5.7 billion inhabitants, there are 157 billionaires, some 2 million millionaires, and more than 1.1 billion people with an income of less than $1 a day. The richest 20 percent corners 82.7 percent of the world's income; the second, 11.7 percent; the third, 2.3 percent; the fourth, 1.9 percent; and the poorest fifth, 1.4 percent. Let us for the moment discard the absurd assumption that the millions or billions of excluded are living their own lives anyway and that an individual can be controlled only to the extent that he or she allows it. And let us assume that all the world's people are bound by a common set of processes with costs and benefits, from plain existence to enjoying nearly boundless freedom of movement. Then we can safely say that very few indeed are in full control over resources, means, and decisions that drive their lives. And this lack of control is expressed in various other forms.

In a sense, no one—not even the richest and most powerful—may be in complete control at all. The Cold War brought with it weapons of mass destruction whose annihilation potential or means of disposal is beyond the capacity of anyone to handle. The more than 100 wars during the past four decades, which took about 20 million lives, and before them the "hot" wars—the two world wars during which even more lives and properties were lost—also attest to how far events could be controlled by the players who waged them or the ordinary mortals who were affected by them.

Global poverty, the real major threat in the coming decades now that the Cold War is no more, is well on its worldwide tour, without passport as it were, and in ways that disturb the peace and quiet of the rich and powerful if not the whole of humanity. A threat to stability everywhere, poverty gives rise to various disturbing manifestations that strike deep into the moral fiber of humankind: massive involuntary migration, diseases, drugs, terrorism, wars, civil conflicts, revolution.

Additionally, environmental disasters of transboundary and global proportion have caught up on even those who have the means and resources to move to safer places. Hardly anyone may be spared from the "hot emergencies" of global warming and ozone depletion. Even those who are in the best position to fend off the all-inclusive effects of such disasters are merely buying time.

The Ways and Means of Exclusion

Millions upon millions of people continue to be excluded, by design or as a matter of course, on the grounds of color, nationality, ethnicity, religion, gender, and poverty. Notwithstanding the Universal Declaration of Human Rights, discrimination of every description happens and stubbornly persists almost everywhere.

Many people cannot travel freely on this planet without suffering the unwanted look that normally befalls a stranger. And this has more profound meaning to some than to others. Citizens from developing countries do not get the same treatment as those from industrial ones. Nationality of origin by itself can be an obstacle or an unrestricted passport to one's passage anywhere in this world. Americans or Japanese, for example, can count on the fingers of one hand the number of countries they cannot set foot in, whereas many other nationals agonize over which countries will let them in.

This is the simplest expression of the North-South divide that citizens from both sides are subject to. The problem can be extended to include decisionmaking processes in the U.N. system, where the one-country-one-vote principle does not mean much. The same holds true in other multilateral set-ups, like the World Bank, GATT, and so on. Money talks and makes things happen, so to speak. By implication, citizens get discriminated or favored unduly because they happen to be African or American by birth. Their inclusion or exclusion is carried to the level of relations among nations.

The poor constitute the biggest bunch of excluded citizens on this planet. They have very limited choices, to begin with. The rich blame them for their poverty and misery, and consider them as the cause rather than the consequence of much of the insecurity shaking this world. They are being labelled with all sorts of negative attributes and blamed for being so many, for stressing scarce and depleting resources when in fact others—though less numerous—consume much more.

The poor learn to blame themselves as well. Over time, they develop a culture of poverty that leads them to accept the way things are, to turn against each other in the worst form imaginable, or to be consumed in hopeless civic inertia. Many have tried to rise above their situation through individual strivings, collective nonviolent actions, class wars, rebellion, or revolution, often ending in failure or Pyrrhic victories but sometimes in well-deserved and more enduring successes.

Women continue to be the nonparticipating majority. Often discriminated against from birth, they have to struggle throughout their lives to be able to reach parity with men. Women hold up half the sky, so the saying goes, and more than half the vote, but they have to fight every step of the way to win just a little over the present 10 percent representation in parliaments and less than 4 percent representation in cabinets worldwide. (Although six countries did have women as heads of government in 1993.)

Women are much less likely to be literate or highly educated than men, and the disparity is most acute in developing countries. In South Asia, for example, female literacy rates are only around 50 percent those of males; in Nepal, they are 35 percent; in Sierra Leone, 37 percent; in Sudan, 27 percent; and in Afghanistan, 32 percent. Women account for two-thirds of the nearly 1 billion illiterates in the world. In higher education, women in developing countries lag far behind men. Even in industrial countries women fare more poorly than men, especially in scientific and technical education.

If and when women do find work, they tend to get paid much less and suffer more from extended hours of work and poor working conditions. Even in Japan, women get only 51 percent of male wages.

Of course, women still work even if not paid, and for much longer hours than do men who are jobless. Domestic chores, tending the backyard, and caring for children and the aged do not figure in the national income accounts although these are a necessary building block of national economic activity. Women's chances for self-employment that yields additional cash are hampered by prevailing property rights, inaccessibility of credit, lack of skills, or sheer limitation in mobility. If women's unpaid housework were made visible as a result of a modified national income accounting system, UNDP estimates that 20-30 percent more will be added to the global output.

In many developing countries women continue to be excluded from productive work and political participation because of tradition, discriminatory policies and legislation, and lack of educational and other opportunities. For many years there has been very little improvement in the lives of 500 million rural women in the countryside of the world, although opportunities are increasing that can and should make their situation better.

Minorities and indigenous peoples are a separate nation within each country. Almost every nation has one or more ethnic groups who suffer different forms of exclusion from national affairs usually dominated by majority populations. Their discrimination starts at birth and is even more reinforced by policies and legislation. Minority groups are denied equal access to education and other social services, employment opportunities, and political representation.

Ironically, the United States, which claims leadership in upholding democracy, freedom, and equality, is a classic case of one country with two nations—in fact, many nations, if we include Hispanics and other recent immigrants. African-Americans fall far below U.S. white citizens in all categories of UNDP's Human Development Index. If the index were used separately for the two populations, U.S. whites would rank highest and African-Americans would drop to number 31 in the world, according to UNDP.

The formal end of apartheid in South Africa is definitely a cause for celebration to every advocate of human rights. But the task of undoing the effects of years of racial discrimination is a formidable one. The South Africans can learn additional lessons from the experience of the United States, which was able to legislate racial discrimination out of existence much earlier, although it continues to grapple with its profound negative legacies.

The worldwide phenomenon of migration has been creating minority populations everywhere, especially in the industrial world. No less than 35 million people from the South have moved to the North in the past 30 years. Around 1 million more join them every year. More than a million people work outside their home countries on contracts for fixed periods. There are now an estimated 15-30 million undocumented international migrants.

Social and environmental disasters are producing an increasing number of refugees. Today, nearly 20 million internally displaced people are found in developing countries. And worldwide, even before the tragic developments in Rwanda, about 19 million men, women, and children lived in refugee camps, hoping for some place to go.

Violence has often been a companion of discrimination and exclusion. Since World War II, some 40 ethnic groups around the world have been persecuted or massacred, with a death toll running up to millions. This calls to mind the Nazi persecution and extermination of 6 million Jews during the war.

Indigenous peoples, one of the more enduring links to our primordial roots, are increasingly being marginalized and pushed to extinction by modern development. More than other minority groups, they suffer public neglect and exclusion from the benefits of human progress. And yet, they are forced to bear its costs. Even if they want to be left to themselves, they tend to be uprooted from their homelands in the name of development. Most of the big energy and infrastructure projects funded by multilateral development banks, governments, and the private sector encroach on their habitat. With the loss of their lands come the shattering of the indigenous cultures attached to them.

People in rural areas fall on the wrong end of the urban-rural divide, a natural consequence of a development model fashioned after and driven by the growth of capital. They normally constitute two thirds of the population in developing countries but often receive less than a quarter of the educational, health, water, and sanitation services. The rural per capita income in many countries is only about half that in towns and cities. In contrast to their urban counterparts, people in rural areas have less scope for participation in the economic, social, cultural, and political affairs of any nation.

Disabled people are also often excluded from full participation in society. The disabled now make up at least 10 percent of the world's population. This growing group includes people who have experienced injury, trauma, or disease that leads to long-term or permanent physical or mental damages. In both industrial and developing countries, a fair share of the population is disabled, and the percentage is increasing. Poverty, malnutrition, disease, and wars will continue to swell this less fortunate part of society.

Circles From Below

Citizens facing up to nation-states and the market forces that stand above them want an equal part in changing the present order of things. The least among them, the poorest of the poor, have been adding their numbers and newfound strengths to the growing struggle for inclusive participation in any and all events and processes that affect their lives. Even those who have more in life have been adding their voices to the collective striving to build a better world. In their midst are being created countless small circles of citizen power, tiny circles from below growing into powerful civic movements, and increasingly proving to be a leading edge as humanity marches into the twenty-first century.

Civil society has come of age, so to speak. With long roots in social history and philosophy dating back to the Enlightenment, the concept of civil society has emerged in current discourse with a force and resonance that can probably parallel the dawning of the information age. This may signify the end of monopoly by either state or market. More important, the worldwide emergence of civil society augurs well for moving world development from this point to the next through a new dynamic partnership and constructive engagement among the three key players symbolized by the prince (state), the merchant (corporate community), and the citizen.

Various societies have gone through several historic transitions, for better or worse, always hoping the next social order would be better than the previous one. These passages have been accompanied by advancement toward some emancipatory ideal or complete reversals, by shifts from patronage to private initiative or from a fairly level playing field to power monopoly, or by a coexistence of all these, as in a mosaic. But probably the most crucial lesson is this: in all these changes the main players have always been the prince and the merchant, with the citizen, who is neither prince nor merchant, often left out in the cold. To be a cocreator of the human drama, a person had to be in government or in business. A plain citizen was a nonentity. But not any longer. The citizen as producer, consumer, soldier, clerk, driver, housewife, or as mere nobody has plucked up enough courage and built a level of capability to stand up as just that—a plain citizen.

Ordinary people have stood up for themselves many times in the past. History is replete with such risings, which contributed to the collapse of old empires and to the birth of new ones, to the fall of old dictators and the rise of new ones, or to the various transitions to democracy. But all these movements from below always ended up in reinforcing the modern state and not necessarily the strengthening of popular and civil institutions. And the outcomes of these historic events have often been contrary to what people had originally intended: the government they helped sweep into power tended to alienate itself from them over time.

Two key elements, at least, make today's citizen participation different from that of the past. One, it questions the very nature of development itself. People have been asking why development processes in the past have been reproducing poverty; fragmenting and polarizing society; disempowering ordinary citizens; undermining time-honored cultures, tradition, and communitarian values; and causing ever-increasing damage on the environment. The questions being raised are not addressed merely to parts of the system but to the whole system itself. People have begun to realize that there is something fundamentally wrong about the development model, whether of the capitalist or socialist kind, which has dominated human affairs for at least two centuries now.

Two, civil society has emerged as a worldwide force that is redefining the meaning of development and governance. People today want to take control of the events and processes that shape their lives. They are rebuilding old institutions of civil society and creating new ones, holding them up as equal to those of state and market institutions. Development is too big a question to be left to government or business alone. People want an equal say and to exercise it in ways that can radically transform old concepts and ways of doing things.

Today, national security no longer means only strong state presiding over the development process. A national community will have security only when every man and woman in it feel secure in their private lives, in their workplaces, in their neighborhoods, and in their relationships to the larger society and their environments. People want to see development woven around humanity and not the other way around, they want development to be of the people, by the people, and for the people, with people living in close communion with the natural systems that support them.

The agency of social change and development is radically transforming. The conventional wisdom that development is the exclusive affair of state and market is now a thing of the past, at least in the dominant discourse, although not just yet in reality. The dynamic interplay of state, market, and civil society has come of age. From here on, all three actors will have to engage each other constructively to tackle all and any issues affecting human welfare in an era characterized by an urgent need for integrated and interdependent responses to world-spanning and interconnected problems.

States and markets will not democratize by themselves. Left to their own devices, as experience has shown, they tend to alienate a large part of society and concentrate wealth, resources, and decisions in a few. Citizens must and can rise from civic inertia to push the process of democratization to its farthest possible limits. They must and can make states and markets more accountable and responsive to the problems and needs of society and individual citizens.

The 1980s may be seen as a watershed era. We have seen in this period dramatic shifts away from authoritarian rule towards greater political freedom and democracy. To a large extent, these shifts were forced by popular movements, as convincingly demonstrated in the cases of the Philippines, Eastern Europe, Thailand, the newly industrializing economies of South Korea and Taiwan, Nepal, and many countries of Latin America and Africa where broad citizens' movements have stood up against authoritarian and corrupt regimes and successfully brought about the long-needed democratic transitions.

The experience of South Africa is the most recent, and probably one of the most dramatic, of the transitions. Here, a very popular liberation movement succeeded in sustaining a resistance to the point of electing its own government in a generally free and honest election. Equally important, we see in this case a resounding rejection of one of the worst forms of discrimination that has afflicted humankind—exclusion by color.

In South Africa, as elsewhere, the big challenge is to keep on course, to prevent the kind of backlash that often attended such transitions in the past, and to push the democratization process as profoundly and expansively as possible. It has often been the case that new societies would buckle under the weight of negative legacies from the past combined with new problems and challenges. Very few have been able to see the process through to its desired conclusion.

The end of the Cold War provides a wide scope of possibilities for citizens of the world. For one, it has dramatically reduced tensions among states resulting from superpower rivalries that had wasted so much human and natural resources and held many countries and millions of citizens hostage for too long. For another, it signifies an end to the folly of the arms race, thereby freeing up a huge amount of peace dividends—$935 billion from 1987 to 1994, accumulated from a yearly 3.6-percent average cut in military spending. These resources may now be redeployed to solve poverty, hunger, disease, and environmental problems afflicting human society.

The expected peace dividends can be dedicated exclusively to advancing human development agendas. Although the world continues to grapple with a huge aggregate defense expenditure and continuing arms sales, especially to developing countries, the prospect of total annihilation by nuclear war and gradual change of spending priorities should at least be a cause for relief to humanity.

Citizens must step up their pressures for disarmament. Beyond this, they need to assert a bigger role not only in peacekeeping but also in making and building peace everywhere. Wars did not end with the end of the Cold War. They merely shifted focus away from superpowers to smaller states and groups of people set apart by cultural, ethnic, religious, and racial differences.

National and ethnic differences often erupt in armed conflicts and get settled or stalemated by the power of arms, a situation that was relatively manageable within the Cold War framework. The current shift from war among states to wars among people have their deeper roots in poverty, deprivations, resource competition, and deep-seated biases. A comprehensive human development agenda should be able to address them and bring about a more enduring peace and harmony among different peoples.

The point for engaging the state is to democratize governance. The horizontal spread of power among diverse small circles of decisionmaking groups across society is the preferred scenario. By nature a centralizing institution, government on its own will not promote decentralization, deconcentration, or devolution of power. Citizens will have to do the pressuring, and do so in a sustained and constructive manner. The task is greater in big countries, such as China and India, which probably need decentralization and involvement of local communities most.

Citizens have to interact more closely with the market. This is easier said than done. For this to happen, people must press their governments for a better policy environment and allocation of resources that somehow level the playing field. And through their own efforts, citizens must and can acquire the confidence and ability to engage in the market arena.

As noted earlier, markets are driven by competition that usually ends up narrowing the scope for winning but swelling the ranks of losers. Their life and dynamism revolve around growing boundlessly, through an ever-rising spiral of production of goods and services that exacts an increasingly heavy toll on people and natural resources.

A number of preconditions have to be deliberately put in place to make markets more friendly to people and the environment. An equitable distribution of assets, such as land, especially in agrarian societies, is a critical element. Others include the following: adequate public investment in education and skills training, health care, and needed infrastructures; expanding access to information; credit extension to the poor; property rights reforms and elimination of barriers to entry into the market on the grounds of gender, nationality, ethnicity, race, or religion; fair wages and improved working conditions; laws against monopoly; social safety nets for vulnerable groups; and installation of measures to account for environmental costs. In other words, level the playing field on behalf of the poor and use a new kind of measurement system that takes full account of social and environmental costs and benefits.

In the face of a powerful state-market growth consensus, citizens should all the more speed up efforts at building their own capacities to intervene forcefully in shaping development processes and outcomes. Despite repeated warnings and worldwide clamor for reforms, states and markets continue to pursue a grow now-pay later path. For them, growth is an all-consuming obsession, and they are only too willing to postpone paying the costs to society and the environment until later, if at all. Oftentimes, realization comes too late or the costs are too heavy for society to afford. The impressive growth performance of the newly industrializing economies has now become the fashionable model for most countries struggling to catch up. And yet, these societies are precisely the leading recent models of the tragic scenario we want to avoid.

The world cannot anymore afford the model of South Korea and Taiwan or the earlier capitalist model they copied in a shortcircuited way. This model has brought these countries to where they are now: impressive examples of wealth creation and international competitiveness, but at great costs to society and the environment. They were built by a people who traded their freedoms for bread but are now facing a backlash in terms of unmet social demands and a huge bill for environmental cleanup. We can barely imagine what scenario would lie in store for the world if the biggest countries—China, India, Russia, and Indonesia—were to follow the same path.

But developing countries need to enlarge their economies to be able to address growing poverty and exploding populations. And this is precisely the Catch-22 that must be addressed by state, market, and popular forces everywhere. By growing in the manner and direction made famous by South Korea, Taiwan, Singapore, and Hong Kong, some countries may be successful but growth itself will recreate the problems they intend to solve in the first place. But what are the alternatives? And are these alternatives going to work?

There are no easy choices. Calibrating growth to the needs of society and the environment will require more than just a redefinition of development itself. Guided by such strategic considerations, states, markets, and citizens must together find comprehensive but pragmatic breakthroughs to the current dilemma. Certainly, this will mean great sacrifices, sharing, compromises, and trade-offs, accompanied by profound value changes never before experienced by humankind, except perhaps in very specific situations such as in major natural disasters, which bring the best out of all of us.

Citizen Action Without Borders

Across the globe, citizens are daily creating ties that bind them toward a common future. In Asia and the Pacific, in Africa and the Middle East, in Latin and North America, in the whole of Europe, thousands of groups, movements, and alliances of citizens have sprung up to make their stand on every conceivable issue affecting human welfare at all levels.

Backed by a long and continues tradition of free associations inspired by all sorts of motivations, these civic formations have surged forward to occupy an ever-increasing public space. Quite a few of them have shaken off parochial interests and are now staking bolder claims over resources and processes that shape their lives.

These civic formations span the whole range. There are neighborhood associations, local community groups, boys and girls clubs, mothers' associations, organizations of small farmers, landless peasants, artisanal fishers, women, youth, indigenous peoples, peace and human rights groups, environmental organizations, religious and spiritual movements, cooperatives and trade unions, local philanthropies and foundations, business associations, media and academic circles, professional societies, self-defense and mutual aid groupings, nongovernmental and private voluntary organizations, and whatnot.

Spontaneously rising from the base of society, these groupings constitute extremely diverse structures mediating between the state and individual citizens. They are the springboard of new ideas, values, and social action. From them have emerged powerful movements of social reform, resistance, and revolutionary change. Some of these movements have not only succeeded in stopping destructive development projects but have brought down authoritarian and unaccountable governments in Asia, Latin America, Africa, and Eastern Europe.

What may appear to us as chaotic aggregations of citizens are actually forces of creation and social cohesion. Organized on the basis of human need and interest, social class and caste, religion, language, regional identity, culture, race and gender, these groups form a solid and active backbone of civil society. An old but newly recovered concept, civil society refers to those autonomous centers of citizen action, independent of the state and corporate economy, contributing to the construction and reconstruction of a certain social order. Casting the whole or part of civil society on the side of alternative development merely suggests failure of mainstream development itself.

The globalized character of present human problems has been driving civil society to a rising level of militance. Just as new interstate bodies are forming to address supranational issues, new institutions of civil society are being built across borders in order to scale up their impact on events and processes that shape society. Citizen action has been moving up from the local community level to the national and global level and back, a pattern that translates the dictum "think globally, act locally." Indeed, many citizens' groups have mastered the art of multilevel thinking and action.

Global bonding, aided by modern communications technology and extensive resource access, has enabled the institutions of civil society to forcefully intervene in development discourses and events of international importance. During the Earth Summit in 1992 in Rio, citizens from different parts of the world, represented by some 10,000 organizations, made their presence felt by organizing a parallel Global Forum and intervening in the governmental process at the same time. The World Summit for Social Development in Copenhagen in March 1995 is another welcome opportunity for citizens of the world to advance their own agenda with respect to the shape of future society.

Tremendous advances have been made on global exchange and solidarity among the institutions of civil society, thanks to modern technology. Citizen groups from one end of the world to the other get to know what each one is doing and respond to the call for assistance of those in need. Through various forms of media, people find out about the quiet resource mobilization by women's groups in far-flung villages of South Asia and the waste recycling activities of children in western countries. Or the more high-profile citizen action, as in the case of people's opposition against big dam projects in India, Thailand, and elsewhere. Or the campaigns by women, human rights, indigenous people, and development and environment groups around U.N.-sponsored processes.

Over the years, international institutions organized by citizens have emerged one after the other. Aside from well-known human rights movements such as Amnesty International and environmental organizations—Greenpeace and Friends of the Earth, for example—many more have come to the fore in recent years. There are also cases when national organizations or even individual citizens have gained international recognition by taking a stand and generating world opinion and citizen action on certain issues. These individuals and their institutions are the emerging examples of global citizenship.

Citizen bonds extend far and wide across the globe. People-to-people aid movements for purposes of common advocacy, monitoring of development policies and projects, resource transfer, technology sharing, and the like are now pretty well established. Citizen groups have come to the aid of each other to challenge the policy centers in Washington, New York, Tokyo, and Brussels. Policies and projects originating from these centers or from the U.N. system, the Bretton Woods institutions, the regional multilateral development banks, bilateral aid agencies, and national governments are now better monitored than before. Citizen solidarity and the international institutions built on it have been molded through direct and sustained cultural encounters and mutual learning processes.

The emergence of civil society as a worldwide force, embodying the voices from below, is now duly recognized by states and the corporate community. Many of the heresies of yesteryears attributed to them have landed in the official rhetoric and policy. Global civil society has arrived, and at a time when its voice was most needed.

Citizens have placed their own perspective in the global agenda. They are exercising their public responsibility to keep the hands and feet of states and markets in the fire of reform even as they strive to better their lot on their own.

If nothing else, people have their own lives and little spaces to secure. There, they reserve the ultimate right to be sovereign, with or without a benign state or market. These living spaces are the only ones citizens can claim and promise to control. At the end of the day, they alone are responsible for making these spaces unbearable or livable.

Surely humanity, though in trouble, has good reasons to be hopeful.

Bibliography

Barnet, Richard J. and John Cavanagh. *Global Dreams: Imperial Corporation and the New World Order.* New York: Simon & Schuster, 1994.

Brown, Lester R. et al. *State of the World 1994.* New York: W. W. Norton & Company, 1994.

Keating, Michael. T*he Earth Summit's Agenda for Change. A Plain Language Version of Agenda 21 and the Other Rio Agreements.* Geneva: Centre for Our Common Future, 1993.

Kennedy, Paul. *Preparing for the Twenty-First Century.* London: Fontana Press, 1993.

Ponting, Clive. *A Green History of the World. The Environment and the Collapse of Great Civilizations.* New York: Penguin, 1993.

U.N. Development Programme. *Human Development Report 1993.* New York: Oxford University Press, 1993.

U.N. Development Programme. *Human Development Report 1994.* New York: Oxford University Press, 1994.

ABOUT THE AUTHORS

African Women Development and Communication Network (FEMNET) — Located in Nairobi, Kenya, FEMNET aims to strengthen the role of nongovernmental organizations focusing on women's development and the integration of women in the development process in Africa, as well as creating an infrastructure and channel through which NGOs may share information, knowledge, and experience. Their activity includes the publication of a newsletter, *FEMNET News.*

Alain Anciaux — Anthropologist teaching at the Université Libre in Brussels (Belgium) and in France. He is Director of CRITIAS (Interdisciplinary Institute on Social Work and Innovations), and has authored five books and numerous articles.

Miguel Darcy de Oliveira — Co-founder and Executive Secretary of Instituto de Ação Cultural. Currently, he is a consultant to the International Labor Organization and UNESCO. He is also a post-graduate instructor at the Catholic University, a lecturer and workshop leader, and author of books and essays about education, people's empowerment, democracy, and development.

Rubem César Fernandes — Professor of Anthropology at the Universidad Federal de Rio de Janeiro (Brazil) and Columbia University (USA). For many years, he has been Executive Secretary of the Instituto de Estudos da Religião. He is also Coordinator of the Inter-Religioso Movimento and President of Viva Rio. His works include *Vocabulario de Ideas Pasadas - Ensayos sobre el fin del socialismo* and *Romerías de la Pasión.*

Dirk Jarré — Head of the international department of the German Association for Public and Private Welfare in Frankfurt, Germany. His other responsibilities include being President of the International Council on Social Welfare, President of the European Council of Voluntary Organizations, and member of the Liaison Committee of the international non-governmental organizations enjoying consultative status with the Council of Europe.

Amani Kandil — Professor of Political Science at Cairo University and the National Center for Social and Criminological Research. She is an advisor for the Follow-Up Committee for Arab NGOs. Her works include several publications on civil society in Egypt and the Arab world.

Michael Keating — Author of five books and numerous reports and articles, principally about the environment and sustainable development. He was a journalist for more than 20 years. Since 1988, he has been an independent writer and consultant, who has advised a number of organizations, including governments, the United Nations, businesses, and non-governmental organizations.

Ewa Les — Assistant Professor of Political Science at Warsaw University, Institute of Social Policy, and a co-founder and former President of the Polish Association of Social Workers. Her works include a collection of interviews with prominent scholars on Social Policy in the Period of Systemic Change (1992). She also co-authored a collection of articles on Social Work Education (1991) and a book on Selected Forms of Self-Governing Institutions (1988).

Amaury Nardone — Lawyer working at the lawyers and barristers office DMG since 1993. He is co-author of *Associations et fondations en Europe - Régime juridique et fiscal.*

Isagani R. Serrano — Vice President of the Philippine Rural Reconstruction Movement (PRRM). He works on development policy and advocacy. His publications include a collection of essays on environment and development, *Pay Now, Not Later* (1994), *On Civil Society* (1993), and a poetry collection, *Firetree* (1985). He also co-authored *Bataan: A Case of Ecosystem Approach to Sustainable Development in the Philippines* (1991).

Rajesh Tandon — Founder and Coordinator of the Society for Participatory Research in Asia (PRIA). He is also the President of the Asia-South Pacific Bureau of Adult Education, Asian Vice President of the International Council for Adult Education, and International Coordinator of the Participatory Research Network and editor of its newsletter. His writings and studies include the history and roles of voluntary development organizations.

Sylvie Tsyboula — Formerly Deputy Director of Fondation de France, she has left this position to take up the responsibility of being Coordinator for the new European Third Sector Training Network based in Brussels. She will continue working with Fondation de France as a Senior Advisor.

About CIVICUS: World Alliance for Citizen Participation

CIVICUS is an alliance for creating and strengthening regional, national, and local initiatives. It will establish linkages across such efforts, transcending boundaries that are geographic or political. CIVICUS will be an open forum for discourse, an international dialogue of views from a range of leaders, institutions, and cultures.

As CIVICUS works to facilitate and encourage this kind of dialogue, it will provide structure and linkages for gathering information on international philanthropy and the rapidly burgeoning voluntary sector. It will become a world organization dedicated to civil society, voluntary action, pluralism, philanthropy, and community service.

The uniqueness of CIVICUS is that it includes both donor and donee organizations; it includes the total of the nonprofit nongovernmental sector and is global in nature. Such a wide constituency represents a **conceptual innovation** that opens new opportunities for dialogue and common action. To be more than a name, however, CIVICUS' significance must gain recognition and legitimacy on the local and regional levels. That is why CIVICUS will be based so much on regional activities. That is why the founding Board of Directors comprises twenty-one people from 18 countries representing six continents. That is why CIVICUS' practical operation has started in the regions with reports and meetings on the status of the third sector.

As an international advocacy organization of the voluntary sector, CIVICUS will go beyond individual issues to stress the generic concerns faced by the emerging third sector.

By promoting research and dissemination of information, offering broader meeting and partnership opportunities, supporting exemplary projects and experiences, removing the legal obstacles and promoting a political and cultural environment favorable to giving, volunteering and citizen action, CIVICUS would add new legitimacy and outreach to a common regional and global agenda geared to the building and strengthening of civil society.

Ricardo Govela
PHILOS
Mexico City, Mexico

Milad Hanna
Supreme Council of Culture
Tawfik Coptic Society
Housing Committee, Peoples Assembly
Cairo, Egypt

James A. Joseph
Council on Foundations
Washington, D.C., United States

Graça Machel (Co-chairperson)
Association for Community Development
Maputo, Mozambique

Amin Mekki Medani
Cairo, Egypt

Carlos A. Monjardino (Co-chairperson)
Fundação Oriente
Lisbon, Portugal

Maria Robledo Montecel
Intercultural Development Research Association
San Antonio, Texas, United States

Horacio R. Morales
Philippines Rural Reconstruction Movement
Quezon City, Philippines

Marek Nowicki
Helsinki Committee
Warsaw, Poland

Brian O'Connell (Co-chairperson)
INDEPENDENT SECTOR
Washington, D.C., United States

Gerard Pantin
Service Volunteered for All (SERVOL)
Port-of-Spain, Trinidad

Rajesh Tandon
Society for Participatory Research in Asia (PRIA)
New Delhi, India

Sylvie Tsyboula
European Third Sector Training Network
Brussels, Belgium

Secretariat Staff

Miklós Marschall
Executive Director

Theresa Siegl
Assistant Director

Jennette Smith
Staff Assistant

Jo Render
Staff Assistant

Past and Present Funders

Charles Stewart Mott Foundation, USA
Ford Foundation, USA
W.K. Kellogg Foundation, USA
Carnegie Corporation of New York, USA
Centro Mexicano Para La Filantropía, Mexico
European Foundation Centre, Belgium
Fundação Oriente, Portugal

Fondation de France, France
Stifterverband für die Deutsche Wissenschaft, Germany
European Cultural Foundation, The Netherlands
Charities Aid Foundation, Great Britain
Arab Gulf Programme for the UN Development Organisations, Saudi Arabia
Hitachi Foundation, USA
Rockefeller Brothers Fund, USA
IBM Corporation, USA
John D. and Catherine T. MacArthur Foundation, USA
The Rockefeller Foundation, USA

In-Kind Supporters

Print Concepts, Australia
Fondation de France, France
Independent Sector, USA
Council on Foundations, USA
Fundação Oriente, Portugal
Women's Research and Training Centre, Tunisia

World Circle of Friends

Manuel Arango, Mexico
Michael Kirby, Australia
Rigoberta Menchú, Guatemala
David Rockefeller, USA

For more information, contact:

CIVICUS: World Alliance for Citizen Participation
919 18th Street, N.W., 3rd Floor
Washington, D.C. 20006, U.S.A.
tel: (202) 331-8518; fax: (202) 331-8774